The Great PC Troubleshooting Road Map

Your computer won't start	Windows won't start	A peripheral doesn't work right	Windows freezes or crashes
POSSIBLE CAUSE: No power to system unit	POSSIBLE CAUSE: Bad command in AUTOEXEC.BAT, CONFIG.SYS, WIN.INI, SYSTEM.INI, or MSDOS.SYS files	POSSIBLE CAUSE: Peripheral not connected or installed properly	POSSIBLE CAUSE: Keyboard or mouse disconnected or defective
TRY THIS: Check power cable and power outlet	TRY THIS: Start Windows in Safe mode and edit system files to remove references to bad or missing drivers or programs	TRY THIS: Uninstall and then reinstall peripheral	TRY THIS: Reconnect keyboard or mouse; replace keyboard or mouse
POSSIBLE CAUSE: Bad CMOS BIOS configuration	POSSIBLE CAUSE: Missing, incorrect, or corrupted device driver or file	POSSIBLE CAUSE: No power to peripheral	POSSIBLE CAUSE: Not enough system memory
TRY THIS: Reconfigure your PC setup during bootup	TRY THIS: Start Windows in Safe mode and use the Device Manager in the System Properties dialog box to look for the bad driver	TRY THIS: Check peripheral's cable hookup or card installation	TRY THIS: Close open applications; reboot computer to free up lost memory; add more memory to your system
POSSIBLE CAUSE: Non-bootable diskette in drive A:	POSSIBLE CAUSE: Device conflict	POSSIBLE CAUSE: Windows not configured properly for peripheral	POSSIBLE CAUSE: Not enough free hard disk space
TRY THIS: Remove diskette from drive A:	TRY THIS: Start Windows in Safe mode and use the Device Manager in the System Properties dialog box to look for the device conflict	TRY THIS: Uninstall and then reinstall peripheral; run Add New Hardware Wizard	TRY THIS: Delete unused programs and temporary files from your hard disk; upgrade to a larger hard [...]
POSSIBLE CAUSE: Missing or corrupted system files	POSSIBLE CAUSE: Damaged Windows Registry	POSSIBLE CAUSE: Incorrect, missing, or corrupted device driver	POSSIBLE [...] ware prog[...]
TRY THIS: Copy COMMAND. COM from Emergency Windows Startup Disk to your hard drive; run Microsoft System Recovery from your Emergency Windows Startup Disk	TRY THIS: Start Windows in MS-DOS mode and use the **c:\scanreg /restore** command to restore the previous copy of the Registry	TRY THIS: Uninstall and then reinstall peripheral; run Add New Hardware Wizard; check with peripheral's manufacturer for updated driver files	TRY THIS: [...] close froze[...]
POSSIBLE CAUSE: Computer virus	POSSIBLE CAUSE: Computer virus	POSSIBLE CAUSE: Peripheral conflicting with another peripheral	POSSIBLE C[...] virus
TRY THIS: Run anti-virus software	TRY THIS: Start Windows in Safe mode and run anti-virus software	TRY THIS: Uninstall and then reinstall peripheral; run Add New Hardware Wizard and choose different port or IRQ; use Device Manager in the System Properties dialog box to find and fix port or IRQ conflict	TRY THIS: P[...] reboot Wind[...] Windows in S[...] anti-virus soft[...]
POSSIBLE CAUSE: Bad hard disk		POSSIBLE CAUSE: Peripheral is defective	POSSIBLE CAU[...] error
TRY THIS: Run disk diagnostic program; consult a technician		TRY THIS: Return peripheral to manufacturer	TRY THIS: Press Ctrl+Alt+Del to reboot Windows; run ScanDisk or other hard disk utility

ALPHA

Your modem isn't working properly

POSSIBLE CAUSE: Modem not installed or connected properly

TRY THIS: Uninstall and then reinstall modem; use Add New Hardware Wizard, if necessary

POSSIBLE CAUSE: Incorrect modem configuration in Windows

TRY THIS: Check modem settings in the Modem Properties dialog box; if necessary, uninstall and then reinstall modem

POSSIBLE CAUSE: Bad, missing, or corrupt modem device driver

TRY THIS: Uninstall and then reinstall modem; run Add New Hardware Wizard; check with modem's manufacturer for updated driver files

POSSIBLE CAUSE: IRQ or COM port conflict with another peripheral

TRY THIS: Use the Device Manager in the System Properties dialog box to find and fix the conflict; run Modem Troubleshooter (in Windows 98)

POSSIBLE CAUSE: Bad, noisy, busy, or disconnected phone line

TRY THIS: Try connecting via another phone line; contact telephone company to check line

You can't connect to the Internet

POSSIBLE CAUSE: Dialing wrong number for ISP

TRY THIS: Check ISP dial-up number; change number in Dial-Up Networking

POSSIBLE CAUSE: Incorrect user ID or password

TRY THIS: Check user ID or password with ISP; change user ID and password in Dial-Up Networking

POSSIBLE CAUSE: Incorrect Dial-Up Networking configuration

TRY THIS: Check settings in Dial-Up Networking with those settings provided by ISP

POSSIBLE CAUSE: Modem speed mismatch with ISP

TRY THIS: Select lower connection speed in Modem Properties dialog box

POSSIBLE CAUSE: ISP's phone lines are busy (too many users)

TRY THIS: Connect again at a later time

POSSIBLE CAUSE: ISP's Internet gateway is overloaded

TRY THIS: Connect again at a later time

Your online session gets disconnected

POSSIBLE CAUSE: Inactive too long (automatic disconnect)

TRY THIS: Reconnect; don't leave connection open but inactive

POSSIBLE CAUSE: Noisy phone line

TRY THIS: Reconnect, using a different phone line if possible; contact telephone company to check line

POSSIBLE CAUSE: Call Waiting not disabled

TRY THIS: Dial *70 before connecting, or reset Dialing Properties to compensate for Call Waiting

POSSIBLE CAUSE: Not enough system memory

TRY THIS: Close other open applications; reboot system to free up lost memory; add more memory to your system

POSSIBLE CAUSE: Another application is trying to use your modem

TRY THIS: Close other application

You can't connect to a specific Web page

POSSIBLE CAUSE: Incorrect URL

TRY THIS: Recheck URL for accuracy and then try again

POSSIBLE CAUSE: Internet traffic overload

TRY THIS: Wait a few minutes and then try again

POSSIBLE CAUSE: Web site traffic overload

TRY THIS: Wait a few minutes and then try again

POSSIBLE CAUSE: Web site temporarily out of service

TRY THIS: Wait a few minutes and then try again; wait a day and then try again

POSSIBLE CAUSE: Web page has been moved or deleted

TRY THIS: Attempt to access another page on the same site; contact site administrator about "dead" page

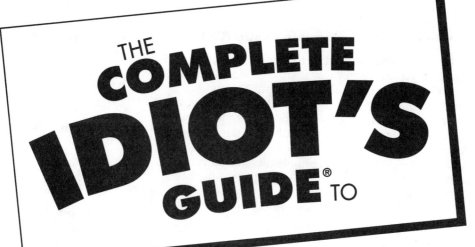

THE COMPLETE IDIOT'S GUIDE® TO

Fixing Your #$%@ PC

by Michael Miller

ALPHA

A member of Penguin Group (USA) Inc.

**The Complete Idiot's Guide to Fixing
Your #$%@ PC**

Copyright © 1999 by Penguin Group (USA) Inc.

International Standard Book Number: 0-7897-2092-2

Library of Congress Catalog Card Number: 99-65640

Printed in the United States of America

First Printing: *August 1999*

06   05   04   10   9   8   7   6   5   4   3   2

Trademarks

All terms mentioned in this book that are known to be trademarks or service marks have been appropriately capitalized. Alpha Books and Penguin Group (USA) Inc., cannot attest to the accuracy of this information. Use of a term in this book should not be regarded as affecting the validity of any trademark or service mark.

Warning and Disclaimer

Executive Editor
Greg Wiegand

Acquisitions Editor
John Pierce

Development Editor
Sue Hobbs

Managing Editor
Thomas F. Hayes

Project Editor
Karen S. Shields

Copy Editor
Kate Givens

Indexer
Chris Barrick

Proofreader
Tricia Sterling

Technical Editor
Wes Gates

Illustrator
Judd Winick

Interior Designer
Nathan Clement

Cover Designer
Michael Freeland

Copy Writer
Eric Borgert

Layout Technician
Lizbeth Johnston

Contents at a Glance

Contents

xiii

30 The Course of Last Resort...Editing the Windows Registry   349

Appendix A: The OOPS! Glossary: Technical Terms for the Technically Timid   357

Appendix B: Online Troubleshooting and Help Resources   369

About the Author

Michael Miller is a writer, speaker, consultant, and the President and Founder of The Molehill Group, a strategic consulting and authoring firm based in Carmel, Indiana. More information about the author and The Molehill Group can be found at www.molehillgroup.com, and you can email the author directly at author@molehillgroup.com.

Mr. Miller has been an important force in the book publishing business since 1987. In his most recent position of Vice President of Business Strategy for Macmillan Publishing, he helped guide the strategic direction for the world's largest reference publisher and influence the shape of today's computer book publishing market. There are few who know as much about the computer industry—how it works, and why—as does Mr. Miller.

As the author of 30 best-selling non-fiction books, Mr. Miller writes about a variety of topics. His most recent books include *The Complete Idiot's Guide to Online Auctions, The Complete Idiot's Guide to Online Search Secrets, Sams Teach Yourself MORE Windows 98 in 24 Hours,* and *Webster's New World Vocabulary of Success.*

From his first book (*Ventura Publisher Techniques and Applications*, published in 1989) to this, his latest title, Michael Miller has established a reputation for practical advice, technical accuracy, and an unerring empathy for the needs of his readers. Many regard Mr. Miller as the consummate reporter on new technology for an everyday audience.

Dedication

To Lloyd Short, who had the initial idea for OOPS! What to Do When Things Go Wrong (the spiritual predecessor to this book) back in 1992, and has been a valued colleague, an inspiration, and a good friend in the years since.

Acknowledgments

Special thanks to the usual suspects at Macmillan, including but not limited to John Pierce, Greg Wiegand, Sue Hobbs, Karen Shields, and Wes Gates. Also a big tip of the hat to the gang at Lulu's Electric Cafe—keep my chair warm and start me another tall mocha!

Tell Us What You Think!

As the reader of this book, *you* are our most important critic and commentator. We value your opinion and want to know what we're doing right, what we could do better, what areas you'd like to see us publish in, and any other words of wisdom you're willing to pass our way.

As a Publisher for Que, I welcome your comments. You can e-mail or write me directly to let me know what you did or didn't like about this book—as well as what we can do to make our books stronger.

Please note that I cannot help you with technical problems related to the topic of this book, and that due to the high volume of mail I receive, I might not be able to reply to every message.

When you write, please be sure to include this book's title and author as well as your name and phone or fax number. I will carefully review your comments and share them with the author and editors who worked on the book.

E-mail: cigfeedback@pearsoned.com

Mail: Alpha Books
           800 East 96th Street
           Indianapolis, IN 46240

Introduction

This is a book for people with problems.

Computer and Internet problems, that is.

You don't have to be a computer nerd to have computer problems. And you're not a complete idiot if you can't figure them out on your own.

This book was written to help you—a normal, average, non-geek, non-technical computer user—find and fix common computer and Internet problems. Nothing too complex is presented, and the solutions are easy enough for people like you and me to try without fear of creating more problems.

In short, if you want to attempt some simple solutions for common problems, this book is for you.

My personal background probably helps to make this book useful. You see, even though I like computers, I'm not a technonerd—I'm a normal guy, just like you. But I do like computers and technology, and for all my adult life I've been the guy people turn to if they have computer problems—neighbors, friends, co-workers, you name it. I'm not sure why, but I think it has something to do with the fact that I take the time to figure out what's wrong and then show people how to fix the problem themselves. Or maybe I'm just a soft touch. Whatever the case, I have a lot of experience helping people through the rough times with their computer systems—and that experience can help you through the rough times when you have a problem with your computer system.

This Isn't My First Troubleshooting Book...

Back in the ancient past (1992, to be exact), I wrote a book titled *OOPS! What to Do When Things Go Wrong*. It was a lot like this book, offering simple troubleshooting advice for non-technical computer users. As it turned out, that book sold more than 100,000 copies in three editions and was the spiritual predecessor to *The Complete Idiot's Guide to Fixing Your #$%@ PC*.

Like the book you hold in your hands, *OOPS!* was written for my father and my brother and my friends and neighbors and other "average" computer users. Back then—in the glory days of MS-DOS and WordPerfect and Lotus 1-2-3—I used to get several calls a month from people I knew, along the lines of: "Mike, my computer is doing something kind of funny. Could you come over and take a look at it?" Those calls inspired the first *OOPS!* book—and the fact that I *continue* to get those calls today led the folks at Que to consider publishing this new troubleshooting book for today's users of Windows, Word, Excel, and the Internet.

I take the same approach in this book as I do when I help my friends with their computer problems. That approach—and this book—isn't fancy, and it isn't overly technical. What I try to offer is good old-fashioned problem solving on a level normal folks can understand—nothing more, nothing less.

Now if my friends would only call when they *didn't* have a computer problem...

Who Should Read This Book?

This book is designed to be used by "normal" computer and Internet users. You don't have to be a technical expert to read this book because I don't go into a lot of technical mumbo-jumbo. I help you cope with common computer and Internet problems and help you figure out how to get things back to normal. My comments and advice mix common sense with some tricks regular computer users might not be aware of. The goal is to get you back up and running in the shortest possible time with the least possible fuss.

In writing this book, I assume you have a computer system purchased in the past five years or so, and that you're running either Windows 95 or Windows 98 as your operating system. If you have an older computer or are running an older version of Windows (or, God forbid, Microsoft's pre-Windows MS-DOS operating system!), some of the information in this book will be useful to you, but not all of it. (Search out—if you can find it—the third edition of *OOPS! What to Do When Things Go Wrong*, published in 1994, if you're having trouble with an older system.)

Why should you read this book? Obviously, you should read this book if you're having trouble with your computer hardware or software, or with your journeys on the Internet. In addition, reading this book *before* you experience trouble can help you *avoid* problems in the future. You'll be surprised at the simple steps you can take to minimize the chances for things going wrong with your computer system.

What Does This Book Discuss?

The Complete Idiot's Guide to Fixing Your #$%@ PC is divided into three major sections.

I recommend that everyone read Part 1, "Start Here Before Things Go Wrong: Computer Basics for the Technically Timid." This section contains a lot of useful information for anyone wanting to get the most out of their computers and protect themselves from possible problems.

Part 2, "Figuring Out What Went Wrong: Troubleshooting for the Technically Timid," is the "What to Do When…" section. Here is where you find specific solutions to specific problems you may encounter.

Part 3, "A Quick Course in Problem Solving: Technical Details for the Technically Timid," serves as a reference to the more technical side of troubleshooting. Think of it as "extra credit" reading if you really want to know more about technical stuff— things like error messages, system settings, and the Windows Registry.

In addition, the tear-out card contains "The Great PC Troubleshooting Road Map" (on one side) and "The Great Internet Troubleshooting Road Map" (on the other). These easy-to-follow flow charts will help you narrow your search for the cause of your specific problem.

Conventions Used in This Book

While reading *this book*, you should note the following conventions that will help you more easily understand the text:

UPPERCASE letters are used for filenames and commands—for example, AUTOEXEC.BAT.

Italic text indicates words or phrases introduced and explained for the first time—for example, *hard boot*.

Text that you enter or type is indicated in boldface—for example, **CD C:\DIR01**.

Web page addresses and links are monospaced—for example, `www.molehillgroup.com`.

Onscreen prompts and messages (including error messages) are also indicated by a special typeface—for example,

`File not found.`

Keyboard keys are usually represented as they appear on your keyboard—for example, Tab.

Key combinations are represented with the plus sign and indicate that you press and hold one key while you also press the other—for example, Ctrl+Shift.

In addition, interesting information not necessarily key to the point at hand is presented in sidebars, such as the "This Isn't My First Troubleshooting Book…" sidebar earlier in this introduction.

One Last Thing…

I hope this book helps you correct whatever is currently wrong with your system and, in the process, makes you feel more comfortable with your computer and the Internet. There's really little to be afraid of inside that ugly beige box, once you know how things work. If I do my job right, your job will be easier and less stressful—because you'll have fewer computer problems to bother with!

Michael Miller
September, 1999

Part 1

Start Here Before Things Go Wrong: Computer Basics for the Technically Timid

Let's call this part of the book "preventive medicine." If you want to keep your PC from falling apart, the information and advice in these chapters could prove invaluable. After all, wouldn't you rather spend a few minutes a week preventing problems than spend countless frustrating hours fixing them?

Chapter 1

The 10 Most Common Computer and Internet Problems

In This Chapter

➤ Learn how to methodically troubleshoot common problems

➤ Find the causes of most computer problems

➤ Discover the 10 most common computer problems—and how to fix them

---

IMPORTANT: Please read this chapter first!

We all know how mischievous your personal computer can sometimes be. That's why I'm starting this book with a list of the 10 most commonly encountered computer and Internet problems. In this chapter, I describe what causes these problems and how you might be able to fix them. Chances are you can find your current problem on this list, and not have to bother with the rest of the book. So if your computer is misbehaving, look here before you read any further.

Now, I don't mean to imply that you shouldn't read the rest of the book. (I especially recommend Chapters 2 through 10, which teach you how to prepare for and protect yourself against many problems.) But if you can find the answer to your problem in these first few pages, more power to you!

First, a Few Troubleshooting Tips

Before we look at specific problems (and solutions), it might help to get a little advice on how to troubleshoot through the things that go wrong with your computer system.

My first tip, stated simply, is—**DON'T PANIC!** In the grand cosmic scheme of things, a malcontent microcomputer just doesn't register on the significance scale. Besides, if anything major really went wrong, there's not much you could do about it *after* the fact, anyway. The thing to do is keep your cool and use the advice in this book to minimize the damage—and get things back to normal as soon as possible. (In fact, you might just want to walk away from your computer for awhile, so you can approach your problem later with a clear head.)

After you've not panicked, you should try to reproduce the problem. If you're lucky, the problem won't occur again. And, after all, if it only happens once, it's not really that bad of a problem, is it? If you can't reproduce the problem, it means that the problem magically fixed itself (unlikely) or that your problem was caused by a one-time user error (quite common).

If you *can* reproduce the problem (too bad!), the next thing to do is to check your system's hookup and configuration. You need to examine every cable going into and out of your system unit, the installation of any add-in cards, the setup of specific software programs (including Windows), and anything else you can think of that might cause the problem. Then, after you've confirmed that everything is plugged in and set up properly, restart your system—correcting a poorly connected cord or misselected option doesn't always register with your system until it starts up again (hence the reboot).

If you still have problems, it's now time to start thinking methodically and logically. Begin by tracing the steps that led to your problem. Did you do anything wrong—or different from normal? Have you recently added anything new to your system—or changed anything old? It's not unheard of for new hardware or software to induce changes in your system's behavior—and even affect things seemingly unrelated to the new items. If you can isolate the cause of the problem, it's easy enough to remove the new peripheral or program and get your system back to pre-problem operating status.

Finally, if you can't fix the problem—and not all problems are easily fixed, unfortunately—it's time to call in a professional. Don't get discouraged if you can't figure everything out yourself; there are just some problems that are beyond the abilities of mortal men (and women). That's why computer technicians exist. If you need to, call one. It's okay.

What Causes Most Problems?

Although there are literally thousands of potential computer and Internet-related problems you could face, most stem from one of three causes:

➤ **You** did something wrong, such as clicking the wrong item, typing a command incorrectly, or accidentally hitting the wrong key.

➤ Your **hardware** is not turned on, plugged in, connected, or configured correctly.

➤ **Windows** or another piece of software is not installed or configured correctly.

So when you encounter a problem, following these simple steps could very well resolve the situation:

1. Try the procedure again. (You'd be surprised how often this "fixes" problems!)

2. If the problem persists, make certain that all your hardware is turned on and that all cables are connected properly. (Many problems are the result of something coming unplugged—or not being powered up!)

3. Undo the last change you made to your system—either hardware- or software-related.

Some elaboration on that last point. Your computer system itself doesn't suddenly go bad. Most problems happen because you change something on your system, and that change upsets a previously working configuration.

What problems can be caused by change? A new piece of hardware can conflict with an existing device. A new software program can reconfigure parameters originally set for other programs. Even resetting a common Windows option can throw the delicate harmony of your system out of balance.

So, if something goes wrong, figure out what you changed, and change it back to the way it was!

What Are the Most Common Problems?

Okay, enough background information. It's now time for the 10 most common problems faced by computer and Internet users. Most users can find their solutions right here; if you don't find yours in this list, you have to read the rest of the book!

1. Your Computer Won't Start

If your computer doesn't start when you flip on the power, check first for some obvious causes. First, make sure that you turned on the *power switch* (or button) and not some other switch or button. (Do you have any idea how many times I've hit the disk eject button instead of the power button on my own system—and vice versa?)

Next, make certain that your computer's power cord is plugged in. Now, make sure *again* that it's plugged in—both into a power outlet *and* into the back of the computer. (You'd be surprised how easy it is to jiggle the power cord loose from the back of your machine!)

Then make certain that the power outlet has power. (Do you see a trend here?) Make sure that the wall switch, if any, is turned on and that all fuses and circuit breakers are securely in place. If you use a surge suppressor, check that it, too, is turned on.

If none of these recommendations work, then you really *do* have a problem—one that could have one of many potential causes. Just look at what can cause a dead computer:

➤ **The cord from your computer to your power outlet might be bad.** Try replacing your power cord with a cord from another computer.

➤ **The power supply transformer in your computer might be faulty.**
Call a technician and get your bad power supply replaced.

➤ **If your computer makes noise but nothing appears on your screen, something might be wrong with your monitor.** Try adjusting your monitor's brightness and contrast settings, or replacing your monitor with a monitor from another computer system.

➤ **If you receive a message about a non-bootable disk in drive A, you forgot to remove a disk before you turned on your system.** Your computer can't start with a normal disk in the disk drive; remove the disk from drive A and press any key to restart your PC. This same problem can also result in other error messages, such as Operating system not found and Invalid or non-system disk.

➤ **You might have a major problem with your hard disk that prevents your computer from starting.** It might have a damaged boot sector, or it might not be connected properly, or it might be missing the key system files, or it might even be completely dead. Try starting your system from your Emergency Windows Startup Disk—described in Chapter 7, "Preparing a PC Survival Kit." Then use ScanDisk to check for hard disk errors. If you can't track down and fix the problem yourself, call a computer technician for more help.

In addition, your so-called dead computer might actually be a live computer with a problem that won't allow Windows to launch. If your computer appears to start (lots of noise and flashing lights) but *Windows* doesn't start, your problem is probably with Windows, not with your computer hardware.

The first thing to do if you have trouble starting Windows is to restart your computer with Windows in Safe mode. *Safe mode* is a special Windows operating mode that uses a very simple configuration which should run on all computer systems—even those that are experiencing operating problems. Safe mode is *not* your standard operating mode; it's a mode you use only when Windows won't work otherwise.

You enter Safe mode by rebooting your computer (just press **Ctrl+Alt+Del** together until your computer turns off and then back on), and then carefully watch the onscreen messages as your computer goes through its start-up procedure. When you see the line Starting Windows..., press the **F8** key. When you do this, you'll be presented with a Windows Startup menu. Select **Safe Mode** from the menu, and then—after Windows has launched into Safe mode—examine all the configuration settings to find out what could be causing your problem.

In particular, check your system's display and device settings, using the **Device Manager** tab in the System Properties dialog box. Correct any misconfigured settings and reboot your computer; if all is well, Windows will start in its normal mode. In a worst-case situation, you might need to uninstall a particular device and then reinstall it to reset the configuration. (See Chapter 29, "Getting It Right...System Settings and Technical Maintenance," for more information about checking and changing system settings.)

If you still can't get your computer or Windows to start, go directly to Chapter 11, "What to Do When...Your System Won't Start," for a multitude of possible solutions that might get you back in shape and ready to roll.

2. Your Computer Locks Up While Running

Sometimes your computer comes on and runs perfectly—then it suddenly just freezes up. Your keyboard doesn't work, nor does your mouse. In fact, repeatedly pressing keys on the keyboard elicits nothing but a series of obnoxious beeps. What gives?

If you're lucky, something came unplugged. Surprisingly, a loose cable between your keyboard and your system unit can cause your entire system to freeze up. Try unplugging and replugging the keyboard cable to see if that fixes the problem.

Sometimes, however, your software is the culprit, not your hardware. Programs can occasionally become stuck in endlessly repeating loops that make your system *appear* to lock up. Try pressing the **Esc** key a few times; with most programs, this cancels the operation in progress. If that doesn't work, try the **Ctrl+C** or **Ctrl+Break** key combinations. Again, pressing these keys often interrupts any software operation in progress, breaking the loop.

If your system is still frozen, try switching to another open program. Click another program button on the Windows Taskbar, or press **Alt+Tab** to shuttle through all open programs.

If you can't change to another program, or if that program is also locked up, then you have a systemwide lockup—and it's now time to do the "three-finger salute." Press the **Ctrl+Alt+Del** keys simultaneously. This brings up the Close Program dialog box. All your active programs will be listed here, even programs you didn't even know were running. (These mystery programs are actually Windows system programs that run in the background all the time.) If you have a locked-up program, the words Not Responding should appear next to the program name. Select the non-responding program, and then click the **End Task** button. After a few seconds a Wait/Shutdown dialog box appears; confirm that you want to shut down the selected application by selecting **End Task** again. This should close the offending program and return your system to normal.

The operative word here is "should." If you can't close a non-responding program, or if there is no frozen application, or if your system is still frozen, then click the **Shut Down** button in the Close Program dialog box. If *this* doesn't have any effect, you need to reset your entire system and start over again. Press **Ctrl+Alt+Del** again, and then a second time. This will perform a *soft boot* of your system, essentially turning it off and then back on. This action—while causing you to lose any unsaved data in any open program—works 88 percent of the time.

Be Patient!

It might take a minute or so for the Wait/Shutdown dialog box to appear; if it hasn't appeared in this time, press **Ctrl+Alt+Del** again.

If your system is *really* locked up, however, even this won't have any effect—that is, pressing **Ctrl+Alt+Del** won't reboot your system. The only solution might be what hard-core techies call a *hard boot*: Use the Reset button or the main on/off switch to turn off your PC manually. Wait about 30 seconds, and then turn the machine back on.

Just to Be Safe

If you're running Windows 98, when your system restarts after an abnormal termination, ScanDisk will automatically be run to check for any potential disk problems.

After you *reboot*, you'll probably discover that you've lost any data you entered after you last saved your file to disk. (If so, let this hard-earned lesson encourage you to save your data frequently while working at the keyboard.) Fortunately, rebooting without first exiting a program doesn't usually damage the data files themselves. Just to be safe, however, make sure that you try every other option *before* you reboot your computer.

What causes Windows to freeze? There could be any number of problems, although the most common culprit is too many programs using too much memory. If your system freezes on a regular basis, consider upgrading the amount of memory on your computer system.

Sleep Isn't Always Good

Windows 95 and 98 include new Always On technology that lets your PC enter a special energy-saving sleep mode when it isn't being used. Under normal conditions, pressing any key on the keyboard or moving the mouse will cause your PC to "wake up" from sleep mode. When these actions *don't* wake up your computer, you need to manually restart your computer, using your system's Reset button.

In some cases a restarted computer will immediately enter sleep mode again—from which it still can't be awakened. If this happens, restart your computer (using the Reset button) and then press the **F8** key during the startup sequence to enter Safe mode. From within Safe mode, go to the Power Management dialog box (found in the Control Panel) and disable all power management schemes (including any options to turn off your monitor and hard disk). Then restart Windows (in normal operating mode).

Note that not all computers have Always On technology, and that Always On doesn't always work well. If your system continues to hang on wake up, permanently disable Always On as described in the previous paragraph. (You should also check your system's CMOS BIOS settings; some PCs come with built-in power management that will have to be disabled outside of Windows.)

3. An Individual Program Locks Up

Sometimes a program just seems to stall—it locks up, and just won't do anything, either with the mouse or the keyboard. You can change to other programs (by using the mouse to click on another window, by pressing another program button on the Windows Taskbar, or by pressing **Alt+Tab** to manually switch to another open program), but this particular program just isn't moving. What can you do?

First, you might want to give it a few more minutes. Sometimes, when Windows is low on memory (or disk space) or you're working with a particularly big file, Windows gets a little pokey. Your program might actually be working fine, but just working slow!

If your patience begins to wear thin, however, you'll want to close the program and get on with other things. Make sure that the offending program is the active program (by clicking anywhere in the program's window), and then press the **Ctrl+Alt+Del** keys simultaneously. You should see the Close Program dialog box, with all your programs listed. Select the frozen program from the list, and then click the **End Task** button. After a few seconds, a Wait/Shutdown dialog box appears; confirm that you want to shut down the selected application by selecting **End Task** again. This should close the frozen program.

When you're back in Windows, check to see if everything else is running fine. In most cases, Windows does a good job of isolating a problem to a single program; forcing one program closed typically doesn't affect any other open program. However, if you notice problems with other programs, or if your system seems to be running slower than it was before, select the **Start** button, select **Shut Down**, and when the Shut Down Windows dialog box appears, select **Restart**.

Even if all your other programs continue to run fine, there's one other situation where you might want to restart Windows. If you can't relaunch the program you just shut down (or if you can launch the program but can't load the document you were working on), you need to restart your computer to clear any phantom memory still in use from before the program shut down.

4. Windows Runs Slower Than Normal

The most likely culprit behind a system slowdown is memory—or rather, the lack of it. Check for the following:

➤ Are you running any new applications—or upgrades of older applications—that might consume more memory? You might need to add extra memory to your system to accommodate the needs of some newer software programs.

➤ Are you running more programs than usual at the same time? Try closing some programs to free up extra memory.

➤ Do you leave Windows running all the time? If so, your computer might have a great deal of *unreleased resources*. Because not all Windows programs release all the memory and other resources they've used after they're closed, little chunks of unreleased memory are left floating around in your system's RAM. Other programs can't access these hoarded resources, which in turn slows down your system. The only way to release these "leaked" resources is to exit and restart Windows.

Any of these factors consumes more memory and forces Windows to slow down. If you're dissatisfied with the performance of Windows on your system, the answer is simple: Add more memory!

While you're looking at your memory, you should also look at the amount of free space on your hard disk. Because Windows uses your hard disk for "virtual" memory, too little disk space has the same impact as too little memory. It doesn't hurt to periodically go through and delete unused files from your hard disk, just to keep Windows happy.

5. Your Printer Won't Print

Printing can sometimes be a problem. Fortunately, however, the most common printer problems also are the simplest to solve.

Here's a short list of some of the more common printing problems:

➤ **You might have the wrong printer driver installed.** Follow the instructions in Chapter 16, "What to Do When...Your Printer Won't Print," to make sure your printer is configured correctly.

➤ **You might not have enough disk space to print.** Windows sometimes uses temporary disk space to store data while a print job is in progress. Try deleting some old files to free up disk space.

➤ **Your programs might not be configured correctly.** Some Windows programs provide additional printer configuration options that go beyond those available through the standard Windows printer setup. Check your programs to make sure they're set up correctly.

➤ **You could be trying to print from both a DOS and a Windows program at the same time (or even from two DOS programs).** You can't do this because the output becomes garbled. Stop printing, and then restart with just one program at a time.

➤ **You might be out of paper.** If you receive an error message to this effect, reload your printer, and then select the **Retry** option to restart the print job.

➤ **Your printer connections might be faulty.** Remember to check all your cables, and make certain that the printer is plugged in and turned on.

One more thing—if you have more than one printer on your system (or you have both a printer and a fax driver installed), make sure you have the right printer selected. You do this via a **Printer Setup** option in your software program, or you can check your system-wide printer selections by selecting the **Printers** icon in the Windows Control Panel.

If you check all these factors and your printer *still* doesn't work, turn to Chapter 16 for more detailed troubleshooting information. The software you're using might not have been installed correctly for your particular printer, or your printer might really be out of whack. If it's the latter, get ready to spend some bucks—printer repair isn't cheap. (In fact, if your printer is really kaput, it might be cheaper just to buy a new one!)

6. You Accidentally Delete a File

Nothing is more frustrating than realizing you've just deleted a file you didn't want deleted. Fortunately, Windows provides a way to recover deleted files from among the dearly departed.

When you use My Computer or Windows Explorer to delete a file, the file isn't really deleted—it's just been sent to the Windows Recycle Bin. The Recycle Bin (which has an icon on your desktop) is actually just a folder that serves as kind of a "holding bin" for deleted files. Files you delete are stored in the Recycle Bin until the Bin fills up—at which point they're truly and finally deleted, on a first-come, first-gone basis. (By default, the Recycle Bin can get as large as 10 percent of your disk drive before it starts to delete files—oldest deleted first.)

To recover a file recently sent to the Recycle Bin, just select the Recycle Bin on your desktop. This opens the Recycle Bin and displays its contents. Select the file(s) you want to undelete and click your *right* mouse button. (Not the normal left one!) When the pop-up menu appears, select **Restore**. This will restore the selected file(s) to the original location(s).

What if you want to recover a file that has been "emptied" from the Recycle Bin? Well, at this point, you're too late—once it's gone from the Recycle Bin, it's really gone, no way to bring it back. (Well, that's not *completely* true...there are some third-party utilities, such as Norton Utilities, that let you find and undelete files that have been emptied from the Recycle Bin, although Windows has no such utilities built-in.)

By the way, the Recycle Bin only holds files deleted from your hard disk. Any files deleted from network drives, disks, or other removable media are permanently deleted when they're deleted, no interim "recycle bin" involved. So be extra careful when deleting files from these auxiliary storage devices!

7. You Have Problems Installing New Software

In most cases, installing new software is a breeze. You pop an installation CD into your system's CD-ROM drive, the installation program starts up automatically, and everything gets installed with a minimum of fuss and muss.

However, you can still run into problems installing new software, especially when upgrading an existing software program to a new version. Just take a look at these common problems (and solutions):

➤ **Your new software doesn't work.** This is either due to a bug in the new software, a bad or incomplete installation, some sort of incompatibility with your system, or an error (probably on your part) in starting the program. You might want to try reinstalling the program, just in case something went wrong with the initial installation.

➤ **Your new software causes your old software not to work.** Some new programs alter the Windows Registry (which is the "bible" used to store all the configuration settings for all Windows programs); it's possible your new software altered the Registry in a way that changed the settings for an older program. It's also possible that your new program has some sort of memory conflict with an older program, or is causing a device conflict of some sort. Try *uninstalling* the new software, and then reinstalling it again. (If you can't formally uninstall the program—not all programs come with uninstall utilities—then just manually delete the program's files from your hard disk and then reinstall.)

➤ **The upgraded version of your old software doesn't work with your old data files.** This used to be a fairly common problem; a lot of software publishers didn't ensure perfect compatibility between different versions of their own programs! If this happens to you, you should contact the publisher of your software to obtain some sort of conversion program. Of course, it's also possible that the new version of your program simply doesn't know where your old files are; you might need to change some program option settings to direct the new software to your old file folders.

If you still have problems with your new software, see Chapter 22, "What to Do When... Your New Software Causes New Problems."

8. You Have Problems Upgrading Your Hardware

Major changes to your system can cause major problems—even if you seem to be doing everything right. The most common problems are either that your new hardware doesn't work, or that your old hardware doesn't work after you've installed your new hardware. While you can find a more detailed analysis of this situation in Chapter 23, "What to Do When...Your Hardware Upgrade Downgrades Your System," here are a few things to look for:

➤ **Your new hardware isn't properly installed.** Check all your connections; make sure that all boards are properly seated and that all cables are firmly connected.

➤ **Your system isn't configured properly for your new hardware.** While Windows embraces the so-called *plug-and-play* technology (and Windows 98 plug and play works better than the Windows 95 version), sometimes you can plug all you want and Windows still won't play—for some reason, it doesn't recognize the new device you added. Try manually adding the new hardware by selecting **Add New Hardware** from the Control Panel; this launches the Add New Hardware Wizard, which kind of overrides the plug and play stuff. It's also possible that Windows recognized your new hardware, but that an individual program didn't get the news; if your problem is isolated to a specific program, you'll need to reconfigure that program for your new hardware.

➤ **Your system has an interrupt conflict.** This happens when two different parts of your system try to use the same interrupt, or IRQ, setting. The easiest fix for this is to change the COM port setting for your newest component (if the device actually uses a COM port—not all do); note that some devices (such as mice and modems) don't work well together if they share even or odd numbered ports. (For example, avoid hooking a mouse to COM1 and a modem to COM3—you're better off using ports 1 and 2 or 1 and 4, if possible.) If this doesn't work, you'll have to reconfigure the IRQ settings for one or more of your hardware devices. (This is sometimes done via software programs, and sometimes via switches located on the boards themselves.)

If you still can't get your new hardware to work, check out Chapter 23.

9. You Can't Establish a Connection to the Internet

If you have an Internet connection (through an Internet service provider) but you can't connect, you could have one of several common problems:

➤ **Your ISP's lines are busy.** Listen to your modem as it tries to connect. If you hear a busy signal, that means that all the telephone lines leading into your ISP are busy. (This often happens in big cities at busy times of the day—typically early evening hours.) You might even connect to your ISP, but then get hung up while logging in; again, this is most often caused by too many people trying to connect at the same time. You should hang up and try again later.

➤ *Your* **lines are busy.** You can't dial out while your phone line is engaged. Make sure nobody else is using the phone before you try to reconnect.

➤ **The Internet is busy.** If you get connected and you log on, but then you can't go anywhere (you can't connect to any Web sites, and you can't send or receive email), it's possible your ISP's connection to the Internet is down. Try disconnecting and then reconnecting later.

➤ **Your dial-up configuration is wrong.** If you repeatedly can't log on to your ISP—if you get connected but can't get through the automatic log on routine—then you might have something configured wrong in your dial-up networking settings. Check your configuration, or (if you have Windows 98 or a later version of Internet Explorer) rerun the Internet Connection Wizard.

➤ **Your modem isn't configured properly.** Most modem problems are caused by either incorrect configuration or conflict with other hardware devices. If you're running Windows 98, you can use the Modem Troubleshooter in the Windows Help system to help you track down the problem. Otherwise, go to the Modem Properties dialog box (by selecting **Modems** in the Control Panel) and running through the diagnostics there.

➤ **Your modem isn't connected properly.** As always, check all the cables (if you have an external modem) or the card installation (with an internal modem). Don't forget to check the cable from your modem to your telephone jack.

17

➤ **Your system's network (or TCP/IP) settings aren't configured properly.**
This is less of a problem in Windows 98, where the networking protocol is built-in
and configuration is relatively automatic, but on older systems you might need to
check the advanced networking settings for accuracy.

If you still have connection problems, it's time to go to Chapter 24, "What to Do When…
Your Internet Connection Goes Offline."

10. You Have Trouble Accessing a Specific Web Site

Don't you just hate this? You enter a URL (that's computerese for "Web site address,"
and stands for *Uniform Resource Locator*) and you get a message saying This Page
Cannot Be Displayed or Unable to Locate the Server or 404 Error. What went
wrong—why *can't* you access that Web page?

More often than not, this problem is caused by a bad address. Either you entered the URL
incorrectly (and that's easy to do, given the length and complexity of some addresses) or
the link you just clicked had the wrong address coded in. It's also possible that the page is
temporarily down (for editing or upgrading) or that the Internet is so busy you just can't get
to that page right now. In all cases, recheck the URL, and then try accessing the page again.

If the address is definitely wrong, maybe you can go elsewhere on that same site to
get to where you really want to go. If you have a long URL, try cutting back to the
next highest directory. For example, if the address looks like this: www.website.com/
directory1/directory2/page.html, try entering www.website.com/directory1/
directory2/; if that doesn't work, try www.website.com/directory1/ or even
www.website.com. Sometimes individual pages on a site go away or change locations,
but the site itself remains.

If you still can't get to where you want to go, you might have to search for a new
address. To learn how to find sites on the Web, go to Chapter 26, "What to Do When…
Your Web Surfing Wipes Out."

The Least You Need to Know

➤ Most computer problems are caused by either user error, a bad connection, or
an incorrect system configuration.

➤ If you encounter a computer problem, first try executing the procedure again,
and then check all the cables (including power cables) between your system
unit and peripherals.

➤ If you're still having problems and you've recently installed a new program or
peripheral, uninstall the new item (to delete recently installed device drivers)
and then reinstall it again; this often resets any bad system settings.

Chapter 2

Hardware Basics for the Technically Timid

In This Chapter

➤ Discover the various parts of your computer system—what they are, and how they work

➤ Learn what can go wrong with each of your system's components

➤ Find out how to upgrade your system's hardware

Before you begin undeleting files, checking printer ports, and editing the Windows Registry, it might be a good idea to take a quick refresher course in computer basics. The best way to start is by examining each component of your system—what that part does and what problems it could experience.

Don't let all this initial attention to technical detail disturb you, however. This book is written for *you*, the average computer user, not some techno-dweeb who carries a screwdriver set in a pocket protector.

By the way, if you want more details about Windows and the Internet, read ahead to Chapters 3, "Windows Basics for the Technically Timid," and 4, "Internet Basics for the Technically Timid." In this chapter we'll stick pretty much to hardware and system basics. So…, let the class begin!

All About Your System Hardware

Computer *hardware* comprises those parts of your system that you can actually see and touch. (Contrast this to your computer software, which consists of data stored in magnetic form on your disks. You can see and touch the disks, but not the actual data they store.)

Technical Troubleshooting

If you're *really* interested in the technical mumbo-jumbo about computer hardware that I *don't* cover in this book, there's help in the form of another fine Que book. Check out *Upgrading and Repairing PCs*, now in its 10th edition; it's a really comprehensive book about almost everything you can find inside your computer.

Your hardware, therefore, includes your *system unit* (that big ugly box that houses your disk drives and many other components) and all the parts inside it. Anything connected to your system unit also is called hardware, including your monitor, your printer, your keyboard, and your mouse.

Always keep your system unit in a well-ventilated location free of excess dust and smoke. (The moving parts in your computer don't like dust and dirt or any other such contaminants that can muck up the way they work.) Because your computer generates heat when it operates, you must leave enough room around the system unit for the heat to dissipate. *Never* place your computer in a confined, poorly ventilated space; your PC might overheat and shut down if it isn't sufficiently ventilated.

For extra protection for your computer, connect the power cable on your system unit to a *surge suppressor* rather than directly into an electrical outlet. A surge suppressor—which looks like a power strip with multiple outlets—protects your PC from power line surges that could damage its delicate internal parts. When a power surge temporarily *spikes* your line voltage (causes the voltage to momentarily increase above normal levels), a surge suppressor shuts down power to your system, acting like a circuit breaker or fuse.

All the different components of your computer system connect to one another through various cables and adapters. These cables can be a source of trouble if they're not connected correctly. Make sure that you plug all cables securely into their sockets; in fact, screw them into place if you can. Make certain, too, that the cables don't have abrupt bends or kinks in them. If your cables aren't as straight as possible, the wires inside them might break or become damaged.

When You Need More Than a Surge Suppressor

A surge suppressor does what it does by shutting down your system when a power spike occurs. Although this protects your computer, you do lose any data you were working on when the surge suppressor did its job. Of course, this is better than losing your entire hard disk to a voltage spike, but if you use your PC for applications in which you can't afford even a momentary shutdown (in a retail store, for example), you might want to invest in a battery-operated backup power supply (also called an *uninterruptable power supply*, or *UPS*). These devices send auxiliary power to your PC during power outages—and, when used in conjunction with a surge suppressor, give you *complete* power protection. In addition, a UPS can provide "clean" power in areas where power line spikes and brownouts are common—it kind of evens out the bumps, as it were.

Under the Hood—Evaluating Your System Unit

When you open up the case on your system unit, you see myriad computer chips and circuit boards. The really big board located at the base of the computer is called the *motherboard* because it's the "mother" for your microprocessor and memory chips, as well as for the other internal components that enable your system to function. (Microprocessors are described in the section "The Brains Behind It All—Evaluating Microprocessors," later in this chapter.)

Your PC—The Inside Story

Opening up your computer's system unit isn't for the faint of heart. Not only is it terribly intimidating, but you stand a good chance of breaking something if you really don't know what you're doing. So if you're the least bit unsure of whether you should be poking around inside your PC—*don't poke!* Let someone more technically qualified do the dirty work so you can get back to your keyboard and mouse that much faster.

The motherboard contains several slots into which you can plug additional *boards* (also called cards) that perform specific functions. A *video card*, for example, enables your microprocessor to transmit video signals to your monitor. (See the following figure for a picture of a typical video card.) Other available cards enable you to add sound, modem, and fax capabilities to your system.

A typical add-on board—this one happens to be a video card.

Most PC motherboards contain six or more slots for add-on cards; if you try to add too many cards to a low-end system, however, you might run out of slots! If that happens, either reevaluate your need for some of the cards or consider buying a new system with enough slots to hold the additional cards.

If add-on cards aren't inserted correctly, your entire system could fail to function. In addition, some cards contain physical *switches* that must be configured for your system. These switches might be physical switches (often called "dip" switches) or they might be *jumpers*, little wire prongs that have to be connected in the proper pattern. Set these switches in the wrong positions, and that card—or your entire system—might seriously malfunction.

Some cards also require you to run software-based setup programs to configure parts of your system. Whatever the case, always be sure to consult the instructions that come with each card to make certain everything is set correctly before you button up the case and turn on the power again.

You might even find it necessary to make adjustments to your operating system or to specific software programs so that you can use your new cards. Check each program to determine whether it must be adjusted or set up individually to operate with your new card.

The Brains Behind It All—Evaluating Microprocessors

Deep inside your system unit lurks the one component that controls your entire system: the microprocessor chip. The *microprocessor* (also called the *central processing unit*, or *CPU*) chip resides atop the motherboard, surrounded by many other chips and transistors that help it do its job.

The microprocessor is the brains inside your system. It processes all the instructions necessary for your computer to perform its duties. The more powerful its microprocessor chip, the faster and more efficiently your system runs.

Microprocessors carry out the various instructions that enable your computer to compute. Every input and output device hooked up to a computer—the keyboard, the printer, the monitor, and so on—either issues or receives instructions that the microprocessor must process. All your software programs also issue instructions that must be implemented by the microprocessor. This chip truly is the workhorse of your system because it affects just about everything your computer does.

Several different types of microprocessor chips currently exist. Most IBM-compatible computers use chips originally designed by Intel; others use Intel-compatible chips designed by AMD and other firms. Other types of computers use other kinds of chips; the Apple Macintosh chips, made by Motorola, for example, are of a totally different design than Intel's.

Certain program types require certain chips to run on a particular system. If your PC contains an older chip, make sure that you buy only software that can run on your system. (Chip requirements usually are listed on the software package.)

Apples and Oranges Don't Mix

It's because of the different processor configurations that software written for the Apple Macintosh (which uses Motorola-compatible chips) won't run on IBM-compatible computers (which use Intel-compatible chips)— and vice versa.

Even within the same chip family, different chips run at different speeds. CPU speed is measured in megahertz (MHz); a CPU with a speed of 1MHz can run at one million clock ticks per second! The higher its megahertz, the faster the chip runs. When you purchase a new PC, look for one with the combination of a powerful microprocessor and a high clock speed for best performance.

Fortunately, not much can go wrong with a microprocessor, short of it completely failing— and microprocessor failure is normally pretty rare if you keep your PC in a well-ventilated place. You might, however, notice that some software programs run very slowly on under-powered machines—that is, machines with slower chips. If you own an older PC that is equipped with an 8086, 80286, 80386, or 80486 chip, you probably can't run most of the newer programs sold today. If in doubt, check the software's packaging or documentation, or ask the software publisher (or your dealer) if a particular program is designed to run on your PC. You might just have to avoid purchasing certain programs—or else upgrade to a newer, more powerful computer that can run all the programs you want it to.

What CPU—and How Much RAM—Do You Have?

If you want to know which microprocessor is installed in your system, Windows will tell you. Just open the **Control Panel** and select the **System** icon; when the System Properties dialog box appears, select the **General** tab. The **System** section will tell you which version of Windows you're running; the **Registered To** section will tell you who you are (or, rather, how your version of Windows is registered); and the **Computer** section will tell you which processor you have, and how much memory (RAM) you have installed.

Temporary Storage—Evaluating Memory

Before your CPU can process any instructions you give it, your instructions must be stored somewhere, in preparation for access by the microprocessor. These instructions—along with other data processed by your system—are temporarily held in the computer's electronic *random access memory* (RAM). All computers have some amount of memory, which is created by their memory chips. The more memory that's available in a machine, the more instructions and data that can be stored at one time.

Memory is measured in terms of *bytes*. One byte is equal to approximately one character. A unit equaling approximately one thousand bytes (1,024, to be exact) is called a *kilobyte* (*KB*), and a unit of approximately one thousand (1,024) kilobytes is called a *megabyte* (*MB*). A thousand megabytes is a *gigabyte* (*GB*).

Cashing In the Chips

If you're adding memory to your PC, make sure that you get the right configuration for your system. Not only do you have to choose how much memory to add (and different RAM chips have different capacities), but you also need to make sure you select either *SIMMs* (single inline memory modules) or the less-common *DIMMs* (dual inline memory modules), as required by your system. The instruction manual for your PC should tell you what kind of memory you need to add; if not, a good computer technician can figure it out for you.

Most computers today come with at least 32MB of memory, and some of the more expensive machines have 128MB or more. To enable your computer to run as many programs as quickly as possible, you need as much memory installed in your system as it can accept—or that you can afford. Extra memory can be added to a computer by installing a new memory module, which is as easy as plugging a "stick" directly into a slot on your system's motherboard.

If your computer doesn't possess enough memory, its CPU must constantly retrieve data from permanent storage on its hard disk. This method of data retrieval is slower than retrieving instructions and data from electronic memory. In fact, if your machine doesn't have enough memory, some programs will run very slowly (or you might experience random system crashes), and other programs won't run at all!

Data Central—Evaluating Hard Disk Drives

The second main physical component inside your system unit is the *hard disk drive*. The hard disk *permanently* stores all your important data. Some hard disks can store more than 10 *gigabytes* of data. (Contrast this to your system's memory, which stores only a few dozen megabytes of data temporarily; your computer's memory often acts as a short-term storage bin for data that's been read from its hard disk but not yet fed into its microprocessor.)

A hard disk consists of numerous metallic platters. These platters store data *magnetically*. Special read/write *heads* realign magnetic particles on the platters, much like a recording head records data onto magnetic recording tape. (The next figure shows a typical hard disk.)

Data is recorded on your hard disk in circular *tracks*, which are much like the tracks on a record album or compact disc. Each disk is further divided into *sectors*. Your computer uses the intersection of track and sector as a sort of electronic road map to locate individual pieces of data on the disk. This tracking data is stored in a special section of the disk, called the *file allocation table* (*FAT*). Your system refers to the FAT data to determine where to find specific files on your hard disk.

Before data can be stored on any disk, including your system's hard disk, that disk must first be *formatted*. A disk that has not been formatted cannot accept any data. When you format a hard disk, your computer prepares each track and sector of the disk to accept and store data magnetically and, in the process, creates a blank FAT on the disk.

Your hard disk can cause you a great deal of trouble if you don't treat it right. Because a hard disk is a physical device that spins at a high rate of speed, it can actually wear out over time. The disk might start spinning at the wrong speed, or the platters that make up the disk might themselves become damaged. If your system is located in an area with too much dust or smoke, the disk platters can become contaminated; a contaminated disk might not read or write data correctly. In addition, a rough jolt to your system unit (and thus to the hard disk) can cause the disk's read/write heads to collide with the platters and result in damaged hardware and data—which is a good reason to turn off your PC before moving it.

The insides of a hard disk drive—see the platters?

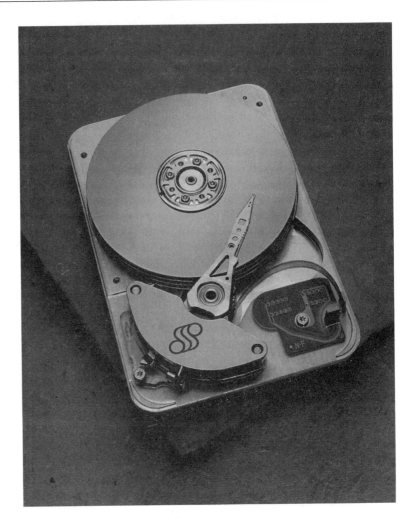

Eventually, too, the platters and the read/write head might become misaligned, due to nothing more to age and use. When this happens, consult a technician. Your disk might be salvageable, or it might have to be replaced.

The data on your hard disk also can be subject to various problems, many of which have human causes. If you accidentally format a hard disk that has data on it, for example, you lose all that data. You can accidentally erase varying amounts of data on your hard disk, too, if you're careless in deleting files. What's more, if computer viruses manage to infect your system, they can scramble your valuable data, making your hard disk function abnormally, if at all. So always take extra care when working with your hard disk; if you don't, all its gigabytes of data can very suddenly—and quite painfully—become inaccessible.

If you think you have disk-related problems, turn to Chapter 17, "What to Do When... Your Disk is Damaged," for help.

Data to Go—Evaluating Diskettes

Along with its hard disk drive, every computer has one or more *diskette drives*. (In fact, most early computers didn't even have hard disks; they relied totally on diskettes to store their data.) Removable diskettes—often called "floppy" disks—work much like hard disks except that they consist of thin sheets of a magnetic-tape-like material instead of hard metallic platters.

Older PCs stored data on 5 1/4-inch diskettes; all new PCs use the smaller, higher-density 3 1/2-inch diskettes. Because diskettes are more portable than hard disks, the former are used to store data that's transported physically from PC to PC. And diskettes are useful, too, for storing backup copies of the data on your PC's hard disk.

The head in a diskette drive works just like the read/write head of a hard disk drive. The only difference is that the diskette drives aren't sealed from the elements, as are hard disk drives. Diskette drives, therefore, are even more suscep-tible to dirt, dust, and smoke than are their "hardier" cousins. If you seem to encounter more than a few read/write errors when you use different diskettes, the disk drive itself might require realignment or even replacement.

Better Safe Than...Well, You Know

For extra safety, you might want to store your backup diskettes in a different location from your computer system, such as in a safe deposit box at your bank. This way, if your computer is lost through theft or damaged by fire, your backup data is still safe.

Diskettes are susceptible to every ailment that can possibly befall a hard disk—and then some. Because diskettes are portable, they can become damaged during transit. And because data is stored on diskettes magnetically, placing a diskette too close to a magnetic source (such as a stereo speaker, a ringing telephone, or your computer monitor) can erase its data.

The main warning to heed is to be as careful with your diskettes as you would with any other computer part or peripheral. Don't assume that just because they are made of flexible material they can't be seriously harmed. (You can actually cause data problems just by opening the little "window" on the diskette and touching the storage surface with your finger!) And always make sure that you have copies of any important files stored on diskette as well as on your hard disk—just in case. (In fact, making an extra diskette copy of your really vital files couldn't hurt either!)

Other Types of Portable Storage

In addition to standard 3 1/2-inch diskettes, you can use other types of portable storage media—most of which offer much more capacity than the 1.44MB found on a standard diskette. For example, Iomega's Zip drive offers 100MB of portable storage, and their Jaz drive offers 2GB of storage. Sony's new Superdisc can store up to 120MB on a diskette that is physically compatible with—and can thus fully replace—traditional 3 1/2-inch drives.

Laser Data—Evaluating CD-ROMs and DVDs

There's a third type of disk that is now standard on personal computer systems. This disk is called a *compact disc—read-only memory*—although you know it by its abbreviation, *CD-ROM*. (The ROM part means that you can only read data from the disk; unlike normal hard disks and diskettes, you can't write new data to a standard CD-ROM. There are, however, recordable (CD-R) and rewritable (CD-RW) drives available that *do* let you write data to CD discs—although they're a bit more expensive than standard CD-ROM drives.

Beyond the CD-ROM is the new *DVD* (*digital versatile disc* or *digital video disc,* depending on who's doing the abbreviating) medium. DVDs can contain up to 4.7GB of data (compared to 650MB for a typical CD-ROM), and thus are ideally suited for large applications or games that otherwise would have required multiple CDs. Like standard CD-ROMs, DVDs are read-only, but DVD drives can also read CD-ROM discs. In addition, many full-length movies are now being produced on DVD discs; you can play these movies in a computer DVD drive.

CD-ROM and DVD discs look just like the compact discs you play on your audio system. In fact, they're very similar in the way they contain data (audio data in the case of regular CDs and computer data in the case of CD-ROMs and DVDs). Information is encoded at a disc-manufacturing plant, using an industrial-grade laser. This information takes the form of microscopic pits (representing the 1s and 0s of computer binary language) below the disc's surface. Like hard and floppy disks, the information is arranged in a series of tracks and sectors, but the tracks are so close together that the disk surface is highly reflective.

Data is read from the CD-ROM or DVD disc via a drive that uses a consumer-quality laser. The laser beam follows the tracks of the disc and reads the pits, translating the data into a form your system can understand.

Most CD-ROM and DVD problems have to do with dirty or scratched discs, or with dirty laser assemblies. Cleaning a disc is easy—just use a soft cloth. If you have a scratch on a disc, you can try one of the so-called "CD scratch repair" kits sold at some stores, although I've found they really don't work that well; once a disc is scratched, the damage is generally permanent. (Which argues in favor of handling your discs as carefully as you do your audio CDs—and only by the edges, never touching the surface of the disc itself.)

If the lens that focuses the laser in your CD-ROM or DVD drive gets dirty, the laser can become unfocused and have difficulty reading the information from the disc. The solution to this problem is to use a commercial laser lens cleaner that you insert just like you do a CD-ROM disc.

Another major CD-ROM/DVD problem concerns the setup for your particular system. Most CD-ROM and DVD drives, whether internally or externally installed, require that a *device driver* be loaded into memory before the drive can work. (Device drivers are small files that control peripheral devices, such as video cards and sound cards.) If you don't have a driver installed—or don't have the *correct* driver installed—your CD-ROM or DVD drive won't work at all.

For more information on fixing CD-ROM and DVD-related problems, see Chapter 18, "What to Do When...Your CD-ROM or DVD Doesn't Spin Right."

Keys to Success—Evaluating Keyboards

Computers receive data by reading it from disk, accepting it electronically over a modem, or receiving input directly from you, the user. Users provide input by way of what's called, in general, an *input device*; the most common input device you use to talk to your computer is the *keyboard*.

A computer keyboard looks and functions just like a typewriter keyboard, except that computer keyboards have a few more keys. Some of these keys (such as the arrows, **PgUp**, **PgDn**, **Home**, and **End** keys) enable you to move around within a program or a file. Other keys provide access to special program features. (The following figure shows one of the newer keyboards on the market, with a split layout for better ergonomics.)

A popular PC keyboard— Microsoft's Natural Keyboard Elite—with an ergonomic design that's easier on the wrists.

When you press a key on your keyboard, it sends an electronic signal to your system unit that tells your machine what you want it to do. If for any reason the system unit doesn't receive this signal, your keystrokes do absolutely nothing (except perhaps exercise your fingers). The most common keyboard problems can usually be traced to some sort of obstacle that's preventing the signals from reaching your system unit. The culprit might be a loose connection, excess dirt or dust—or maybe even a crumb from that Twinkie you ate while working with your files the other night.

To avoid loose connections that could interrupt signals from your keyboard, always make certain the keyboard is securely connected to your system unit. Try also to keep your keyboard free of dust, dirt, and other foreign matter that could block signals to the system unit. And always take care when handling or transporting your keyboard so as not to damage it.

Food and Keyboards Don't Mix

Unfortunately, because computer keyboards do consist of complex electronic components, damaging one can sometimes be far too easy. That's why you never want to eat or drink around your computer. Spilling food and beverages on the keyboard can short out its electronic circuits and wreak havoc on your entire system. Soft drink residue can also cause your keys to stick, and a stuck key can actually cause your computer not to start!

Some "third-party" keyboards feature unique key configurations that might not work with some PCs. If you're experiencing difficulty inputting data manually into your machine and you think that it might be because your keyboard is incompatible with your computer, try using another keyboard. If the different keyboard works, your problem almost certainly lies within your original keyboard, which means you probably should replace it.

If you're having any sort of trouble with your keyboard, turn to Chapter 13, "What to Do When...Your Keyboard Won't Type."

The Mighty Mouse—Evaluating Pointing Devices

At one time it was considered merely a novelty, but in recent years it has become a must-have input device. "It" is the *mouse*.

The mouse is a small hand-held device usually consisting of an oblong case containing a roller underneath and two or three buttons on top. When you move the mouse along a desktop, an onscreen pointer (called a cursor) moves in response. When you click (press and release) a mouse button, this motion initiates an action in your program.

A mouse is just one kind of input device you can hook up to your PC. Trackballs, joysticks, game controllers, and pen pads all count as input devices, whether they work in conjunction with a mouse or replace it. Make sure you have enough free ports before you start adding too many input devices—and be forewarned that multiple input devices can sometimes cause conflicts among themselves.

If you have a portable PC, you don't have a separate mouse, but rather a built-in pointing device of some sort—a touchpad, a rollerball, or a TrackPoint (the thing that looks like a little rubber eraser). These devices are typically less troublesome than freestanding mouse devices because they're sealed against dirt and dust. (Not that you have to use the built-in pointing device on a portable PC; most portables let you attach an external mouse, which then overrides the internal device.)

Just as with the keyboard, the most common mouse problems result from loose connections. These usually occur when the mouse somehow becomes unplugged from the computer (such as when you tug too hard on it or accidentally roll it off the desk). Because the mouse is a mechanical device, its roller ball can eventually wear out with use, making cursor movement difficult. The constant movement of the mouse across a desk surface can often damage the mouse cable, too. If your mouse's behavior becomes too erratic, it might be time to either clean or replace the little rodent.

If you have more than one input device connected to your computer—a mouse and a joystick, for example—these two devices can sometimes interfere with one another. I've seen instances where changing the settings on a joystick affected the behavior of a mouse. Always look for unwanted interaction when you have two similar devices connected to one PC.

If you're plagued by mouse problems, find more solutions in Chapter 14, "What to Do When...Your Mouse Won't Point."

Sounding Off—Evaluating Sound Cards and Speakers

Every PC comes with its own built-in speaker; in fact, some systems (like the one shown in the following figure) come with multiple-speaker audio systems, complete with subwoofers and so-called "3D" sound. These higher-end sound systems are driven by a special sound card inside your system unit; if you want better sound, buy a higher-priced sound card and speakers.

One of the better speaker systems for personal computers, from Cambridge SoundWorks—the big thing in the middle is a subwoofer, for better bass.

Because speakers have no moving parts, they seldom go bad. If your PC goes silent, the problem probably lies in the configuration of a specific software program, in the workings of your sound card, or in the connection of the speakers to your system unit—but *not* in the speakers themselves.

Note that when you add multiple speakers to your system, the hookup can sometimes get a little complex. Make sure you follow the manufacturer's wiring diagram to hook the right speaker up to the right cable; this is especially tricky if your system includes a powered subwoofer.

If you're having problems with your system's sound, you can probably find the solution in Chapter 19, "What to Do...When Your Sound System Doesn't Sound Right."

What You See Is What You Get—Evaluating Video Cards and Monitors

It would be difficult to operate a computer if you didn't constantly receive visual feedback showing you what your machine is doing. This vital function is provided by your computer's monitor.

The monitor is very much like a little television set. Your microprocessor electronically transmits to your monitor words and pictures (*text* and *graphics*, in PC lingo) in some approximation of how these visuals would appear on paper. You view the monitor and respond according to what you see onscreen.

The monitor itself doesn't generate the images it displays. These images are electronically crafted by a *video card* installed inside your system unit. To work correctly, both video card and monitor must be matched to display images of the same resolution. Resolution refers to the size of the images that can be displayed and is measured in pixels. (A pixel is a single dot on your screen; a full picture is composed of thousands of pixels.)

Early PCs could not display graphics at all. They were strictly *character-based* and could display only text. As technology progressed, however, graphics standards were developed, and virtually all PCs available today can display some level of graphics. The current "base" graphics standard is called *VGA* (for *video graphics array*); VGA monitors are capable of displaying 640×480 pixels. Many video cards and monitors can display much higher resolutions, with 800×600 pixels, 1,024×768 pixels, or even higher combinations being readily available. As you probably guessed, the higher the resolution, the better and more colorful the picture.

Sadly, your system's video setup can be the source of numerous problems. If your card and monitor are mismatched, for example, you might receive distorted images on your monitor—if, in fact, you see anything at all. (You might have to reset the switches on the video card itself to establish the correct setup for your system.) Configuring Windows for the wrong video card can result in display problems, too. And, as with most peripheral-based problems, a loose connection between the monitor and the system unit is Public Enemy Number One. So, to ensure great reception on your monitor, just as you would with your television, make sure that everything is plugged in, set up, and adjusted correctly.

If you're experiencing problems with your computer's display, turn to Chapter 15, "What to Do When...Your Display Looks Funny."

All That's Fit to Print—Evaluating Printers

Your monitor displays images in real-time, but in a transitory manner. For permanent records of your work, you must add a printer to your system. Printers create *hard copy output* from your computer programs.

You can choose from various types of printers for your system, depending on your exact printing needs. The two main types of printers today are *laser* and *inkjet* printers.

Laser printers work much like copying machines, applying toner (powdered ink) to paper by using a small laser. *Inkjet* printers shoot jets of ink to the paper's surface to create the printed image. Inkjet printers are typically lower priced than laser printers, and often offer affordable color printing; laser printers cost more, but have higher-quality output.

All printers can cause you trouble. Not only are the usual problems with hookup and setup to be expected, but printers also require constant maintenance to stay in top operating condition. For example, laser printers require regular replacement of their toner cartridges as well as frequent paper-path cleaning; inkjet printers require new ink cartridges and maintenance to keep the ink jets from getting clogged.

If you're having problems printing, turn to Chapter 16, "What to Do When…Your Printer Won't Print," for help.

Going Online—Evaluating Modems

The last major peripheral you might consider adding to your PC system is a *modem*. Modems allow your computer to connect to telephone lines and transmit data to and from the Internet and commercial online services (such as America Online).

Modems come in either internal (card-based) or external (hooking up to an open port on the back of your system) models. Internal modems usually fit into a slot on your motherboard and connect directly to a telephone line. External modems are free-standing devices that connect to your system unit by cable and hook directly to a phone line.

When you connect a modem to your system, take care that all its settings are configured correctly for your computer—and that you have the correct device drivers installed. You also must create a dial-up connection in Windows to connect to an Internet service provider; you need to input the right information to establish your connection and account.

If all this sounds somewhat complex, well, that's because it is. I don't mean to scare you away from the joys of online communications, but you should be made aware that modems can cause you some headaches. Getting everything hooked up and configured correctly *can* be a chore. Add in the potential for *port conflicts* (when your modem actually interferes with other parts of your system), *dirty telephone lines* (which interrupt or slow down data flow), and protocol mismatches (resulting from incompatible configurations between your system and the system you're trying to reach), and you see how problems can arise.

If you do have trouble using your modem or connecting to the Internet, turn to Chapter 24, "What to Do When…Your Internet Connection Goes Offline."

How to Upgrade Your Hardware—Without Calling a Technician

If your PC is more than a year old, chances are you can significantly improve its performance by upgrading one or more components. Whether you're adding more memory, moving to a larger hard disk, adding a faster modem, or changing audio or video cards, you can keep your system up-to-date without buying a completely new system.

Fortunately, Windows makes it relatively easy to add new components to your system. Windows works with both *Plug and Play* and older *legacy* (non-Plug and Play) hardware. Plug and Play hardware is automatically identified by Windows when you add it to your system; older hardware sometimes needs to be manually identified (via the Add New Hardware Wizard) before it can be installed.

Which One Should You Buy?

Although it might be tempting to buy the lowest-priced device when you want to upgrade, be aware that the cheapest option isn't always the best. Low-priced peripherals often come with inadequate instructions, out-of-date driver files, and limited (or non-existent) technical support. You get what you pay for; sometimes spending a little more money gets you a much easier upgrade.

Also, make sure that the device you want to add is fully compatible with your system. Different system units have different types of expansion slots, and not all cards will work in all PCs. When in doubt, check with your PC's manufacturer for compatibility—and don't be afraid to let a qualified technician do the installing for you.

In general, you need to turn off your system before you add new hardware—whether the hardware is installed internally or externally to your system. The next time you boot up your PC, Windows will recognize that a new device has been added, and proceed to install the proper drivers for the new device. If Windows *doesn't* recognize the new device, you have to configure Windows manually.

Before You Begin—Create a System Hardware Report

It's good practice to know what your PC's settings are before you install any new equipment. Device Manager, found in both Windows 95 and Windows 98, can provide you with various reports that detail the devices installed on your system and which resources they're using.

Just click the **Start** button, select **Settings**, select **Control Panel**, and then select the **System** icon. When the System Properties dialog box appears, click the **Device Manager** tab; select **View Devices by Type** to list all devices by class. To print a report for a specific class or device, select the name in the devices list box, and click **Print** to open the Print dialog box. When the Print dialog box appears, select the type of report to print, as described in Table 2.1. Click **OK** in the Print dialog box to print the report on the selected output device.

Table 2.1   System Hardware Reports

Report	Description
System Summary	Lists the resources on your system, as well as which hardware is using each resource.
Selected Class or Device	Lists the resources and device drivers used by the device selected in the device list.
All Devices and System Summary	Lists all the hardware on your system, including a list of all resources used by the hardware.

Use the All Devices and System Summary report to determine whether you have a potential conflict with new hardware that you are preparing to install in the computer. Print the report, highlight all IRQ, I/O, and MEM settings, and then compare these to the settings that the new device(s) can be set to.

In Windows 98, you can also use the Microsoft System Information utility (shown in the next figure) to print out more detailed reports on your system status. Because Microsoft System Information gives you a snapshot of your entire system configuration, this is a great resource for anyone—including technical support staff—trying to troubleshoot Windows problems; this kind of specific information is necessary to figure out what might be conflicting with what.

The Microsoft System Information utility—a great way to learn about your system components.

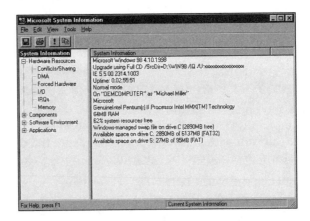

Just click the **Start** button, select **Programs**, select **Accessories**, select **System Tools**, and then select **System Information**. When Microsoft System Information appears, click on the item in the left-hand pane you want to examine. The contents of that view will appear in the right-hand pane.

Microsoft System Information organizes your system data into three major categories, displayed in a kind of resource "tree" in the left-hand pane:

➤ **Hardware Resources**   This view displays hardware-specific settings—DMA, IRQs, I/O addresses, memory addresses, and so on. Select **Conflicts/Sharing** to identify devices that are sharing resources or are in conflict.

➤ **Components**   This view displays information about your Windows configuration. Look here to determine the status of your device drivers and network resources. Select **History** to see changes made to your system components over time.

➤ **Software Environment**   This view displays a snapshot of the software loaded in your system's memory.

To print out a complete listing of all system parameters, click the **Print** button. (Note: Depending on your particular system, the printout can run up to 100 pages!) If you'd prefer to save your system information in a text file for future viewing, pull down the **File** menu and select **Export**, and then select a filename and location for the text file.

Even *More* Troubleshooting Tools

There are several other advanced system tools useful for troubleshooting located within the Microsoft System Information utility. Pull down the **Tools** menu to access Windows Report Tool, Update Wizard Uninstall, System File Checker, Signature Verification Tool, Registry Checker, Automatic Skip Driver Agent, Dr. Watson, System Configuration Utility, ScanDisk, and Version Conflict Manager.

To learn more about Windows' system reporting and configuration utilities, turn to Chapter 29, "Getting It Right...System Settings and Technical Maintenance."

Adding New External Hardware

Perhaps the easiest way to add new peripherals to your system is to add them via an external port; this way, you don't have to open up your PC's case.

Follow these steps to attach a new external device to your system:

1. Turn off your computer and unplug its power cable.
2. Find an open port on the back of your system unit, and connect the new peripheral.
3. Plug your system back in, and restart it.
4. If necessary (see the instructions provided by the device's manufacturer), enter your PC's Setup program and reconfigure the CMOS settings.

5. After Windows starts, it should recognize the new device and automatically install the appropriate driver. If Windows doesn't recognize the device you might be prompted to insert a disk containing the driver; you can also install drivers manually with the Add New Hardware Wizard.

Listing to Port

There are several types of ports that might be available on the back of your PC. These include *parallel ports*, used primarily to connect printers; *serial ports*, used to connect communications devices, such as modems; *SCSI ports*, used for fast communications devices, such as digital cameras or Zip/Jaz drives; *USB ports*, used for newer plug-and-play devices; *network ports*, used to connect your PC to an office LAN; *video ports*, used to connect your monitor; *mouse ports*, used to plug in your mouse or trackball; *game ports*, used to plug in both a joystick and MIDI musical instruments; and *keyboard ports*, used to connect your keyboard.

When attaching new devices to most ports, it's recommended that you turn your system off first, connect the new device, and then restart your system. If your system has a Universal Serial Bus (USB), however, you don't have to turn off your system to add new peripherals; the peripherals are "hot swappable." Just plug the new device into the USB port, and Windows will automatically recognize it in real-time.

Whichever type of port you use, make sure you follow the directions from your peripheral manufacturer to plug the right kind of device into the right port—using the right cable!

Most new peripherals are Plug and Play, meaning that Windows will recognize them automatically the next time it starts; adding a new device is truly as easy as shutting off your PC, plugging in the new device, and then starting your PC again. Adding older devices to your system, however, can be more problematic and less automatic. For these older devices, you'll most probably need to use the Add New Hardware Wizard, described later in this chapter.

Adding New Internal Hardware

Adding an internal device—usually through a plug-in card—is slightly more difficult than adding an external device, primarily because you have to use a screwdriver and get "under the hood" of your system unit. Other than the extra screwing and plugging, however, the process is pretty much the same as with external devices.

Follow these steps to add a new card to your system:

1. Turn off your computer, but leave the power cable plugged in (to protect your system against unwanted electrostatic discharge).

2. Take the case off your system unit, per the manufacturer's instructions.

3. If the card has switches or jumpers that need to be configured, do this before inserting the card into your system unit.

4. Find an open card slot inside the system unit, and insert the new card according to the manufacturer's instructions.

5. After the card is appropriately seated and screwed in, put the case back on the system unit, plug your system back in, and restart it.

6. If necessary (see the instructions provided by the card's manufacturer), enter your PC's Setup program and reconfigure the CMOS settings.

7. After Windows starts, it should recognize the new device and automatically install the appropriate driver. If Windows doesn't recognize the device you might be asked to install a disk containing the driver, or you might need to run the Add New Hardware Wizard.

Test It Before You Put It Back Together

You probably want to see if the new component configures properly and works fine before you button your system unit back up; save putting the case back on until you're convinced everything is working okay and you don't need to do any more fiddling around inside your PC.

In most cases, both your system and Windows will recognize the new card without any manual prompting. Note, however, that you can run into conflicts if you install two cards of the same type in your system—for example, installing two modem cards can confuse Windows to no end.

If you run into problems after you've installed a new device, see Chapter 23, "What to Do When...Your Hardware Upgrade Downgrades Your System."

Adding a Disk Drive

It's fairly easy to insert a new card—be it a video, audio, modem, or other such device. Adding a new disk drive however, can be more of a chore; you have to find an open drive bay, mount the new drive, connect a power cable, and connect the drive to a free drive controller. You'll need to get explicit instructions from the drive's manufacturer and your PC's manufacturer, and follow the instructions accordingly.

Using the Add New Hardware Wizard

Windows provides the Add New Hardware Wizard to aid in the configuration of drivers for new hardware devices. If Windows doesn't automatically detect your new device, you need to use the wizard to manually install and configure the new hardware.

To start the wizard, click the **Start** button, select **Settings**, **Control Panel**, and then select the **Add New Hardware** icon. When the first screen of the wizard appears, click the **Next** button.

When the second screen appears, click **Next** and Windows will search for any new Plug and Play devices installed on your system. The wizard will now prepare to search for any hardware that isn't Plug and Play. In most cases, you'll want to have Windows identify your hardware automatically; select **Yes** and click the **Next** button.

The next screen in the wizard tells you that it is now going to look for new hardware. Choose **Next** to start the search (which can take awhile). When your new hardware has been identified, the wizard displays a message that it is ready to begin installing the device(s). Click the **Details** button to view the device(s) Windows has identified; click **Finish** to complete the installation.

If the Add New Hardware Wizard cannot locate the required files on your hard drive, you are prompted to identify the type of hardware you're installing and then to choose the manufacturer and model of your hardware. If your specific model isn't listed, click the **Have Disk** button and place the CD-ROM or diskette containing the driver files into the appropriate drive. When the necessary files have been loaded, follow the onscreen instructions to complete the installation.

The Add New Hardware Wizard will, in most cases, detect the proper driver for your newly installed hardware. You should almost always opt to accept Windows' recommended drivers, unless the drivers supplied by your peripheral's manufacturer are newer—or unless Windows doesn't recognize the device at all.

Changing Your PC's Internal Configuration

Your PC has its own internal configuration stored in nonvolatile CMOS memory. When you install a new peripheral, in most cases your system will recognize the device and automatically update the CMOS settings. However, if your system doesn't automatically recognize the new device, you will have to update your CMOS memory manually through a special Setup program.

See More CMOS?

CMOS stands for Complementary Metal-Oxide Semiconductor, and is a type of low-power battery-backed memory that stores very basic system information (and the time for your PC's clock). This information stays in CMOS memory until you change it or the battery runs down. CMOS memory settings are sometimes called *BIOS* (basic input/output system) settings.

If your computer is currently on, you'll need to exit Windows and restart your system. When your computer restarts, watch your screen for a message that tells you how to enter your system's Setup program. In most cases you will be instructed to press a certain function key (**F1**, **F2**, **Del**, and so on); press this key to enter the Setup program.

When the Setup program starts, write down the current settings. (This is a good precaution in case you change something you shouldn't— you can simply reset all the settings to those in place before you made any changes.) You can now make the appropriate changes to the settings for your new device; in most cases, this means following the instructions provided by the device's manufacturer.

Can't Get In?

If you don't see instructions on how to enter the Setup program, or if you cannot enter the Setup program, contact your computer's manufacturer for instructions.

After you've edited your settings, save the new settings in CMOS memory and exit the Setup program. Your computer will continue with its startup procedure, with the new settings in place.

The Least You Need to Know

➤ Your system unit contains your computer's microprocessor, memory, disk drives, and add-on cards; connected to the system unit are your machine's keyboard, mouse, monitor, and printer.

➤ If any of these parts fails to work or communicate with the other parts, your system itself ceases to function normally.

➤ You should take the utmost care with your computer system, either when initially installing its various parts or when operating it on a daily basis.

Chapter 3

Windows Basics for the Technically Timid

In This Chapter

➤ Discover the key features of Windows 98

➤ Learn how to perform common Windows operations

➤ Uncover 10 ways to upgrade your system for better Windows performance

Windows is a piece of software called an *operating system*. An operating system does what its name implies—it *operates* your computer *system*. Every program that runs, every command you issue, every option that is selected, must be filtered through the operating system to be executed by your computer hardware. Your computer won't run without an operating system—and Windows is the operating system used by almost all personal computers today.

All About Windows

Windows—published by Microsoft Corporation—is the friendly "face" of your computer system, the thing you see every time you power on, the system you interface with on a constant basis. Not only does it control your hardware, but it also presents a variety of functions and features you can use to ease the pain of personal computing.

The version of Windows on your personal computer isn't the first version of Windows ever released. There have been numerous versions of Windows released over the years, starting with version 1.0 back in the late 1980s. Both the original version of Windows and its 2.0 replacement weren't very good, to be quite honest, and not many people used them. But Windows 3.0 (released in May 1990) actually worked quite well, and was embraced by PC users—who had previously been using a text-based operating system called *DOS* (which literally stands for *disk operating system*).

Windows 3.0 (and its subsequent 3.1 and 3.11 upgrades) changed the face of personal computing, literally. In the DOS environment, users had to issue a series of obscure text commands to perform even the simplest of tasks; with Windows, these same tasks could be executed by using a mouse to click on an icon or pull down a menu. Windows 3.0, with its *GUI* (pronounced "gooey" and standing for *graphical user interface)*, made computing easier, and within a few years DOS-based computers were nowhere to be found.

The Big Move—Upgrading from Windows 3.1 to Windows 98

You don't have to progress in perfect order; it's fully acceptable to upgrade from Windows 3.1 (or 3.11) to Windows 98, skipping Windows 95 altogether.

Note, however, if you make this big jump there are several significant differences between Windows 3.1 and Windows 98, as outlined in Table 3.1.

Table 3.1   Major Differences Between Windows 3.x and Windows 98

Task/Item	In Windows 3.1	In Windows 98
Open applications	Program Manager	Start menu
Manage files	File Manager Directories	Windows Explorer or My Computer Folders
Store files in filenames	Eight characters plus three character extension	Long filename and extensions (up to 256 characters)
Delete files	Are deleted	Are sent to the Recycle Bin, from where they can be undeleted
Minimize windows	Becomes temporary icons at bottom of screen	Becomes temporary buttons on Taskbar
Close window button	Top-left corner	Top-right corner
Right mouse button	Does nothing	Displays context-sensitive pop-up menu
Install new hardware	Difficult	Uses Plug-and-Play technology to automate most hardware installations

In 1995, Microsoft released a radically revised version of Windows called *Windows 95*. This new Windows did away with Windows 3.0 staples like Program Manager and File Manager and replaced them with My Computer, the Windows Taskbar, and a Start button—along with an interface that more closely resembled the Apple Macintosh. Where previous versions of Windows didn't really do away with the DOS operating system (they kind of ran "on top of" DOS), Windows 95 was a true operating system, the only thing users saw when they powered on.

What Happened to File Manager and Program Manager?

Even though they're not readily visible, Program Manager and File Manager still exist in both Windows 95 and Windows 98, if you absolutely insist on using them. To run Program Manager, click the **Start** button, select **Run**, and type **PROG-MAN** when the Run dialog box appears. Likewise, to run File Manager, click the **Start** button, select **Run**, and type **WINFILE** when the Run dialog box appears. Note, however, that any new programs you install after the upgrade will not appear in Program Manager; File Manager, however, will continue to show the contents of all your disk drives.

Windows 98, released in (you guessed it!) 1998, made some minor but important changes to Windows 95. The desktop stayed pretty much the same, but the operating itself was a little more bullet-proof, and included more "wizards" to help users more easily perform various tasks.

If you're using an older version of Windows, should you upgrade to Windows 98? My answer is yes—and no:

➤ If your system is working perfectly with an older version of Windows and you don't need to install any new software or hardware devices, you don't need to upgrade. (And, in fact, if you have an older PC system, you might not have the horsepower to run Windows 98, anyway.) Why mess with a good thing?

➤ If you install any new software (or upgrade any old software), or want to add any new hardware peripherals, you should upgrade to Windows 98. The newest version of Windows crashes less frequently than older versions, and makes it easier to add new hardware to your system. Before you upgrade your hardware, especially, upgrade to Windows 98.

So if your system is stable and you're happy with things, don't upgrade. If you're an active user, however—and add *any* new software or hardware to your system—then order a copy of the Windows 98 upgrade today!

Windows 2000?

You might have heard about another version of Windows called *Windows 2000*. This operating system (previously referred to as Windows NT 5.0) is a networked operating system that looks and feels a lot like Windows 98, but is optimized to run on large networks in a corporate environment. Windows 98, on the other hand, is a *personal* operating system, designed to run on individual computers. If you control your own PC, you should run Windows 98; if other people (like an IT department) controls your PC, they might elect to run Windows 2000. From a user's perspective there shouldn't be much difference between the two.

Focusing on Windows 98

For the balance of this chapter, I'll focus on how you use Windows 98. Most of my instructions and advice will also apply to Windows 95, but there is some Windows 98–specific information presented. (I had to pick one version to use for examples—so I picked the most recent version!)

Starting and Stopping Windows

Before you can use Windows, you have to launch it. And, after it's started, it helps to know how to stop it, as well.

Launching Windows

There is only one way to launch Windows: Turn on your computer!

Windows starts automatically every time you turn on your computer. Although you will see lines of text flashing onscreen during the initial startup (and you have the option of interrupting the boot process to configure your system's CMOS settings), Windows loads automatically and goes on to display the Windows desktop.

Shutting Down Windows

When you finish running Windows applications and want to turn off the computer, you first must correctly exit Windows by using the Shut Down command—you shouldn't just turn off your computer with Windows still running (or you could damage your system!).

Shut Down Properly!

Try not to turn your computer off without exiting Windows. You could lose data and settings that are temporarily stored in your system's memory. Wait for the message saying it is safe to turn off your computer.

What if your computer just hangs there, without displaying the shut off message? If you've waited at least 60 seconds without any activity on your PC (lights flashing, disk drives whirring, and so on), it's probably hung up—and you'll have to shut down your PC manually, using the on/off button. When you do this, Windows will automatically run ScanDisk (a utility that analyzes the status of your hard disk) the next time you start up, just in case any files were damaged during the emergency shutdown.

To shut down Windows, first save any documents and other data in applications that are open, and then exit all applications. Now click the **Start** button and select **Shut Down**. When the Shut Down Windows dialog box appears, select one of the following options (which might vary depending on your configuration):

➤ **Stand By**
➤ **Shut Down**
➤ **Restart**
➤ **Restart in MS-DOS Mode**

Choose **Shut Down**, and then click **OK**. If prompted as to your real intentions, choose **Yes**, and then turn off your computer when you see the message that says it is safe to do so. (Note, however, that many newer computers—including most laptops—automatically shut off your computer when the "safe to shut off" message appears; no action is necessary on your part.)

To restart your computer (reboot) without shutting down completely, choose the **Restart** option in the Shut Down Windows dialog box. To simply restart Windows without restarting your entire computer system, hold down the **Shift** key when you choose the **Restart** option, and click **OK**. (This performs a much faster "soft" reboot.)

Many new PCs now come with special "sleep" modes (also called *stand by* or *suspend* modes) that let you power down your system without shutting it off. When you select **Stand By** from the Shut Down Windows dialog box or the **Start** menu, your PC doesn't have to go through the lengthy "boot" process when you next use it, it just "wakes up" instead.

To Sleep, Perchance to Dream

When your PC is in sleep mode, it looks like it's completely shut down. The difference is that "awakening" from sleep mode takes much less time than fully booting up your PC from a complete shutdown. Note, however, that going into sleep mode doesn't reboot your machine, so if you need to turn your computer on and off for any reason (to recover "lost" memory, or refresh your system in the wake of a program crash), sleep mode won't do the job. Also note that your computer will go into sleep mode after a preset time of inactivity—and that means inactivity from you, the user. Activation of a screen saver will not affect the timing of sleep mode activation.

Understanding the Windows Desktop

The Windows desktop (whether you're using Windows 95 or Windows 98) includes a number of shortcut icons, a Taskbar, and other recognizable elements. However, if you elect to activate Windows 98's *single-click mode*, the desktop changes a bit—you still have all the old elements, but now they behave like hyperlinks on a Web page; you highlight icons by hovering over them, and you launch applications by single-clicking icons. (*Without* single-click mode activated, you still single-click to highlight and double-click to launch, just as you do in Windows 95.)

Activating Single-Click Mode—and Learning How to Hover

To make your Windows 98 desktop work like a Web page (single-clicking instead of double-clicking), click the **Start** button, select **Settings**, and then select **Folder Options**. When the Folder Options dialog box appears, select **Web Style**, and then click **OK**. (To return to the traditional double-click mode, select **Classic Style** from the Folder Options dialog box.)

By the way, if you activate single-click mode, you have to learn a new way to highlight items. This new technique is called *hovering*, which involves placing the cursor over an item without clicking your mouse. When an object is hovered over, it is automatically highlighted, and the cursor turns from an arrow into a hand shape.

This single-click feature was actually launched with Internet Explorer 4 as a feature called the *Active Desktop*, which integrated with Windows 95 to provide the Web-like desktop. Active Desktop continues into Windows 98 with additional features, such as the ability to put "active" Web content on your desktop—much less useful and much less used than the single-click feature.

Learn More About Windows

This book is only so big; there isn't enough space here to deal with typical troubleshooting topics *and* Windows basics, too. So if you're a complete Windows novice, I recommend that you examine one of the following excellent Que books to learn more about the subject at hand:

➤ *Easy Windows 98*, a good step-by-step, full-color, visually oriented introduction for beginning users.

➤ *The Complete Idiot's Guide to Windows 98*, an unintimidating overview of Windows ins and outs.

➤ *Special Edition Using Windows 98*, a comprehensive reference that tells you everything you could ever want to know about Windows.

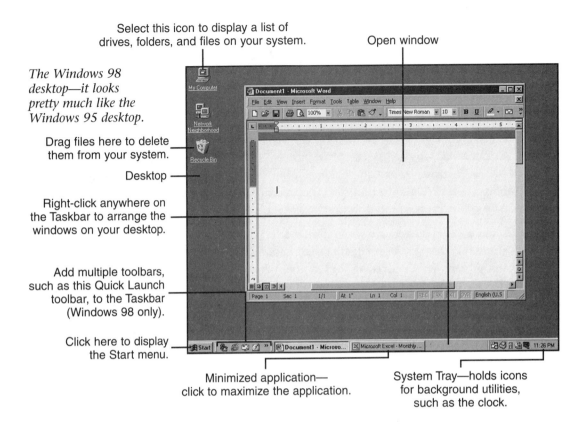

Select this icon to display a list of drives, folders, and files on your system.

Open window

The Windows 98 desktop—it looks pretty much like the Windows 95 desktop.

Drag files here to delete them from your system.

Desktop

Right-click anywhere on the Taskbar to arrange the windows on your desktop.

Add multiple toolbars, such as this Quick Launch toolbar, to the Taskbar (Windows 98 only).

Click here to display the Start menu.

Minimized application— click to maximize the application.

System Tray—holds icons for background utilities, such as the clock.

As shown in the previous figure, the major parts of the Windows desktop are as follows:

➤ **Start button** Opens the **Start** menu, which has submenus leading to many other folders and applications.

➤ **Taskbar** Displays buttons for your open applications and windows, as well as different toolbars for different tasks.

➤ **Toolbar** A separate button bar that can be attached to the main Taskbar, specific to Windows 98. Windows 98 includes toolbars for URL addresses, Links to favorite Web sites, Desktop icons, and Quick Launch of Web utilities; in addition, you can create your own personalized toolbars.

➤ **System Tray** The part of the Taskbar that holds the clock, volume control, and icons for other utilities that run in the background of your system.

➤ **Shortcut icons** Allows you to launch applications and load documents with a single-click of the mouse.

➤ **Windows** When open on the desktop, they can be moved around and resized.

Important Windows Operations

Now, to use Windows efficiently you need to master a few simple operations—such as pointing and clicking.

Left Is Right

For the purposes of discussion, I'll assume that you're right-handed, and therefore using the left mouse button as your main mouse button and the right mouse button as your secondary mouse button. If, however, you're a southpaw, you can select the Mouse icon in the Windows Control Panel to reconfigure Windows so that your mouse operates backwards—that is, so the right mouse button is your main mouse button and the left mouse button is your secondary mouse button. So if you're left-handed, when I refer to the right mouse button, you need to transpose that to mean the left mouse button, and vice versa. Right?

Pointing and Clicking

The most common mouse operation is *pointing and clicking*. Simply move the mouse so that the pointer is pointing to the object you want to select, and then click the left mouse button once. Pointing and clicking is an effective way to select menu items, directories, and files.

Double-Clicking

If you're using Windows 95 or the double-click mode of Windows 98, you'll need to *double-click* an item to activate an operation. This involves pointing at something onscreen with the pointer, and then clicking the left mouse button twice in rapid succession. For example, to open program groups or launch individual programs, simply double-click a specific icon. (With Windows 98's single-click mode activated, you just single-click to perform the same operations.)

Right Is Right

Windows and many Windows applications use the right mouse button to display a pop-up menu containing commands that directly relate to the selected object. Refer to your individual programs to see if and how they use the right mouse button.

Dragging and Dropping

Dragging is a variation of clicking. To drag an object, point at it with the pointer, and then press and hold down the left mouse button. Move the mouse without releasing the mouse button, and drag the object to a new location. When you're done moving the object, release to mouse button to drop it onto the new location.

Launching Applications

The easiest way to launch an application is to either click (in single-click mode) or double-click (in double-click mode) its desktop icon or **Start** menu item. There are several other ways you can start a program, however.

If you know the path and name of the program you want to launch, you can click the **Start** button and select **Run**. When the Run dialog box appears, type the program path and name into the Open box and click the **OK** button; the program launches automatically.

If you don't know the name of the program, you can still launch it via My Computer or Windows Explorer. Simply scroll through the folders and files until you find the file you want, and then click or double-click on the filename, and the program launches. It's as simple as that.

Using Dialog Boxes, Tabs, and Buttons

When Windows or an application requires a complex set of inputs, you are often presented with a *dialog box*. A dialog box is like a form where you can input various parameters and make various choices—and then register those inputs and choices when you click the **OK** button.

There are various types of dialog boxes, each one customized to the task at hand. However, most dialog boxes share a set of common features, including the following:

➤ **Buttons**   Most buttons either register your inputs or open an auxiliary dialog box. The most common buttons are **OK** (to register your inputs and close the dialog box), **Cancel** (to close the dialog box without registering your inputs), and **Apply** (to register your inputs without closing the dialog box). Click a button once to activate it.

➤ **Tabs**   These allow a single dialog box to display multiple "pages" of information. Think of each tab, arranged across the top of the dialog box, as a "thumbtab" to the individual page in the dialog box below it. Click a tab to change to that particular page of information.

➤ **Text boxes**   These are empty boxes where you type in a response. Position your cursor over the empty input box, click your left mouse button, and begin typing.

➤ **Lists**   These are lists of available choices; lists can either scroll or drop down from what looks like an input box. Select an item from the list with your mouse; you can select multiple items in some lists by holding down the **Ctrl** key while you click with your mouse.

➤ **Check boxes**   These are boxes that let you select (or deselect) various stand-alone options.

➤ **Option buttons**   These are the round "boxes" that you check to select an option; typically, selecting one option *deselects* all other options.

➤ **Sliders**   These are sliding bars that let you select increments between two extremes—like a sliding volume control on an audio system.

➤ **Spinner arrows**   These are controls that let you "spin" through a number of selections by clicking the up or down arrow buttons.

This figure shows a common dialog box—the Display Properties dialog box. (To display this dialog box, right-click an empty part of the desktop, and then select **Properties** from the pop-up menu.) As you can see, this dialog box includes buttons, tabs, lists, and check boxes—everything *except* a text box and a slider.

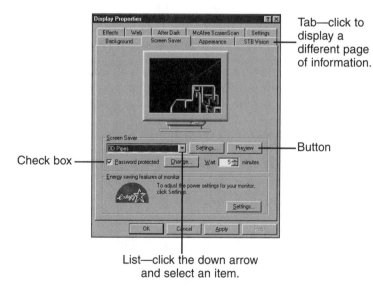

Tab—click to display a different page of information.

The Display Properties dialog box—where you can set all sorts of parameters for your desktop and display.

Button

Check box

List—click the down arrow and select an item.

Windows Pains

Windows is an incredibly complex environment and, as such, the cause of many headaches. Not only can you inflict countless problems on yourself through user error, but also Windows often seems to go screwy all on its own. Because the program uses so much system memory, Windows occasionally creates or exacerbates memory conflicts among various programs. If your system operates slowly to begin with, or

Shades of Gray

If an option in a dialog box is dimmed (or "grayed"), that means it isn't available for the current task.

has insufficient memory to run Windows efficiently, be prepared for long waits when you attempt to execute operations—and expect plenty of system errors. (A distinct inverse correlation exists between the amount of memory your system possesses and the number of system errors you experience when running Windows.)

You can take certain measures to entice Windows to run cleaner (such as expanding your computer's memory and watching the number of programs you run at one time), but like nearly everything else, Windows is not—and probably never will be—perfect.

10 Tips for Upgrading Your System for Windows 98

If you have an older PC that you've just upgraded to Windows 98, you might be somewhat disappointed with your system's performance. If so, consider these tips to speed up your Windows 98–enabled PC:

1. Add More Memory

The biggest effect you can have on your system's performance is by adding more memory. Microsoft recommends a "minimum" of 16MB for Windows 98; I say it's more like 32MB to get acceptable performance, with a personal recommendation for 64MB or more.

2. Install a Bigger Hard Disk

Windows 98 itself takes up a lot of disk space—as do most other state-of-the-art software programs (such as Microsoft Office). In addition, Web browsers (including *both* Internet Explorer and Netscape Communicator) "cache" recently viewed Web pages on your hard disk. The net of all this is that space on your hard disk can rapidly diminish. Add a big hard disk to your system—2GB is probably the minimum you should consider—and also think about augmenting your hard disk space with a large portable storage device, such as a Zip or a Jaz drive from Iomega.

3. Get a Faster Modem

If you connect to the Internet with any regularity, you know how slow the Net can be. One way to speed it up is to use a faster modem. If—heaven forbid!—you still have an old 14.4Kbps model, or even if you have a 28.8Kbps model, spend the bucks for a 56Kbps model *now*.

4. "Overdrive" Your Processor

Some older Pentium processors are capable of being upgraded to faster speeds through the use of what Intel calls an Overdrive chip. Piggybacking an Intel Overdrive processor to your existing Pentium chip can increase your system's processing speed by 50 percent or more.

5. Use a Bigger Monitor

Let's face it—a standard 14" or 15" monitor running at 640×480 resolution just doesn't cut it in these days of big and graphically intensive Web pages and applications. Spend the bucks for a 17" monitor and run it at 1,024×768 resolution. You'll wonder how you ever put up with a smaller monitor!

6. Get an IntelliMouse

Used to be, a mouse was a mouse was a mouse. Not anymore. Microsoft's IntelliMouse includes a special wheel in between the left and right buttons that lets you scroll through Web pages and applications without rolling your mouse all around the desktop. After you've used one, you'll never go back to using scrollbars.

7. Replace Your Old Keyboard

There are two reasons you might want to replace your old keyboard. First, most newer keyboards include special Windows menu keys that let you access Windows 98's pop-up menus and other functions right from the keyboard, without using your mouse. Second, investing in an ergonomic keyboard—one with a split-keyboard design—can help relieve wrist tension and prevent carpal tunnel syndrome.

8. Upgrade Your Audio System

If you play a lot of loud multimedia games on your PC, or if you use your PC to listen to music CDs or watch DVD movies or television broadcasts (via a TV tuner), the standard built-in PC sound just doesn't cut it. A good sound card hooked up to decent left and right speakers—and a subwoofer for punchy bass—can really enhance your listening experience.

9. Add a DVD Drive

You have a CD-ROM drive in your PC; why would you need a DVD? Well, DVD discs hold more than seven times the data of a CD-ROM, so you can get more sophisticated games and applications on a single disc. In addition, you can use your PC's DVD drive to watch movies on DVD discs. It's the wave of the future, which you can get today.

10. Clean Up Your System—and Load Windows Faster!

If you don't want to, you don't have to add anything to your system to speed it up—in fact, taking some things out of your system will do the job! Read ahead to Chapter 5, "Staying Alive: Simple Steps to Keep Your System in Tip-Top Shape," to discover maintenance activities—such as the Disk Defragmenter and Disk Cleanup Manager—that can speed up your PC's performance. In addition, removing all unused files—including unused fonts—will also speed up your system. (The more fonts installed on your system, the longer Windows takes to load; deleting unused fonts can make a significant difference in system boot-up speed.) Just remember: clean systems run better!

The Least You Need to Know

➤ Windows is an operating system with a graphical user interface.

➤ The latest version of Windows is Windows 98, which isn't much different from Windows 95.

➤ Most of the important parts of Windows are easily accessed from either the desktop or the Start menu.

➤ You can make Windows run better by adding more memory and hard disk space to your computer system.

Chapter 4

Internet Basics for the Technically Timid

In This Chapter

➤ Find out what the Internet is—and what it isn't

➤ Learn how to establish a connection to the Internet

➤ Discover the different activities available on the Internet—including email, chat, newsgroups, and the World Wide Web

---

It used to be that most people bought personal computers to do work—word processing, spreadsheets, databases, that sort of thing. But today, most people buy PCs to access the Internet—to send and receive email, surf the Web, and chat with other users.

If you're not yet on the Internet, you will be, soon—and you'll need to know how to get connected, and what to do when you get there. If you are already connected, I don't have to tell you how frustrating the Internet can be, with dropped connections, dead links, junk email, and the like. But before you get too frustrated, let's take a quick trip around the Internet and see what it takes to get connected—and *stay* connected!

What the Internet Is—and What It Isn't

If you're new to the Net, keep one thing in mind—the Internet isn't a thing. You can't touch it or see it or smell it; you can't put it in a box and buy it. The Internet is like the huge power grid that provides electricity to homes across the country—it exists in-between the points that matter.

So if the Internet isn't a physical thing, what is it? It's really more simple than you might think; the Internet is nothing more than a really big computer network. In fact, it's a computer network that connects other computer networks—what some would call a "network of networks." Computers connect to the Internet (typically through larger networks, most often supplied by an *Internet service provider*), and thus have access to other computers and devices that are also connected to the Internet. After you're connected, you can access anything or anybody else also connected to the Internet, seamlessly and practically invisibly. With a single click, you connect through the Internet to a computer down the street or half way around the world; on the Internet, distance doesn't matter.

Get Networked

A network is a group of two or more computers or electronic devices connected together. A local area network (LAN) is a network of computers that are geographically close together; a wide area network (WAN) is a network with computers not all in the same place. The Internet is the widest-area network today, connecting computers and computer networks from all around the world.

By my estimate, there are more than 150 million users connected to the Internet today. According to the Computer Industry Almanac, that number is expected to grow to 320 million by the end of the year 2000, and to 720 million by 2003.

Just being connected to the Internet, however, really doesn't accomplish anything. It's much the same as having electricity run to your home—that wall outlet doesn't do anything until you plug something into it. The same thing with the Internet; the Internet itself just kind of sits there until you plug something into it that takes advantage of it.

There are many activities that are plugged into—or sit on top of—the Internet, including the following:

➤ **Chat** lets groups of users "talk" to each other (via their keyboards) in real-time chat rooms.

➤ **Email** is a type of electronic "letter" sent from one user to another.

➤ **FTP** lets you download files from servers on the Internet.

➤ **Instant Messaging** is a one-on-one kind of chat, again in real-time.

➤ **Usenet Newsgroups** are electronic message boards for communities of users, organized around specific topics.

➤ The **World Wide Web** presents information—both text and pictures—in a virtual "web" of linked sites and pages (such as the one shown in the following figure).

The Internet itself doesn't perform any of these activities—but it does *enable* these activities to happen. And when you connect to the Internet—through your personal computer—you have access to all these activities and more.

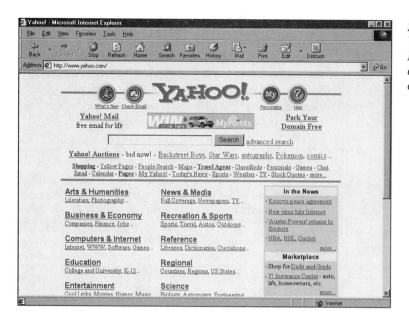

Surfing the World Wide Web with Microsoft's Internet Explorer—just one of many activities available on the Internet.

America Online—It's Not the Internet, Although It's Connected to It

You probably know someone who is connected to America Online—or you might be an AOL subscriber yourself. America Online is a *commercial online service,* in that it exists independent to the Internet, with its own distinct connections and its own proprietary software, content, and interface. However, AOL also functions as a *gateway* to the Internet, so that AOL users can connect to the Internet through the AOL service. So if you're on AOL, you can access the Internet—even if the AOL service itself can't be accessed by non-AOL users.

How an Internet Connection Works

All Internet connections work pretty much the same way. First, your personal computer connects to an *Internet service provider* (ISP) via standard telephone lines. (If you use your computer at work to connect to the Internet, you actually go through your company's

Mo' Better Modems

A modem (which stands for *modulator-demodulator*) is a piece of hardware that enables a computer to transmit data over telephone lines. Because computer information is stored digitally and phone lines can only transmit analog data, the modem must convert (modulate) the digital data into analog format—or, when receiving data, demodulate the analog data back into digital format.

Talk or Surf—Your Call

While you're connected to your ISP, your phone line is busy—which means that you can't place or receive normal telephone calls while you're surfing the Internet. If you use the Internet a lot, you might want to invest in a second phone line just for your modem.

local area network to a dedicated line to the Internet, bypassing conventional phone lines.) Your computer uses a piece of hardware called a *modem* to translate the signals from your keyboard to signals that can be sent over standard phone lines. Your ISP has a modem on the other end of the line that converts the signals back into digital format for transmission over the Internet.

An Internet service provider is a company that does nothing more than connect individual users to the Internet. Some ISPs (such as America Online and CompuServe) are also commercial online services, and provide their users with an easy-to-use onscreen interface and proprietary content and navigation. But these commercial online services also function as traditional ISPs, consolidating thousands of incoming telephone lines into a single gateway to the Internet for their users.

So you connect to an ISP with your phone line, and your ISP then plugs you into the Internet. After you're on the Internet, you're on your own, free to use (or not to use) individual Internet services, to visit (or not to visit) individual sites and servers connected to the Internet, and to communicate (or not) with individual users who are also plugged into the Internet. When you disconnect from your ISP (hang up your phone line), you're no longer connected to the Internet, and you can't access any Internet services or contact any other users—and they can't contact you, either—until you connect again.

Finding an ISP

Before you can explore the wonders of the Internet, you first have to find and subscribe to an Internet service provider. There are thousands of ISPs in America alone, some of them large and national in scope, many of them smaller and local. You can find ISPs listed in your local yellow pages, in local computer magazines and newspapers, and at various online sites.

Here are some things to keep in mind when you're looking for an ISP:

➤ Does it have a local dial-up number? (You don't want to incur long distance charges every time you surf the Internet.)

➤ Does it have a national network of local numbers? (If you're going to be traveling, you want to connect via a local call—and not be forced to dial long distance to connect via your home number.)

➤ Does it have a local or toll-free technical support number? (If you run into problems, you'll need technical support.)

➤ What are the hours for its technical support? (Don't ask me why, but chances are you'll have connection problems outside of normal business hours.)

Check the List

For a comprehensive listing of both local and national ISPs, go to CNET's Ultimate ISP Guide (`www.cnet.com/Content/Reviews/Compare/ISP`) which lists 4,200 ISPs, or to The List (`thelist.internet.com`) which ranks 7,100 ISPs.

➤ What is the monthly charge or hourly rate? (If you think you'll be online a lot—and you probably *will*—opt for a flat monthly rate; if you only expect to connect occasionally, consider a per-hour charge.)

➤ How busy is it? (Ask other subscribers how often they get a busy signal when they dial in; a growing ISP with too little capacity can be difficult to connect to during busy times of the day.)

➤ What speeds can it connect at? (Make sure its connect speeds match your modem speed; for example, some ISPs don't yet offer 56Kbps connection speeds for all locations.)

Setting Up Your PC for a New ISP Account

After you create an account with an ISP, you can then proceed to create a new Internet connection for that ISP on your personal computer. You'll need to get the following information from your ISP:

➤ The area code and telephone number of your ISP (its dial-up number, *not* its voice number!)

➤ Your username and password as assigned by your ISP

➤ Your email address (in the form of *xxx@xxx.xxx*) as assigned by your ISP

➤ The names of your ISP's incoming and outgoing email servers (with some ISPs, the incoming and outgoing servers might be the same)

➤ Your email POP account name and password as assigned by your ISP

➤ The name of your ISP's news server

➤ If your ISP offers LDAP "white pages" service (not all do), the name of your ISP's LDAP server

Note that, for most ISPs, your username, email name, and POP account name will be the same name. It's also likely that your login password and POP password will also be the same.

Alphabet Soup

Don't get confused by all the initials in the preceding list. POP stands for **P**ost **O**ffice **P**rotocol, which is how your ISP's email server is identified on the Internet. LDAP stands for **L**ightweight **D**irectory **A**ccess **P**rotocol, which is a way to access directory services on the Internet.

After you have that information, the easiest way to create a new Internet connection is by using the Internet Connection Wizard found in Internet Explorer (version 4 or later) or in Microsoft Windows 98. When you use the wizard, just answer the questions by using the information provided by your ISP; Windows will automatically create a new dial-up connection (complete with email and newsgroup accounts) for your ISP.

If you're using Windows 95 (and not using Internet Explorer as your browser), you don't have the Internet Connection Wizard installed on your system. Instead, you'll need to create a new Dial-Up Networking connection manually. Click the **Start** button, select **Programs**, **Accessories**, and then select **Dial-Up Networking**. When the Dial-Up Networking window appears, select the **Make New Connection** icon, and then follow the directions in the Make New Connection Wizard.

If You're Using an Older PC to Connect to the Net...

Windows 95 and Windows 98 make it relatively easy to establish an Internet connection; all the technology and protocols that you need to connect are built into the operating system. Versions of Windows prior to Windows 95, however, didn't have the necessary Internet protocols built in, so you had to install even more software and utilities—with names like SLIP and PPP—to get connected. If you're still using Windows 3.1 (or before!), my advice is to upgrade your system to Windows 98 before you try to create an Internet connection—it's so much easier, and you'll thank me for the advice.

Of course, it's possible that you won't have to go through any of these procedures to configure your system for your ISP. Many ISPs supply you with their own installation software; run this software to configure all of Windows' settings automatically.

After You Configure—Install the Software

As I said at the start of this chapter, just connecting to the Internet doesn't get you much. To do anything on the Internet, you have to install the proper software. Table 4.1 details what you can do on the Internet, and what software you use to do it.

Table 4.1   Internet Activities and Software

Internet Activity	Software
Chat	mIRC (www.mirc.com); PIRCH (www.pirchat.com)
Email	Eudora (www.eudora.com); Microsoft Outlook Express (www.microsoft.com/ie/ie40/oe/); Netscape Messenger (home.netscape.com/computing/download/)
FTP (file download)	BulletProof FTP (www.bpftp.com); WS_FTP (www.csra.net/junodj/ws_ftp32.htm)
Instant Messaging	ICQ (www.icq.com); AOL Netscape Instant Messenger (www.newaol.com/aim/netscape/adb00.html)
Usenet Newsgroups	Free Agent (www.forteinc.com/agent/freagent.htm); Microsoft Outlook Express (www.microsoft.com/ie/ie40/oe/); Netscape Messenger (home.netscape.com/computing/download/)
World Wide Web	Microsoft Internet Explorer (www.microsoft.com/windows/ie/); Netscape Navigator (home.netscape.com/computing/download/)

You can find the software (generally for free) at the Web sites listed in the table, or at most general Internet software repository sites, such as Download.com (www.download.com) or Tucows (www.tucows.com). Many of these programs are also available (not for free) at your local computer retailer. You don't have to install every type of program, just those necessary for the activities you want to participate in.

Connecting to the Internet Via Your ISP

After you've created the Internet connection for your ISP account, you can connect to the Internet in one of two ways:

➤ Launch any Internet application (Internet Explorer, Netscape Navigator, Outlook Express, and so on) and Windows will automatically dial your ISP and establish a connection.

➤ Launch your Internet connection via Dial-Up Networking by clicking the Windows **Start** button, and selecting **Programs**, **Accessories**, **Communications**. Then select **Dial-Up Networking**. When the Dial-Up Networking window appears, click the icon for your ISP; when the Connect To dialog box appears, fill in your **User Name** and **Password** and click the **Connect** button. After you're connected to your ISP, you can then launch any of your Internet applications.

After you're connected, you can launch any Internet application and get down to business. In fact, you can run multiple Internet applications at one time—so you can surf the Web while checking your email, or instant message another user while posting an article in a Usenet newsgroup.

Connecting to the Internet Via America Online

Using an ISP is only one way to connect to the Internet. You can also connect to the Internet via a commercial online service, such as America Online (AOL). In addition to a gateway to the Internet, America Online also offers proprietary content and communications services, such as channels and chat rooms.

If you use America Online to connect to the Internet, you can use AOL's built-in Internet applications, or launch third-party applications (such as Internet Explorer or Netscape Navigator) on top of the AOL software. Many users like AOL because of its ease-of-use—and because of how easy it is to establish an account and get connected.

What Can Go Wrong Online

Online connections aren't the most stable environments in the world. Not only do you have to worry about problems in your own system, you also have the potential for problems in your connection to your ISP, in your ISP's connection to the Internet, and in the multitude of connections between Internet sites. Even if you dial in and connect to your ISP without problems (and this is a problem-prone area, to be frank), your ISP might not establish a clean or fast connection to the Internet itself. And even when you're on the Net, your attempts to visit any particular site might be thwarted by bad connections or too much traffic. (Too many people online slow things down—and slow connections are a big problem on the Internet.)

And all this assumes that you know where you want to go online—if you have a bad address (or no address!), a perfect connection won't ensure you find the site or user or information you're looking for.

In other words, you're darned lucky if you can do anything at all online!

To be fair, it isn't all that bad—but it *can* be, if you're not careful. You have to start with your modem, and make sure it's connected and configured properly. You have to be sure that you have the correct information from your ISP—the right addresses and phone numbers and other settings. Then you have to *hope* that you have a clean phone line, and that your ISP has enough capacity to connect you and your fellow users to the Internet backbone, simultaneously. And you have to *hope* that you have the right email and Web site addresses, and that Internet traffic is light enough to get you where you want to go without too long a wait.

If everything performs as promised, you'll be online and surfing in no time. If not...well, that's what this book is for!

More Books to Read!

I've written several Internet-related books in the past year that might be useful or interesting to you. If you're interested in finding things online—using search engines and directories—then check out *The Complete Idiot's Guide to Online Search Secrets*. If you're interested in bidding or selling via online auctions—such as eBay—then check out *The Complete Idiot's Guide to Online Auctions*. If you're connecting to the Internet via a WebTV box, check out *The Complete Idiot's Guide to Surfing the Internet with WebTV*. All these books are published by Que, and all should be available where you purchased your copy of this book.

The Least You Need to Know

➤ You configure your system's modem to connect to an Internet service provider (ISP), who then connects you to the Internet.

➤ Your ISP will provide you with your own unique email address and account.

➤ After you're connected to the Internet, you have access to different activities—including email, Web pages, chat, and Usenet newsgroups.

➤ You use different software programs to perform different Internet-related activities.

Chapter 5

Staying Alive: Simple Steps to Keep Your System in Tip-Top Shape

---

In This Chapter

➤ Learn to perform simple maintenance for each part of your computer system

➤ Discover how to automate necessary maintenance activities

➤ Find out if you have the latest version of key system files

---

One of my goals in writing this book is to not only help you recover from problems, but also to help you *prevent* problems. After all, wouldn't it be nice if you didn't have to read anything else in this book? (And don't worry—I won't take your answer personally!)

Why You Need to *Prevent* Problems... Before They *Become* Problems

Even though this book is about *solving* problems, I think it's better to *prevent* problems before they occur, if possible. Let's face it—even if you can fix problems when they do happen, you save yourself a lot of grief if you can avoid those problems completely. It's worth it to spend a little time on preventive maintenance *now* if it saves you hours of problem-solving and disaster recovery *later*.

That said, let's look at some simple things you can do to reduce your chances of contracting computer problems.

Soothe the Soul of Your System Unit

Your system unit has a lot of stuff inside—everything from memory chips to disk drives to power supplies. Check out these maintenance tips to keep your system unit from flaking out on you:

➤ Keep your system unit in a clean, dust-free environment. Keep it away from direct sunlight and strong magnetic fields. In addition, make sure your system unit and your monitor have plenty of air flow around them, to keep them from overheating.

➤ Hook your system unit up to a surge suppressor to avoid deadly power spikes.

➤ Avoid turning your system unit on and off too often; it's better to leave it on all the time than incur frequent "power on" stress to all those delicate components. However...

➤ Turn off your system unit if you're going to be away for an extended period—anything longer than a day or two.

➤ Check all your cable connections periodically. Make sure all the connectors are firmly connected, and all the screws properly screwed—and make sure your cables aren't stretched too tight, or bent in ways that could damage the wires inside.

➤ If you're really adventurous, open up the system case periodically and vacuum or wipe the dust from the inside. (Just make sure the system unit is unplugged at the time!) Using a can of "compressed air" is also a good way to blast the dirt out of your system. You should also "dust" the inside of your CD-ROM drive, and even use a swab or commercial cleaner to clean the laser lens.

➤ Defragment your hard disk on a periodic basis. (Windows 95 and Windows 98 both include the Disk Defragmenter utility, discussed later in this chapter.)

➤ Back up your hard disk regularly, as recommended in Chapter 7, "Preparing a PC Survival Kit."

➤ Run a disk diagnostic program from time to time. Windows includes ScanDisk (discussed later in this chapter), which automatically checks your hard disk for errors and bad files.

➤ *Always* run anti-virus software, such as McAfee ViruScan or Norton AntiVirus, both discussed in Chapter 10, "Germ Warfare—Protecting Your Computer from Viruses."

Keep Your Keyboard Klicking

Even something as simple as your keyboard requires a little preventive maintenance from time to time. Check out these tips:

➤ Keep your keyboard away from young children and pets! They can get dirt and hair and Silly Putty™ all over the place, and have a tendency to put way too much pressure on the keys.

➤ Keep your keyboard away from dust, dirt, smoke, direct sunlight, and other harmful environmental stuff. You might even consider putting a dust cover on your keyboard when it's not in use.

➤ Use a small vacuum cleaner to periodically sweep the dirt from your keyboard. (Alternately, you can use compressed air to *blow* the dirt away.) Use a cotton swab or soft cloth to clean between the keys. If necessary, remove the keycaps to clean the switches underneath.

➤ If you spill something on your keyboard, disconnect it immediately and wipe up the spill. Use a soft cloth to get between the keys; if necessary, remove the key-caps and wipe up any seepage underneath. Let the keyboard dry thoroughly before trying to use it again.

Make Sure Your Mouse Keeps Rollin' Along

If you're a heavy Windows user, you probably put over 10,000 miles a year on your mouse. Just like a car tire, anything turning over that often needs a little tender loving care. Check out these mouse maintenance tips:

➤ Periodically open up the bottom of your mouse and remove the roller ball. Wash the ball with water (or perhaps a mild detergent). Use a soft cloth to dry the ball before reinserting it.

➤ While your mouse ball is removed, use compressed air or a cotton swab to clean dust and dirt from the inside of your mouse. (In extreme cases, you might need to use tweezers to pull lint and hair out of your mouse—or use a small knife to scrape packed crud from the rollers.)

➤ Always use a mouse pad—they really do help keep things rolling smoothly, plus they give you good traction when you're working on those fast documents! (And while you're at it, don't forget to clean your mouse pad with a little spray cleaner—it can get dirty, too!)

Monitor Your Monitor

If you think of your monitor as a little television set, you're on the right track. Just treat your monitor as you do your TV and you'll be okay. That said, look at these preventive maintenance tips:

➤ As with all other important system components, keep your monitor away from direct sunlight, dust, and smoke. Make sure it has plenty of ventilation, especially around the back; don't cover the rear cooling vents with paper or any other object, and don't set anything bigger than a Beanie Baby on top of the cabinet.

➤ Don't place any strong magnets in close proximity to your monitor. (This includes external speakers!)

➤ *With your monitor turned off,* periodically clean the monitor screen. Spray standard glass cleaner on a soft cloth (anti-static type, if possible), and then wipe the screen clean.

➤ Don't forget to adjust the brightness and contrast controls on your monitor every now and then. Any controls can get out of whack—plus, your monitor's performance will change as it ages, and simple adjustments can often keep it looking as good as new.

Patronize Your Printer

Your printer is a complex device with a lot of moving parts. Follow these tips to keep your printouts in good shape:

➤ Use a soft cloth, mini-vacuum cleaner, or compressed air to clean the inside and outside of your printer on a periodic basis. In particular, make sure you clean the paper path of all paper shavings and dust.

➤ If you have an inkjet printer, periodically clean the ink jets. Use a small pin to make sure they don't get clogged.

➤ If you have a laser printer, replace the toner cartridge as needed. When you replace the cartridge, remember to clean the printer cleaning bar and other related parts.

➤ *Don't* use alcohol or other solvents to clean any rubber or plastic parts—you'll do more harm than good!

Minimize Modem Madness

Modems don't generally give you too much trouble. There are a few things to watch out for, however, if you do a lot of online computing:

➤ If you're using an external modem, make sure its power cord is plugged into a surge suppressor.

➤ If you know a big electrical storm is coming, unplug both the power cord and the phone line from the back of your modem. Otherwise, you risk possible damage from power surges and lightning strikes (which are just as apt to happen via the phone line as via the power cable!).

➤ When you download files from the Internet, make sure you're running a good anti-virus program to protect your system from computer viruses.

➤ Periodically clear the history file and cache in your Web browser. (This is typically done from the Options or Configuration menu.) Most Web browsers store copies of visited Web pages in a cache on your hard disk; this can absorb a lot of disk space if left unchecked.

➤ Periodically clean up your email folders. If you're like most users, you end up saving a lot of messages that you never read again; these can eat up a lot of disk space, and actually make your email program run slower. While you're at it, make sure you check the Sent Messages folder; many email programs *never* delete your sent messages unless instructed to!

Let Windows Tune Up Your System

Windows 95 and Windows 98 include several utilities to help you keep your system running smoothly. In fact, Microsoft completely overhauled almost all of Windows' system maintenance features with Windows 98, making it easier for you to clean up your system—and providing the means for you to do so automatically.

The next few sections discuss the system maintenance utilities found in Windows 98; in many cases, similar utilities are included in Windows 95, but my instructions and recommendations are Windows 98 specific. (And why haven't you upgraded to Windows 98 yet, anyway?)

Make Your Hard Disk Run Better by Defragmenting

If you notice that opening files seems to take longer than usual or your hard drive light stays on longer than usual, you might need to defragment your hard drive.

You create fragments on your hard drive any time you run an application or when you edit, move, copy, or delete a file. Fragmentation is like taking the pieces of a puzzle and storing them in different boxes along with pieces from other puzzles; the more dispersed the pieces are, the longer it takes to put the puzzle together. So if you notice your system takes longer and longer to open and close files or run applications, you probably need to defragment your system—in effect, putting all the pieces of the puzzle in one box.

New to Windows 98 is the capability of Disk Defragmenter to rearrange files on your hard drive according to how often you use them. In essence, Disk Defragmenter places those files you use most frequently near the front of your hard drive, so that they can be accessed more quickly.

To defragment your hard drive, click the **Start** button, select **Programs**, **Accessories**, **System Tools**, and then select **Disk Defragmenter**. When the Select Drive dialog box appears, choose the drive you want to defragment and then click **OK**.

Stop Before You Defragment

You should close all applications and stop working on the system while Disk Defragmenter is running. (This includes disabling your screen saver and turning off power management's sleep mode.) Defragmenting your drive can take awhile, especially if you have a large hard drive or your hard drive is especially fragmented. So you might want to start the utility and let it run while you're at lunch.

Perform a Hard Disk Checkup with ScanDisk

As you run applications, move files, delete files, or accidentally turn the power off while the system is running, you can introduce disk errors. ScanDisk can locate these problems and correct many of them automatically.

Sometimes ScanDisk Starts All By Itself

If your system shuts down unexpectedly or if you have to reboot your system manually, Windows runs ScanDisk automatically the next time you start up your system.

Any time you are having difficulty with your drive, you should run ScanDisk to look for errors. These difficulties include slow access, failure to open a file, or a system hang when saving or opening a file. Normally, a standard scan will take care of your difficulties. If you suspect serious errors with the physical mechanics of the drive, you can choose a thorough scan. Thorough scans take much longer, however, so allow extra time when performing one.

To run ScanDisk, click the **Start** button, select **Programs**, **Accessories**, **System Tools**, and then select **ScanDisk**. When ScanDisk launches, choose the drive you want to scan. Select the **Standard** option and check **Automatically Fix Errors**. Click the **Start** button to start the scan.

Delete Unused Files with Disk Cleanup

Windows 98 includes a new utility that helps you identify and delete unused files on your hard disk. Disk Cleanup is a great tool to use when you want to free up extra hard disk space for more frequently used files.

To use Disk Cleanup, click the **Start** button, **Programs**, **Accessories**, **System Tools**, and then select **Disk Cleanup**. Disk Cleanup will now start and automatically analyze the contents of your hard disk drive. When it's finished analyzing, it presents the dialog box shown in this figure.

Use Disk Cleanup to identify and delete unused files from your hard disk; select the file types you want to delete, and then click **OK**.

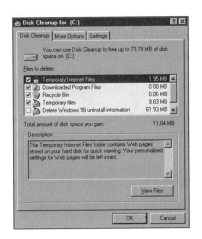

Start by selecting the **Disk Cleanup** tab. You can have Disk Cleanup delete the following types of files:

➤ **Temporary Internet Files**   These are Web pages cached by your Web browser for faster reloading. It's normally okay to delete these.

➤ **Downloaded Program Files**   These are ActiveX controls and Java applets associated with Web pages you've recently visited. It's normally okay to delete these; if you need them again, they'll be automatically downloaded at that time.

➤ **Recycle Bin**   This clears all recently deleted files from the Windows Recycle Bin. Check this one if you're sure you won't need to undelete any of these files. (Remember—after you clear a file from the Recycle Bin, it's really truly deleted— you can't get it back!)

➤ **Temporary Files**   These are hidden files that Windows creates while running various programs. It's normally okay to delete these.

➤ **Non-Critical Files**   These are regular files on your hard disk that haven't been used for awhile. If you select this option, you'll be prompted whether you want to delete each individual file. I recommend *not* checking this option—just because you haven't used a file in awhile doesn't mean you won't ever use it in the future! (Note that this option doesn't appear on all systems.)

If you want to remove infrequently used programs or Windows components (or convert your hard disk to the more efficient FAT32 file system), select the **More Options** tab and make those choices. Otherwise, click **OK** to begin cleaning up your hard disk. (To learn more about FAT32 and other disk-related issues, check out Chapter 17, "What to Do When…Your Disk is Damaged.")

Schedule Regular Tune-Ups with the Maintenance Wizard

Windows 98 includes a new *Maintenance Wizard*—a scheduling utility that lets you automatically run other Windows utilities. The Maintenance Wizard lets you automatically run various system maintenance tasks—including ScanDisk, Disk Defragmenter, and Disk Cleanup—while you're away from your computer.

To use the Maintenance Wizard, click the **Start** button, select **Programs**, **Accessories**, **System Tools**, and then select **Maintenance Wizard**. When the Maintenance Wizard appears, you have the choice of an **Express** tune-up (which runs the most common utilities—Disk Cleanup, Disk Defragmenter, and ScanDisk— with the most common settings) or a **Custom** tune-up.

If you choose the **Express** tune-up, click the **Next** button to select a maintenance schedule. You can choose to run your tune-up **Nights** (Midnight to 3:00 a.m.), **Days** (Noon to 3:00 p.m.), or **Evenings** (8:00 p.m. to 11 p.m.). Choose a time frame where you're likely to be away from the computer, and then click **Next**. When the final screen appears, click **Finish** and the Maintenance Wizard will be set to do its job, according to the schedule you selected.

You Have to Turn It On to Use It

For the Maintenance Wizard to run, your computer has to be turned on during the scheduled maintenance periods. The Maintenance Wizard will *not* turn on your PC for you! If your PC is turned off when maintenance is scheduled, the Maintenance Wizard simply skips that scheduled activity.

If you choose the **Custom** tune-up, you have a few more options than you have with the Express tune-up. For example, when you click the **Next** button to select a maintenance schedule, you'll see the same choices as with the Express tune-up—plus the ability to select a Custom time for maintenance. As you progress through the wizard, you'll have the opportunity to choose from the following maintenance options:

➤ **Start Windows More Quickly**   This lets you select which programs load when you launch Windows. The more items selected, the longer it takes for Windows to start.

➤ **Clean Up Your Start Menu**   This removes nonworking items and empties folders from the Windows **Start** menu. (Not available on all systems.)

➤ **Speed Up Programs**   This runs Disk Defragmenter.

➤ **Scan Hard Disk for Errors**   This runs ScanDisk.

➤ **Delete Unnecessary Files**   This runs Disk Cleanup.

For most of these items you can select when you want them to run; this is the Custom schedule referred to on the **Select a Maintenance Schedule** page.

In my mind, the Maintenance Wizard alone is a good reason to upgrade to Windows 98. System maintenance is never fun (and you always forget to do it); program the Maintenance Wizard once and you never have to worry about tuning up your system again!

Update Important Files with Windows Update

Windows is constantly changing. Microsoft often releases updated versions of critical system files to improve performance or fix bugs; peripheral manufacturers often issue updated versions of their driver files.

How do you make sure your system has the latest versions of these critical files? If you use Windows 98, you have access to a new Windows System Update utility that compares the files on your PC with a database of files on Microsoft's Web site—and automatically downloads and installs any new or updated files your system needs for best operation. (Naturally, you need to have an Internet connection on your system to use this utility.)

To update your system with Windows Update, click the **Start** button, select **Settings**, and then select **Windows Update**. Windows 98 now starts Internet Explorer and navigates to the Windows Update Web page. When the Windows Update Web page displays, click the **Update Wizard** link. The Update Wizard launches and runs a special program that scans your hard disk for files that might need updating. (It might take several minutes for the Update Wizard to completely scan your hard disk.)

After scanning your hard disk, Windows Update lists those items on your computer that need updating. To update each item, select it and then click the **Install** link. Follow any onscreen instructions to complete the updates.

Updating System Files in Windows 95

Windows Update is exclusive to Windows 98; how do you keep your system updated if you have Windows 95? You *can* update system files in Windows 95, but you have to do it manually, from the Microsoft Windows 95 Web site (www.microsoft.com/windows95/). Of course, the *best* way to update Windows 95 is simply to upgrade to Windows 98!

The Least You Need to Know

➤ Simple preventive maintenance will help keep your system running in optimal condition.

➤ Windows includes several system maintenance utilities; these utilities can be scheduled to run automatically with the Maintenance Wizard.

➤ Windows Update will automatically check to see whether you have the latest versions of key system files—and download new files if you need them.

Chapter 6

Why Bad Things Happen to Good Users

In This Chapter

➤ Discover what causes most computer problems

➤ Learn how to be a better—and safer—computer user

I'm sure you're a good person. (Really!) So why should you be the victim of computer problems? Don't you deserve better than that?

Of course you do! But the reality is that computer problems can befall *anyone*. And no matter how careful you are, the chances are good that at some time in your computing career *something* will go wrong. Your goal, then, is to ensure that nothing major goes wrong, and that you're thoroughly prepared just in case something nasty does happen, however minor.

What Causes Most Problems

Most computer problems are easy to solve because they're really not major problems. Oh, they might *appear* to be major—especially because any problem that happens to *you* is major! But in reality, most problems result from causes that are easily fixed. So, take a look here at some of the most common sources of computer problems and how you can avoid them.

Garbage In, Garbage Out

It's a Load of Garbage!

The phrase *garbage in, garbage out* (or GIGO, for short) refers to a phenomenon not necessarily unique to computing. When you put garbage into the system (that is, when you make a mistake), the computer is too stupid (actually, too literal) to interpret what you meant to do, and outputs exactly what you input—mistakes and all. So, if you put garbage in, you get garbage out. After all, computers can't read your mind...yet.

I hate to be the one to break this to you, but computers very rarely make mistakes. You can't always blame your problems on the computer. That's because the most common cause of computer problems is *you*!

You see, most problems result when the user (yes, that's *you*!) does something wrong. You might not *know* you're doing something wrong—and, most certainly, you don't have evil intentions—but you do it anyway.

You know and I know that no one makes mistakes on purpose. When you make an error at your computer, you almost always do so accidentally, and you usually remain unaware of your blunder—at least until something goes terribly and unmistakably wrong with your work. The key to correcting the problem, then, is to remain calm and retrace your steps to figure out exactly what you did wrong.

One way you communicate with your computer is with your keyboard, and many errors occur when you type something wrong. If you're like me, your fingers occasionally fly across the keyboard faster than you're actually able to type—and they usually do so while you're looking at anything but the screen.

This means you can quite easily type the wrong Web page or email address, or misspell the name of a file you're trying to save or open. Any of these mistakes will cause what appears to be an error—which can be easily corrected by simple retyping.

If you often encounter these or similar errors or find yourself regularly retyping commands, you might want to try typing a little more slowly in the future. Sometimes s-l-o-w-e-r is more appropriate than faster. (Remember the tortoise and the hare?) If you find that you have trouble typing accurately even at slower speeds, perhaps consider taking a typing course or buying a typing-instruction program for your computer. You'd be surprised how much these can help increase both your typing speed and your accuracy.

You don't have to type something wrong to make a mistake, however—especially in Windows. You can make mouse mistakes, too!

It's all too easy to position your cursor over the wrong option or file; when you click your mouse, the mistake is registered immediately. If you find yourself clicking on a lot of the wrong things, maybe the items on your screen are too small for you to see well; consider changing your display to a lower resolution (so things appear larger)— or maybe you just need bifocals!

The bottom line? If your computer doesn't seem to do what you tell it, make sure that you're telling it to do the right thing. When you input an error, you get an error in return. (That's the whole idea behind "garbage in, garbage out.")

Somebody Else's Fault

Sometimes errors are generated through no fault of your own. This happens a lot online; you try to go to a specific Web page, and find that the URL or link leads to a dead end. If you check the address and try again and *still* end up empty handed, you have a bad address. Either someone has given you the wrong address, or someone has coded the wrong address into a hypertext link, or the address *used to be* good but the page has since moved or been deleted. In any case, it's not your fault—it's *somebody else's fault*.

Anytime you're dealing with Internet addressing—in Web pages, or emails, or even chat channels or instant messaging usernames—you run the risk of someone else screwing up the address. More often than not, there's not much you can do at this point, save for searching for the correct address (which is discussed in Chapter 26, "What to Do When...Your Web Surfing Wipes Out").

Those Pesky Plugs!

After you eliminate people problems as the source of your troubles, check for the next most common cause of computer malfunctions: improper hookup. Hooking up a handful of cables might sound simple, but it's easy to do wrong. If you plug a cable into the wrong connector, whatever is connected to that cable—on either end—won't work. If the connection isn't solid—if the plug is loose—operation can be intermittent. If the cable is old, frayed, or sharply bent, the wires inside the cable might not transmit data effectively, again causing intermittent operation. And, of course, if you forget to turn the power on—well, nothing happens at all!

If a *peripheral* (such as a printer, a monitor, or a modem) isn't working, the problem most likely lies in the connection. Make sure that all cables are solidly connected and, if necessary, securely screwed into their ports. Make certain that the printer cable actually is connected to the printer port, the keyboard cable to the keyboard port, and so on; it's easy to plug the right cable into the wrong connector. Finally, check that *both ends* of the cable are connected; a cable can work its way loose from the back of the monitor just as easily as it can from the back of the system unit.

If your entire system refuses to start, a faulty connection could be to blame here, too. In this case, however, you need to examine the *power cable*. Make sure that the power cable is securely connected to your system unit and firmly plugged into a power outlet. Then make certain that the power outlet actually is *turned on*. You can't imagine how many "major problems" can be caused by a wall switch in the "off" position. And while you're at it, make sure that all your peripherals are also turned on; it doesn't do you any good to have a functioning system unit with a monitor that's switched off.

Of course, you're positive that all *your* cables are connected correctly. After all, you're a good computer user—and besides, everything worked fine the last time you used your system! Forget it, pal. Cables come loose. Trust me. No matter how conscientious you are, *cables come loose*. So if you're experiencing difficulties with your hardware, swallow your pride—and check the wall switch and start wiggling your cables. Nine times out of ten, you'll find your hardware problem right there.

It's a Setup!

Okay, so your entire system is hooked up and turned on—and you *still* have hardware problems. Then again, maybe not. In some cases, your "hardware problems" actually turn out to be *software problems*.

Living in a Changing World

If you change any aspect of your computer system—for example, if you upgrade to a better monitor/video card, or add a new printer—you have to go back through all your software programs and change their settings to reflect your new hardware. If you don't, your computer won't know you've changed anything, and will keep on acting the same old way—which might not be the best way to work with your new equipment.

Any time you add a new peripheral to your system, Windows must be configured to recognize and properly work with the new device. Now, both Windows 95 and Windows 98 use so-called Plug-and-Play technology to automatically recognize most new components when they're first installed. Theoretically, this should alleviate the need to manually configure your system each time you change it. *Theoretically.*

Although Microsoft would be loathe to admit this, Plug and Play isn't perfect. It does not recognize 100 percent of the devices you can potentially add to your system. (I won't venture what percent it *does* recognize, but it's definitely less than 100 percent—sometimes *much less*.) And sometimes, it thinks it recognizes one device but configures itself for *another* device instead. So don't assume that Windows will do all the work for you; manually check your configuration every time you add a new peripheral, and be prepared to manually adjust Windows' settings. (See Chapter 2, "Hardware Basics for the Technically Timid," for instructions on how to add new hardware to your Windows-based system.)

In addition, just adding a device to your system doesn't mean that that device will automatically be *used* by Windows or by any specific software program. If you add a new printer, you'll probably have to manually instruct Windows to select the new printer as your *default* printer—and you'll probably have to configure your software programs individually, as well.

The bottom line is that your hardware might be working properly, but Windows and your software might not know it.

Bugs in the Machine

After you check for human error, make certain that everything is hooked up and turned on, and ensure that Windows is configured correctly for your hardware, what do you do if you still have problems? Well, the possibility exists—however slight—that your system actually is infested with software or hardware bugs.

Yes, I'm afraid it's true: not every software program is programmed perfectly, and not every piece of hardware comes from the factory totally free of mechanical inconsistencies. It's entirely possible that your software program truly doesn't do what you instruct it to do or that some component really has broken down inside your system unit or a peripheral. Can you believe it? Some problems actually are caused by *computer* error!

But how can you tell whether your software has bugs? First, read the README file included with most new software programs. This file (variously labeled README, README.DOC, README.TXT, or READ.ME) contains last-minute instructions, changes, and additions that were developed too late to include in the standard software documentation. If certain features of a program malfunction, the README file probably discusses those problems.

Next, go to the software publisher's Web site. (The address is typically listed in the software manual or on the software box.) Click around the site looking for pages related to your specific program; look for technical notes or information, or *FAQs* (lists of Frequently Asked Questions). If there are any last-minute changes to your software, they should be noted somewhere on the Web site—and you might even find software "patches" that you should download and install to bring your "new" program even more up-to-date.

Two other potential sources of information about any glitches in your software include your dealer and other users of the program. The latter group especially might be aware of bugs in the program that could be causing your problem. (You can often find comments from other users in Usenet newsgroups devoted to your specific software.)

As a last resort—if README, the publisher's Web site, your dealer, and other users can't help—call the software publisher's technical support line. The call might cost you a few pennies, but the publisher's technical support staff often can warn you of bugs in their company's programs and sometimes even help you exterminate your own particular pest.

If your software seems okay, how do you determine whether a bug in your *hardware* is causing the problem? The simplest thing to do—although not always the most convenient—is to replace the offending peripheral with one from a friend's computer system. If you think your printer is acting up, for example, try hooking up a friend's printer to your system. If your friend's printer works, your printer is probably at fault. (An alternative is to hook up your printer to your friend's system to see whether your device works there. If it doesn't, you definitely have problems with your printer. If it *does*...turn to *The Great PC Troubleshooting Road Map*—on the tear-out card—to help track down the real cause of your problem!)

Another good resource is your hardware manufacturer's Web site. Most PC manufacturers have good tech support resources on their sites, including troubleshooting information and email access to technical staff.

Finding a Reliable Repairman (or Repairwoman)

Make sure that you take your computer to a repair shop you can trust. Call your computer's manufacturer and have them recommend a repair center in your area. (They might also have quick factory service via Federal Express or overnight mail.) You should also ask your friends (or the office techno-nerd) where they get their computers repaired. It's worth your peace of mind (and your PC's ongoing health) to do a little legwork before you entrust your computer to a stranger.

After you find a repair center, you might want to do a little work *before* you hand over your PC to them. If your PC is still running, think about removing any sensitive files you have on your hard disk, such as online banking data, confidential documents, and dirty pictures you downloaded from the Internet. And if you think your hard disk might need replacing, back it up *before* you ship it off (if you can); most repair centers won't bother to transfer data from one hard disk to another unless it's a specific request.

You might not be able to identify every hardware problem you experience yourself; that's why so many people train to be computer repair technicians. When all else fails, never be afraid to call a repair tech; often, these specialists can fix your machine in less time than it takes you to determine if you even have a problem and, if so, where the problem originates.

Catching a Virus

There is one final category of computer problems to discuss. Unfortunately, it is one that is growing in seriousness almost daily—the dreaded *computer virus*.

Chapter 10, "Germ Warfare—Protecting Your Computer from Viruses," explains about viruses in greater detail. Basically, a virus is a computer program or file designed to deliberately cause other programs and data to malfunction. Viruses can infiltrate regular programs and inflict extensive damage to these and other programs and data on your hard disk. Viruses are truly evil and can be enormously destructive.

How do you catch a computer virus? Like other computer data, viruses are transmitted through the exchange of infected disks, by downloading infected programs from the Internet, or through files attached to email messages. Whenever you allow new programs from an outside source into your system, the chance exists—however slight—that within that data might lurk a hidden computer virus.

So, how exactly can you tell whether your computer has a virus? If your old reliable programs suddenly start acting funny, they might be infected. If you experience sudden data loss, your system might have contracted a virus. If your computer suddenly shuts down and displays a weird message on its screen, or starts performing unusual tasks of its own volition (such as sending out batches of email messages to people in your personal address book), it's almost certainly suffering from a virus infection. In short, any sudden, unusual, unexplained computer behavior could be a sign that your system is infected.

How do you avoid viruses? The only foolproof way is to sever your connection to the Internet and never use any disks given to you by other users. However, such extreme measures are often impractical. Fortunately, you can take any of several more practical precautions, including the installation of special anti-virus software. See Chapter 10 for more information on how to practice safe, virus-free computing.

How to Be a Better Computer User

Now that you know why *even you* can be plagued by computer problems, what can you do about it? How can you become an even better computer user than you already are? The next few sections provide you with some helpful suggestions.

Careful, Careful, Careful

First, always take extra care to prevent making mistakes whenever you use your computer. If you type a command, address, or filename, be sure to type it correctly. It helps if you actually look at the screen while you're typing, especially before you press the **Enter** key—in other words, look before you execute. It will save you *a lot* of headaches.

Second, be very cautious when you communicate with other users. Whether you trade disks with another user, receive unsolicited email messages, or download programs from the Internet, always be aware that *any* new files you introduce into your system could contain a hidden computer virus. The rules of safe computing are much like those of safe sex—know your partners and take reasonable precautions. If you don't know where the data has been and what it might contain, don't copy it onto your system.

(And don't just automatically save or install everything everyone sends to you or that you find on the Internet. Not only will some of this stuff contain viruses, you'll very quickly clog up your hard disk with useless files—most of which will also modify your configuration files and quite possibly cause conflicts with other, more useful, programs. In other words—only install the programs you really need and are sure you will use.)

Third, connect the various parts of your system together *very* carefully—and with the power turned off! Make sure that you hook up everything correctly and that all the connections are solid. And don't forget to turn the power to your system back on when you're done, preferably through a surge protector.

Finally, make sure that Windows is configured correctly for all the components of your system. Don't simply assume that the installation routine and Plug and Play worked as advertised—check out Windows' setup information yourself to be certain it's correct.

It's an old saying but a true one: You can never be too careful. When things go wrong—no, even *before* things go wrong—double-check anything and everything involved with your system that could possibly cause problems. Someday, you'll be glad you did.

Save, Save, Save

When you're working on a file—whether it's a word processing document, an Excel spreadsheet, or a large Access database—you're making important changes as you go along. If you happen to experience computer problems in the middle of a work session, you could lose any changes you've made to that file. Think about it—I'm sure you've experienced a program freeze or a computer crash that wiped out the document you were working on at the time.

The only way to save your data is to *save your data*. Until you've clicked the B button, everything you've typed exists only in memory. After you save it, it's on your disk, and will still be on your disk even if your system crashes.

Whenever you work on an important file, save your work at least every five minutes and make copies *every half hour* (or even more frequently!) on a separate disk or portable storage device. (I like keeping my copies on a Zip disk.) This ensures that you always retain a relatively up-to-date copy of your work, even if your system experiences a severe data loss. You should even consider turning on your program's "autosave" feature, if it has one.

In other words: Be safe and save frequently.

Back Up, Back Up, Back Up

When something is important to you, *always* keep a copy in case you lose the original. Whether we're talking about personal papers or computer files, anything can be damaged or misplaced. If a copy exists, you're protected should even the worst happen.

Back up your important data *frequently*. If your hard disk suffers damage, a virus invades your system, you accidentally delete several files, or you inadvertently reformat your hard disk, you can recover the lost data from your backup tapes or disks. Make it a point to back up your hard disk on a regular basis—at least once a week and perhaps even daily. See Chapter 7, "Preparing a PC Survival Kit," for detailed information on exactly *how* to back up your important data.

The Least You Need to Know

➤ Most computer problems are caused by user error, bad information, broken or poorly connected cables, incorrect system configurations, software bugs, or computer viruses.

➤ For maximum protection, remember to be *careful* when you use your computer, to always *save* files while you're working on them, and to *back up* key files frequently.

Chapter 7

Preparing a PC Survival Kit

In This Chapter

➤ Learn how to back up the data on your hard disk

➤ Discover how to create an Emergency Windows Startup Disk

➤ Find out what should be part of every user's PC Survival Kit

---

You know, the Boy Scouts have it right. "Be Prepared" is a *great* motto—especially when you're dealing with personal computers!

If you're reading this book, you know the value in preparing for potential disaster. If you're prepared, the odds of recovering your valuable data are much higher than if you're not prepared. Just think of it as a way of "buying" insurance for your computer: You invest a little time today to protect yourself should the unthinkable happen to your PC and its data tomorrow.

Backing Up Your Data

If all heck breaks loose and your hard disk gets trashed, you're pretty much up the creek without a paddle, right?

Not necessarily.

If you were *prepared*, you had anticipated this situation and *backed up* the important files from your hard disk. If your files are backed up, it's an easy job to *restore* your files to your hard disk—and you don't lose key data when disaster strikes.

Windows provides two utilities that can help you prepare for disaster: Microsoft Backup (discussed next) and Microsoft System Recovery (discussed in Chapter 8, "Recovering When "The Big One" Hits"). Armed with these tools—and a Windows Startup disk (also discussed in this chapter)—you'll be ready just in case something really big happens to your system.

Third-Party Backup Solutions

In addition to the Microsoft Backup utility included with Windows 95 and Windows 98, there are many high-quality commercial backup programs available. These include Backup Exec (www.veritas.com/products/be98/), NovaBackup (www.novastor.com), and Tape-It (www.pgsoft.com). All these programs let you perform backups with even more sophistication than Microsoft Backup allows.

For the ultimate in protection, you can use an *online backup* service, which lets you back up your files online to a special Internet site. The advantage of an online backup service is that if your house burns down, your key files are stored *offsite*, completely free of any harm that could happen to the rest of your computer system. Note, however, that with current modem speeds, backing up your data over a telephone-based Internet connection can be *very* time consuming! Given bandwidth constraints (and ongoing subscription costs—which can really add up over time), some of the more popular online backup services are @Backup (www.backup.com), Connected Online Backup (www.connected.com), and Internet FileZone Plus (www.atrieva.com).

Backing Up with Microsoft Backup

Microsoft Backup is a utility that helps you store important files on disks or backup tapes or Zip disks; in the event of a hard drive crash, you can restore your backed-up files, and thus minimize your data loss. Even if you've never had a hard drive fail or become corrupted, you should always make regular backup copies of your critical files—*just in case*.

With Microsoft Backup you can choose to back up the entire contents of your hard disk, or just selected files. How often you need to back up your files depends on how often the files change and how critical the changes are. For many users, once a month is often enough. If your system crashes, you'll lose some information, but nothing you can't reproduce with a little time. If you store critical information that changes rapidly, however, you should consider backing up more regularly.

The following steps show you how to use the Windows 98 version of Microsoft Backup to back up your files. (If you're using Windows 95, the procedure is similar, with a few minor differences).

1. To start Microsoft Backup in Windows 98, click the **Start** button, and select **Programs**, **Accessories**, **System Tools**, **Backup**.

2. When Backup launches, you are presented with a dialog box asking you what you'd like to do. Check **Create a New Backup Job**, and click **OK**.

3. Windows launches the Backup Wizard. If you want to back up your entire hard disk, select **Back Up My Computer** and proceed to step 5. If you want to back up only selected files on your computer, select **Back Up Selected Files, Folders, and Drives**, click **Next**, and then proceed to step 4.

Can't Find Microsoft Backup?

Microsoft Backup isn't always installed on all computer systems. If you can't find Microsoft Backup on your PC, use the Add/Remove Programs utility to install it from your Windows installation CD.

4. In the left pane of the screen shown in this figure, select the drives and folders that contain the files you want backed up. In the right pane, select the individual files you want to back up. To back up an entire drive, click the check box next to the drive in the left pane. Click **Next** to proceed.

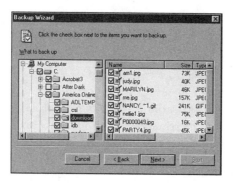

To back up files with Microsoft Backup, click the + next to each drive and folder to display its contents, and then check the box next to those items you want to back up.

5. When asked *what* you want to back up, specify to back up **All Selected Files**, or only those **New and Changed Files**. Click **Next** to proceed.

6. When asked *where* to back up, select a destination for the backup files. You can back up files to a disk, to a tape drive, to a removable disk (such as a Zip or Jaz disk), or to a second hard disk. Click **Next** to proceed.

7. When asked *how* to back up, make sure both options (**Compare** and **Compress**) are selected; then click **Next** to proceed.

Full, Differential, and Incremental Backups

There are three different types of backups you can make: Full, Differential, and Incremental. Which type of backup you choose depends on your backup strategy (discussed later in this chapter).

A *Full* backup makes a copy of all the files on your hard disk. Given the large size of today's hard disks, a Full backup can be quite time consuming—and use multiple disks, Zip disks, or backup tapes. However, restoring data from a Full backup is a simple procedure. Because of the time and size of a Full backup, you probably won't do this every day—once a month is probably the right timing for a full system backup, and even then only if you have high-capacity backup media.

A *Differential* backup is a copy of all the files that have changed since your last Full backup. Maintaining a Differential backup means that you actually keep two sets of backup files—one Full backup set, and a smaller Differential backup set. Differential backups, because they back up much less data than a Full backup, are faster and consume less time and fewer disks or tapes. To restore a Differential backup, you first have to restore the Full backup, and then do a Differential restore.

An *Incremental* backup is a copy of all the files that have changed since your last Incremental backup (*not* the last Full backup!). If you choose an Incremental backup strategy, you need to have a separate set of disks or tapes for each Incremental backup; for example, if you do a Full backup once a week followed by six Incremental backups, you'll need six sets of Incremental backup media. To restore an Incremental backup, you first restore the Full backup, then the first Incremental backup, then the second Incremental backup, and so on. Incremental backups are the least time consuming to create but are the most tedious to restore.

It's a good idea to perform some sort of backup daily, whether that's a Differential or Incremental backup. This way your frequently used data files (Word documents, Excel spreadsheets, Quicken records, and so on) are never more than a day out-of-date in the event of a system failure.

8. You are now prompted for a name for this backup job. Enter a name and click **Start** to begin the backup. (Hint: When labeling your backup set, include the date in the filename so that you can see at a glance when the files were last backed up.)

What media should you use to perform your backups? When determining what backup media to use, look at both cost and ease of use, and then make your choice.

Given the gigabytes of data stored on a typical hard disk, backing up to 1.4MB disks is highly impractical. Zip disks (with 100MB of storage) are probably the minimum acceptable alternative, with backup tapes more common and recordable or rewritable CDs more ideal (but also more expensive).

Restoring Files from a Backup

If you do experience a hard disk problem (or lose files for any reason), you might need to restore to your hard disk the files you previously backed up. Although it can be traumatic to lose files in a hard disk failure, restoring files from your backup disks will help to get you up and running in no time.

If you're using Windows 98, follow these steps to restore your backed-up data:

1. Click the **Start** button, and choose **Programs**, **Accessories**, **System Tools**, **Backup**.
2. When Backup launches, you are presented with a dialog box asking you what you'd like to do. Check **Restore Backed Up Files** and click **OK**.
3. When the Restore Wizard appears, select where the backup files are stored, and then click **Next**.
4. When the Select Backup Sets dialog box appears, select which backup set you want to restore, and then click **OK**.
5. When the next dialog box appears, select the files (or folders) you want to restore. Click **Next** to proceed.
6. When asked *where* you want to restore these files, select either **Original Location** or **Alternate Location**. If you select **Alternate Location**, a new text box appears in this dialog box; enter the location you want for the restored files in this box. In most cases, however, you'll want to restore the files to their original locations. Click **Next** to proceed.
7. When asked *how* to restore, select one of the following options and then click **Start**:

   ➤ **Do Not Replace the File on My Computer**   This prevents you from overwriting existing files.

   ➤ **Replace the File on My Computer Only if the File Is Older**   This allows you to restore only those files that are newer than those on your computer—that is, those files that have changed recently.

   ➤ **Always Replace the File on My Computer**   This allows you to replace all files on your computer with the versions contained in your backup set.

In most instances, the second option (**Replace the File on My Computer Only if the File is Older**) is the safest, because it prevents you from overwriting a newer file with an older version.

8. When the Media Required dialog box appears, make sure you have the right disks/tapes ready for restoration, and then click **OK**.

9. A Restore Progress dialog box appears during the restore process. When the restoration is complete, a dialog box appears with the message Operation completed. Click **OK**.

Remember that restored files might not be the most recent versions, especially if the files were used any time after your most recent backup. Still, recovering a slightly older version of a file is better than not having any version of that file at all.

Miller's Recommended Backup Procedure

There is no need to back up your entire hard disk—for one thing, it's just too darned big! Even if you have a tape backup system or a large Jaz drive, it still takes a long time and a lot of space to back up today's multi-gigabyte hard drives.

Besides, you don't *need* to back up every single file on your hard disk. If you keep all your software installation disks and CDs, it's easy enough to reinstall software programs—just as it's relatively easy to reinstall Windows 98 itself.

The key files to back up are your data files—the files created by your software programs, like Word documents and Excel spreadsheets and PowerPoint presentations and Access databases and Quicken financial records and PhotoShop graphics. In other words, back up any file that cannot easily be recreated.

One easy way to remember *what* you need to back up is to segregate your data files into their own special folder. For example, on my home PC I have a folder called **\My Documents**. (This folder is created by default by Microsoft Office; you can create your own version of it if you're not an Office user.) Within this folder I have subfolders for different types of data; my Word files are in a **\My Documents\Word** folder, and my Excel files are in a **\My Documents\Excel** folder. This way I can back up the entire **\My Documents** folder (and all its subfolders) and have a complete backup of all my data files, in one place.

I recommend that you initiate a backup schedule that involves a Full backup of your data files once a week, and Differential backups on the remaining days. The procedure is simple:

1. On day one, perform a Full backup of your data files (and any program files you can't easily reinstall in the event of a hard disk crash).

2. On days two through seven, perform Differential backups of any data files that have been modified or added that day, using the same set of Differential backup disks or tapes each day.

3. On day eight, start the process all over again with a new Full backup (reusing last week's Full backup media).

This procedure offers you the benefit of a Full backup on a weekly basis, while protecting modified or new files daily. If you follow this procedure, you'll never lose more than a day's worth of data in the event of a hard disk disaster; restoring your files will be as easy as restoring your Full backup first, and then your Differential backup.

Making a PC Survival Kit

Every smart computer user keeps a PC Survival Kit close at hand, just in case a computer emergency does develop. The contents of such a kit often are indispensable if you are to recover your data after a complete or partial hard disk crash. Thus, I consider these items to be required accessories for every PC user. You probably already have most of these components, and I'm going to show you how to complete your kit.

Here is what your PC Survival Kit should contain:

➤ Windows Emergency Startup Disk

➤ Original Windows installation CD

➤ Original installation disks/CDs for all your software programs

➤ Set of backup disks/tapes

➤ Disk utility software

Now let's take a quick look at each of the kit's components.

The Windows Emergency Startup Disk

The most important component of your PC Survival Kit is the Windows Emergency Startup Disk. You can use such a disk to boot your computer in the event of total hard disk failure.

To create an Emergency Startup Disk, you must instruct Windows to format a disk so that it can "boot" your computer. (Booting is just a fancy name for starting your system.) To understand how booting works, you must understand what happens when you first turn on your computer.

After you turn on your computer, the system immediately tries to read from drive A. If a disk is in drive A, Windows tries to boot from this disk. If a normal disk (that is, a nonbootable one) is in the drive, Windows finds no system files on the disk, and the following error message appears:

```
Non-System disk or disk error
Replace and press any key when ready
```

If you receive this message on startup, remove the nonbootable disk from drive A and press any key to restart the system.

If drive A is empty, your computer proceeds to your hard disk (drive C), and searches for the system files it needs to start itself. If your hard disk is inaccessible (due to some sort of hard disk error or failure) and drive A is empty, your system doesn't start at all. And, if your computer won't start, all your valuable data is suddenly inaccessible. This nonevent is known as "the big one," and it is not a pleasant experience—unless you have an Emergency Startup Disk ready.

The Emergency Startup Disk is vital in case you have to restart your computer in an emergency, such as when corrupted system files are detected at normal Windows startup or if your hard disk crashes. With a Startup disk, you essentially start your system from the disk instead of your hard disk.

In both Windows 95 and Windows 98 you're prompted to create a Startup disk when you first install Windows. Maybe you did this; maybe you didn't. In any case, you can create a Startup disk at any time by clicking the **Start** button and selecting **Settings**, **Control Panel**, and then selecting the **Add/Remove Programs** icon. When the Add/Remove Programs Properties dialog box appears, select the **Startup Disk** tab and then click the **Create Disk** button.

As Windows prepares to create the Startup disk, it prompts you to label and insert a disk in drive A; do so, and then click the **OK** button. (If you insert a disk that contains data, that data will be erased during this process; if you insert an unformatted disk, that disk will be automatically formatted.) When the Startup Disk has been successfully created, you are returned to the Add/Remove Programs Properties dialog box. Click **OK** to close the dialog box and return to the desktop.

The so-called Startup disk you just created isn't quite the Windows Emergency Startup Disk I recommend, however. To create Miller's version of the Emergency Startup Disk, you need to copy a few more files to your Startup disk.

If you're using Windows 98, you should also copy the SYSTEM.INI and WIN.INI files (found in the \Windows folder) to your disk.

A Better Startup with Windows 98

One big difference between Windows 95 and Windows 98 is in the contents of the Startup disk. In Windows 95 the Startup disk didn't include any CD-ROM drivers, making it difficult to use the Startup disk to reinstall Windows from a CD-ROM. Windows 98 adds CD-ROM drivers to the Startup disk, so if you need to reinstall the entire operating system from scratch, you can use the CD-ROM version of Windows 98 to do so.

If you're using Windows 95, you should copy FORMAT.COM, SCANDISK.EXE, SCANDISK.INI, WIN.INI, SYSTEM.INI, AUTOEXEC.BAT, CONFIG.SYS, and your system's CD-ROM device drivers to the Startup disk. (Consult your CD-ROM's instruction manual for the names of the driver files, and then search for them and copy them from where they reside on your hard disk.)

A Startup Disk for Older Versions of Windows

If you're still using a pre-Windows 95 version of Windows, you have to exit to DOS to create a Startup disk. From the DOS prompt, put a blank disk in your A drive and enter this command:

```
FORMAT A: /S
```

When the disk is fully formatted, copy these files (found in various directories and folders, depending on the version of your specific operating system):

➤ ATTRIB.EXE   ➤ MODE.COM
➤ AUTOEXEC.BAT   ➤ MORE.COM
➤ CONFIG.SYS   ➤ MOUSE.COM
➤ DEBUG.EXE   ➤ MSCDEX.EXE
➤ DELTREE.EXE   ➤ SCANDISK.EXE
➤ DISKCOPY.EXE   ➤ SCANDISK.INI
➤ EDIT.COM   ➤ SYS.COM
➤ EDIT.HLP   ➤ SYSTEM.INI
➤ FDISK.EXE   ➤ WIN.INI
➤ FORMAT.COM   ➤ XCOPY.EXE
➤ HIMEM.SYS   ➤ XCOPY32.EXE
➤ MEM.EXE

In addition, if you have a CD-ROM drive, you should copy your CD-ROM drivers to the disk.

To use the Windows Emergency Startup Disk, insert it into your PC's A drive, and then turn on your machine. Your PC should start and, after some simple system diagnostics, display an A:\ prompt. From here you can use simple disk utilities (such as ScanDisk) to diagnose problems.

Original Windows Installation CD

If your hard disk gets trashed, you'll need to reinstall Windows. The best way to reinstall Windows is from the original Windows Installation CD; make sure you hold on to your copy of this after the initial Windows installation! (One other reason why the original CD—and its packaging—is important: You'll need to access the original installation "key" code, located on the CD package, to reinstall the software.

Original Software Installation Media

Although you *could* restore all your program files from backup files, it's actually just as easy to reinstall your programs in the event of a hard disk crash. So hang on to all your old software disks and CD-ROMs, just in case. (And remember to keep the software *package*, as well—in case you need to access any installation codes or passwords.)

Backup Data

If you've been reading along, you know the value of backing up your data files on a regular basis. For this reason, your PC Survival Kit should include (per Miller's Recommended Backup Procedure) both your Full weekly backups and your Incremental daily backups.

Useful Disk Utilities

Now, if you really want to play it safe, include in your survival kit at least one third-party disk utility program. These programs—such as Norton Utilities (www.symantec.com/nu/), Nuts & Bolts (store.mcafee.com), or CheckIt (www.touchstonesoftware.com/products/fsetcit98.html)—contain utilities that enable you to repair most of the damage your hard disk might incur. My own favorite utility

is the Norton Disk Doctor, part of Norton Utilities. This useful program analyzes your hard disk for any damage and even repairs the damage it discovers. I consider the Disk Doctor an excellent addition to anyone's PC Survival Kit.

Protect Your Startup Disk

Open the write-protect notch of your Startup disk to minimize the possibility of erasing or overwriting the disk.

(Microsoft's ScanDisk—included free with Windows 95 and Windows 98—is an okay disk utility, but not nearly as full-featured as a Norton Utilities program. If you ever do run into catastrophic problems, it's unlikely that ScanDisk will be enough to get you up and running again.)

The Least You Need to Know

➤ You should use Microsoft Backup to create backup copies of the key files on your hard disk.

➤ You need to have a Windows Emergency Startup Disk handy, in case you can't start your system from your hard disk.

➤ Every user should create a PC Survival Kit, containing the Windows Emergency Startup Disk, your original Windows installation CD, the original installation disks/CDs for all your software programs, a set of backup disks/tapes, and some sort of disk utility software.

Chapter 8

Recovering When "The Big One" Hits

In This Chapter

➤ Learn how to troubleshoot catastrophic system failures

➤ Discover how to fix and restore data to a damaged hard disk

➤ Find out how to use Microsoft System Recovery to recover from a disaster automatically

When I talk about "The Big One," I'm not talking about Dolly Parton, Elvis, or the Pope; I'm talking about that rarest of situations—when your hard disk completely and irrevocably shuts down.

Dead.

Kaput.

Deceased.

Not working at all.

As you can guess, this isn't a desirable situation. So what do you do? Well, begin by turning the page, and I'll tell you what to do when you have a "late" computer.

Don't Panic!

The first thing to remember when your hard disk dies is—*don't panic!* If you followed the precautions advised in Chapter 7, "Preparing a PC Survival Kit," you have every reason to believe that you can at least partially, if not completely, recover your important data. (Of course, if you *didn't* follow these precautions, my advice is—*panic!*)

But how exactly do you know that you're facing "The Big One" and not another, lesser catastrophe? Check for one of the following symptoms; either is a dead giveaway—and I *do* mean *dead!*

Bad Disk Symptoms

If your computer doesn't boot correctly—if, in fact, it can't even access your hard disk—you'll notice one of two symptoms. Symptom One is that nothing happens—nothing at all. You have a blank screen, no lights and no noises, and your system just sits there like Monty Python's proverbial dead Norwegian Blue parrot with its claws nailed to the perch. (Not a pleasant thought, eh?)

Symptom Two is that your system tries to start but then displays one of the following error messages (before launching Windows):

```
Bad or Missing Command Interpreter

Cannot load COMMAND, system halted

Cannot read file allocation table

Disk boot failure

Error loading operating system

File allocation table bad, drive C

Abort, Retry, Fail?

Invalid COMMAND.COM, system halted

Missing operating system

No system on default drive

Non-System disk or disk error

Replace and strike any key when ready
```

If you receive one of these error messages, there are eight things you can do to try and get your system up and running again.

When Death Is Near

In some instances, you might get warning signs that your hard disk is about to go south. If your hard disk begins to run slower and slower, for example, or starts sending you too many error messages, or no longer copies data the way it used to, the poor thing is probably on its deathbed. If you think your hard disk might be about to give up the ghost, back up all your data and then put in an emergency call to your local repair center.

And here's one thing *not* to do if your hard disk is on Death's door—*don't* run any disk repair utilities! ScanDisk and other similar utilities can actually scramble some of the data on a dying hard disk, making it harder for a data recovery service (discussed later in this chapter) to recover any data you haven't backed up.

Troubleshooting a System Failure

Any number of problems can cause your system not to boot. The key to diagnosing your specific problem is to follow a detailed troubleshooting procedure, outlined in the following eight steps. In order, then, try the following:

1. Make sure that everything is plugged in and turned on. It's possible that your system is actually booting but your monitor isn't working. Trust me, I've seen it happen.

2. Try booting again. That's right. Turn your system off, wait about 30 seconds, and then turn it back on again. Don't ask why, but sometimes this fixes things.

3. Make sure that you haven't left a (nonbootable) disk in drive A. If there's a disk in drive A, remove it and reboot your system by pressing **Ctrl+Alt+Del**.

4. If your hard disk still doesn't boot, insert your Windows Emergency Startup Disk (explained in Chapter 7) into drive A and restart your system. After your system boots from this disk, type the following command to copy a fresh version of the command interpreter to your hard disk:
   COPY A:\COMMAND.COM C:\COMMAND.COM

   Now remove the disk from drive A and reboot your system by pressing **Ctrl+Alt+Del**.

5. If an error message tells you that you can't copy COMMAND.COM to your hard disk, or if suggestion 4 doesn't get you up and running, you might have a completely trashed hard disk. Try using the DIR command to see what, if anything, is left on drive C. From the Windows Startup Disk (in drive A), type
   DIR C:

If you get an error message, you probably have a damaged or accidentally refor-matted or repartitioned hard disk. If you don't get an error message, but no files are listed, something has erased the files from your hard disk; proceed to step 6 for more instructions.

6. If there are no files on your hard disk, something has wiped the disk clean. (This something could be a computer virus, a vengeful ex-employee, or some other fiend out to destroy your data.) To get your hard disk back to normal, use Microsoft System Recovery (on your Windows Emergency Startup Disk) to re-install key systems files (and the Windows operating system!) to your hard disk.

7. If your hard disk is totally inaccessible, try to repartition and reformat the disk, and then restore your data files. This procedure is described later in this chapter.

8. If you can't reformat your disk, or if you continue to encounter problems after reformatting, you probably have more serious hard disk problems. You might need to consult a computer repair technician.

Recovering from Disaster

If you've walked through these eight troubleshooting steps and come to the conclu-sion that your hard disk is toast, stay calm. Before you call in the pros, you can try rebuilding your disk yourself.

Sounds Easy—Not!

Okay, so rebuilding a hard disk really doesn't sound that easy. If you're not com-fortable doing it yourself, that's okay too. Besides, you should only try rebuilding your hard disk if you're extremely confident of your skills and if you have a com-plete set of recent backup disks. If you don't want to do it yourself—*or if you don't have backup disks/tapes*—you should take your entire system to a qualified com-puter technician, who might be able to salvage most or all of your data through professional means. Remember, if you try to do it yourself and screw up, there's a very good chance that not even the best technician in the world can recover any of your data if you haven't backed everything up!

Rebuilding Your Hard Disk

The procedure of rebuilding a damaged hard disk includes two required steps and one optional step. The required steps can be accomplished by anyone familiar with DOS commands. The optional step, which I'll discuss first, requires the use of a third-party disk utility.

Fix the Disk

Before you go to all the bother of reformatting your hard disk, you should check the disk itself for physical damage and fix that damage, if possible. Although you can perform some rudimentary inspection with Microsoft's ScanDisk (included free with Windows 95 and Windows 98), if ScanDisk can't fix the errors, you really need a more powerful third-party utility, such as Norton Disk Doctor (included with Norton Utilities), to make major repairs. If you don't have access to a copy of Norton Disk Doctor or some similar utility, or you feel uncomfortable with this level of complexity, the time to call a professional technician has arrived.

Where's ScanDisk If Your Hard Disk Is Gone?

When you create your Windows Emergency Startup Disk from Windows 98, several key utilities are compressed onto the disk. When you boot your computer with the Emergency Disk, the utilities are uncompressed and extracted into a *RAM disk* (a "virtual" disk residing in your system's random access memory). The RAM disk is assigned to drive D; to access any of these utilities, you have to switch to drive D (enter **d:** at the DOS prompt) and then issue the command to start the utility.

Among the utilities extracted to the RAM disk are ScanDisk (type **scandisk** to launch), Chkdsk (a simpler DOS-based disk utility; type **chkdsk** to launch); Edit (a DOS-based text editor; type **edit** to launch); and Format (type **format** to launch).

Partition the Disk

To prepare your hard disk for formatting, you first have to *partition* the disk. (This involves dividing the disk into one or more usable sections; you don't need to know all the technical details involved, as long as you remember that you have to partition before you can format.) In most cases, you configure your hard disk to have a single partition; for very large hard disks you might need to create multiple partitions.

To partition your hard disk, you issue the following command from your Windows Emergency Startup Disk:

FDISK

Follow the onscreen instructions to create the partition on your disk.

Format the Disk

After your hard disk has been partitioned with FDISK, you're ready to format it. (In fact, you *have* to format your disk after you've repartitioned it, in order to access it at all!) The command is straightforward, and you use the /S switch to add key system files to the disk. Just type

FORMAT C: /S

Wipe Out!

Don't type the FORMAT /S command if your hard disk is functioning normally and contains data. This command wipes out any data present on the disk and should be used only in an emergency!

You'll be prompted that all data on the drive will be lost, and you'll answer **Y** to proceed with the format. When the format is complete, your system will display the following message:

```
Format complete
```

Your system will now automatically copy key system files to your hard disk, and then display this message:

```
System Transferred
```

Next, you are prompted to supply a name for your disk by the following message:

```
Volume label (11 characters, ENTER for none)?
```

If you don't want to name your disk, just press **Enter**. If you *do* want to assign a name to your disk, type a name of no more than 11 characters and then press **Enter**.

Finally, your system displays an onscreen report showing the disk space formatted, the bytes used by the system files, any defective sectors, and the number of bytes available on the disk.

After your hard disk is formatted, you can restore your backed-up data, as discussed next.

Recovering from a Disaster with Microsoft System Recovery

Although you could reinstall Windows and restore your backed-up files manually, Windows 98 provides a neat little utility that automates these tasks for you. *Microsoft System Recovery* provides an easy way to restore your system after a catastrophic failure.

When Bad Sectors Are Okay

Don't get upset if your system reports that your disk has defective sectors. Almost all disks have a few small bad sectors due to normal imperfections in manufacturing. During formatting, your system marks these sectors as unusable and avoids them in future operations, so they're no threat to your system's day-to-day operation.

To rebuild your system (to a "clean" hard drive), start by inserting the Windows Emergency Startup Disk in drive A, and then turning on or rebooting your PC. When the A:\ prompt appears, type **e:** and press **Enter**. (The Windows Emergency Recovery Disk automatically assigns your CD-ROM to drive E; drive position D is assigned to a virtual RAM disk containing key utilities.)

Now you should insert your Windows 98 Installation CD in your CD-ROM drive. Next, type **cd\tools\sysrec** and press **Enter**, and then type **pcrestor** and press **Enter**. Follow the onscreen instructions to automatically reinstall Windows 98, start the System Recovery Wizard, install any necessary drivers, and restore your data files with the Microsoft Backup Restore Wizard.

Although you can do all the tasks necessary to restore your system manually, Microsoft System Recovery provides an easier, more automated way to make your system whole again.

Restoring Data Manually

If you're using Windows 98, Microsoft System Recovery will lead you step-by-step through the process of restoring your backup files to your hard disk. If you're running an earlier version of Windows—or if you've misplaced your Windows 98 installation CD—you might have to restore your backup files manually.

Restoring backed-up files is relatively easy—after you have Windows reinstalled on your hard drive. (The following instructions are specific to Windows 98; backing up in Windows 95 is similar.)

First, you'll need to launch the Microsoft Backup utility. Do this by clicking the **Start** button, and selecting **Programs**, **Accessories**, **System Tools**, **Backup**. When Backup launches, you are presented with a dialog box asking you what you'd like to do. Check **Restore Backed Up Files** and click **OK**.

When the Restore Wizard appears, select where the backup files are stored, and then click **Next**. When the Select Backup Sets dialog box appears, select which backup set you want to restore, and then click **OK**. When the next dialog box appears, select the files (or folders) you want to restore. Click **Next** to proceed. When asked *where* you want to restore these files, select **Original Location**. Click **Next** to proceed.

When asked *how* to restore, select **Replace the File on My Computer Only if the File Is Older**, and then click **Start**. When the Media Required dialog box appears, make sure you have the right disks/tapes ready for restoration, and then click **OK**.

A Restore Progress dialog box appears during the restore process. When all files have been restored, a dialog box appears with the message `Operation completed`. Click **OK**, and you're finished.

Turning to Professional Help

When all else fails, don't be embarrassed about turning to a pro for help. A qualified computer technician often stands a better chance of fixing your system and restoring your data after a major disk disaster than you do. If you try and try and try again and still can't bring your hard disk back from the dead, by all means call someone who gets paid to do the dirty work.

What to Do If You Didn't Back Up Your Data

If you have backup data and your hard disk crashes, you can simply restore the backup to your new or repaired hard disk. If you *don't* have a back up, however, the situation is more dire—but not hopeless.

At this point you need to turn to a *data recovery service*. These firms specialize in "saving" lost data from crashed drives—and do a surprisingly good job of it, in most cases. You send them your disk, they analyze it and tell you what's salvageable— and if you agree to the price, they transfer the remaining data to another storage medium, so you can then copy it to your replacement hard disk.

These services aren't cheap, however; depending on the size of your disk and the extent of the damage, prices can range from $200 to $2,000 (although most firms won't charge you if they can't recover the data). Obviously, this is not something you would do for a hard drive full of PC games, but if truly vital data is at stake, this might be your only option, at any price.

If you need data recovery, some of the larger firms providing this service are ACR Data Recovery Services (www.atl-datarecovery.com), Data Recovery Labs (www.datarec.com), Drive Service Company (www.driveservice.com), DriveSavers (www.drivesavers.com), and Ontrack Data Recovery Solutions (www.ontrack.com).

The Least You Need to Know

➤ You can recover from minor hard disk problems by booting from the Windows Emergency Startup Disk, running ScanDisk, and restoring key files to the fixed disk.

➤ In more serious situations, you might need to manually repartition, reformat, and restore your hard disk.

➤ In Windows 98, you can use the Microsoft System Recovery utility to perform recovery operations automatically.

➤ If you can't rescue your hard disk, you can use a data recovery service to try and recover lost data from the bad drive.

Chapter 9

Coping with the Year 2000 Problem

In This Chapter

➤ Find out what the year 2000 problem *is*, and what caused it

➤ Learn how to test your hardware and software for Y2K compliance

➤ Discover online resources to help you understand and cope with the Y2K problem

---

The Year 2000 Problem. Y2K. The Millennium Bug.

Whatever you call it, it's something that can play havoc with any computerized device—from large mainframe computers to personal computers to the computer chips that control your corner stoplights or local ATM machines. When the year rolls over from 1999 to 2000, some of these devices could misinterpret the date (as 1900!) and start working in unpredictable ways. Some computers and devices will quit working altogether; some will begin to execute unreliable calculations; others won't be affected at all.

But how will the Y2K problem affect your personal computer?

Just What Is the Year 2000 Problem?

The so-called Year 2000 (Y2K) problem is all about digits—and sloppy computer programming.

For years, programmers have been a bit lazy in how they store date information in computer programs. Historically, programmers specified a year using two digits (99) rather than four digits (1999). By "assuming" the first two digits of the year (as "19"), computer memory and storage were maximized—and less coding was required.

But what made sense 25 years ago (when the turn of the century was a lifetime away) doesn't make sense as we approach the year 2000. If a program only looks at the last two digits of the date, how is it supposed to interpret "00"—as the year 2000, or the year *1900*?

And so you see the problem.

It's a simple fact that some computer software (including the "burned-in" software on some microprocessor chips) might have difficulty interpreting any year data after January 1, 2000. If a computer system relies on a date to perform critical processes— and if that date is *wrong*—any information, calculations, or processes based on that date could produce unintended results.

Given that so many devices and systems rely on computers, and given that any computer could be affected by this Y2K bug, the potential impact of this issue is huge. And the only way to fix the problem is to go back and recode any offending programs, changing two-digit date storage and calculation to the more accurate four-digit configuration.

If You're Reading This Book *Before* January 1, 2000, Start Here

Before we get into the nitty-gritty of Y2K-compliance checking, I want to offer my opinion of the whole Y2K issue.

My opinion? There probably isn't much to worry about.

I seriously doubt that we'll see worldwide chaos and the collapse of civilization as we know it when the clock rolls over on the first day of the new millennium. Frankly, so many systems rely on forward dating that if there were going to be major problems, we would have seen them already. (For example—what is the expiration date on your credit cards, or insurance policy, or driver's license? All of these databases are already dealing with year 2000 dating, and all appear to be working fine.)

Not that there won't be *any* Y2K problems at 12:01 on January 1st. There has been enough sloppy programming over the years to convince me that *something* will go wrong—I just don't think *everything* will blow up!

Still, it doesn't hurt to be prepared. Better safe than sorry, and all that. And, although most of the Y2K-issue focus has been on larger computer systems—and those systems that are widely used, such as the ATM network—personal computers are not immune from Y2K problems.

How your personal computer system might be affected by the Y2K problem depends not only on the hardware and software that you use, but also on *how* you use your system. For example, if you only use your PC to play games, write memos, and surf Web sites, you probably won't notice any problems. On the other hand, if you're a heavy spreadsheet user, if you use Quicken or Microsoft Money to manage your personal finances, or if you rely on database programs to store a lot of numerical data, you're at a higher level of risk.

To analyze the potential for Y2K-related problems on your particular computer system, you have to look separately at your computer hardware, your computer software and operating system, and your personal data files.

Y2K and Your Computer Hardware

If Y2K is a programming problem, why should you worry about your hardware—it doesn't contain any software that could be affected, does it?

Actually, every personal computer in existence relies on a battery-powered internal clock (called a *Real-Time Clock* or RTC) to keep track of your system's date and time. But the RTC only keeps track of the last two digits of the year, not the century. Instead, your computer's *BIOS* (Basic Input/Output System—a set of instructions "burned into" every microprocessor chip) oversees the century digits—and is susceptible to the Y2K bug. If your BIOS—and thus your entire PC system—doesn't know the correct date, various aspects of your computer system could be affected.

So how do you find out if your computer hardware is Y2K-compliant?

First, check with the manufacturer of your PC. Many PC manufacturers have Y2K information, tests, and solutions on their Web sites.

Second, test your hardware to see how it handles the year 2000 rollover. You can find an automated test for hardware readiness at the National Software Testing Labs site (`www.nstl.com/html/nstl_ymark2000.html`), or perform the following manual test:

Don't Test from Your Hard Disk!

Perform any Y2K test by booting from a disk—*not* from your hard drive. If you perform a Y2K test from your hard drive *and your system fails the test*, you could lose valuable information. If possible, boot the PC using a bootable disk, so that you don't access programs or data on your hard drive. And, of course, remember to reset your PC's date to the current date when you're finished testing!

1. Start your PC using the Windows Emergency Startup Disk.
2. After your system is up and running, set the date and time to December 31, 1999, 23:59:00. (At the DOS prompt, type **date:** followed by the new date, and then press **Enter**. Then type **time:** followed by the new time, and press **Enter**.)
3. Turn off your computer.

4. Wait a minute or so for the "rollover" to the next century to occur.

5. Restart your PC, again using the Windows Emergency Startup Disk.

6. After your system restarts, check to see whether the system date is January 1, 2000.

7. With the Windows Emergency Startup Disk in the disk drive, warm boot your computer by pressing **Ctrl+Alt+Del** simultaneously.

8. After your system restarts, check to see if the system date is January 1, 2000.

9. Reset your system to the current date and time, remove the Windows Emergency Startup Disk, and reboot your computer for normal operation.

If your PC fails this test—if it doesn't hold the new date, or reports an erroneous date—then you should check with the PC's manufacturer for an update to your system's BIOS. (Most BIOS updates are user-installable—you don't need a technician to update your BIOS.) If your BIOS isn't upgradeable (and some cheaper, older systems *aren't*)...well, then you have real problems.

Of course, you could also solve any potential Y2K problems by purchasing a brand new computer. Most PCs manufactured in the past few years have already addressed the issues and are fully Y2K-compliant.

Y2K and Your Computer Software

In general, newer computer software is more likely to be Y2K-compliant than is older software. Also, commercial software programs (the stuff in a box) is more likely to be Y2K-ready than are custom-developed programs (such as those your company's IT department might supply).

So if you just bought a brand-new PC complete with brand-new preinstalled commercial software (Windows 98 and Office 2000, for example), you probably don't have much to worry about.

However, if you have an older system running custom applications, it wouldn't hurt to be a little concerned.

Here's what you can do if you think you have Y2K issues with your operating system or software:

➤ Nothing. Take your chances; if you work more with text than numbers, or if all you do is play games or surf the Internet, even if your programs have Y2K problems, you'll probably never notice them. On the other hand, if you do a lot of number crunching or database sorting, you could be tempting fate.

➤ Install a special Y2K update "patch." Many software publishers are providing patch programs to correct known Y2K problems with their software. Check with the publishers of your programs for any Y2K updates; most of these can be downloaded via the Internet and easily installed on your system.

➤ Upgrade to a newer version of your software. This is the fail-safe solution to your Y2K problems. If you're running an old version of a program, just upgrade—and get all your Y2K problems taken care of at the same time.

Because Microsoft publishes the operating systems and application software used by practically every PC user, you can get a good head-start on your Y2K compliance just by analyzing Microsoft's most popular programs. Table 9.1 details the recommendations for various versions of Microsoft's two most popular pieces of software, Windows and Office:

Table 9.1 Y2K Solutions for Microsoft Windows and Microsoft Office

Software and Version	Recommendation
Office 4.x	No action necessary (fully Y2K-compliant).
Office 95	Install the Office 95 Year 2000 Update (officeupdate.microsoft.com/articles/ O95y2kfactsheet.htm). Download OLEAUT32.DLL version 2.20.4118 (http://support.microsoft.com/ download/support/mslfiles/msvbvm50.exe).
Office 97	Install the Office 97 Service Release 2 Update (officeupdate.microsoft.com/articles/sr2fact.htm).
Office 2000	No action necessary (fully Y2K-compliant).
Windows 3.1	Install the updated Wfwfilup.exe file (support. microsoft.com/download/support/mslfiles/Wfwfilup. exe). Read the article "File Manager Shows Garbled Date for Year 2000 or Later" in Microsoft's Knowledge Base (support.microsoft.com/support/ kb/articles/Q85/5/57.asp). Note, however, that this update doesn't address all the year 2000 issues in Windows 3.1; your better solution is to upgrade to Windows 98.
Windows 95	Install the Windows 95 Year 2000 Update (www.microsoft.com/windows95/downloads/contents/ wurecommended/s_wufeatured/win95y2k/default.asp).
Windows 98	Install the Windows 98 Year 2000 Update. Click the **Start** menu, select **Windows Update**, then select **Product Updates**. The Windows 98 Year 2000 Update will be listed under critical updates (if it has not already been installed on your system).

To request any of these Microsoft Y2K updates on CD-ROM, call 1-888-673-8925. You can also check Y2K compliance for other Microsoft products at the Microsoft Product Information page (`computingcentral.msn.com/guide/year2000/msy2k/learningmore/microsoftprod.asp`), or run the Microsoft Product Analyzer (`computingcentral.msn.com/guide/year2000/msy2k/learningmore/analyzer.asp`), which analyzes and displays the Y2K readiness status for most Microsoft products.

Y2K and Your Data Files

You can make sure your hardware, software, and operating system are all Y2K-ready and still run into problems if your own personal data files—word processing documents, spreadsheets, financial records, and so on—rely on two-digit year dating. Depending on how the "date" field is understood by the software program, digits you enter as "00" might be interpreted as 1900, which is probably not what you intended.

You need to be concerned about this issue when your files use dates that are included in some type of calculation. This is typically a spreadsheet, accounting, and database problem, *not* a word processing, presentation graphics, or computer game problem.

To protect against this problem in the data files you personally created, you have to manually go through your files, looking for date fields. If you find a two-digit date field, change it to a four-digit field (so you use "2000" instead of "00").

There is an easier way to perform this task, however—if you're lucky. It's possible that the publisher of your software program provides a utility to check your data files for Y2K compliance. For example, Microsoft provides "wizards" to change errant dates in Excel workbooks; you can find these Y2K utilities at `support.microsoft.com/support/kb/articles/Q176/9/43.asp`. Check with your program's publisher for such Y2K utilities *before* you start analyzing all your files by hand.

Commercial Solutions to the Y2K Problem

In addition to the Y2K solutions provided by hardware manufacturers and software publishers in support of their own products, several third-party software publishers are selling utilities designed to sniff out and fix the Millennium Bug. For example, Norton 2000 (`www.symantec.com/sabu/n2000r/index.html`) scans for Y2K problems in a variety of data files (including Microsoft Excel, Microsoft Access, Lotus 1-2-3, Quattro Pro, dBase III, dBase IV, Paradox, FoxPro, and Clipper files), audits your software programs for Y2K compliance, and even tests and fixes hardware BIOS issues. Check with your local computer retailer for this and other Y2K-fix utilities.

If You're Reading This Book *After* January 1, 2000, Start Here

I'm writing this book during the summer of 1999; the book itself is being published in the fall of 1999. If you purchased your copy *after* January 1, 2000, all the previous blather about the Y2K problem is old news. Either the world came to an end due to the Millennium Bug, or nothing major happened and life went on. In either case, you can look back at all the hand-wringing and prognostications and laugh at how wrong everyone was, one way or another.

If you're reading this book in a well-lit office, with your personal computer turned on and connected to the Internet, my prediction of little Y2K impact proved true. Aren't you glad you didn't spend a lot of time preparing for a disaster that didn't happen?

On the other hand, if you're reading this book by candlelight in a fortified bunker while snacking on canned Spam, my prediction was obviously a bit off base, and things turned out a lot worse than I anticipated. Sorry!

More Y2K Resources

One short chapter in a general computer book can only scratch the surface of the larger Y2K problem. To learn more about this issue, check out the following Web sites:

➤ CNET Year 2000 Center (www.news.com/Categories/Index/0,3,87,00.html?st.ne.nav. .y2kidx). The best tech news site on the Web presents news and commentary on the Y2K issue.

➤ CNN In-Depth Special: Looking at the Y2K Bug (www.cnn.com/TECH/specials/y2k/). CNN's Web site presents a guide to recent stories about the Y2K problem, and includes compliance deadlines, a Y2K primer, and a guide on how the Y2K problem will affect different industries.

➤ Microsoft Year 2000 Challenge: A Guide for Home Computers (computingcentral.msn.com/guide/year2000/msy2k/Introducing/y2home.asp). Microsoft's informative site about the Y2K problem, featuring information and updates to make your Microsoft operating systems and software programs Y2K-ready. (See the next figure.)

➤ PCY2000 Alliance (www.pcy2000.org). This alliance, comprised of the industry's largest PC hardware manufacturers and software companies, presents a top-notch resource for all PC users confronting Y2K issues, including Y2K tests and direct links to the year 2000 Web sites of member companies.

➤ President's Council on Year 2000 Conversion (www.y2k.gov). The U.S. government's take on the Y2K problem, including information on efforts to prepare government computer systems and links to information on Y2K compliance for critical sectors of the economy.

➤ U.S. Small Business Administration: Help for the Year 2000 (www.sba.gov/y2k/). The SBA presents a variety of Y2K resources for small businesses, including a five-step plan for small businesses to achieve year 2000 readiness.

➤ ZDNet Year 2000 Briefing Center (www.zdnet.com/anchordesk/bcenter/ bcenter_287.html). Another large collection of articles and information, from Ziff-Davis' many computer-oriented publications.

Microsoft's Year 2000 Challenge site—a good resource for Y2K issues in general, with links to compliance information for all Microsoft products.

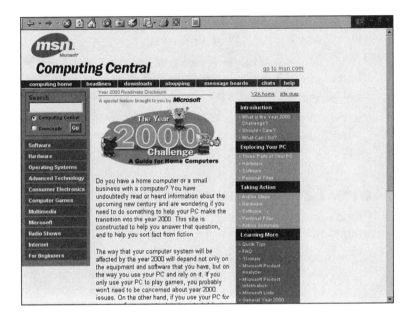

The Year 2000: A Personal Observation

One of my friends recently commented that if the Y2K bug does its worst and disables all our computer-assisted devices and services, our society will be forced all the way back to...*the early 1970s.*

That's right, most of the ubiquitous use of computers that we've come to depend on has only happened in the past 25 years or so. (I remember back to my college days—I graduated in 1980—and realize that I didn't have access to ATM machines, charge card-operated gasoline pumps, *or* personal computers!)

Would it be so bad if we had to live life in 1970s terms? Could we survive without computer-assisted systems, ATMs, and the Internet? Or would we have to start wearing leisure suits and listening to ABBA again?

If worse comes to worst, civilization will survive. Besides, if you can't use *your* PC or access *your* ATM, you'll be no worse off than anyone else—your neighbors will also be PC-less and ATM-less. Although I personally doubt that the Y2K problem will have any widespread effects, period, I think we can easily withstand even the worst of what some Cassandras are predicting. So you won't see me stockpiling canned food and barricading myself from the coming hordes; on New Year's eve, I'll have a glass of champagne in my hand as I toast the new millennium with my closest friends, Y2K problems be damned.

The Least You Need to Know

➤ The so-called year 2000 problem is caused by a programming shortcut that only used two digits to record the current year (such as, "99" for "1999").

➤ Most newer commercial software programs and most newer computer systems won't be affected by the Y2K problem.

➤ There are numerous resources available that can check your hardware and software for Y2K readiness.

Chapter 10

TSSSss

Germ Warfare— Protecting Your Computer from Viruses

In This Chapter

➤ Learn what a computer virus is—and the damage it can do

➤ Find out how to decrease your chances of catching a computer virus

➤ Discover how anti-virus software can guard your system and help you recover from a virus attack

---

Computer viruses are not the figment of some computer geek's imagination. They're all too real, and they can cause real damage to your computer system. You must protect your system from the danger they pose—or run the risk of catastrophic system failure and data loss.

What Is a Computer Virus?

A computer virus actually is similar in many ways to a biological virus: A biological virus invades your body's system and replicates itself; likewise, a computer virus invades your computer's system and also replicates itself. Computer viruses can be destructive (like the HIV virus) or simply annoying (like any of several viruses that cause the common cold). Just as you try to protect your own body from biological viruses and find a cure when you become infected, you want to protect your computer from computer viruses and find a cure if its system ever becomes infected.

Unlike biological viruses, a computer virus is not alive (although it might seem like it if one of the pesky things manages to infest your computer). A virus is actually a rogue computer program that injects copies of itself into other programs on your computer system. Viruses typically invade executable program and system files—the very heart of your computer system. Some viruses merely display an annoying message on your screen;

other more deadly viruses actually destroy your software programs or system information. The worst of this loathsome bunch are difficult both to detect and dislodge because they craftily conceal themselves from observation and doggedly defend against removal.

How Viruses Work

A computer virus is a computer program that places copies of itself in other programs on your system, or that somehow manipulates other files on your system. Most viruses infect program files or work through macro code in data files; plain-text email messages are not capable of being infected (although email attachments *can* include viruses).

Literally thousands of different viruses have been detected to date, and are typically classified by the way they work:

➤ **Boot-sector virus**   A boot-sector virus overwrites or deletes the startup sector on a disk, making it impossible for your computer to start.

➤ **File infecting virus**   These viruses infect executable files (with .EXE, .COM, or .SYS extensions) on your system. A file-infecting virus activates each time an infected file is run; the virus code typically searches for an uninfected file and infects it, even though the original program might run normally.

➤ **Multipartite virus**   This is a virus that infects both boot sectors and executable files—and is very difficult to detect.

➤ **Polymorphic and stealth viruses**   A polymorphic virus changes its appearance with each infection and is sometimes encrypted, making it difficult to detect. A stealth virus attempts to hide from anti-virus software by hiding any changes it makes to other files (both file sizes and directory structure).

➤ **Trojan Horse**   A Trojan Horse is a program that performs other functions in addition to its declared function. This type of program enters your system under the guise of peace, but then goes to war when you're least expecting it—similar to the Trojan Horse of ancient legend.

➤ **Worm**   This type of virus spreads copies of itself through networked computers, or over the Internet.

➤ **Macro virus**   The newest and most common type of virus is one that actually infects data files, such as Word or Excel files. These viruses rely on the pseudo-programming code in application documents to perform specific operations *in the background* when you load a document into your application program.

Common Virus Symptoms

How do you know whether your computer system has been infected with a virus? You might notice one or more of the following symptoms:

➤ Strange messages appear on your monitor screen, such as
`You've been stoned.`

➤ Strange graphics appear on your monitor screen, such as bouncing balls or a simulation of your screen "melting."

➤ Strange noises ("beeps," "boops," "squeals," "phfffts," and so on) emanate from your computer speaker.

➤ Normally well-behaved programs start operating erratically or crash intermittently.

➤ Files you know you haven't erased turn up missing.

➤ Common program files appear to have grown in size since your last analysis.

➤ Your system begins to act sluggish.

➤ Your system fails to boot.

➤ Your system starts performing an action totally on its own—such as sending rogue email messages to people in your personal address book.

If your computer exhibits one or more of these symptoms—and if you have recently engaged in behavior conducive to contracting a virus (see the next section)—the prognosis is not good: It might very well be infected.

How to Catch a Virus

Whenever you share data with another computer or computer user, you risk exposing your computer to potential viruses. When you use a disk given to you by another user, you take the chance that the disk harbors a virus. If you download programs from the Internet, or open attachments to emails from unknown senders, you're tacitly accepting the risk that this data could transmit a virus to your computer. In fact, even when you load a brand-new, shrink-wrapped piece of software onto your computer system (after removing the shrink wrap, of course), you should be aware that it's possible— if unlikely—for even this new, direct-from-the-factory software to carry a virus! Egads! Is *nothing* safe?

Home Alone

If by chance you do operate a completely isolated computer, never sharing disks or using the Internet, you're probably safe from virus infection. So if you *never* interact with other computer users—and why are you so antisocial, anyway?—you shouldn't get overly concerned about all the warnings and advice in this chapter.

Is It Safe?

Is it possible to completely protect your system against computer viruses? Unfortunately, the answer is no— unless you never add another piece of software (even *new* software) to your system, never accept disks from strangers, and never access the Internet, not even for email. The reality is that computer viruses are created by evil people with destruction on their minds, and—just like real-world terrorism—it is impossible to completely guard against these random acts of computing terrorism. That doesn't mean you have to live the rest of your computing life in fear, but it does mean you should take whatever precautions are prudent to reduce your risk factors.

Using an Anti-Virus Program

Anti-virus software programs are capable of detecting known viruses and protecting your system against new, unknown viruses. These programs check your system for viruses each time your system is booted—and can be configured to check any programs you download from the Internet, as well. (To be safe, you should download any programs from the Internet to a separate directory and scan them with the anti-virus program before you run the new programs on your system.)

You can find several popular anti-virus programs at your local computer software retailer. My favorites are McAfee VirusScan (a free version of which is included with Microsoft Plus! 98) and Norton AntiVirus.

Practicing Safe Computing

If you live in the real world, you can't be 100 percent safe from the threat of computer viruses. You can, however, take these steps to reduce the risk associated with these havoc-inducing programs:

➤ Share disks only with users you know and trust. If you don't know where a disk comes from, don't stick it in your disk drive.

➤ Download programs only from reliable sources. If you're connecting to a non-commercial Web site run out of some guy's basement, avoid the temptation to download any files from that site. If you must download files from the Internet, use only those established and reliable Web sites (such as CNET's Download.com or the ZDNet Software Library) that actually check their files for viruses before they post them for downloading.

➤ Don't open email attachments from people you don't know. If you get an unsolicited email message from someone you've never heard of before, and that message includes an attachment (a Word document, or an executable program), *don't open the attachment!* The attached Word file could contain a macro virus, and the attached program could wipe out your entire hard disk! (In fact, I would even caution against opening unsolicited attachments from people you *do* know!)

➤ Don't execute programs you find in Usenet newsgroups. Newsgroup postings often contain attachments of various types; executing a program "blind" from an anonymous newsgroup poster is just asking for trouble.

➤ Use anti-virus software. Anti-virus programs protect you against all types of viruses—including both executable and macro viruses. Purchase, install, and run a program such as Norton AntiVirus or McAfee VirusScan—and let the anti-virus program check all new files downloaded to or copied to your system.

These precautions, taken together, should provide good insurance against the threat of computer viruses.

Recovering from a Virus Attack

What should you do if your computer has been infected by a virus? A lot depends on the type of virus you've been blessed with, and the damage that it has done.

If your system is still working and you have full access to your hard disk, you can use one of the anti-virus programs to "clean" infected files on your system. If specific files can't be cleaned, they should be deleted.

If you can't start your system or access your hard disk, you should follow the instructions in Chapter 8, "Recovering When "The Big One" Hits," to boot from the Windows Emergency Startup Disk and repair/rebuild/restore your hard disk. After your system is up and running again, run an anti-virus program to perform additional cleaning.

Know, however, that one of the dangers of catching a virus is that you could lose key data files. If your system has been hit, you might have to essentially start from scratch with a "fresh" system—losing any data that wasn't previously backed up.

Which is one of the main reasons everyone hates viruses.

The Least You Need to Know

➤ A computer virus is a software program that infects your system and damages or manipulates key files.

➤ You can protect against virus infection by avoiding disks given to you by strangers, not downloading files from non-commercial Web sites, and not opening unsolicited email attachments.

➤ Commercial anti-virus programs can also guard against computer viruses—and help you "clean" any infected files.

Part 2
Figuring Out What Went Wrong: Troubleshooting for the Technically Timid

Got problems? Then these chapters are for you! Just turn to the chapter that covers the kind of problem you're having, and read on to discover how to troubleshoot and fix the problem. Anybody—even you!—can follow the instructions in these chapters and get their computers up and running again in no time!

Chapter 11

What to Do When...Your System Won't Start

In This Chapter

➤ Discover exactly what happens when you turn on your PC

➤ Find out what can cause your computer not to start

➤ Learn how to use Windows Safe mode to troubleshoot problems that keep Windows from launching normally

---

You're all ready to start computing. Your desk is clean, your chair is positioned *just right,* your mouse is all warmed up, you've just loaded some cool tunes into your audio system, you turn that big power switch or button *on,* and then...

Nothing.

Nothing at all.

Your computer is dead, dead, dead. It just sits there, like a big, beige, beached whale, refusing to start.

Well, before you panic and do something stupid (like throw your PC out the window!), turn the page and let me tell you how to get your system up and running.

What Happens When You Turn On Your Computer

So what happens when you first turn on your computer? What complex chain of events is initiated when you flip your power switch to the "on" position?

The first thing that happens is that power is sent through the PC's power supply to the boards in the system unit. This initial power surge (called a *power-on reset*) resets your system's memory, microprocessor, and other electronics. Then your system, using instructions stored in a special battery-powered memory called CMOS RAM, does a *power-on self test* (POST). During this test, you see some messages scroll down your screen, letting you know how much RAM is available and that the system checks out as expected.

After the self-test, your computer tries to access drive A, looking for a bootable disk. A bootable disk, as explained in Chapter 7, "Preparing a PC Survival Kit," contains important system files necessary for your system to operate—files that are normally "hidden," and not displayed in a normal directory listing. If a bootable disk is in drive A, your system proceeds based on the startup files on this disk; if not, your system proceeds to drive C to look for the system files.

Getting the Boot

"Serious" computer users never can use simple, understandable names for common procedures. For example, these techno geeks never "turn on" their computers; they "boot" their computers. The term *boot* comes from the old expression "pulling yourself up by your own bootstraps," and refers to the way old computers used to "bootstrap" themselves from a launch disk. (Don't ask.)

When your computer accesses drive C, it reads into memory the contents of the disk's *boot sector*, which tells the system how to load the operating system. Surprisingly, the operating system that is loaded isn't Windows; your computer actually loads a copy of the older DOS operating system to begin with, to maintain compatibility with older programs and files on your system.

After DOS is loaded (and this all happens in the background, by the way; you don't actually see DOS on your screen), your system then loads a key system file named IO.SYS. This file contains much configuration information about your basic system. When this file loads, it reads the contents of a second configuration file (named MSDOS.SYS), which contains additional configuration information. After the contents of MSDOS.SYS have been read, IO.SYS then reads the contents of CONFIG.SYS, a third configuration file (if it exists—it was necessary pre–Windows 95, but not so with Windows 95 and Windows 98).

After the IO.SYS file has been loaded, your system runs the AUTOEXEC.BAT file. Like CONFIG.SYS, this file was a mainstay pre–Windows 95 (containing commands that loaded drivers and programs), but might not contain any information in "pure" Windows 95 or Windows 98 systems.

Your system then begins to load Windows and reads important settings from the Windows Registry, a database that contains all of your system configuration settings. (Older versions of Windows—pre–Windows 95—didn't have a Registry, and instead relied on the SYSTEM.INI, WIN.INI, CONFIG.SYS, and AUTOEXEC.BAT files to hold these settings; these "legacy" files can cause lots of problems on boot-up—more on this later.)

As Windows loads, it also loads a variety of device drivers, as specified by the Registry. Device drivers are small files that enable various pieces of hardware—such as modems and printers—to operate; the driver files are loaded into your system's memory, where they're immediately available for use. (These files are sometimes called *virtual device drivers*, and often are called *VxDs*.)

See for Yourself

If you want to take a look at everything that happens during the boot process—including the dozens and dozens of VxDs loaded into your system's memory—use Windows Notepad or WordPad to look at the contents of the BOOTLOG.TXT file, located in the main folder (root directory) of your hard drive. This figure shows the first page of a typical BOOTLOG.TXT file—just look at all those drivers that are loading!

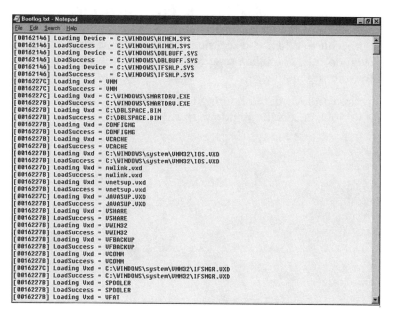

Examine the BOOTLOG.TXT file to view everything that happens when your system starts up.

Finally, after all the settings have been checked and all the drivers loaded, Windows itself is launched. You see a "loading" screen (which replaces the text-based screen you've seen up till now), hear "The Microsoft Sound," and then the Windows interface begins to build, element by element, until you can see the entire desktop and can use your system.

All this activity during startup is accompanied by beeps and whirrs and clicks and flashing lights, which just indicate that your system is doing its job. If you don't hear all the beeps and whirrs and clicks and see the flashing lights, and if your system doesn't load the boot program, the system files, and Windows, you have a problem.

Starting Windows in Safe Mode

Safe mode is a special mode of operation that loads Windows in a minimal configuration, without a bunch of pesky device drivers. This means the screen will be low-resolution VGA, and you won't be able to use a lot of your peripherals (such as your modem your scanner, or your printer)—but Windows will load, which it might not have, otherwise.

Any time you can't load Windows normally, you should revert to Safe mode. In addition, Windows will automatically start in Safe mode if it encounters major problems while loading.) Safe mode is a great mode for troubleshooting, because Windows still works and you can make whatever changes you need to make to get it up-and-running back in normal mode.

You enter Safe mode by restarting your computer (do the **Ctrl+Alt+Del** "three-fingered salute"), and then carefully watch the onscreen messages as your computer goes through its startup procedure. When you see the line `Starting Windows...`, press the **F8** key. When you do this, you'll be presented with a Windows **Startup** menu. Select **Safe Mode** from the menu.

Once in Safe mode, there are various troubleshooting techniques you can employ. I'll go over some of these as we look at specific Windows startup problems.

Other Startup Menu Options

When you press the **F8** key when Windows is starting, **Safe Mode** is just one of the options available on the Windows Startup menu. Here are some of the other options (which might differ from system to system):

➤ **Normal**   This starts Windows in its normal mode—as if you hadn't pressed F8 to begin with.

➤ **Logged (BOOTLOG.TXT)**   This logs all remaining startup operations to the BOOTLOG.TXT file.

➤ **Safe Mode**   Starts Windows with a minimal number of device drivers loaded, and also skips the CONFIG.SYS and AUTOEXEC.BAT files.

➤ **Safe Mode with Network Support**   A version of Safe mode that also loads key network drivers.

➤ **Step-by-Step Confirmation**   Loads all drivers and files one at a time, allowing you to load or not load each individual driver.

➤ **Command Prompt Only**   Boots to the DOS command prompt, after processing the CONFIG.SYS and AUTOEXEC.BAT files.

➤ **Safe Mode Command Prompt Only**   Boots to the DOS command prompt *without* loading the CONFIG.SYS and AUTOEXEC.BAT files.

Depending on your system configuration, you might have even more options available on the Windows **Startup** menu. In particular, systems that have been upgraded from a pre–95 version of Windows or from DOS may have options pertaining to the previous version of the MS-DOS operating system.

What to Do When You Can't Turn On Your Computer

There can be many possible reasons for your computer not starting. In fact, a computer might not start in several different ways. Read on for some analysis.

Problem 1:

Your computer doesn't start—you hear no noises and see no lights

First things first—*don't panic!*

Now, very calmly, look at the back of your system unit. Is the power cable plugged into the right connector? Now follow the power cord to the other end. Is it firmly connected to a power outlet? Now check the wall switch. Is it turned on? Now walk to your fuse or circuit-breaker box. Is the fuse good or the circuit breaker set? Now go back to your computer. If it still isn't working, unplug the computer from the power outlet and plug in something that you know works (a lamp or a radio, perhaps). If the appliance doesn't work, you have a bad power outlet. If the appliance *does* work, you really do have computer problems.

If you're positive that your computer is getting power and that you're turning it on correctly, you probably have a hardware problem. The most likely suspect is the power supply in the system unit. To determine the culprit and fix the problem, however, you'll need to call in professional help at this point. Take your system to a certified repair center and let its technicians get to work.

Problem 2:

Your computer doesn't start, but it makes the normal startup noises

If your system is making noise, at least you know that it's getting power. Because you can rule out a bad power cord, the most common things to look for are poorly connected cables or a nonfunctioning monitor.

Begin by checking your monitor. Is it turned on? Is it plugged into a power outlet? Is the power outlet turned on? Is the monitor connected to the correct port on your system unit? Is the connection solid? Is the connection solid in the back of the monitor? Are the brightness and contrast controls turned up so that you can actually see a picture?

If everything is connected and adjusted properly, you might have a monitor that needs repair. Is the monitor's power light on? If not, your monitor might have power supply problems that need attention from a professional. If your monitor's little green light is on but nothing shows onscreen, the video card in your system unit might be loose or set up incorrectly. Turn off your system, open the computer case, and check the video card to make sure it's installed, seated, and connected properly.

It's also possible that your keyboard isn't plugged in properly, or that you have some other internal problem that causes your system to halt during startup. See Problem 5 for more suggestions.

Problem 3:

Your computer doesn't start, and it generates a series of beeps

No, aliens aren't trying to contact you via Morse code. This strange audio communication is supposed to alert you to a wrong video card setting on the motherboard. (Some engineer had the bright idea that if your video wasn't working you couldn't see an error message, so the error message would have to be transmitted audibly.)

If you've recently changed video cards, you might need to change some switches on your motherboard to accommodate your new card. This process gets pretty technical, so I recommend either reinstalling your old card for the time being or taking your computer into the repair shop to have switches set. If you're brave, you can dig through all your instruction manuals (for your system unit *and* your new video card) and try to set the switches yourself.

The beeping can also occur if your video card is not firmly seated in its slot. Open the system unit and make sure that the card is plugged snugly into position; then close the case and reboot. If the problem persists, you might have a defective video card or a problem on the motherboard, both of which require professional attention.

Turn Off the Power!

Remember always to turn off the power before you open the case to do any work.

Another cause of these beeps could be the video settings in the CMOS setup. Your CMOS RAM chip stores certain system settings in battery-operated memory; if the CMOS battery is weak or dead, these settings might be corrupted. Have your local repair person replace your CMOS battery and reset your system settings.

Finally, some systems will beep if something is wrong with the memory setup—if there is no memory installed, or if the wrong memory chips are installed. When in doubt, read your computer system's manual for clues, or contact your system's manufacturer for technical support.

Problem 4:

Your computer starts, but the monitor displays an error message (before loading Windows)

Your system uses error messages to communicate with you when it encounters certain problems. Table 11.1 details some of the most common error messages you might encounter on startup (*before* Windows loads), their causes, and how to fix the problem.

Table 11.1   Startup Error Messages

Error Message	Causes/Solutions
`Non-system disk or disk error Replace and press any key when ready`	You see this message when you have a nonbootable disk in drive A. Check the disk drive and remove the disk, and then press any key to restart the boot procedure using your hard disk drive. (You *can* boot from drive A, of course, but you must have a *bootable* disk in that drive—such as the Windows Emergency Startup Disk, discussed in Chapter 7—and the disk must be inserted correctly.)
`Keyboard error, press F2 to continue`	It sounds kind of silly to ask you to use your keyboard to confirm that your keyboard isn't working, doesn't it? This message is generated when the rest of your system works but the PC can't find the keyboard. If you receive this message, your keyboard probably is disconnected, has a loose connection, or has a stuck key. Check the connecting cable (at both ends) and reboot. If you still receive this message, you have a keyboard problem. Verify this fact by plugging in a keyboard from a friend's machine. If you do have a keyboard problem, it's probably cheaper to buy a new keyboard than to get your old one fixed.

Error Message	Causes/Solutions
`File allocation table bad, drive x:`	This message is not good. Something has messed up your FAT (File Allocation Table), the part of your hard disk that holds vital information necessary for your system to operate. One of the most common causes of this problem is a computer virus. Another cause is some sort of physical damage to your hard disk, caused by contaminants or plain old wear and tear. If you have actual physical damage to your disk, you might need to use a third-party utility program, such as Norton Disk Doctor, to repair the damage—or you might want to drop back ten and punt by letting a technical professional handle the situation from here.
`General failure reading drive X` `General failure writing drive X`	These very serious messages mean that something is wrong with your computer—but it has no idea what the trouble is. Try shutting down your system for a few minutes and then rebooting; sometimes this message is generated when your system gets a little cranky. More likely, however, there is something seriously wrong with your hard disk, which means it's time to hop in the car and drop your PC off at your local computer repair center. The pros there have diagnostic software and equipment that can pinpoint problems much more easily than can you or me.
`Bad or missing filename.SYS` `Error in CONFIG.SYS line XX`	This message is generated when your old CONFIG.SYS file tries to load a driver that didn't exist. Although Windows 95 and Windows 98 don't actually need the CONFIG.SYS file to load drivers, pre–Windows 95 operating systems *did* use this file; if you upgraded from a previous version of Windows (or even DOS), Windows 95/98 kept this file pretty much as-is to deal with previously installed drivers. So if you see this message, it means that one of your older device drivers has been deleted or corrupted. (This happens sometimes when you delete very old programs from your hard drive.) You need to examine your CONFIG.SYS file (using Windows Notepad or WordPad) and edit the specified line to correct any mistakes or erase the line if the driver no longer exists.

continues

Table 11.1   CONTINUED

Error Message	Causes/Solutions
System halted	This message, typically generated when your system is trying to execute the old CONFIG.SYS file, is caused by an invalid, incompatible, or corrupted device driver. You might need to reinstall any drivers in question, or delete references to these drivers from the CONFIG.SYS file.
Invalid drive specification Drive not ready	Either of these error messages indicates that you're having problems with the drive you're trying to boot from. If you're booting from a disk drive, your bootable disk might be bad. Try using another bootable disk. If the problem persists, or if you're booting from a hard disk drive, the problem might reside in the drive mechanism itself. Sometimes an older drive can operate too slowly to always boot properly; try rebooting your system. If the problem persists, have a professional check out your system. The drive in question might need to be replaced.
CMOS RAM error	This message appears when something is bad in the setup held in memory by your system's CMOS RAM chip. (This chip holds important system information in permanent, battery-powered memory.) When you see this or any similar message, you are given the opportunity to press the **F1** key to continue. Do this, and adjust your CMOS setup accordingly. (See your system's documentation for information on how to do the latter.) If this message persists, you might have a dead CMOS battery; see your repair center to replace the battery.

Error Message	Causes/Solutions
Memory size error Memory size mismatch Not enough memory Insufficient memory Parity check xxx Parity error x	Any of these messages indicate that something is wrong with your computer's memory. Your CMOS setup might be in correct, or you could have some bad or improperly seated memory chips. It's also possible that you recently added extra memory to your system and it isn't configured correctly; if this is the case, enter your CMOS Setup menu and reconfigure your system for the new memory. If you can't fix this problem via the setup routine, you should probably consult a computer professional for further assistance.

Use the Emergency Startup Disk!

At any point in this process you might find it impossible to start *anything* using a normal hard-disk boot. If this is the case, you need to use your Windows Emergency Startup Disk (created back in Chapter 7, remember?) to reboot your system from drive A. When you use the Emergency Startup Disk, you can't get into Windows—but you *can* use ScanDisk to analyze any hard disk problems you might be having that could be causing Windows not to load.

Problem 5:

Your computer starts but then suddenly halts during startup—before Windows is launched

This problem occurs most often when your computer is trying to execute the CONFIG.SYS file. Although this file isn't necessarily used in brand-new Windows 95 or Windows 98 setups, it can still remain on your system if you upgraded from Windows 3.x or MS-DOS, and it is executed as part of the normal Windows startup procedure.

The difficulty is caused by an invalid, incompatible, or corrupted device driver. It's quite possible that you deleted an old program from your hard disk—along with the program's drivers—and the CONFIG.SYS file is still telling your system to look for the deleted driver before it starts.

To get going again, you should reboot your system and enter Windows Safe mode, and then check your CONFIG.SYS file for any bad or deleted drivers. You might also want to reboot your computer, press **F8** during the system startup, and select **Step-by-Step Confirmation** from the **Startup** menu; see Problem 7 for more details on this troubleshooting method. (Then you can reboot Windows in Safe mode and edit that command out of the CONFIG.SYS file.)

Your system can also halt if you accidentally press **Esc** or **Ctrl+C** or **Ctrl+Break** during the startup procedure. If you do this, reboot your system by pressing **Ctrl+Alt+Del**.

Another cause of startup halts is when a cable accidentally becomes disconnected, which often occurs with the keyboard cable. Check your connections and reboot.

Problem 6:

Your computer starts, but Windows doesn't—and you receive an error message

If Windows doesn't load—if your system, after the standard boot procedure, just "hangs" in place—then there is probably something wrong with your Windows installation or configuration. This typically happens after you add something new (hardware or software) to your system; the new thing changes the settings that *used to* work okay to a configuration that doesn't work okay anymore. But it's also possible for Windows to have trouble loading even when you've done nothing new or different to your system—to be quite frank, Windows is a finicky little operating system, and can surprise you with what it does or doesn't do seemingly of its own accord.

If you receive an error message while Windows is loading, it's probable that Windows is trying to load a bad or incorrect device driver of some sort. In fact, Windows will more often than not tell you exactly which driver it's having trouble with in the error message itself. After you know which driver is causing problems, you can either reinstall that driver, or eliminate that driver from the loading process—either by editing the driver out of the CONFIG.SYS, AUTOEXEC.BAT, WIN.INI, or SYSTEM.INI files, or by editing that driver's entry in the Windows Registry. (See Chapter 30, "The Course of Last Resort…Editing the Windows Registry.")

If the error message doesn't tell you which driver is causing the problem, you can determine that yourself by doing a *selective startup*. If you're running Windows 98, you can start Windows in Safe mode. Then click the **Start** button, and choose **Programs, Accessories, System Tools**, and then select **System Information**. When the Microsoft System Information utility launches, pull down the **Tools** menu and select **System Configuration Utility**. When the System Configuration Utility appears, select the **General** tab and choose **Selective Startup**. Now uncheck all the options under **Selective Startup** *except* **Process System.ini File** and **Process Win.ini File**. Make sure these options are the *only* options checked, and then click **OK**. When you're prompted to restart your computer, do so.

A Fast Way to Edit *All* Your System Files

The CONFIG.SYS, AUTOEXEC.BAT, WIN.INI, and SYSTEM.INI files are simple text files that can be edited with any text editor, such as Notepad or WordPad. If you want to edit these files all at once, however, Windows includes a "hidden" utility called the System Configuration Editor that opens *all* these key files at one time, ready for editing, automatically. To run the System Configuration Editor, click the **Start** menu, select **Run**, and when the Run dialog box appears, enter **sysedit** in the **Open** box and click **OK**. Select a window to edit a specific file; pull down the **File** menu and select **Save** to save any edits you make.

This procedure restarts Windows *without* any carryover drivers or instructions from Windows 3.x or DOS. If your system starts fine without the pre–Windows 95 startup files, you need to use Notepad or WordPad to edit the CONFIG.SYS and AUTOEXEC.BAT files to remove any offending commands.

(Note that the above procedure is Windows 98–specific; Windows 95 doesn't have a similar selective startup option. Also note that after you've fixed your problem, you'll need to manually *turn off* the Selective Startup option to return your system to normal startup mode.)

If this *doesn't* fix your problem—if you still receive an error message on Windows launch—then there is probably a bad entry in either the SYSTEM.INI or WIN.INI file. Use Notepad or WordPad or the System Configuration Editor to open each of these files, and look for the line that matches the error message you received. Either remove the offending entry or *disable* that entry by placing a semicolon (;) in front of it. If the entry refers to a program that you recently unin-stalled or deleted, *reinstall* the program, and then uninstall it *correctly* via the **Add/Remove Programs** option in the Windows Control Panel.

If after performing these actions you still have problems starting Windows, proceed to Problem 7.

Problem 7:

Your computer starts, but Windows doesn't—and you don't receive an error message

What if you can't load Windows and *don't* receive an error message? In this instance you want to start Windows in Safe mode, and then run some diagnostics.

Begin by clicking the **Start** button and selecting **Programs, Accessories, System Tools,** and then selecting **System Information**. When the Microsoft System Information utility launches, pull down the **Tools** menu and select **System Configuration Utility**. When the System Configuration Utility appears, select the **General** tab and select **Diagnostic Startup**. You'll now be prompted to restart your computer; do so.

When your computer restarts, you'll be presented with the Windows **Startup** menu. From this menu, select **Step-by-Step Confirmation**. In this special startup mode, you're prompted to load or not load every system file and device driver, instead of them loading automatically. As each file/driver is ready to load, press **Enter** to load the file/driver and **Esc** to *not* load the file/driver. This time around, go ahead and load everything *except* the AUTOEXEC.BAT and CONFIG.SYS files; when these options appear, press **Esc**.

If the rest of the files/drivers load properly and Windows starts successfully, you need to clean up some of the startup files left over from your older installation of Windows. (If this is a "clean" installation of Windows 95 or Windows 98, these files will still exist but probably won't contain any commands to start with.) Use Notepad or WordPad or the System Configuration Editor to open the AUTOEXEC.BAT and CONFIG.SYS files, and then type the word **REM** (followed by a space) in front of *every* line. (This "remarks" out the line, essentially telling Windows *not* to execute the command or load the associated driver.) Then, just to be safe, use Notepad or WordPad to open WIN.INI and put a semicolon (;) in front of the RUN and LOAD lines. (This has the same effect as the REM in AUTOEXEC.BAT and CONFIG.SYS.) Now restart your computer and you should be okay going forward.

If disabling these old files *didn't* get Windows running normally, the next step is to disable any other programs that might be loading when Windows starts up. Right-click the **Start** button, select **Open** from the pop-up menu, open the **Programs** folder, and then open the **Startup** folder. Use your mouse to drag and drop all items in the **Startup** menu to another folder (any folder will do, as long as you remember which one it is!). Now restart Windows again and see what happens.

If Windows now starts properly, that means that one of the programs that *used to* start up when Windows started is causing you problems. One at a time, drag those programs back to the **Startup** menu (using the same procedure as before), and then restart Windows. Each time Windows starts properly, you know that particular program is okay. When Windows *doesn't* start properly, you know that particular program is a problem—so leave it out of your Startup folder.

If, on the other hand, removing the programs from your Startup folder *didn't* fix your problem, you have a problem with a specific device driver. Restart Windows and, when you see the line Starting Windows..., press the **F8** key. When the Windows **Startup** menu appears, select **Step-by-Step Confirmation**. Now you go through the loading procedure manually, pressing **Return** to load each driver individually. Wait a moment after you press **Enter** each time, to see how your system responds. The first time your system hangs, you know that the driver you just loaded (make a note of it, now!) is somehow bad. You'll want to delete that driver from your system, and then reinstall it.

If you can't isolate your problem driver through this method, there's a more involved (yet more precise) way to find the culprit. Restart Windows in Safe mode, and then go to the **Control Panel** and select the **System** icon. When the System Properties dialog box appears, select the **Device Manager** tab, and get ready to *disable* a bunch of devices. To disable a device, right-click the device listing, select **Properties** from the pop-up menu, and when the Properties dialog box appears, check **Disable in This Hardware Profile**. Then click **OK**. You want to disable *all* devices in the following categories: Display Adapters, Floppy Disk Controllers, Hard Disk Controllers, Keyboard, Modem, Mouse, Network Adapters, PCMCIA Socket, Ports (COM & LPT), SCSI Controllers, Sound Video and Game Controllers, and Universal Serial Bus Controller. Exit out of this dialog box and then restart your computer.

Windows should now load properly—but only because practically all devices on your system have been disabled! Now you want to go back to the System Properties dialog box and *reenable* (by *unchecking* the **Disable in This Hardware Profile** option) your individual devices *one at a time*, in the following order: COM ports first, followed by Hard Disk Controllers, Floppy Disk Controllers, and then all your other devices. After you enable each device, restart your computer. The first time Windows doesn't start properly, you know that the last device you reenabled is causing your problems. You'll want to delete that driver from your system, and then reinstall it. (Don't forget to reenable all your other devices, too!)

If Windows *didn't* start properly after you disabled all your devices, you have a problem with the Windows Registry. (See Chapter 30 for more information on this crucial configuration database.) It's likely your Registry is damaged; you need to restore the Registry from a backup. Fortunately, Windows 98 (but not Windows 95) makes daily backups of your Registry automatically. To restore the Registry, restart your computer again and when you see the line Starting Windows..., press the **F8** key. When the Windows **Startup** menu appears, choose **Safe Mode Command Prompt Only**. This will essentially bypass Windows and start you in a version of the old DOS command-mode operating system. When the C:\ prompt appears, type **scanreg /restore** and press **Enter**. When you're prompted, select **Previous Day's Registry**, and then press **Enter**. This restores your Registry to the version that existed yesterday; restart Windows and, if everything works properly, reinstall any applications you installed in the past 24 hours.

If restoring the Registry *still* doesn't fix your problems (or if you're running Windows 95), you need to back all the way up to an original, "clean" copy of the Registry. Restart Windows in the Safe Mode Command Prompt Only mode, as before. At the C:\ prompt, enter the following four commands, pressing **Enter** after each entry:

```
c:\windows\command\attrib -h -s -r c:\system.1st
c:\windows\command\attrib -h -s -r c:\windows\system.dat
ren c:\windows\system.dat *.dax
copy c:\system.1st c:\windows\system.dat
```

Now restart your computer. Theoretically, Windows should start properly, but all information about your installed programs and configuration will be lost. (Because the Registry holds all program and configuration information, installing a "new" Registry causes your system to "forget" all the programs you've installed.) You'll need to reinstall all the programs on your computer in order to update the "new" Registry.

If, after all this work, Windows still doesn't launch properly, it's time to reinstall Windows. (In fact, if you're running Windows 95, use this opportunity to upgrade to Windows 98.) Use your Windows 98 installation CD to initiate a complete installation and setup—and if *this* doesn't fix your problem, it's time to contact a technical professional.

Problem 8:

Your computer starts, but Windows doesn't—and you can't enter Safe mode

Sometimes Safe mode isn't safe enough. Any number of conditions can cause Windows not to start in Safe mode:

➤ Your system is infected with a computer virus. You might need to reinstall Windows to eliminate the effect of the virus, and then use an anti-virus program to initiate a more complete cleansing of your system.

➤ Your computer's CMOS settings are incorrect. During boot-up, check your CMOS settings, and make corrections as necessary. If your CMOS battery is weak and not holding its settings, replace the battery.

➤ You have a hardware conflict. Some device in your system is conflicting with some other device; the most common conflicts are IRQ conflicts. Ask a technical professional (or just an old geek who knows how to use DOS) to hunt down the errant device from the DOS prompt.

➤ A setting in the MSDOS.SYS file needs to be changed. This file holds some configuration settings that are read at startup—especially if you have an older system that has been upgraded to Windows 95 or Windows 98. Reboot using the Windows Emergency Startup Disk, use the DOS **edit** command to launch the MS-DOS Editor, and then open the MSDOS.SYS file and look for any incorrect settings. In particular, check the Windows directory settings for accuracy.

If you have persistent problems starting in Safe mode, you probably should just reinstall Windows (from your Windows installation CD) to clear all your settings and start from scratch.

Problem 9:

Your computer starts, and Windows enters Safe mode automatically

Windows starts up in Safe mode automatically when it senses a major driver problem or conflict. Follow the steps in Problem 7 to track down the source of the problem.

Problem 10:

Your computer starts, Windows starts—and so does another program or utility that you don't want to start

Many programs, when first installed, have the audacity to think that you want them to run whenever you start up your PC—so they configure themselves to launch when

Windows launches. If you want to *stop* a program from launching automatically when Windows starts, you first have to find out from *where* it is being launched. There are several places to check:

➤ **Startup menu**   Click the **Start** button, select **Programs**, and then select **Startup**. If the offending program is here, right-click it and select **Delete** from the pop-up menu. (This doesn't delete the program itself; it just removes it from the **Startup** menu.)

➤ **WIN.INI file**   Use Notepad or WordPad or the System Configuration Editor to open the WIN.INI file, located in the **\windows** folder. Look for the **load=** and **run=** lines, and delete the offending program if it appears there. (Even though WIN.INI is a file used by pre–Windows 95 versions of Windows, some older programs might still use it for their autoloading instructions.)

➤ **AUTOEXEC.BAT and CONFIG.SYS files**   These are two autoexecuting DOS files, located in your main or root folder, that load when your PC is first turned on. Use Notepad or WordPad or the System Configuration Editor to check these files for the offending program; if it's there, delete that line. (As with WIN.INI, these programs aren't really used in Windows 95 or Windows 98, but some older programs might still be hiding there.)

➤ **Windows Registry**   Now we're into trickier territory. When I first turned on my brand new Gateway 2000 PC last year, I found several little applets loading into the Windows Tray on startup, and I couldn't find hide nor hair of them in the **Startup** menu, or in any of the configuration files mentioned previously. Where were they loading from? From "hidden" entries in the Windows Registry! There are several keys in the Registry that can contain autoload instructions; if the offending program is in any one of these, delete it! Here are the keys to check:

```
HKEY_LOCAL_MACHINE\SOFTWARE\Microsoft\Windows\CurrentVersion\RUN
HKEY_USERS\.DEFAULT\SOFTWARE\Microsoft\Windows\CurrentVersion\RUN
HKEY_CURRENT_USER\SOFTWARE\Microsoft\Windows\CurrentVersion\RUN
```

See Chapter 30 for information on how to edit the Registry.

10 Do's and Don'ts When Starting Your System

1. *Do* plug your system's power cable into a surge suppresser for added protection against power-line surges.

2. *Don't* leave a nonbootable disk in drive A. (Unless, of course, you're trying to boot from drive A—then make sure that it's a *bootable* disk!)

3. *Do* be patient—there's so much stuff to load, sometimes it takes a few minutes for your system to boot and Windows to fully launch.

4. *Don't* turn on your system unit and *then* turn on your monitor or plug in your keyboard; these items must be up and running before your machine starts its boot procedure.

5. *Do* make sure that all your Windows files match the same version of Windows; never copy a file from a Windows 95 installation CD onto a system running Windows 98.

143

6. *Don't* try to jump-start your computer by hooking up jumper cables from the battery of your Land Rover.

7. *Do* press the **Esc** key or the **Ctrl+C** keys if your booting procedure hangs up for some reason; if these keys don't do the job, restart the computer by pressing **Ctrl+Alt+Del**.

8. *Don't* delete any key system files (such as IO.SYS or MSDOS.SYS) from your hard disk.

9. *Do* upgrade to the latest version of Windows—and then use the Windows Update feature to keep constantly up-to-date with new drivers and files.

10. *Don't* boot a portable computer on an airplane during takeoff or landing; you'll make the flight attendant *really* mad!

The Least You Need to Know

➤ If your computer doesn't start at all, the problem is typically caused by a lack of power to your system unit, a key device (such as an internal card) not being installed properly, or your hard disk going bad.

➤ If you receive an error message on startup, the message will generally give you a clue as to the cause of the problem.

➤ If Windows doesn't start, chances are that there is a reference to a bad, missing, or incorrect driver file in one of the key system files.

➤ More often, if there is a problem loading Windows, Windows will launch in the stripped-down Safe mode, from which you can troubleshoot the cause of the problem.

➤ If you have trouble starting Windows, you can enter Safe mode manually by pressing **F8** during startup and selecting **Safe mode** from the resulting **Startup** menu.

Chapter 12

What to Do When... Your Computer Freezes Up

In This Chapter

➤ Learn the "three-fingered salute" necessary to reboot a frozen computer system

➤ Discover the sorts of things that cause your computer to freeze or crash

➤ Find out what to do if your system totally freezes up

It's happened to everyone. You're computing along, everything is going fine, no problems, when all of a sudden you realize that...

Your computer has frozen.

Stopped working.

Given up the ghost.

Just like that. No warning, no nothing.

So what do you do?

How to Keep Your System Up and Running

Don't panic!

That's the best advice when your computer freezes up. You see, whatever harm could be done *has* been done, and there's not much you can do about it at this point. Not very comforting, I know, but true.

In any event, about the only thing you can do (assuming the problem isn't something simple, like a loose connection) is reboot your computer. The good news in this situation is that—should rebooting be your only recourse—you probably won't damage any of your software programs. (A pretty weak consolation prize, eh?) The bad news is, of course, if you reboot your computer, you lose all the data you've entered since you last issued the Save command.

Sorry.

Why Your Computer Quits

What makes a computer simply stop in its tracks? Several common causes come readily to mind, including:

➤ Something came loose. Yes, it's the old loose connector trick again. Likely culprits are your keyboard cable and mouse cables, although on occasion your monitor cable can cause you fits, too. Sometimes you can just reconnect the cable and pick up where you left off. Other times, you must reboot after you reconnect the cable.

➤ You typed too fast. I know this probably sounds strange, but at times you might type too fast for your computer. Some keyboards and systems can accept only so much data in a given period. In other words, you can actually out-type your keyboard! Sometimes, when this happens, you just have to sit back and let your keyboard catch up to you; other times, you might even have to reboot your system.

➤ You clicked too fast. Just as you can type too fast, you can sometimes confuse Windows by clicking too many things too fast. This seems to happen particularly when you try to execute a new command in a program before the last command has finished executing. *What's your hurry?* Slow down, take your time, be patient— and let Windows finish one thing before you start another.

➤ You did something wrong. I know, I know. You never do anything wrong. But sometimes clicking the wrong element, inserting the wrong disk, or even just pressing the wrong key can make your computer freeze up. If you suspect this to be the case (be honest, now!), and then retrace your steps, try to figure out exactly what you did wrong, and either correct it or reboot your system.

➤ Your memory is full. No, not *your* memory, your *computer's* memory! Occasionally a program can use too much memory and provoke what is called a *memory allocation error*. This doesn't happen often, but when it does, you need to either manually close down a frozen program or reboot your entire system to correct the problem. If it happens too often, however, you need to add more RAM to your system.

➤ Your programs are in conflict. The world is a pretty dismal place if your own software programs can't even live together peacefully. Unfortunately, some programs just don't get along with other programs—they want to use the same memory space, or they try to access the hard disk at the same time, or they just plain don't like each other. You probably have no choice but to reboot if two (or more) warring programs lock up your system. After you have your machine up and running again, however, experiment with your programs to determine which ones are in conflict. If you normally load one program before the other, for example, load them in reverse order this time to see if that does the trick. (This affects which program gets what memory when and can resolve some conflicts.) If not, well, you might be forced to admit defeat and forevermore avoid running the two rival programs at the same time. Let that be your personal contribution to (computer) world peace.

➤ A virus has attacked your computer system. Oh no! Not that! Anything but that! (Oh, calm down, will you?) Refer back to Chapter 10, "Germ Warfare—Protecting Your System from Viruses," for information about fighting those nasty viruses.

➤ Somebody turned off the power. It sounds stupid, but make sure that you didn't accidentally flip off your PC's power switch, turn off the juice at the wall switch, flip off the switch on your surge suppressor, or trip over the cord and unplug it from the wall. (If all the lights in your house went off at the same time, it's also possible your entire circuit has gone dead—or your metropolitan area is experiencing a blackout!)

➤ Your computer broke. Well, it happens. Maybe your microprocessor stopped processing, or a transistor ceased transisting, or your power supply lost power. If the entire system goes down (no lights, no beeps, nothing), you might indeed have serious hardware problems.

➤ The stars are not in alignment today. If you can't ferret out any other reasons for your system stalling, and it reboots okay, the only possible answer must be that your biorhythms and your horoscope are in conflict, the moon is in the seventh house, the tide is high, and gravity is especially strong today. In other words, some things you never figure out—so don't lose any sleep over it. Just reboot and get on with your life.

What to Do When Your System Freezes or Crashes

When the system freezes, more often than not, you must reboot to get your computer working again. Rebooting loses whatever you typed since you last saved the file you were in when the machine froze, but the process really doesn't hurt either your computer or your software programs. (Of course, this is another reason why you should *save* and save *often* when you're working on important documents!)

Try first to reboot from the keyboard by pressing the **Ctrl+Alt+Del** key combination. This *should* bring up the Close Program dialog box. If you're lucky (!), your entire system really isn't frozen and you only have a problem with a single program not responding. If you have a frozen program, it will be listed in the Close Program dialog box as (not responding). Select that program from the list and click the **End Task** button. After a few seconds (well, up to 10 seconds or so) a Wait/Shutdown dialog box appears; confirm that you want to shut down the selected application. This should close the offending program and return your system to normal.

If you can't close a non-responding program, or if there is no frozen application, or if your system is still frozen, click the **Shut Down** button in the Close Program dialog box. If *this* doesn't have any effect, you need to reset your entire system and start over again. Press **Ctrl+Alt+Del** key again, a second time to reboot your system.

If you can't reboot your system via the "three-fingered salute," use the reset button or the main power switch on your system unit.

Is It Really Dead?

Before you reboot, make sure that your system is really and truly locked up. Don't mistake a long wait time during a complex operation for a complete system freeze. Look for signs that your computer is still working, such as noises from your disk drive or blinking lights on your system unit. The last thing you want to do is reboot and lose your current data when you don't have to.

Naturally, your computer's system can stall for any number of reasons. Some of the most common causes of this annoyance, along with their solutions, are described in the following sections.

Problem 1:

Your system halts—nothing remains onscreen, and all power is off

This is a scary one. Two probable causes exist for this problem. First, you (or someone for whom you will soon have an intense dislike) accidentally cut the power to your system by turning off the system unit, turning off the wall switch, tripping over the power cord and yanking it from the socket, or tapping the off switch on your surge suppresser. Second, a major calamity has just struck your system's power supply. (This is a heavy-duty device inside your computer that "transforms" AC electrical current to a different type of current used by your system's electrical components.) If you discover the cause of its inaction to be the former problem, simply turn your machine back on by whatever means necessary. If you decide that it must be the latter—well, it's time to take your electronic buddy to the shop.

Problem 2:

Your system halts—your system unit has power, but your keyboard isn't working

If no error messages appear onscreen but you can't type a thing, you probably face a simple problem: Your keyboard is unplugged. So plug it back in.

Of course, the solution might not be quite that simple. If replugging your keyboard doesn't work, reboot your computer. (You'll probably have to turn off your system with the main power switch or button; if your computer isn't working, you won't be able to execute a **Ctrl+Alt+Del** reboot!) If you still experience difficulties after rebooting, you actually might be the not-so-proud possessor of a bad keyboard. Try plugging another keyboard into your PC, or your keyboard into another PC, to determine whether keyboard failure is at the root of your problem.

This predicament also can be caused by two software programs interfering with each other. Maybe the culprits attempted to access the same peripheral at the same time or to use the same memory area simultaneously. If so, you probably must reboot to get your keyboard functioning again. If you continue to experience such difficulties when using the same two programs together, you almost certainly are caught in the cross-fire of a serious program conflict. Try reversing the order in which you normally load these programs, as described earlier in this chapter. If that doesn't work, and all else fails, well, just don't use those two programs together, okay?

If, on the other hand, your keyboard freezes *and* an error message appears, turn immediately to either Problem 4 or Problem 6 for instructions.

Problem 3:

Your system halts—your system unit has power, but your mouse isn't working

This is the rodent equivalent of Problem 2—your mouse is unplugged. Plug it back in.

Problem 4:

Your system halts and Windows displays an error message

Windows can sometimes exhibit perplexing behavior. (Computer people refer to this type of behavior as "unstable." I prefer to call it "screwy.") When Windows freezes up, it sometimes displays some sort of error message (in a pretty-looking little Windows dialog box, of course). These messages are just nice ways to say that something (who knows what) has bombed.

More often than not, it's just your current program that has frozen, and not all of Windows. In this case you get a `Program Not Responding` error message. Try pressing **Ctrl+Alt+Del** to manually shut down any unresponsive program.

If the error message you get is displayed on a blue screen (known in the industry as the "blue screen of death"), follow the onscreen instructions to get rid of the blue screen; you might have to press **Ctrl+Alt+Del** to close the program causing the error. After you encounter the blue screen, your system typically gets unstable, so I recommend rebooting your entire system, even if you're able to close that particular program manually.

Blue screen messages are often caused when you start running out of space on your hard disk. You need more than 25MB free on your hard disk for Windows to run properly; it uses this space to create temporary files when certain programs are running. Sometimes these temporary files become permanent—that is, Windows doesn't always delete the temporary files when it's done with them. To delete the temporary files, open **My Computer** and look for files with the .TMP extension. (Typically, temporary files are found in the \windows\temp folder.) Delete any of these files that you find—but note that Windows won't let you delete any .TMP files that are currently in use.

The blue screen error messages can also be caused by errors on your hard disk. If you get a lot of these error messages, it wouldn't hurt to run ScanDisk to check for any disk errors.

As to specific error messages, see Chapter 28, "Windows Error Messages...What They Mean and How to Deal With Them," for more detailed information.

GPFs and UAEs: Old Windows Error Messages

Windows 95 and Windows 98 are much more stable than older versions of Windows. Pre–Windows 95, specific error messages were common enough for all users to know them by their initials!

In Windows 3.1, the most common error message was the GPF (General Protection Fault). In Windows 3.0, the most common error message was the UAE (Unrecoverable Application Error). Both of these error messages occurred when either a single program or the entire system crashed, and typically could be alleviated by adding more memory to your system.

Windows 95 and Windows 98 don't have an equivalent of these "all purpose" error messages; instead, error messages are now more situation-specific, to help you better track down the cause of any individual problem. Not that they're any less common, mind you, just less generic!

Problem 5:

Your system halts while running Windows—no error message appears

Sometimes Windows freezes without displaying an error message. One of two things has happened: (1) Windows itself has locked up, or (2) Your current Windows application has locked up.

In either case, the solution is the same: Press **Ctrl+Alt+Del**.

If Windows itself has frozen, either nothing will happen (in which case you'll need to press **Ctrl+Alt+Del** to fully reboot, or you might have to press the **Reset** button on your system unit), or every press of the keyboard and click of the mouse results in nothing more than an annoying beep (yeah—time to reboot again), or you'll be shown a screen saying Windows has frozen and you need to press **Ctrl+Alt+Del** again (which you should do). In other words, if Windows freezes, you need to reboot!

If, on the other hand, it's an errant program that freezes up, you should see the Close Program dialog box when you first press **Ctrl+Alt+Del**. Select the "not responding" program and click **End Task**; if and when the Wait/Shutdown dialog box appears, go ahead and shut down the offending program.

If the Close Program dialog box doesn't appear, or if you try to shut down a program but your system is still locked up, it's time to fully reboot by pressing **Ctrl+Alt+Del** twice in a row.

What causes Windows to freeze? There can be many different causes of a Windows freeze, including the following:

➤ You might be running an application that isn't compatible with your version of Windows. If so, upgrade the program.

➤ You might not have enough memory to run Windows effectively. Upgrade the amount of RAM in your PC.

➤ A memory conflict might exist between applications or between an application and Windows itself. Try running fewer programs at once, or running problematic programs one at a time to avoid potential memory conflicts.

➤ You might not have enough free hard disk space for Windows to use for temporary files. Delete any unnecessary files from your hard drive.

➤ Your hard disk might be developing errors or bad sectors. Use ScanDisk to check your hard disk for errors.

If your system crashes or freezes frequently, call in a pro. These kinds of problems can be tough to track down by yourself when you're dealing with Windows.

Problem 6:

Your system halts—it appears to be stuck in a loop

This problem really *is* caused by a *loop*—an endless program loop, to be exact. Loops often result when programmers use improper *GOTO* statements—programming commands that instruct a program to loop to another part of the program until a certain event takes place. A poorly thought-out program can actually loop perpetually from point to point within itself, allowing you no chance to input a loop-ending command.

If you believe your problem stems from a runaway loop, try pressing **Ctrl+C**. This often "breaks" the loop and temporarily halts the program. (The **Esc** key and the **Ctrl+Break** keys sometimes have the same effect.) Occasionally, you must reboot your system with the **Ctrl+Alt+Del** keys to escape the loop.

However, if this problem happens a lot with a specific piece of software, you have a definite software bug. Contact the software publisher about the problem—they might have a patch that will fix it!

Problem 7:

Windows won't let you exit

The most common cause for this situation is that you have a misbehaving program. Try closing all your open programs, one at a time. If any individual program is frozen, use **Ctrl+Alt+Del** to close that "not responding" program.

Beyond a single misbehaving problem, a number of things can cause Windows to not shut down. Believe it or not, one of these things can be a bad sound file! It's that stupid sound you hear every time you go to shut down Windows; if that file is corrupted, the shutdown sequences stops there, leaving Windows running. To fix this problem, open the **Control Panel** and select the **Sounds** icon; when the Sounds Properties dialog box appears, highlight the **Exit Windows** event, select **None** in the Name box, click **OK**, and then try shutting down your system again. (If you do have a corrupted sound file, you can reinstall this particular file from your Windows installation CD.)

It's also possible that Windows' Power Management technology is keeping you from closing Windows. Disable Power Management by opening the **Control Panel** and selecting the **System** icon; when the System Properties dialog box appears, select the **Device Manager** tab and click the + next to **System Devices**. Highlight **Advanced Power Management** and click the **Properties** button; when the Advanced Power Management Support Properties dialog box appears, select the **General** tab, check **Disable In This Hardware Profile**, click **OK**, and try to exit Windows normally. If this fixes your problem, you might want to leave Power Management (which manages the so-called sleep or standby mode) turned off.

Problems in the Windows file system can also cause Windows to hang. To check on this, open the **Control Panel** and select the **System** icon; when the System Properties dialog box appears, select the **Performance** tab and click the **File System** button.

When the File System Properties dialog box appears, select the **Troubleshooting** tab, check all options, click **OK**, and then try to exit Windows normally. If you're able to exit Windows, the next time you start your system, return to the File System Properties dialog box and uncheck the options, one by one, trying to exit Windows after each step, so you can determine which option is causing Windows to hang.

Windows 98 utilizes a special "fast shutdown" technology that, if it's not working properly, can stop *all* shutdowns. To shut down the fast shutdown, click the **Start** button and select **Programs, Accessories, System Tools**, and then select **System Information**. When the Microsoft System Information utility appears, pull down the **Tools** menu and select **System Configuration Utility**. When the System Configuration Utility appears, select the **General** tab and click the **Advanced** button. When the Advanced Troubleshooting Settings dialog box appears, check **Disable Fast Shutdown**, click **OK**, and try to exit Windows normally. If this fixes your problem, you have some sort of conflict between fast shutdown and your system hardware, and probably want to keep fast shutdown shut off.

If this doesn't fix your problem, you can try shutting off a few more system procedures. Return to the Advanced Troubleshooting Settings dialog box, and check **Disable System ROM Breakpoint, Disable Virtual HD IRQ**, and **EMM Exclude A000-FFFF**. Click the **OK** button and try exiting Windows normally. If you're now able to shut down Windows, one of these three settings was causing your trouble. Try turning each back on, one at a time, to isolate your problem, and then contact your hardware manufacturer for further advice.

If you still can't shut down Windows after trying all these actions, there is probably a "fragment" of a program still running somewhere in your system's memory. It's nearly impossible to track down that fragment; instead, you need to reboot via the double **Ctrl+Alt+Del** procedure.

Problem 8:

Windows won't wake up from sleep mode

Windows 98 added a "sleep mode" (also called a standby or suspend mode) where the operating system essentially hibernates when not used, as opposed to shutting all the way down. This theoretically lets you "wake up" your computer faster than it would take for you to reboot it normally. But what do you do when Windows doesn't wake up from sleep mode? Normally you "wake up" your computer by moving your mouse, or pressing any key on your keyboard. Some keyboards have special "wake up" keys that need to be pressed to exit sleep mode. In any event, if you move and click your mouse a bit and then type furiously on your keyboard and Windows stays fast asleep, you have problems. (Make sure, however, that your monitor is actually plugged in and turned on; a switched-off monitor looks suspiciously like sleep mode!)

The solution here is to reboot your computer—*somehow*. Try the **Ctrl+Alt+Del** method first. However, if your system is in a really deep sleep, it might not recognize any keyboard input. So you'll probably have to turn your system off at the main power switch/button, wait a few seconds, and then turn it back on again.

Use BOOTLOG.TXT to Find Your Problem

The BOOTLOG.TXT file (found in your main, or root, folder) keeps a record of all startup and shutdown activity on your system. Use Notepad or WordPad to open the BOOTLOG.TXT file and look for the last entry from your problematic shutdown.

With a perfect shutdown, this last line should be EndTerminate=KERNEL. If the last line is Terminate=Query Drivers, you have a possible memory management problem. If the last line is Terminate=Unload Network, you have a possible conflict with a network driver (probably loaded in the CONFIG.SYS file). If the last line is Terminate=Reset Display, you might need to update your video driver or have a technician disable your BIOS' video shadowing. IF the last line is Terminate=RIT, you need to check either your sound card or your mouse driver, and possibly update one or both of these drivers. If the last line is Terminate=Win32, it was an individual program that blocked your shutdown.

In addition to this type of oversleeping, sleep mode can sometimes cause other problems. I've had sleep mode screw up my video display (dropping me down to a lower-resolution mode!) and cause some programs not to run at all post-wake up. It's fair to say that I've found sleep mode to be the most bug-ridden of the new features in Windows 98.

If you experience constant sleep mode-related problems—*disable sleep mode!* Open the **Control Panel** and select **Power Management**. Select the **Power Schemes** tab and, if you have an option for **Standby Mode**, disable it. Note that not all PCs support this feature; if your hardware isn't Standby-compatible, you won't have this option, and you won't be having this problem, either.

It's possible that your system has a different kind of "sleep" function built into the PC's BIOS. If so, you'll need to enter the CMOS BIOS setup during system startup and disable the sleep mode there.

Finally, it's possible that your system woke up but your *monitor* stayed asleep! Yes, some monitors have their own sleep modes, and if they get stuck in that mode, you won't know if your system is awake or not. It doesn't hurt to turn your monitor off and then back on (which definitely wakes it up!) just in case the sleep problem is the fault of your monitor, not your PC. (If this problem persists, of course, you might need to repair or replace your monitor.)

Problem 9:

Windows runs slower than normal

The most likely culprit behind a system slowdown is memory—or rather, the lack of it.

Are you running any new applications or upgrades of older applications that might consume more memory? Are you running more programs than usual at the same time? Are you running any programs in the background during a heavy computing session—programs such as ICQ or AOL Netscape Instant Messenger or mIRC? Do you have any hidden utilities taking up space in the Windows Tray? Any of these factors consumes more memory and forces Windows to slow down. If you're dissatisfied with the performance of Windows on your system, the answer is simple: *Add more memory!*

Something else to check: Do you leave Windows running all the time? If so, your computer might have a great deal of *unreleased memory*. Not all Windows programs release all the memory they've used after they're closed—especially if you have to manually shut them down for unresponsive behavior. This leaves little chunks of unreleased memory floating around in your system's RAM. Because other programs can't access this hoarded memory, your system starts to run out of free memory, and thus slow down.

Fortunately, all this "lost" memory is released whenever you exit and restart Windows. If you never exit Windows, however, all those little unreleased memory clots begin to accumulate, clogging up your system and deteriorating its performance. I make it a habit to exit Windows at least once a day just to free up this unreleased memory.

Problem 10:

The Windows 98 Active Desktop crashes

In Windows 98 you can configure the Windows desktop as an *active desktop*, complete with HTML links and other neat stuff. (Just click the **Start** button, select **Settings**, select **Active Desktop**, and then check **View as Web Page**.) This can, however, make your desktop a tad less stable than the traditional Windows desktop. If you have something get a little wonky elsewhere (such as a program freezing), it's not uncommon for the Active Desktop to crash. When this happens, your entire desktop becomes a giant error message, and you're asked if you want to restore the Active Desktop. Click the Restore My Active Desktop link to get things back to normal, and consider restarting Windows because this problem is a red flag for other system instabilities.

10 Do's and Don'ts to Keep Your PC Running

1. *Do* check all your cables, especially your keyboard cable; if your keyboard isn't connected, the system freezes up.

2. *Don't* press **Ctrl+Alt+Del** unless you're really, *really* sure that the system is irreparably locked up; you might lose data if you reboot while working on an important (but probably not yet saved) document.

3. *Do* have patience; many times a so-called frozen system is just an application that is running *very* slowly (probably because it's working with a very large document).

4. *Don't* unplug your computer from the wall while it's turned on, even if it's locked up; not only do you lose all work in progress, but you might even damage parts of the system or your program files in the bargain. If necessary, press **Ctrl+Alt+Del** instead, or use the computer's on/off switch.

5. *Do* try pressing the **Esc** and **Ctrl+C** and **Ctrl+Break** and **Ctrl+X** keys, in case you're merely stuck in a slow program or an endless batch-file loop.

6. *Don't* hit the keyboard with a hammer; as tempting as this might be, it will only make matters worse.

7. *Do* remember that if a Windows application freezes, all might not be lost. Pressing **Ctrl+Alt+Del** will often let you close *that particular program* without effecting all of Windows and your other open Windows applications.

8. *Don't* engage the services of a professional magician; you won't be able to talk to your dead computer, even during a seance!

9. *Do* call your friendly neighborhood computer repair person if you're accessing a really important file and don't want to lose your work; it's just possible he or she can help.

10. *Don't* sell your computer just yet; whatever is wrong is probably fixable.

The Least You Need to Know

➤ If your system freezes, reboot your computer (either by pressing **Ctrl+Alt+Del** or by using your system unit's power button/switch).

➤ When you reboot a frozen computer, you'll lose all unsaved documents you were working on—so make sure you frequently save your work in progress.

➤ Always check to make sure that your entire system is frozen—quite often the problem is a frozen *program*, which can be manually shut down without rebooting your entire computer.

Chapter 13

What to Do When... Your Keyboard Won't Type

In This Chapter

➤ Learn how keyboards work—and why you might want to buy a new Windows-compatible ergonomic keyboard

➤ Find out why it pays to keep your keyboard clean

➤ Discover the causes of common keyboard problems

If you can't type, you're fairly limited as to what you can do with your computer. Fortunately, keyboard problems are few and far between, and easily corrected. If you have a quirky keyboard, however, this is little consolation—so let the information in this chapter show you what to do when your keyboard starts acting up!

More Than You Ever Wanted to Know About Computer Keyboards

Just what do you need to know about your keyboard? Fortunately, not a great deal. It's one of the least complicated parts of your computer system.

A keyboard is basically just a bunch of switches that send electrical impulses to the system unit when you press a key. In fact, some of the original computer keyboards didn't even have keys; they had flat touch pads. These "Chiclet" keyboards weren't too popular with touch typists, however, because they didn't have the same "feel" as the old mechanical typewriters. So hardware manufacturers added mechanical devices to provide a stiffer action and add clicking sounds. (In fact, you'll find that the feel and sounds of keyboards vary from manufacturer to manufacturer.) Touch typists were happier, and the computer revolution was free to continue.

All PC keyboards include a few keys you won't find on normal typewriters. You'll find keys that move the cursor around the screen (the arrow, or *cursor control*); keys that let you page through entire screens in a single keystroke (**Page Down**, **Page Up**, **Home**, and **End**); and function keys, which perform special functions for specific software programs (**F1**, **F2**, and so on). Pressing **F1**, for example, accesses the Help system in many programs.

All PC keyboards also have a **Caps Lock** key, which shifts the keyboard to type all capital letters; a **Num Lock** key, which shifts the numeric keypad keys to type numbers instead of serving as directional keys; and a **Scroll Lock** key, which keeps the screen from scrolling in some programs. There are also keys that enable you to print the screen contents (Print Screen), insert new characters (Insert), and delete old characters (Delete).

Don't Drink and Type!

About the worst thing you can do to your keyboard is to spill something on it. When you spill the contents of your glass onto your keyboard, several things might happen:

➤ **Nothing**   You're lucky. You should still turn off your computer, unplug your keyboard, and let it dry out for a day or so before using it again, just to make sure that none of the electronics are damaged.

➤ **It shorts out**   Liquids and electronics don't mix. Spilling water or any other liquid onto your keyboard could cause the circuitry to short-circuit. If this happens, take it into the shop or buy a new one. Whatever you do, don't use the keyboard again until it dries out or you get it fixed!

➤ **It gets gummed up**   The sugar in most soft drinks can get down into the switches under the keys on your keyboard, which can cause them to malfunction or stick. If this happens, take your keyboard to a repair center where they can clean out all the sticky gunk and get things clicking back to normal. (Some techies recommend trying to *wash* the keyboard, but this can often cause more problems than you had to begin with!)

Whichever happens, make sure that you turn off your PC before you unplug your keyboard—or even worse stuff could happen!

Most keyboards for desktop computers have both the regular number keys and a separate numeric keypad for quick entry of numbers; some portable PCs leave off the keypad to save space. Finally, all PC keyboards have **Esc**, **Ctrl**, and **Alt** keys, which—when pressed with other keys—access special program operations.

A newer class of Windows-specific keyboards adds a few new keys to the old lineup. The Windows key (which has a little Microsoft Windows icon on it) displays the **Start** menu when pressed; the Menu key displays a relevant pop-up menu when pressed. This type of keyboard is nice if you're more of a typist than a mousist forced into a Windows world.

Finally, some keyboards feature a special *ergonomic* design, splitting the left and right halves of the keyboard for more comfortable wrist positioning. If you have experienced wrist or arm pain when typing for extended periods—or, worse yet, are developing carpel tunnel syndrome—think about switching to one of these ergonomic keyboards.

Why Good Keyboards Go Bad

What can go wrong with your computer keyboard? Fortunately, it's a rather short list:

It can become unplugged. The keys can start sticking. (This is exacerbated when you pour soda or coffee on the keyboard; try to avoid doing this.) The key mechanisms can simply go off and not transmit the proper electrical impulses. Some of the other electronic parts in the keyboard can go bad. You can type so fast that your system can't keep up with you. (Keyboard signals are stored in a kind of temporary memory called a *buffer* until your system can get around to processing them; you can actually fill up the buffer if you type quickly enough, causing a "buffer overflow" effect.) And, finally, you can set up parts of your system incorrectly so that your keyboard seems to be messed up.

If your keyboard does happen to go bad, you probably should just throw it away. Most new keyboards cost less than $50, and you'll probably pay that much to get your old one fixed. It's actually cheaper to buy a new one.

Keep Your Keyboard Kleen!

It's good to perform some periodic maintenance on your keyboard. Use a mini-vacuum or small brush to blow or wipe dust from between the keys. If necessary, *carefully* pull individual keys off to clean underneath. (And do all of this *with your computer turned off!*) You might even think about putting a *dust cover* on your keyboard when it's not in use, to keep the dust and dirt away in the first place.

What to Do When Your Keyboard Won't Work

Fortunately, only a few things can go wrong with your keyboard, and here they are, along with some suggestions on how to correct them:

Problem 1:

Your keyboard won't type—no characters appear onscreen

First, check to make sure that the keyboard is firmly connected to the system unit. If need be, reboot so that your system realizes that the keyboard is actually there.

If that doesn't solve your problem, you probably have a bad keyboard. Try hooking another keyboard to your computer. If the new keyboard works and your own keyboard doesn't, you have a bad keyboard.

If another keyboard doesn't work on your system either, you might have some weird problem in your system unit—maybe a bad connector. Call the repair shop, and take it in for repairs.

It's also possible that a frozen keyboard is caused by an incorrect keyboard driver within Windows. Click the **Start** button, select **Settings**, **Control Panel**, and then select the **System** icon. When the System Properties dialog box appears, select the **Device Manager** tab, make sure **View Devices by Type** is checked, and scroll down to the Keyboard section. Open this section (by clicking on the +) and highlight the keyboard driver. If the driver is nonfunctional, it will appear with a large red X over its icon.

If this is the case, click the **Remove** button to delete the driver, then return to **Control Panel** and select the **Add New Hardware** icon. Use the Add New Hardware Wizard to reinstall your keyboard driver; if necessary, use a driver from your Windows installation CD.

Problem 2:

Your keyboard quits working after you install a new peripheral

I've warned you before—you add something new to your system and it can screw up anything you've previously had running right.

The most probable cause of a frozen keyboard after a major system change is a memory conflict. Your new device is now trying to share the same memory space needed by your keyboard.

The first thing to do is to remove the device that is causing the conflict. Whatever you just installed—uninstall it! (You also might need to uninstall the driver manually via the System Properties dialog box—see Problem 1.)

Now reinstall the new device again, and see if there are any settings you can affect manually during installation. (There probably aren't.) If you continue to have keyboard problems after reinstalling the new device, contact the device's manufacturer for assistance.

Problem 3:

Your keyboard won't type—every time you press a key, you hear a beep

Type What You're Supposed To!

If your keyboard doesn't respond to what you type, maybe you're not typing the right thing! If you're in a program that expects a certain kind of input, and you type something entirely different from what it expects, your system probably won't accept it. So if your keyboard beeps at you, always check first to make sure that you're actually typing what you're supposed to type!

Your keyboard is probably connected, but maybe not correctly. Make sure that the connectors are firmly plugged into one another. If that isn't it, something funny has happened while you were typing—maybe you typed too fast and filled the keyboard buffer. Try rebooting. (If your keyboard is really dead, you can't reboot by pressing **Ctrl+Alt+Del**, so you have to turn the system on and off from the reset button or the main power switch.)

If, after rebooting, you still have keyboard problems, try hooking up another keyboard to your PC; if the replacement keyboard works, you need to buy a new keyboard. Fortunately, keyboards aren't that expensive to replace.

Problem 4:

You spill some liquid on the keyboard

Are you a complete idiot, or just a clumsy goof? Whatever the case, all might not be lost.

The first thing to do is turn off your computer and unplug your keyboard. Then use a soft cloth to wipe up the spill, as much as possible. You can then pull off individual keycaps, taking care not to damage the switches underneath, and clean up any excess liquid there.

It's a good idea to let the keyboard dry overnight, before testing it again. After drying, plug it back in and fire up your PC; if you're lucky, everything will work fine.

The worst that can happen is that you spill liquid with a high sugar content (like a cola or other soft drink), and the residue gunks up your keyboard switches. If this happens, you can take the keyboard in for a professional cleaning, or just spring for a new keyboard.

Problem 5:

You type a lowercase letter, but an uppercase letter appears onscreen

You have the **Caps Lock** key on. Press **Caps Lock** again to turn it off. (The Caps Lock light should reflect the position of the key; if the light is on, the key is on.)

Sometimes your system can get confused and think that Caps Lock is on when it really isn't supposed to be. I don't know what causes this, but it happens to me sometimes when I type just a little too fast in some programs. If this happens to you, you might have to reboot to reset the system.

Problem 6:

You type a number, but the onscreen cursor moves instead

You have the **Num Lock** key off. Press **Num Lock** again to turn it on. (The Num Lock light should reflect the position of the key; if the light is on, the key is on.)

As noted in Problem 5, sometimes your system can get confused and think that Num Lock is on when it really isn't supposed to be. If this happens, you might have to reboot to reset the system.

Problem 7:

Your Num Lock or Caps Lock light doesn't reflect the true position of the key

As noted in Problems 5 and 6, sometimes your system gets confused and thinks Caps Lock and Num Lock are on when they're supposed to be off. Exit your current program, and reboot your computer to reset this configuration.

Problem 8:

You type one key, and a different character appears onscreen

This is an interesting problem with five possible causes:

➤ You really didn't type what you thought you did. Look at your fingers. Now look at the screen. Now look at your fingers again. Is everything the way it should be? Good!

➤ You or someone else might have configured your keyboard to emulate a foreign-language keyboard. Open the Windows **Control Panel** and select the **Keyboard** icon. When the Keyboard Properties dialog box appears, select the **Language** tab. Look at the Installed Keyboard Languages and Layouts list; if you're in the U.S., you want **English (United States)** to be selected. If this option isn't highlighted, select it and then click the **Set as Default** button. If this option doesn't appear at all, click the **Add** button, and select **English (United States)** from the Add Language dialog box.

➤ If you have a programmable keyboard, you or someone else might have repro-grammed the keys so that they don't do what they normally do. Refer to the keyboard's manual for instructions about how to reprogram the keys.

➤ If you're in a specific software program, some programs let you reprogram the keyboard from within the program. When you exit the program, your keyboard should be back to normal.

➤ It's possible your keyboard is broken. Try hooking another keyboard up to your system and see how it works.

Problem 9:

Your keyboard isn't responding properly

What do you do if you hold down a key and it repeats too fast—or too slow? Windows lets you make adjustments to your keyboard via the Keyboard Properties dialog box. Just open the **Control Panel** and select **Keyboard**, then select the **Speed** tab. Adjust the **Repeat Delay** and **Repeat Speed** settings to your liking, and then test your settings by clicking in the blank box and holding down a key. When you have things adjusted to your liking, click **OK**.

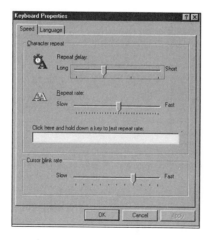

Use the Keyboard Properties dialog box to adjust your keyboard's repeat rate—and to change to a different language.

163

Problem 10:

You press the Page Up or Page Down keys, but your window doesn't scroll

Check to see if the Scroll Lock on your keyboard is activated. Sometimes having Scroll Lock on will cause strange scrolling problems with some programs.

10 Do's and Don'ts to Keep Your Keyboard Clicking Away

1. *Do* try typing an entry again, but slower this time—and with feeling.

2. *Don't* press the **Caps Lock** or **Insert** keys accidentally.

3. *Do* check to make sure that your keyboard is plugged in properly.

4. *Don't* pour 10W40 on your keyboard, in the hopes that "oiling it up" will make it go faster.

5. *Do* upgrade to a keyboard with special Windows keys.

6. *Don't* hunt and peck your way through your computing tasks—if you don't know how to touch type, take a typing class or use a "typing tutor" software program!

7. *Do* use an ergonomic keyboard if you are prone to wrist pain.

8. *Don't* change your keyboard's COUNTRY or KEYB setups unless you really want to use a foreign keyboard layout.

9. *Do* clean your keyboard periodically with appropriate kits available at office supply stores.

10. *Don't* line up a bass player and drummer to accompany you on the "keys;" it's not *that* kind of keyboard!

The Least You Need to Know

➤ Most keyboard problems are caused by age and poor maintenance; remember to clean your keyboard regularly and avoid spilling anything on the keys.

➤ Typing too fast can cause commands to jam up the keyboard buffer—and cause your keyboard to freeze.

➤ If you have a bad keyboard, just replace it—new models aren't that expensive.

Chapter 14

What to Do When... Your Mouse Won't Point

In This Chapter

➤ Find out how a mouse works

➤ Learn about other types of input devices

➤ Discover how to fix common mouse-related problems

Next to your keyboard (both metaphorically and physically), your mouse is the part of your system you use most often. Your mouse is constantly in your right hand (unless you're left-handed, of course), rolling along your mouse pad as you point your cursor at one or another part of Windows.

So what do you do if it quits working?

Well, you *could* learn how to use Windows without a mouse (which is possible, but darned difficult). Or you could read this chapter to get more of Miller's advice on coping with recalcitrant rodents.

How a Mouse Works

A mouse is nothing more than a little roller ball in a case with a couple of buttons on top. The mouse connects to your PC through one of the ports on the back of the system unit.

Alternate Rodents

If you don't like a mouse, there are other options. First, you can get a trackball, which is kind of like an upside-down mouse. If you're a games junkie, you could try using a joystick in place of a mouse. If you're a graphics wizard, you can always use a tablet pointer as a mouse. And, if you're using a portable PC, you have some sort of built-in pointing device—a touch pad, or a trackball, or a TrackPoint. All in all, I recommend you stay with the rodent you know—your friendly Microsoft-compatible mouse.

For a mouse to operate, a mouse driver must be loaded into the system's memory. (*Drivers* are memory-resident files that tell the system how to use specific devices.) This should be done automatically when you install Windows, or you can do it manually if you add a new mouse to your system.

A standard mouse has two buttons; the left button typically initiates an action, where the right button typically displays a pop-up menu related to the selected item onscreen. It's not uncommon for a newer mouse to include a small wheel in-between the two buttons; this "IntelliPoint" design lets you scroll through a window or Web page by using the wheel.

Some mouse manufacturers equip their products with a third button, which can be programmed for specific actions in specific programs. This type of additional feature is configured via an enhancement to the standard Mouse Properties dialog box, (shown in the following figure), which is accessible by selecting the **Mouse** icon in the Windows **Control Panel**. The Mouse Properties dialog box lets you adjust various mouse settings, such as pointer and double-click speed. Because each type of mouse works differently, refer to your mouse documentation for instructions.

Keeping Your Rodent Clean

Mouse maintenance is important. Most manufacturers let you open up the bottom of your mouse to clean the roller ball mechanism, which you can do with a small brush or mini-vacuum. If your mouse is in really bad shape, you might need to physically remove lint or animal hair, or even use a knife to scrape built-up crud off the roller. You should do this once a month or so, or if your mouse starts acting erratically.

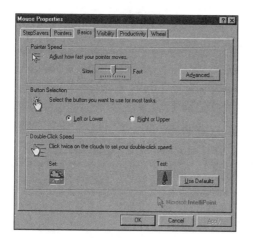

Use the Mouse Properties dialog box to configure your mouse.

What to Do When Your Mouse Doesn't Work

A mouse is relatively easy to set up and relatively easy to use. It needs little maintenance, and few things can go wrong with it. But given the right circumstances, something will go wrong. Look at this list to determine what problems your mouse might be causing you.

Problem 1:

Your mouse doesn't work at all

First, make sure that your mouse is connected correctly to the back of your system unit. You might have the mouse connected to the wrong port on your machine, or it might have come loose or become disconnected.

Next, check to see whether the right mouse driver is loaded. Open the Windows **Control Panel** and select the **System** icon. When the System Properties dialog box appears, select the **Device Manager** tab and click the **+** next to **Mouse**. Confirm that the mouse driver listed is correct; if there is no driver listed or if the icon has a red X through it, you'll need to reinstall your mouse driver by selecting **Add New Hardware** in the **Control Panel**. If there is more than one mouse listed, highlight the one that you're *not* using and click the **Remove** button.

Finally, your mouse driver might conflict with some other device on your system, which is not an uncommon occurrence. Your mouse is probably using your system's COM1 port. This is fine and dandy, but if another device in the system (like a modem) is using the COM3 port, conflicts might develop between the two devices. (Don't ask me why, but it all gets pretty technical and has to do with IRQ lines and interrupts and other stuff regular people don't understand.) If you can reconfigure your mouse to use port COM2, or your other device to use port COM4, you might solve the problem. Each type of device has its own methods for changing ports, so you'll need to check the instructions for your specific mouse and other devices.

(More often than not, you'll have to *uninstall* the device you want to change, and then reinstall it to a different port.) If this adjustment is beyond you, call in a computer pro, who can do it faster than you can microwave a hot dog.

Problem 2:

Using other peripherals causes your mouse to act up

If your mouse quits working after you initiate a print job or use your modem, chances are you have this peripheral on a conflicting interrupt with your mouse. (It's the old COM1/COM3 problem again.) You'll need to change the port assignment of either your mouse or your other peripheral to resolve this conflict.

Problem 3:

Your mouse moves erratically

If you find your mouse jumping around of its own accord (hah! a mouse with a mind of its own!) or just not holding its position correctly while you're moving it around, chances are you have a bad or incorrect mouse driver loaded on your hard drive. Check with your mouse manufacturer to make sure you have the latest version of your mouse driver (it's just a computer file you can copy to your hard disk). It's also possible that your mouse is dirty or broken; try taking the mouse apart and cleaning it, as discussed earlier in this chapter. In addition, the old interrupt conflict (COM1 versus COM3) also can cause this problem; make sure that you have your mouse hooked up to a port that it doesn't conflict with other accessories in your system.

It's possible, too, that you need to adjust the settings in the Mouse Properties dialog box; select the **Mouse** icon in the **Control Panel** and make any necessary changes.

I've also found that changing the configuration of *other input devices* can affect your mouse operation. As an example of this, one weekend last winter my brother-in-law discovered that the cursor on his PC had started moving (all by itself) slowly from left to right across his screen. After about an hour of checking all the mouse-related advice in this chapter, we happened to open his Game Controllers dialog box (accessible from the **Control Panel**). We went ahead and recalibrated his joystick, and discovered that this fixed his roving cursor problem. The moral to this story—if you're having mouse problems, check your joystick (or trackball or pen pad or whatever) configuration!

Problem 4:

You receive an error message about your mouse

If you receive an error message saying that the mouse driver could not find the mouse, the mouse was not connected correctly when you booted your computer. Reconnect your mouse and reboot. If you still receive this message, you could have a dead mouse. Buy a new one.

Problem 5:

Your mouse moves too fast (or too slow)

This is a matter of taste, of course, but a setting that is easily adjustable. Select the **Mouse** icon from the Windows **Control Panel** to open the Mouse Properties dialog box. Select the **Motion** or **Basics** tab (depending on the type of mouse you have) and adjust the **Pointer Speed** slider to your liking.

Problem 6:

You can't find your pointer onscreen

Many displays—especially those on portable computers—have trouble tracking fast motion (like that of your mouse pointer), making it look like the pointer disappears when you're moving the mouse. Normally, the cursor reappears when you're finished moving your mouse. There are several solutions to this problem, all enabled by tweaking settings in the Mouse Properties dialog box.

The first thing to do is to change the size (and possibly the color) of your mouse pointer. Select the **Pointers** tab and choose a new pointer "scheme" (which changes the shape, size, and color of all the different cursors used by Windows).

You also might be able to leave a "mouse trail" behind the cursor. (This puts a trail of pointer images onscreen behind the movement of your mouse pointer.) Select the **Motion** or **Visibility** tab (depending on your mouse), check **Show Pointer Trails**, and use the slide to select how long a trail you want to leave.

Problem 7:

You spilled something on your mouse

Just like a keyboard, your mouse doesn't like liquids (or even solids) entering its innards. (Which means: Don't spill stuff on your mouse!)

If you do create a wet or dirty mouse, all hope is not lost. First, if possible, take your mouse apart and remove the roller ball. Carefully wash the ball with soap and water (*don't* use rubbing alcohol or anything similar!), and use a soft cloth to soak up any excess liquid on the outside and inside of the mouse. Dry the mouse (and all mouse parts) overnight, and then reassemble your mouse. If you plug it in and all works fine, good job! If not...well, fortunately a new mouse isn't that expensive. Just remember to delete your old mouse driver (from the **Device Manager** tab in the **System Properties** dialog box) before you add the new mouse to your system.

Try Before You Buy!

You might want to try swapping your (apparently) dead mouse with a friend's still living rodent. If your friend's mouse works and yours doesn't, that means you really do have a dead mouse. If your friend's mouse *doesn't* work, that means you have problems inside your system unit—or with some system settings!

10 Do's and Don'ts for Keeping Your Mouse Running

1. *Do* check out different types of pointing devices; find a mouse or a trackball (or *whatever*) that fits the shape of your hand and feels right to you.

2. *Don't* connect another peripheral to the same port (or a conflicting port) as that used by your mouse.

3. *Do* clean your mouse by removing the roller ball and cleaning out any dirt and debris.

4. *Don't* roll your mouse over your computer screen—the proper signals are transmitted by the cable, thank you.

5. *Do* adjust your mouse settings from the Mouse Properties dialog box.

6. *Don't* pick up your mouse and talk into the bottom of it, saying things like "Beam me up, Scotty."

7. *Do* use a mouse pad; it gives you better traction.

8. *Don't* try to use your keyboard arrow keys instead of a mouse; you can do it, but it's a real chore.

9. *Do* configure Windows for the specific mouse hooked up to your system.

10. *Don't* swing your mouse by the tail and use it to swat flies.

The Least You Need to Know

➤ A mouse can get quite dirty over time, which can affect movement; remove and clean your mouse's roller mechanism periodically.

➤ One common cause of mouse-related problems is a COM port conflict.

➤ There are a variety of adjustments you can make to your mouse's configuration (through the Mouse Properties dialog box) that affect the speed and visibility of the onscreen cursor.

Chapter 15

What to Do When... Your Display Looks Funny

> ## In This Chapter
>
> ➤ Learn how images are displayed on your computer monitor
>
> ➤ Discover how to adjust the properties for your video display
>
> ➤ Find out how to find and fix common display-related problems

It's a complicated procedure to put a picture on your computer monitor. First, your operating system (Windows) has to generate the instructions to display a character or image. Next, a video card has to interpret this command and generate the electronic impulses that create the image. Finally, these impulses have to be transmitted (via cable) to your display monitor, which fires up a series of phosphor dots in such a way that a picture is displayed.

Okay, you're saying, so why do I care about all this?

Simple. Any one of these things can go bad, causing you to have display problems.

And fixing problems is what this book is about, so read on and learn all about finding and fixing problems with your computer display!

How Your Monitor Works

Most computer systems come out of the box with the video card and monitor already set up and ready to run. That doesn't mean that you can't change cards and monitors, however. Before I proceed with the troubleshooting part of this chapter, look at how the words and pictures get put on the monitor screen.

A monitor really does work like a TV set. It receives a video signal from the system unit through a standard video cable. This cable is different from the kind used on your home TV set, however, because PC video is different from TV video. It's impossible to view normal TV on a PC monitor without a special TV tuner card installed in your system unit.

Not *All* Monitors Work Like TV Sets

Okay, I lied when I said a monitor works like a TV set. Traditional monitors certainly do, but the screens on laptop computers and the new class of flat-panel computer displays work somewhat differently. These displays—though still receiving a video signal from a video card inside your PC—use LCDs to display the picture instead of the cathode-ray tubes used in traditional monitors. The theory is the same; it's the execution that's different.

It's the Frequency That Counts

For your monitor to work at all, you need a PC video card installed in the system unit. (On some PCs—especially portable PCs—the video function is built into the system's motherboard, so no additional video card is needed.) This card generates video images at a specified *resolution*, the measurement of how detailed your picture is (the higher the resolution, the sharper the picture). These video images then are displayed on the monitor. The resolution of the card must match the resolution of the monitor, or you get gibberish onscreen. The resolution is actually a by-product of the *video frequency* generated by the card.

What's the Frequency, Kenneth?

Video signals—such as radio and television signals—are transmitted electronically, at specific frequencies. In the case of PC video, the higher the frequency transmitted, the higher the resolution of the picture.

Almost all current monitors can reproduce images at a variety of frequencies and resolutions. Where some older monitors operated at a fixed frequency (so that you had to change your monitor when you changed video cards), today's multi-frequency monitors immediately adapt to any change of resolution from your video card.

There are several display standards for personal computers. Today's base level display is 640×480 pixels, which is sometimes called the VGA standard. If you have a larger monitor, however, you're probably running at a higher resolution—800×600, 1,024×768, or more. The more pixels in the display, the more detailed the information you can display onscreen—or put more simply, the higher the resolution, the better the picture.

More Colors, Slower Speed

When you choose to display either a higher resolution or more colors, or both, you run a good chance of slowing down the performance of your system. Because more complexity requires both more processing speed and more memory, the more complex the video images you choose to display, the more slowly your system runs.

Getting in the Driver's Seat

For your video card/monitor combination to display all the resolution it's capable of, you have to have the right video driver installed in Windows. If you have the wrong driver installed or selected, you'll either get no video, or generic VGA (640×480) low-color resolution.

You can check your driver information in the good old System Properties dialog box. Just select the **System** icon in **Control Panel**, and then select the **Device Manager** tab when the System Properties dialog box appears. Click the + next to **Display Adapters**, and confirm that the driver listed is correct; if there is no driver listed or if the icon has a red "X" through it, you'll need to reinstall your video driver by selecting **Add New Hardware** in the **Control Panel**. If there is more than one display adapter listed, highlight the one that you're *not* using and click the **Remove** button.

You might also want to upgrade your display driver to a newer version. To do this, open the Display Properties dialog box (see the next section), select the **Settings** tab, and then click the **Advanced** button. When the Properties dialog box appears, select the **Adapter** tab, click the **Change** button, and follow the instructions in the Upgrade Device Driver Wizard. This will lead you through a series of steps to upgrade your driver, either via disk, CD, or from the Web.

Don't Go Too Far!

Never try to select a driver type that is beyond the capability of your monitor. You could cause damage to the monitor or make the display unreadable. If your selection makes the screen unreadable, shut off your computer immediately. Now restart your PC, but press **F8** when you see the phrase Starting Windows.... When the Windows Startup menu appears, select **Safe Mode**. When Windows loads in Safe mode, use the Display Properties dialog box to select a driver and resolution that your monitor can display.

Configuring Your Display Properties

Assuming you have a powerful enough video card, you can configure your display to run at a variety of screen resolutions. Make sure you've selected the proper display setup for your video card, however—if you set up your display to run at a higher resolution than your card is capable of supporting, you could end up with a lot of gibberish on your screen.

All your display properties are found in the (surprise!) Display Properties dialog box, shown in this figure. You access this dialog box by selecting the **Display** icon in the Windows **Control Panel**, or by right-clicking on any empty space on the Windows desktop and selecting **Properties** from the pop-up menu.

Change all your video settings from the Display Properties dialog box— which might look different, depending on the particular video card you have installed.

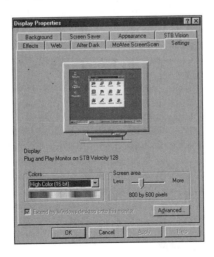

174

To change the color and resolution of your display, select the **Settings** tab. From here you can select a color level from the **Colors** pull-down list, and a resolution from the **Screen Area** slider. (The sample display will change to reflect your new settings.)

You can also use the Display Properties dialog box to change your Windows desktop background, color scheme, and other settings. Just select the appropriate tab to make specific adjustments.

Watching TV on Your PC

Computer monitors aren't just for displaying computer programs anymore. With the appropriate video and TV tuner cards, you can watch video clips, DVD movies, and television programs on your computer monitor—and display them in windows on your screen while you're performing your normal computing tasks. Assuming you have the proper equipment installed, Windows 98 includes all the utilities you need to turn your PC screen into a full-motion video display.

You can adjust the manner in which Windows 98 displays video clips by using the Multimedia Properties dialog box, which is displayed when you select the **Multimedia** icon in **Control Panel**. From this dialog box you can choose to display your video clips either in a window or using your entire screen. Note, however, that choosing to display moving video in a larger window will often result in a choppier, lower-resolution picture. Better performance often results from using a smaller window for video display.

What Can Give You Bad Video

All this video card and monitor business sounds fairly complicated to set up, but should run fine after setup, right? Sure, and I have some swamp land in Florida to sell you, too. No, as with any other part of your computer system, things can go wrong with your video setup. Let me count the ways....

➤ Your cables could be disconnected. If the cable from the card to the monitor isn't firmly connected, all sorts of strange images can show up onscreen—or absolutely nothing at all shows up. *Always* check the connections, including the power cable. And while you're at it, make sure that you don't have any bent pins on your cable plugs.

➤ Your monitor might need adjusting. Most monitors have the same type of picture controls as your TV set—contrast, brightness, and even vertical and horizontal hold on some models. Some monitors let you adjust the size and position of the display image itself. If your display doesn't look right, adjust it.

Monitor Your Monitor

To keep your monitor in tip-top shape, avoid dusty areas and strong magnetic fields. You should also use a soft, static-free cloth (or special "screen cleaner" wet pads) to clean your monitor screen at least once a week.

➤ You might have a bad monitor-card combination. Believe it or not, some cards don't work with some monitors. In particular, you can't use a higher-resolution card with a lower-resolution monitor. Check with your dealer to make sure that you have the right monitor-card combination.

➤ Your video card might be inserted improperly. The video card is just like any other card in your computer. If the video card isn't seated in its slot properly, it won't work right.

➤ Your video card might be set up incorrectly. Some video cards use either separate software programs or switches on the card itself to adapt to a particular monitor and system. If the card's switches are set wrong, the display might not work at all. Check your card's switch settings against those recommended in the card's documentation.

➤ Your drivers might be set up incorrectly. If you've loaded the wrong video driver for your card or monitor, you could get gibberish on your screen. If Windows doesn't recognize your video card, it will run a generic video driver—which will display the lowest possible resolution. It's also possible that Windows will recognize the *wrong* video card, mistaking your card for another card and causing all sorts of havoc. The moral of this story: Always check your driver setup.

➤ You might need a new video driver. Check with the manufacturer of your video card to make sure that you have the latest version of their video driver. Older drivers might not work with newer versions of Windows or individual programs.

➤ Your monitor might be on the fritz. If your TV can go on the fritz, your PC monitor can go on the fritz, too. If you get lots of lines onscreen, or smoke out the back of the monitor, or if nothing at all happens, suspect the worst.

➤ Your video card might be bad. Enough said.

What to Do When Your Display Goes Bad

Now I get down to the juicy part—figuring out what's causing what. Here's a look at some of the most common display problems you might encounter.

Problem 1:

Your monitor is dead—the power light isn't on

Check all the cables. Is the power cable for the monitor plugged into a power source? Is the power source turned on? Is the monitor turned on?

If the cables are okay and the monitor is turned on and has power, you have a problem with your monitor, probably a blown fuse or a bad power supply. See your local repair center—don't try to fix it yourself. (You could get a nasty shock fiddling about inside what is essentially a miniature television set!)

Problem 2:

Your monitor does not display—but the power light is on

If the power light for the monitor is on, all the power cables are okay. The cable from the monitor to the system unit, however, might have a bad connection. You should also check your video card to make sure that it is installed and set up properly. In addition, check your monitor's contrast and brightness controls to make sure that they're turned up enough to display a picture.

If you still don't have a picture, try connecting another monitor to the system. If that monitor displays properly, you have some sort of hardware problem with *your* monitor. If the second monitor doesn't work either, the problem is probably with your video card. Try installing a new card or having your existing setup examined by a professional.

Problem 3:

Your monitor does not display—the system unit issues a series of beeps

Your computer system uses beeps to communicate with you when something is wrong with the video setup. Check the settings on your video card to make sure that they're correct for your system. Also check any switches on the motherboard to make sure that they're set up correctly for your type of video card. (You should consult your system's instruction manual for details on this procedure.) Check to make sure that your video card is seated properly in its slots. If none of these suggestions works, try a new video card, or have your system examined by a professional.

The Big Switch

When your video card is installed and set up properly, you probably will never need to change its switch settings—unless, of course, you hook up a higher-resolution monitor and you set up your card to send higher-resolution signals. About the only time you have to worry about these switches is when you first install the card; if everything works okay then, you'll never have to touch your switches.

In a pre–Windows 98, system, if you have two video cards installed at the same time, they can sometimes interfere with each other and cause neither to work properly. Try removing one of the cards; if this results in the remaining card working, you need to reconfigure one or both of the cards to work together better. (In Windows 98 you can install two video cards to run multiple monitors simultaneously.)

Problem 4:

Your monitor does not display—it makes a high-pitched whine

This whine indicates that your monitor, for some reason, is operating at the wrong frequency. Turn it off *immediately*—this problem could seriously damage your monitor! Now check the settings on your video card. Chances are that it's set to a higher resolution than your monitor is capable of displaying. If this isn't the problem, your video card itself could be defective. If your video card is okay, your monitor might be defective.

Problem 5:

Your monitor works, but displays a screen full of garbage before Windows loads

If the display isn't displaying right, most likely you have a loose connection or a bad cable. Check all your connections and cables, as well as your video card installation. Make it a rule to be certain that all the parts of your system are hooked up and set up properly.

It's also possible that the configuration of the video card itself is wrong. Check the instructions for your video card to see if there are any switches that need to be set; when in doubt, configure your card for the lowest possible (default) resolution—which all monitors can display.

Problem 6:

Your monitor works, but displays an error message before Windows loads

At least, if you see an error message, you know that video signals are getting to your monitor. Look for these common messages:

```
Bad or missing FILENAME
```

In this message, the *FILENAME* refers to your video card's device driver file. Make sure that the driver has been copied to your hard disk and selected properly within Windows.

```
4xx
5xx
23xx
24xx
32xx
39xx
74xx
```

One of these messages indicates that you have a defective video card or a problem on the motherboard, or that you are trying to display in a mode that your system can't display. Check all the switch settings on your card and motherboard, and if the problem persists, see a repair technician.

Problem 7:

Your monitor works until Windows launches, and then displays a screen full of garbage

This situation indicates that your monitor is working fine, but that you have Windows-related problems, such as:

➤ You've selected a resolution that your monitor can't display.

➤ You're using the wrong video display driver.

➤ You're using an outdated video driver.

➤ You're using a screen saver that Windows doesn't like.

At this point, your challenge is to get into Windows and make the appropriate changes—which you can do from Windows' Safe mode.

Reboot your computer (using **Ctrl+Alt+Del**, if necessary), watch for the message Starting Windows..., and then press **F8**. When the Windows **Startup** menu appears, select **Safe Mode**. When Windows loads in Safe mode, you can change the resolution of the current video driver (from the **Settings** tab in the Display Properties dialog box), update the current driver (from the **Adapter** tab in the

Advanced Properties dialog box), delete the current driver (from the **Device Manager** tab in the System Properties dialog box) and install a new one (with the Add New Hardware Wizard), or disable your screen saver (from the **Screen Saver** tab in the Display Properties dialog box).

Problem 8:

Windows displays at a lower resolution than normal

Chances are that, for some reason, Windows started in Safe mode. This is a special startup mode that launches Windows with a minimal driver configuration—and uses a generic VGA driver for your video display, which explains the lower resolution.

See Chapter 11, "What to Do When…Your System Won't Start," for more information about Safe mode and how to troubleshoot your way out of it.

Problem 9:

Your display is missing lines or text

This problem indicates that your software setup is incorrect for your current video card. You could be forcing a higher resolution on a card that can display only lower resolutions. Check your settings to make sure they're correct.

Finally, it's possible that the monitor might be at fault. A defective monitor might not be switching to the right modes when instructed. If all else fails, have a technician check your monitor—and the rest of your system.

Problem 10:

You can't find your mouse pointer onscreen

Many displays—especially those on laptop computers—have trouble tracking fast motion (like that of your mouse), making it look as though the pointer disappears when you're moving the mouse. Normally the pointer reappears when you're done moving your mouse.

There are several solutions to this problem, all enabled by tweaking the options available in the Mouse Properties dialog box. The first thing to do is to change the size, shape, or color of the mouse pointer. You can also configure Windows to leave a "mouse trail" behind the cursor.

By the way, it's also possible that you changed your cursor to a color you can't see against your screen background. Make sure you haven't done something stupid, such as selected a blue cursor and a blue background.

Problem 11:

Your monitor pops and crackles and starts to smell

Like the rest of a computer system, monitors can get dusty. When dust builds up inside the monitor, it can generate static charges.

It's also possible that the power supply inside the monitor has become defective. If the monitor demonstrates these symptoms, turn it off immediately and take it to a repair center. The technicians can either clean your monitor or replace the power supply, if necessary.

Problem 12:

The display on your portable computer is dim

This problem can happen with an LCD display subjected to temperature extremes. If the screen is too hot or too cold, the liquid crystals might not react properly to the electrical impulses used to generate the display images. If this is your problem, turn off your laptop and let it adjust to normal room temperature before you use it again.

Another cause of this problem is that your computer's battery might be getting weak. It's also possible that your LCD display is going bad or that your contrast or brightness controls are not adjusted correctly—or that you have too much light shining directly on your screen. If the problem persists under *normal* conditions, go to a repair center.

Problem 13:

Your screen display flickers

Some high resolution displays (1,024×768) use what is called *interlaced* display technology. An interlaced display lets you run higher resolutions on lower-cost hardware, but sometimes results in a very annoying screen flicker. Your options are to buy a video card/monitor combination that can run in *noninterlaced* mode, or to select a lower video resolution, such as 800×600 or 640×480.

10 Do's and Don'ts for Your System Video

1. *Do* buy the best video card you can afford, and run it at the highest resolution you can.
2. *Don't* install the wrong video driver in your system, and don't hesitate to contact your video card's manufacturer to get the latest version of your video driver.
3. *Do* use a screen-saver program to prevent phosphor burn-in. This prevents "ghost" images from appearing on your monitor if a static image is left onscreen too long.
4. *Don't* forget to plug in your monitor and turn it on!

5. *Do* adjust the contrast and brightness to obtain the best picture.

6. *Don't* get upset if you measure your monitor and find that it comes up smaller than what was advertised. For some reason, PC manufacturers measure the size of your monitor's picture tube before it's inserted into its case, so that the supposedly 14-inch diagonal monitor you bought only has 13 inches of diagonal viewing space.

7. *Do* spend the bucks for a larger monitor; the small amount you'll pay for a larger monitor might be the best investment you can make in your computer system.

8. *Don't* forget to clean your monitor screen to prevent dirt and dust buildup—and do it when your monitor is turned *off*, to avoid static discharge.

9. *Do* check out Windows 98's new multiple monitor feature, where you can run dual monitors from the same PC (by installing two video cards); it's great for programmers and designers, who can write code on one monitor and display the results on another.

10. *Don't* try to hook up an antenna directly to the back of your monitor; computer monitors operate at a different frequency than do regular television sets, and require your computer to use a special TV tuner card to convert television signals to computer-compatible signals.

The Least You Need to Know

➤ The images you see on your computer screen are generated by a video card inside your system unit and transmitted to your computer monitor.

➤ The *resolution* of your display reflects the amount of detail generated by your video card and displayed by your monitor.

➤ Most display problems are caused by video card/monitor mismatches, bad or outdated display drivers, or improperly connected cables.

GIVE IT ANOTHER 20 MINUTES.

Chapter 16

What to Do When... Your Printer Won't Print

> ## In This Chapter
>
> ➤ Learn about the different types of printers and how to configure them in Windows
>
> ➤ Find out how simple printer maintenance can reduce the chances for major printer problems in the future
>
> ➤ Discover how to find and fix most printer-related problems

The nice thing about a printer problem is that it really doesn't throw all your plans into jeopardy. Even if your printer isn't printing, you can always copy the files you want to print to a disk and take that disk to another PC or a service bureau (such as Kinko's) to print.

Still, if you have a problem, you want to fix it—so read on to learn more about trouble-shooting problematic printers!

How Printers Print

In the early days of personal computing, you needed to be a technical wizard to get your printer set up and printing. You had to worry about DIP switches and serial ports and device names and control codes. It almost made you want to forget the printer entirely and just take Polaroids of your computer screen.

These days, most of the technical stuff is taken care of by smarter printers and a much smarter operating system (Windows), making your life a whole lot easier. All you have to do is plug in the printer, hook it up to your computer, and tell Windows what kind of printer you're using (and that's if Windows doesn't figure it out on its own, via Plug and Play technology). In a matter of minutes, you're printing, and you can use your Polaroid camera for better things.

Printers print when they receive data transmitted from your computer system. In almost all instances, the data is generated by a software program, formatted for your type of printer, translated into a form your printer can understand, and transmitted through ports and cables to the printer. There the information is fed into the printer's memory (yes, even printers have small amounts of memory) and printed on sheets or rolls of paper. Different printers print in different ways, however.

Inkjet Printers

The lowest-priced printer available today is the *inkjet printer*. Inkjet printers produce printout by spraying ink through holes in a matrix onto single sheets of paper. These printers are lower-priced (although slightly slower) than laser printers, and the best of the bunch have print quality indistinguishable from laser quality. You can also get color inkjet printers at affordable prices.

Laser Printers

The highest-quality (and highest-priced) printers available today are laser printers. Popularized by Hewlett-Packard's LaserJet models, these printers use a small laser to transfer toner (a kind of ink in powder form) to paper. Like inkjet printers, laser printers print on single-sheet paper, with the only moving parts being in the paper-feed mechanism. Laser printer output is extremely high quality, and the process is fast and quiet.

All-in-One Machines

One of the hottest trends today is the combo printer/fax/copier/scanner machines, popularized by Hewlett-Packard. These units are very efficient, both in terms of cost and in desktop footprint. They essentially hook up and configure like normal printers, but with additional functions. The problems these units encounter are the same problems encountered by traditional printers—with the caveat that the additional functions increase the complexity, and thus the chance for something to go wrong.

How to Get and Keep Your Printer Printing

Even though you'll need to perform some periodic maintenance to keep your printer in perfect working shape, this extra work pays off in extended life for your printer, and less down time for you. The bottom line, though, is that it's easy to hook up your printer—and even easier to keep it printing.

Hooking Your Printer to Your Computer

Hooking up your printer is a piece of cake. Begin by plugging it into a power source and filling it with paper. (Also make sure that you have a new ink or toner cartridge installed.) Then run the printer cable (normally supplied with your printer) to your computer, and plug it into the appropriate port on the back of the computer. (A *port* is what serious computer users call the connectors that stick out the back of your system unit. Each port serves a specific purpose and can be connected to a printer, a monitor, a modem, a mouse, and so on.) That's it—the hookup is complete.

Follow the Instructions

The best thing to do when installing a new printer is to follow the instructions provided by the printer's manufacturer. Many printers will come with their own proprietary installation routines, available on diskette or CD-ROM. Given that some printers have their own internal setup needs (such as aligning cartridges), I recommend that you use the printer's installation program when available.

Configuring Windows for Your Printer

Now, you still need to configure Windows to recognize your new printer. Theoretically, both Windows 95 and Windows 98 should recognize your new printer the first time you turn on your system after installing the printer. So-called Plug and Play technology tells Windows when something new is connected to your system, and then recognizes the device and installs the proper device driver to make the new device work properly.

A device driver is nothing more than a small file that contains the instructions necessary for your system to use the corresponding device. In this case, the device is the printer, which is physically attached to the back of your PC's system unit, and the device driver is often called a *printer driver*. The printer driver, as with all files, is installed on your hard disk. You must have the right driver for your particular printer present on your hard disk and loaded (during the Windows startup process) into system memory. If you use multiple printers, you install and use multiple printer drivers. If you add a new printer to your system, you must install a new printer driver. This is important to remember.

If Plug and Play becomes "plug and pray" and doesn't automatically recognize your new printer, you can add new printer drivers manually through the Add Printer Wizard. Just click the **Start** menu, select **Settings**, and then select **Printers**. When the Printers window appears, select **Add Printer** and follow the onscreen instructions. You'll be asked to select the manufacturer and model of your printer; you may need to insert the diskette or CD that came with your printer to use the manufacturer's printer drivers, rather than using Windows' more limited set of built-in drivers.

Selecting a Driver

If you can't find your printer's driver listed in the Windows printer list, there are some generic drivers you can use. For example, if you have a laser printer, you can select the HP LaserJet driver because most laser printers can emulate the original Hewlett-Packard LaserJet printer. If worse comes to worst, choose the **Generic Generic/Text Only** driver, which will provide basic text printing for virtually any printer.

After the printer is installed, you can then configure a myriad number of options within Windows that will affect the way your printer prints. Go to the Printers Window, right-click on the icon for any installed printer, and select **Properties** from the pop-up menu. The Properties dialog box, shown in the figure, contains a half-dozen tabs of settings for you to play with, including options for print sharing, port assignments, and color management (on color printers). Because each type of printer has different options, I can't tell you exactly what you'll see in your specific Properties dialog box, although Table 16.1 does list some of the options common to many printers. I will tell you, however, that the default options are generally acceptable, although you may want to call in your resident PC pro to guide you through some of the more obscure features of your printer.

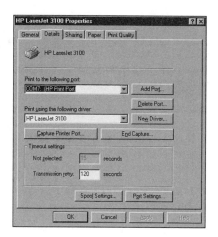

Use the Printer Properties dialog box to adjust your system settings for your specific printer model.

Table 16.1   Common Printer Properties

Tab	Properties
General	Enter comments about this printer, and select whether or not to insert separator pages between each printed page. Click the **Print Test Page** button to test your printer's output.
Details	Select which port and driver to use; select timeout settings (how long your printer will wait for data from your computer before displaying an error message); click the **Spool Settings** button to determine how your printer handles multiple print jobs.
Sharing	Determine whether your printer will be shared by other users on your network.
Paper	Select the default paper size, paper orientation (portrait or landscape), paper source, media choice, and number of copies.
Graphic	Select how your printer will display graphics; the higher the resolution (and the finer the dithering), the more memory is required inside your printer.
Font	Determine how to handle TrueType fonts; the default is to download TrueType fonts as bitmap soft fonts.
Color Management	This is specific to color printers in Windows 98, and lets you determine which color profiles to use.
Device	Determine settings specific to your model printer, such as print density, print quality, and printer memory tracking.

187

Printing by Default

Even though you may have multiple printers installed on your system, only one of these can be your main, or *default*, printer at any given time. (The default printer is the printer that your applications automatically use for printing, unless instructed otherwise.) To set one of the printers listed in the Printers Window as your default printer, simply right-click on that printer's icon and select **Set as Default** from the pop-up menu. The default printer will always appear with a large black check mark in the Printers Window, and come up first in your printer list when you go to print from any Windows program.

Using Fonts

After your printer is connected and you've been using it for a while, you may start to get bored with the selection of *fonts* available to you. Windows uses *TrueType* font technology, which makes it easy to add new fonts that can be printed with good results on just about any printer.

A Font of Knowledge

A font is, technically, a specific combination of typeface and style. Each typeface has a name (such as Helvetica or Times Roman), and can be printed in specific styles (such as bold or italic). Different fonts have different affects on your printed documents; you generally want to use serif fonts (fonts that have those little decorations on the ends of letters) for body text, and sans serif fonts (fonts without those little decorations) for headlines. You also don't want to use too many fonts in a single document; it makes the page less readable, plus it takes more time to print!

To add new fonts to Windows, open the **Control Panel** and select the **Fonts** icon; the Fonts dialog box displays all installed fonts. When you want to add a new font, pull down the **File** menu and select **Install New Font**. When the Add Fonts dialog box appears, tell Windows where to look for the new fonts then click **OK**. Windows will now go through the font installation procedure, during which you'll click **OK** a couple of times to install your new fonts to your hard disk and register them with Windows. Now, when you next access your favorite Windows program, your new fonts will show up in your font listing boxes along with all your previously installed fonts.

Too Many Fonts Slow Down the System

It's tempting to keep adding new fonts to Windows, but know that the more fonts Windows has to load (and it loads them all during the startup operation), the slower Windows will run. Install too many fonts, and Windows will get sluggish. Resist the urge to install every new font you see, and periodically delete unused fonts from your system.

Printing from Windows

When you need to print a document from an application, you normally have two methods available to you—clicking the **Print** button on the toolbar, or pulling down the **File** menu and selecting **Print**.

Clicking the **Print** button is kind of a "shortcut" method, as the document prints automatically, using program defaults, without displaying a dialog box first. If you want to change how your document prints (how many copies, or to print only selected pages) you must pull down the **File** menu and select **Print** to display the Print dialog box.

Windows also lets you print directly from the desktop, which requires that you first create a shortcut icon for the printer on the desktop. After you've created a printer icon on your desktop, all you have to do is drag a document from My Computer or Windows Explorer onto the printer icon, and printing will commence automatically.

Managing Print Jobs with Print Manager

Print Manager is the Windows utility used to control print jobs sent to a printer. There is a separate manager for each printer installed on your system. Although small print jobs (a page or two) print virtually immediately, larger jobs feed into a "buffer" while the printing continues, giving you time to pause or change the job mid-stream.

189

When a print job is being fed to your printer, a printer icon appears in the Taskbar's tray, near the clock. While this icon is visible, you can change the print job via the Print Manager. (After the printer icon disappears from the Taskbar Tray, you can only control your job at the printer itself.)

There are several ways to open Print Manager:

➤ Click the **My Computer** icon and then click the **Printers** folder icon. Click the printer icon for the printer you want to manage.

➤ Click the **Start** button, select **Settings**, and then select **Printers**. Click the printer icon for the printer you want to manage.

➤ If a print job is in progress, double-click the printer icon in the Taskbar's Tray.

If you have several print jobs pending—or even one very long print job—it's helpful to check the in-progress status by using Print Manager. Just double-click the printer icon in the Taskbar Tray and observe the jobs in the queue. Each job's status (such as printing, paused, or spooling) is displayed in the Status column; the number of jobs remaining to be printed is displayed in the status bar.

If you have multiple print jobs on a single printer, you can choose to pause specific print jobs, while allowing other print jobs to proceed as scheduled. From within Print Manager, just select the document(s) you want to pause, and then pull down the **Document** menu and select **Pause Printing**. To resume a paused print job, select the paused document, pull down the **Document** menu, and select **Pause Printing** again.

Faster Pausing

To pause a document quickly, right-click its entry in the print queue and then choose **Pause Printing** from the pop-up menu. Note, however, that pausing a specific print job is not the same as pausing all printing. To pause all current print jobs from Print Manager, pull down the **Printer** menu (*not* the **Document** menu) and select **Pause Printing**.

You can also use Print Manager to cancel a print job—even if it has started to print. From within Print Manager, select the document(s) you want to cancel, and then pull down the **Document** menu and select **Cancel Printing**. When you cancel a print job, it disappears immediately from the print queue. You may want to try pausing the job first to be sure you are canceling the right job.

If you want to cancel *all* pending print jobs, you want to perform what is called a *purge*. From within Print Manager, pull down the **Printer** menu and select **Purge Print Jobs**. Purging all print jobs is faster than canceling multiple jobs individually.

Some Simple Printer Maintenance

It helps to spend a little time on printer maintenance to ensure continued peak performance over the life of your printer. Yeah, it's a little time-consuming, but a lot less so than getting your printer repaired!

In general, you should check the connections on your printer from time to time. Make sure that all cables are securely fastened to the back of the printer and to the back of your computer. Check the cables for flexibility; cables can get stiff over time and the internal wiring inside can actually snap. Also, check the paper feed on your printer, and keep it free of paper shavings and torn paper.

Laser printers require little maintenance. You need to replace the toner cartridge periodically; if you start seeing black streaks down your printouts or your printer's readout displays a "low toner" message, it's time to change the cartridge. When you replace the cartridge, you also need to wipe clean some of the internal parts. Normally, a swab is included with new cartridges for this purpose, along with cleaning instructions.

Inkjet printers also require very little maintenance, save for the replacement of ink cartridges and the cleaning of the individual print jets.

Take Your Printer to Alcoholics Anonymous!

Here's a big no-no for printer maintenance: Don't use alcohol, solvents, or thinners to clean any of your printer's internal parts. These substances cause rubber parts to dry out and become brittle. Instead, use a soft cloth dampened with a mild detergent solution.

What Can Go Wrong When You Print

Now that you have your printer drivers installed and your fonts loaded, what possibly could go wrong with your printer? Plenty, pardner!

First, you may have the wrong printer driver installed in Windows. You may have either simply selected the wrong driver for your printer, or Windows may have mistaken your printer for another model, or the driver selected may be out of date. While we're in this area, it's also possible that various aspects of your printer setup may be incorrect, which can cause some highly unusual problems. You should also check your font setup because fonts themselves can cause perplexing problems if they're not installed correctly.

In addition, any new input or output device you've installed since you installed your main printer could have changed your printer's settings. (It's kind of like the last device installed gets dibs on key system settings.) If you've recently added a scanner or a digital camera or fax software or anything like that and then experienced printer problems, try uninstalling your printer (and all printer drivers) and then reinstalling your printer, so that your printer is now the last device installed—and thus controls key system settings.

It's also possible that if you're printing large or graphically complex documents, you may not have enough disk space or memory to print. Make sure that you have plenty of both because Windows needs all the space it can get to complete the printing operation.

Use the Troubleshooter

Windows 98 includes a special interactive Print Troubleshooter to help you figure your way out of printing-related problems. Click the **Start** button and select **Help**. When the Help window appears, select the **Contents** tab, select **Troubleshooting**, select **Windows 98 Troubleshooters**, and then select **Print**. When the Print Troubleshooter appears, follow the steps onscreen to track down and fix your specific problem.

Finally, you could have real printer hardware problems. These problems range from the mundane—(you're out of paper, you forgot to turn on the printer, you have a bad connection)—to the fairly serious—(your printer is broken!). Check all your cables and connections—and make sure that your printer is actually turned on!

The bottom line is, there are a lot of things you need to check if you have printer problems, both hardware and software related. So if you have printing problems, hunker down and plow through the problems/solutions section, coming up next.

What to Do When Your Printer Doesn't Print

The types of problems you may encounter with your printer fall into four basic categories: The printer has no power, the printer doesn't print, the printout is garbled, or pages of the printout are missing. Read on to find out more about each problem and ways to solve it.

Problem 1:

Your printer has no power

This is the perennial problem with computer hardware. By now you know the drill:

1. Make sure that the power cord is plugged into both the power outlet and the back of the printer.
2. Make sure that the power outlet has power; check all fuses and circuit breakers, as well as surge suppressors.
3. Make sure that the printer is online. (This is normally accomplished by a front-panel button of some sort.)
4. Check the internal fuse in the printer itself.

If all the right parts in your system have power and your printer is online, your problem is more serious. The biggest potential source for this type of problem is the power supply in the printer. At this point, it's time to call the repair center and ready your checkbook.

Problem 2:

Your printer has power but doesn't print

The first item to check is whether your printer is connected correctly to your computer. Check the connecting cable to make sure that the connections are tight. You also should unplug each end of the cable to ensure that none of the connecting wires are bent, making a bad connection. You might also want to change the printer cable. Cables can get old, and the wires inside can break; try a new cable and see whether this change fixes the problem.

Turn It Off to Make It Work

Anytime you change *any* connection between your system unit and any external device (such as your printer), you probably need to turn your computer off and then back on again for the connection change to register with your system. So if you're plugging in cables, reboot your system when you're done.

Next, you should make sure that the printer is connected to the correct port on the back of your computer. Checking the port connection is not always as simple as it seems. Some computers come with more than one printer port, and your printer may be hooked up to the wrong one. If you have multiple printer ports, try plugging your printer into the other ports.

Next, check the paper feed of your printer. If you're out of paper, your printer can't print. You also should check the paper path inside the printer to make sure that no stray pieces of paper are lodged inside. Make certain, too, that your printer is *online*, or set in the *on* position.

Give Your Printer the Boot

If you have a paper-feed problem, you might have to put your printer back online to resume printing. In some cases, you might even have to reboot your printer by turning it off and then back on again to recover from a paper-feed error.

You should also check to see if your printer is paused. Check your front panel buttons to make sure that your printer is online; also check Print Manager to make sure the job isn't paused from within Windows.

Another potential cause of this problem is having the "manual feed" option selected in Windows or on your printer. If this option is selected and there is no paper in the manual feed tray, your printer just sits there waiting for someone (like, oh, *you!*) to insert some paper. The solution to this is to either (1) add some paper to the manual feed tray, or (2) switch off the manual feed option.

It's also possible that you have the wrong driver installed or selected within Windows. Right-click on this printer's icon in the Printers Window and select **Properties**. Check the **Details** tab to make sure you're printing to the right port using the right driver. If you need to change drivers, pick one from the pull-down list, or click the **New Driver** button to add a new printer driver.

It's possible that the right driver is installed, but something has gone screwy with how Windows reads the driver information. Go to the Printers Window and *delete* the current printer, and then use Add Printer Wizard to reinstall the printer driver. You might also want to check with your printer's manufacturer to see if there is an updated version of your driver available.

In addition, it's possible that a recently installed device has somehow mucked with your printer configuration in Windows. Try deleting your printer driver and then reinstalling it, as described in the previous paragraph. Because the last device installed on your system can overwrite previous configuration information, go ahead and make your printer the last installed device.

If none of these suggestions solves your problem, you're looking at a major computer or printer problem. Try hooking up another printer to your computer; if the new printer works, it's time to take your old printer into the shop. If the new printer doesn't work, you more than likely have a defective port in your computer.

(Printing the printer's "self test" page is also a good way to determine if the problem is in the printer or in the computer—or somewhere in-between!)

Problem 3:

Your printer prints, but output is smudged or garbled

If your printout is not as you expected, there may be several causes. The most likely cause, believe it or not, is our old friend the poorly connected cable. If all the instructions don't make it from the computer to the printer, your printout will be incomplete, if not totally out of whack. Check all cable connections to ensure a good throughput of data. If that doesn't fix the problem, just change the printer cable. An old or damaged cable could be causing your problems.

Do As I Say, Not As I Do

The day after I wrote the printing chapter for the first edition of this book back in 1992, I tried to print out the chapter and received a page of garbage in response. Well, because I'm supposedly an expert in these things, I spent the next hour installing new printer drivers and changing setup configurations, all without changing the resulting output. Finally I remembered to check my cables, and—lo and behold—one of the connectors had come loose. A quick push of the plug later and my output was back to normal. So please—*please!*—learn from my experience and *check your cables first!*

Another cause of print garbage may be the printer itself. If you have a low or old toner cartridge in a laser printer or a near-empty ink cartridge in an inkjet printer, your printout will be lighter than normal, perhaps even unreadable. If necessary, change the cartridge and run the print job again.

If you're using a laser printer, you may get black streaks on your output. This problem is most often caused by an old toner cartridge, or by a dirty roller or printer cleaning bar. If you replace the toner cartridge and clean the suspect parts (using a cotton swab) and you *still* experience black streaks, your printer may need service.

If you're using an inkjet printer, it's possible that your print jets are clogged. You'll need to unclog the print jet by inserting a small pin into the jet.

Look Before You Leave

Save yourself a little grief (and a lot of paper)—take a look at the first page or two of any long report as it comes out of your printer. You don't want to print out 75 pages before you discover that you have a problem, do you? (Along the same vein, you might want to test-print overheads and labels on plain paper first, before you waste the expensive media.)

It's also possible that a paper misfeed in your printer caused the printout to become smudged or out of line; if this is the case, straighten the paper feed and start the print job again.

An incorrect printer setup in Windows can also cause unusual printouts. Make sure that Windows is configured for the exact type of printer you're using. Also make sure that you have the correct landscape (horizontal) or portrait (vertical) printing option selected.

If none of this works, you probably have a problem somewhere in your printer. Although a bad printer port on your PC could be the culprit, more than likely some internal problem with your printer is causing the poor printout. (You can confirm this by printing a "self test" page; if it looks bad, the problem is in your printer.) Consult your friendly repair center.

Problem 4:

Your printed page looks half-finished

If you're trying to print a document with a lot of graphics (especially on lower-priced laser printers), you may find that your printer doesn't have enough memory to print the entire document. What you'll get is about half the document—and not always a contiguous half! You can do one of several things to rectify the problem:

➤ Add more memory to your printer. If you do a lot of heavy graphics printing, you probably need at least 1M of RAM installed in your printer. You may be able to add the memory yourself, or you may want to have a qualified laser printer technician do the job for you.

➤ Instruct Windows to print this document at a lower resolution. Go to the Printer Properties dialog box for your printer and select the **Graphics** tab (if your printer has this option). Select a lower resolution (which requires less memory—and gives you less finely detailed output) and see if you can now print your document.

➤ Simplify your document. If you're using a lot of different fonts and graphics, take some out. It's not an ideal solution, but it may be the only way you'll get this particular document printed on time!

It's also possible that there are elements in your document that have been "turned off" for printing. Many applications let you configure each element on the page (such as graphics or text boxes) to be either printable or not printable. If you have an element that isn't printing, right-click it and see if there is a print/not print option on the pop-up menu.

Problem 5:

Your printer prints, but pages are missing

If you're missing the last page of a printout, it's possible that it's still in your printer's memory, waiting for a *form feed* signal from your computer. (The fact that the printer didn't get the signal indicates that your software is probably not set up correctly.) The immediate solution is to press the form-feed button on your printer to eject the page.

It's also possible that the last page is physically stuck in your printer. Check your printer's paper path to make sure that no pages are gumming up the works.

Sometimes an incorrect printer setup can cause bizarre printing problems. If, for example, you have Windows set up for legal-sized paper but your printer thinks it's printing letter-sized sheets, you'll get results that only remotely could be considered readable. Again, check your printer configuration in the Windows program to make sure the setup is correct.

Problem 6:

Your printer prints, but fonts aren't correct

If you create a document on a PC with one set of fonts installed, and try to print it on another PC with different fonts installed, you could be in for a real surprise! Windows will try to "match" missing fonts, but quite often the match leaves a lot to be desired—resulting in different line lengths and page breaks than what you had originally. Your options are to install the missing fonts on the PC you're printing from, or change the fonts in the document in question. (A word to the wise: stick to common fonts—such as Arial and Times New Roman—if you think you'll be sharing a document on multiple PCs!)

Problem 7:

Your color printer doesn't print all available colors

This could be caused by a couple of problems. First, you may not have a color ink cartridge inserted. You can't print color from black-and-white cartridges!

Second, your ink cartridge may be getting old. Typically, some colors will get depleted before others, throwing off your color output. If you're seeing less blue (or red or yellow or black) than normal, chances are it's time to change your cartridge.

Problem 8:

Paper jams in your printer

It's possible that your printer's internal paper feed mechanisms are getting dirty. You can try taking the printer apart yourself to clean out any pieces of scrap paper or other debris, or you may want to take it into the shop to let a pro deal with.

You may also be getting some paper sticking to other sheets of paper in your paper tray. (This happens more often with cheaper paper—spend a little more and get the good stuff!) Try thumbing through the stack of paper before inserting it into the tray; this should loosen up the paper and make it feed easier into your printer.

Finally, you may need to change the grade of paper you use with your laser or inkjet printer. Lightweight papers tend to jam up the works, so switch to something heavier if you experience a lot of problems.

Problem 9:

Your printer is slo-o-o-o-w

Well, sometimes printing *is* slow! Check these hints for speeding up your printer's performance:

➤ Simplify your documents. If you use a lot of different fonts or graphics, they all take longer to print. Along the same lines, printing an entire Web page—graphics and all—can be time consuming; choose the option to print text-only if you want to speed up the printing.

➤ Print at a lower resolution, if available. Many programs let you print in a lower-resolution mode, which takes less time than the normal high-resolution mode.

➤ Make sure that you have the right fonts installed. If Windows has to substitute missing fonts, more processing time is involved. Make sure you're printing fonts that are actually installed on your system.

➤ Add memory to your printer. Most laser printers print faster if they have more memory.

➤ Free up extra memory and disk space. Make sure that you have plenty of free memory and free disk space. Windows printing uses both RAM and disk space to buffer information during printing, and a lack of either can slow things down.

Problem 10:

You used to have a fax program (Microsoft Fax) with Windows, and now you don't (in Windows 98)

Windows 95 included a utility called Microsoft Fax, which was part of Windows Messaging (also known as Microsoft Exchange). Windows Messaging was the email and messaging system in Windows 95, and it included a full-function fax program.

In Windows 98, Windows Messaging has been replaced by Outlook Express, a new email client that is also part of Internet Explorer. With the exit of Windows Messaging, however, Microsoft Fax has been deleted from Windows 98.

So, because Windows 98 doesn't come with its own fax program, what do you do when you need to send a fax? There are several options you can pursue:

➤ Use Outlook in Microsoft Office. If you have Microsoft Office 97 or Office 2000 installed on your PC, and you chose to install Microsoft Outlook, you have a fax program installed. Use it.

➤ Use your modem's fax software. Many modems come with their own fax software. (If your modem came preinstalled with a new PC, the PC manufacturer probably included fax software as part of the package.) This software, though seldom sporting a deluxe feature set, is often adequate for most basic faxing needs.

➤ Buy a third-party fax program. There are plenty of third-party fax programs you can buy and install on your Windows 98 computer system. Among the most popular packages are Delrina WinFax Pro and the full-featured ProComm Plus suite, which includes both faxing and modem terminal software.

By the way, if you upgraded from Windows 95 to Windows 98 on the same PC, you probably still have Microsoft Fax installed; installing Windows 98 doesn't automatically delete Microsoft Fax from your system. So if you still see the Microsoft Fax option when you go to print a document (and you still have a Mail icon in the Windows Control Panel), you don't need to change anything—you can still use Microsoft Fax for all your facsimile needs!

What About Scanners

This chapter is about output (via printers), but many users tend to think of scanners (an input device) like they do printers—and, in fact, some new devices combine printing and scanning (and faxing and copying) in a single machine. So let's look at a handful of common scanner problems and what you can do to fix them:

➤ Other devices freeze when you use your scanner. This is a classic device or IRQ conflict, probably with your mouse, keyboard, or printer. You'll need to switch the port or IRQ for one of the conflicting devices.

➤ Nothing happens when you try to scan. This problem could have one of several causes. Your scanner may have a conflict with another device (like your mouse or your printer). You may have the wrong driver installed for your scanner. You may have your scanner hooked up to the wrong port. You may even have everything connected alright, but just haven't finished the prior scan job; you have to wait for one job to completely finish (which sometimes takes awhile) before you start a new one.

➤ The scanned image is blank. This is another problem with multiple potential causes. You could be scanning the *wrong side* of the page—did you place the document to be scanned in the right direction? The scanner could be misadjusted, with the brightness turned down too low. As always, your scanner could be hooked up or configured incorrectly, or have the wrong driver installed.

➤ Something about the scanned image looks bad or is wrong. This is typically a minor problem with commonplace causes. Your scanner might need to be readjusted, to better "read" the document to be scanned. If you use a clear plastic "sleeve" to hold the document to be scanned, the sleeve might be dirty or scratched. The scanner cover might not be closing all the way, or might need to be cleaned. The scanner *glass* also might need cleaning. If your printer allows different "scan types," you may have the wrong type selected—selecting text when you're scanning a photo, for example. It's also possible that your original document was of too low a quality to scan perfectly—it might be old or wrinkled or faded.

➤ You receive a "disk is full" or "disk I/O error" message when you try to scan. You need space on your hard disk to execute a scan; Windows generates these error messages when you're too low on disk space. (So delete some files and try again!)

10 Do's and Don'ts for Your Printer

1. *Do* keep your printer in a well-ventilated area, free from dust and cigarette smoke.

2. *Don't* pull out a sheet of paper while the printer is still printing; wait for the page to finish printing and deposit itself in the "out" bin before you grab for it.

3. *Do* recycle the toner cartridges on your laser printer—it's good for the environment!

4. *Don't* turn off your printer in the middle of a print job if you can help it.

5. *Do* connect your printer to a surge suppressor, just in case.

6. *Don't* reuse partially used sheets of labels; running the sheet through your printer causes the sheet to heat up and break down the glue on the labels—which can cause the labels to come up and gum up your printer feed!

7. *Do* perform periodic maintenance, such as cleaning dust from the inside of the paper path.

8. *Don't* run your printer 24 hours a day without a break; this kind of continuous use requires an industrial-grade printer, not a consumer model.

9. *Do* reuse old paper in a laser printer by reinserting it upside down in your paper tray to print on the back side.

10. *Don't* use the wrong kind of paper for your specific printer; using paper that is too thin or too thick can really gum up the works.

The Least You Need to Know

➤ Most printer problems are caused by a bad cable connection, a misconfiguration in Windows, or a bad or outdated print driver.

➤ Take the time to perform periodic maintenance on your printer—this will prevent many future problems.

➤ Use the Print Manager to pause and cancel print jobs in mid-stream.

Chapter 17

What to Do When... Your Disk Is Damaged

In This Chapter

➤ Learn how to partition and format disks

➤ Find out what periodic maintenance you should perform on your hard disk

➤ Discover how to find and fix disk-related problems

Your system includes numerous types of storage devices, in the form of disk drives. All PCs have at least two types of disk drives: a 3.5" *diskette* drive (for portable diskettes that can store 1.44MB of data) and a larger *hard disk* drive (that can store anywhere from 100MB to more than 10GB of data).

Unfortunately, disks are physical devices and, as such, are prone to problems. This chapter is about all the problems you can encounter with your disks.

The "Floppy" Diskette

Diskettes are sometimes called *floppy disks*, from the days of relatively flexible 5 1/4-inch diskettes. The newer 3.5-inch diskettes have hard-shell cases and don't flop around, so it's probably best not to call them floppies.

Working with Diskettes

All blank diskettes must be formatted before they can be used. Many diskettes come preformatted from the factory; if you get an unformatted diskette, you'll have to do the formatting yourself. Just insert the unformatted diskette in its drive, select the **My Computer** icon on the Windows desktop, select the drive that holds the diskette you want to format (typically drive A or B), pull down the **File** menu, and select **Format**. Select the correct capacity (typically 1.44MB), check the **Quick Format** type, enter a label for the diskette (optional), and click the **Start** button. Windows will notify you when the format is complete.

Under no circumstances, however, should you format any diskette that contains data. Do so and you lose all the data on the diskette, which is generally not a good thing.

Formatting the Hard (Disk) Way

Hard disks also have to be formatted before they're used, but most new hard disks come preformatted from the factory—so you'll seldom need to format a hard disk. If you need to format a hard disk, you can either use **My Computer** (as explained previously) or, from the DOS prompt, use the old DOS FORMAT command. Beware, however—if you format an existing hard disk, you'll wipe out any files that were stored there!

Before you insert a new diskette, make sure that no other diskette already occupies the drive. (You really don't want to try to insert two diskettes into one drive; some fairly serious damage can result.) Insert the diskette with the label side up and toward you. To remove a diskette, push the button on the drive, and the disk is ejected.

Working with Hard Disk Drives

Hard disks work just like diskettes, except with lots more data. This extra storage capacity sometimes requires a bit more disk management on your part to make the most efficient use of the space—and to keep things up and running effectively.

Check Your Disk for Errors with ScanDisk

As you discovered in Chapter 5, "Staying Alive: Simple Steps to Keep Your System in Tip-Top Shape," Windows' ScanDisk utility should be run periodically to locate and correct any developing problems with your hard disk. To run ScanDisk, click the

Start button, select **Programs**, select **Accessories**, select **System Tools**, and then select **ScanDisk**. When ScanDisk launches, choose the drive you want to scan. Select the **Standard** option and check **Automatically Fix Errors**. Click the **Start** button to start the scan—and fix any errors.

Keep Your Disk Running Smoothly with Disk Defragmenter

Over time, your hard disk gets all fragmented, so that there is very little contiguous free space available. This slows down your disk access, and therefore your entire system. Fortunately, Windows includes a utility that lets you *defragment* your hard disk.

To defragment your hard drive, click the **Start** button, select **Programs**, select **Accessories**, select **System Tools**, and then select **Disk Defragmenter**. When the Select Drive dialog box appears, choose the drive you want to defragment and then click **OK**.

Disk Defragmenter launches and does a quick analysis of your disk. (It even displays a real neat map of your hard disk so you can easily see how Swiss-cheesed things are!) When you begin the optimization procedure, Defragmenter starts to do its thing, moving data from one part of your disk to another to create as much contiguous free space as possible. When Defragmenter is done, exit the program and reboot your computer.

Don't Work When Defragmenting!

Disk Defragmenter can only defragment a disk when the data stored on the disk is stable—and if you're using your computer, data is constantly being written and rewritten to the hard disk! Using your computer *at all* while defragmenting will cause Disk Defragmenter to constantly restart (so that it defragments the most recent data). In fact, even a screen saver kicking in will cause Disk Defragmenter to start from scratch. So plan on not using your computer while defragmenting— and remember to shut off all background applications, including screen savers!

Better Utilize Large Drives with FAT32

Windows' file system uses a special section on each hard disk, called the *File Allocation Table* (or FAT), to store the data needed to track the location of all your files. The 16-bit FAT used prior to Windows 98 was effective in managing data on smaller hard disks, but was inefficient in managing larger hard disks. In addition, it could only track data on disks under 2GB in size; for that reason, larger hard disks had to have multiple partitions of 2GB or less.

Windows 98 (and some later versions of Windows 95) includes a new 32-bit file system called FAT32 that is much more efficient in dealing with large hard disks—and can recognize disks larger than 2GB. If you buy a new PC with Windows 98 preinstalled, chances are it will already have FAT32 enabled. If you're upgrading from an earlier version of Windows, however, you may want to convert from the existing 16-bit FAT system to FAT32.

Start by clicking the **Start** button, selecting **Programs**, selecting **Accessories**, selecting **System Tools**, and then selecting **FAT32 Converter**. When the Drive Converter launches, follow the onscreen instructions to begin the conversion process. After your drive has been converted to FAT32 operation, Windows will automatically launch Disk Defragmenter. Defragmenting your drive after it has been converted is necessary for optimal operation, although it may take several hours.

Should you upgrade your hard disk to FAT32? If you have a new hard disk on a new PC, the choice has probably been made for you; FAT32 is standard on most new systems. If you have an older system with a really big hard drive (2GB or more), it's probably worth it—you'll gain some additional disk space.

Make More Space on Your Hard Disk with DriveSpace 3

What if you have a smaller hard disk—and you're running out of space? If FAT32 isn't an option (and you don't want to add a larger hard disk to your system), check out DriveSpace 3, a *disk compression* utility that comes with Windows 98. DriveSpace allows you to compress the information that you store on your hard drive, thus giving you more space on the hard drive. (Windows 95 uses an earlier version of DriveSpace that works similarly, but is slightly less efficient.) If you have a small hard disk—or are simply running out of disk space—you can use DriveSpace 3 to compress your existing data and free up space for new programs.

Note, however, that drives compressed with DriveSpace run slower than normal disk drives, and can cause all sorts of odd problems. If you have an older, slower system, you may find that compressing your hard disk results in unacceptable performance. Given the low price of today's large-capacity hard disk drives, I'd recommend that you consider adding a new hard disk drive rather than trying to squeeze more space out of your old drive with DriveSpace.

If you insist on compressing your existing hard drive, start DriveSpace by clicking the **Start** button, selecting **Programs**, selecting **Accessories**, selecting **System Tools**, and then selecting **DriveSpace**. When DriveSpace launches, select the drive you want to compress from the drives listed. (Any drive already compressed will have `Compressed drive` shown next to it.) Pull down the **Drive** menu and select **Compress**. When the Compress a Drive dialog box appears, you can graphically see how much extra disk space you get by compressing the selected drive. Click the **Start** button to begin compressing the selected disk. (If you haven't already backed up the files on this disk, be sure to click the **Back Up Files** button when prompted; after backing up, click the **Compress Now** button.) After the disk is compressed, you'll be prompted to restart your computer. Click **OK**; your disk will reflect its compressed status when your computer restarts.

New FAT, No DriveSpace

If you're using the FAT32 file system (discussed earlier in this chapter), you won't be able to use DriveSpace 3. FAT32 does a more efficient job of using disk space than the old FAT16 file system, and thus doesn't need disk compression.

Compressing a Disk Takes a Loooooong Time

Compressing a drive can take several hours, during which time you cannot use your computer.

Any drive you compress can also be *decompressed*—which is a good thing because there are several scenarios that require returning your hard disk to its original, uncompressed condition. For example, if you are changing machines or operating systems and you need to format your drive, you must decompress the drive before you can format it. In addition, if you decide you really don't need the extra space given with disk compression, you should consider decompressing the drive to reduce the amount of time it takes to read and write data to the drive. To decompress a drive, start DriveSpace, back up your files, and then click the **Uncompress Now** button.

Add a New Hard Disk Drive to Your System

Adding a new hard disk to your system is relatively easy these days, especially if it's a supplemental rather than a replacement drive. (If you're replacing an existing hard disk, you'll need to back up all the data on your original drive and restore it to your new drive—or start from scratch with a completely clean system!)

Before you use a new hard disk drive, you first must create one or more partitions on the disk, and then you must format the disk.

In previous versions of Windows, drives larger than 2GB had to have more than one partition because each partition could be no larger than 2GB; the different partitions were then presented to you as separate "virtual" drives labeled C, D, E, and so on. With Windows 98's FAT32 file system, fortunately, even the largest drives can use a single partition. Partitioning a disk can only be done from DOS mode; you can format a disk either from DOS or from Windows proper.

To partition a new hard disk, click the **Start** button and select **Shut Down**. When the Shut Down Windows dialog box appears, select **Restart in MS-DOS Mode**. When your computer restarts, it will automatically launch in a special non-Windows mode called MS-DOS mode. At the DOS prompt, type **FDISK** and press **Enter**; you'll be asked if you want to enable large disk support. Answer yes and you'll see the special **FDISK** menu. Select the drive you want to partition, and then choose option 1 from the menu. When asked if you want to use the entire drive for your DOS partition, answer yes. (If you're asked whether you want to enable FAT32 support, also answer yes.) After the partition is created, exit FDISK, restart your computer, and prepare to format the new hard disk.

FDISK Is for New Drives Only!

Do *not* run FDISK on an existing hard disk drive, unless you're really, really sure you want to return your hard drive to its original from-the-factory condition. Partitioning the drive will delete all data on the drive!

After your new drive has been partitioned, you now have to format it for use. (There are also occasions when you have to format an existing hard disk drive, such as when a virus corrupts your FAT or boot sector; these same instructions apply.)

To format a new hard drive, insert your Windows Emergency Startup Diskette into drive A and turn on your computer. Windows will detect the new drive and ask you if you want to allocate all of the unallocated space on your drive. Answer yes, and the formatting will begin.

You can also format an existing drive from Windows. (This is nice if you're adding or reformatting a *second* hard drive on your system—and have Windows up and running on your main hard drive.) First, make sure you have backed up important files from the drive, and then make sure all applications are closed. Start **My Computer**, right-click the drive you want to format, and choose **Format** from the pop-up menu. Select the **Quick Format** type, enter a label for the disk, and then click the **Start** button.

You Can't Format a Drive in Use!

You cannot format the drive that contains Windows while Windows *is* running. If you need to format this drive, you need the Windows Emergency Startup Diskette because formatting the drive that contains Windows will make your system unbootable without a bootable diskette.

After your new drive has been partitioned and formatted, it's ready to store whatever data you need stored. If you want to use this new drive as your main drive, you'll want to boot from the Windows Emergency Startup Diskette and then install a fresh copy of Windows from your Windows installation CD.

What Can Happen to Your Disks

Your disks are where you store your valuable data. If anything happens to your disks your data is put in jeopardy. What exactly can go wrong?

Take a look at all the potential problems that can befall your hard disks and removable diskettes:

➤ You can accidentally format a disk or diskette that contains data. Oh, this is the big one! Don't do this!

➤ You can try to access a diskette that isn't there. If you try to access a diskette drive that's empty, Windows gives you an error message. You probably need to insert a diskette to proceed.

➤ You can insert a diskette into its drive incorrectly. Of course, sticking a diskette into a drive upside down or sideways doesn't do you too much good, either. In fact, you could even damage your drive. Try not to do this!

➤ You can take a diskette out of its drive while it's still being used. If you remove a diskette that's still being accessed, not only will you confuse the system, but you may scramble some data on the diskette.

➤ Your PC can shut down while a disk is being accessed. Any time you interrupt a disk access, you run the risk of scrambling data, whether it's with a hard disk or a diskette. Do everything you can to avoid doing this.

➤ Your hard disk can become fragmented. A disk gets fragmented when so many files are erased and added and erased and added that whatever free disk space exists is scattered all over your disk—which slows disk access. To defragment a disk, you need to use the Disk Defragmenter utility—in fact, it might not be a bad idea to do this once a month or so just to keep your disk as orderly as possible.

➤ The disk itself can go bad. Yes, it happens. Diskettes endure a great deal of hard use, going in and out of the drive and back and forth to work. Even hard disks can go bad, especially if your computer is in a space subjected to dirt and dust and cigarette smoke. The cleaner the room and the less abuse subjected, the longer your disks last.

➤ A diskette can transmit a computer virus. Be careful about accepting diskettes from strangers. You never know where that diskette has been—or what it carries.

What to Do When Things Go Wrong with Your Disks

Okay, what do you do if you have a disk problem? Read on to examine the most common problems you can experience (or foist upon yourself).

Problem 1:

You can't access a disk

What do you do when your system can't read or write to a disk? First, check and make sure that the disk is really there. If it's a diskette your system can't find, make sure that it's actually inserted into the drive—and correctly. Also make sure that the disk or diskette has been formatted.

You should also check to make sure that you typed the right drive letter. If you typed Q instead of C, naturally your system won't be able to access the drive.

If you can't access your hard disk, you could have major problems. See Chapter 8, "Recovering When "The Big One" Hits," for more information.

Problem 2:

Your system shuts down while accessing a disk

This is not good, but is often not catastrophic. You should get your system up and running again, and then try to access the data that was being accessed when the system went down. If the data is okay, then life is wonderful. If the data is scrambled—well, this is what happens: You either have to re-create that file from scratch or use a backup copy.

Problem 3:

Your disk is running slower than normal

This problem is most often caused by a fragmented disk. As explained earlier in this chapter, you need to run Windows' Disk Defragmenter utility to clean up your disk and get it back up to speed.

Problem 4:

You accidentally format a disk or diskette

Oh boy, you went and did it this time, didn't you!

Back in the pre-Windows days of DOS, computer users had access to a special UNFORMAT command that would automatically undo accidental disk formats. Unfortunately, this command doesn't exist in Windows 95 or Windows 98. (Sorry!)

Today if you need to unformat a disk, you'll have to pick up a copy of Norton Utilities (or some similar disk utility program), which contains unformat and undelete utilities. Otherwise, you're stuck with a newly formatted disk—and you've lost any data that was on the disk, pre-formatting.

Problem 5:

You experience problems while running DriveSpace

Disk compression programs such as DriveSpace can give you fits sometimes. In most cases, it's not really the utility's fault, although I know this is little consolation if trouble happens to you. My advice when using DriveSpace is to back up your data early and often because DriveSpace *can* cause some very specific problems.

First, DriveSpace can trash your files. This can happen if your drive is old or has surface defects; if you turned off your system too soon; or if your files became cross-linked. You see, DriveSpace gives your hard disk a pretty good workout as it reads and writes compressed data to and from your hard disk. If your hard disk has any defects or weaknesses, DriveSpace will expose them. In addition, because DriveSpace holds some compressed data in system memory at all times, you *will* lose data if you shut off your computer before all the data is written to your hard disk.

In addition, DriveSpace can slow down your system. Because DriveSpace essentially compresses and decompresses data "on the fly," you may notice a slight deterioration of your system's performance while using a compressed disk drive. If your system has a fast hard drive and a slow processor, running DriveSpace *will* slow down your system—and there's not much you can do about it.

If you experience a lot of DriveSpace-related problems on a compressed drive, the solution is simple—*uncompress the drive* and buy a new, larger hard drive instead!

Problem 6:

ScanDisk indicates you have damage to your disk

If ScanDisk finds a hard disk problem, let ScanDisk try to fix it. From the main ScanDisk window, check the **Automatically Fix Errors** option, and then click **Start**. ScanDisk will now attempt to automatically fix any damage it encounters.

If ScanDisk can't fix the damage, you're in bigger trouble. You'll probably need to run a third-party utility, like Norton Disk Doctor, or consult someone more technical for help.

10 Do's and Don'ts for Disk Maintenance

1. *Do* clearly label all your diskettes.
2. *Don't* format drive C—*ever!*
3. *Do* use anti-virus software if you're exchanging diskettes with other computer users.
4. *Don't* hesitate to upgrade your system to FAT32 if you have a very large hard disk.
5. *Do* run ScanDisk regularly to check for hard disk errors—and automatically fix them.
6. *Don't* stick more than one diskette into a drive at one time.
7. *Do* use Disk Defragmenter to keep your hard disk running up to speed.
8. *Don't* remove a diskette from a drive while Windows is still accessing the drive— it's a sure-fire way to scramble your data.
9. *Do* keep your diskettes far away from magnets and magnetic fields—such as those generated by large audio speakers, monitors, speakers, and even vacuum cleaners!
10. *Don't* limit yourself to 1.44MB removable media; check out the 100MB Zip drives from Iomega, or the 120MB Superdiscs from Sony.

The Least You Need to Know

➤ Hard disks must be partitioned and both hard disks and "floppy" diskettes must be formatted before they can be used; partitioning or formatting a disk already containing data will permanently remove that data from the disk.

➤ Routine maintenance (such as running ScanDisk and Disk Defragmenter) can extend the useful life of your hard disk.

➤ If a disk is damaged, some damage can be repaired; use ScanDisk, Norton Disk Doctor, or similar utilities if you encounter a damaged disk.

Chapter 18

What to Do When... Your CD-ROM or DVD Doesn't Spin Right

In This Chapter

➤ Discover the differences between CD-ROM, CD-R, CD-RW, and DVD discs and drives

➤ Learn how to find and fix CD-ROM– and DVD-related problems

In the last chapter we talked about the kinds of disks and drives that store data magnetically. In this chapter we're going real high-tech and looking at disks and drives that store data optically—with a laser beam!

CD-ROM and DVD drives work just like the compact discs you play on your audio system; the shiny little discs are encoded with digital optical data, and read with a special kind of laser. As you can imagine, any combination of moving parts (the motor that spins the disc) and fancy technology (the laser itself) provides the potential for plenty of problems!

Looking at CD-ROM and DVD Drives

CD-ROM stands for *compact disc read-only memory*. This doesn't mean that CD-ROMs are memory devices; they're storage devices, just like hard disks or diskettes. The difference is that you can't write data to CD-ROM discs—you can only read data from them.

The other difference between a CD-ROM and a normal computer disk is that information is stored on a CD-ROM *optically*, while a normal disk stores data *magnetically*. In essence, a CD-ROM is composed of concentric circles filled with numerous pits. A laser beam in the CD-ROM drive reads these pits and converts the information into data that can be used by your computer system.

Both computer CD-ROMs and audio compact discs (CDs) store data in the same manner, and both types of drives use laser beams to read the data. But you can't play a CD-ROM disk in an audio CD player because the computer data is stored in a different format than normal audio data; you *can* play audio CDs in computer CD-ROM drives, however. Think of a CD-ROM as a backwards-compatible extension of basic CD technology, kind of a superset of the basic compact disc.

While the standard CD-ROM drive included with most PCs can only read data, there are other types of CD drives that let you store your own data on CD-format discs. The CD-R (compact disc-recordable) format lets you write data *once* onto a blank CD-R disc that can then be read from virtually *any* standard CD-ROM drive. (You can also use CD-R drives to record *audio* CDs!) The CD-RW (compact disc-rewritable) format lets you record multiple times onto special CD-RW discs—which can only be read on CD-RW drives, *not* on normal CD-ROM drives.

Note, however, that recording or writing to a CD-R or CD-RW disc takes longer than it does to *read* the data from the disc. New CD-ROM drives now *read* data at 40× the rate of the original CD-ROM drives; recordable/rewritable drives will *store* data at only 2× or 4× rates. If you're looking for a CD-R or CD-RW drive, make sure you compare both the read and the write/record rates.

Computer DVD Versus Movie DVD

The DVD format allows for the storage of any type of digital data on a DVD disk—which can be either computer data or full-motion audio/video. So a computer DVD is essentially the same as a movie DVD, and you can play DVD movies on your computer DVD drive. In fact, if your PC or DVD drive has audio/video out jacks, you can run these into the corresponding audio/video *in* jacks on your TV set and thus use your PC as a fairly inconvenient DVD movie player. (Don't try playing computer DVDs in a movie DVD player, however; this trick doesn't work going in that direction.)

A DVD is similar to a CD-ROM, but with lots more data storage capability—up to 4.7GB, compared to a CD-ROM's 650MB capacity. Like a CD-ROM, it's a read-only medium, meaning that you can't use it to store your data, only to read data from the disc.

A DVD drive for your computer system can read computer software on DVD discs, play back DVD-format movies, and play back standard CD-ROM discs. (That's right—DVD is fully backwards-compatible with CD-ROM, so you can lay all your CD-ROM discs in your new DVD drive.) While they're still a tad more expensive than CD-ROM drives, DVD pricing is dropping rapidly, and DVD drives are standard equipment on many higher-end PC systems sold today.

As I write these words, there are not yet any commercially viable (re: *affordable*) recordable or rewritable DVD drives. However, rewritable DVDs are expected to hit the market soon, capable of recording up to 2.6GB of data!

Hooking It Up to Your System—and Making It Run

Digressing Very Deeply?

The acronym DVD actually doesn't stand for anything anymore; at one time it stood for Digital Versatile Disc, and at another Digital Video Disc, but the powers that be decided to just go with the initials, to alleviate any confusion.

When you add a CD-ROM or DVD drive to your system, it can be added internally or externally. Both function identically; they just hook up differently. An internal drive hooks up into a spare drive bay in the front of your system unit. An external drive hooks up to a spare port on the back of your system unit. An external unit also needs external power; an internal unit gets its power directly from your system unit.

After your CD-ROM or DVD drive is installed, you need to load a device driver (normally included with your new drive) into system memory so your system can recognize the presence of the new peripheral. This is theoretically done automatically the next time you start Windows, via Plug and Play technology. If Plug and Play fails to recognize your new drive, however, you'll have to use the Add New Hardware Wizard to configure your system manually for your new drive.

Using CD-ROM and DVD Drives

Using your CD-ROM or DVD drive is just like using a diskette or hard disk drive. My Computer displays an icon for your CD-ROM/DVD drive, labeled with the next letter of the alphabet after the last installed hard drive on your system. If you only have one hard drive, labeled C, the CD-ROM/DVD drive will be labeled D.

To view the contents of the CD-ROM or DVD drive, make sure a disc is inserted in the drive, and then click the drive icon in My Computer. You can launch any program from your CD-ROM or DVD drive just as you do from any other drive. (Note that if your CD or DVD contains a software program, chances are that the program will start up auto-matically when you insert it in your drive, thanks to Windows Autorun technology.) You can also copy files from the CD-ROM/DVD to your hard drive or to a diskette (assuming the file will fit on the smaller storage medium!).

What Can Go Wrong with Your CD-ROM or DVD Drive

The bad thing with CD-ROM and DVD drives is that they don't always work right! Just look at the things that can go wrong when you add a CD-ROM or DVD drive to your system:

➤ Things might not be hooked up right. Remember to properly seat all the internal cards and connect all the cables—including power cables for external CD-ROM/DVD drives!

➤ Things might not be loaded correctly. Windows must be configured to load the device drivers for your CD-ROM/DVD drive; if Windows is configured incorrectly, or loads the wrong drivers, or if the driver files are corrupted, things won't run right.

➤ Things might be in conflict—in particular, ports (also called input/output addresses) and DMA channels! It's *very important* to make sure that your CD-ROM or DVD drive is set up so that it doesn't use ports, or channels assigned to other devices on your system. If you have conflicts, you might find that *several* devices don't work right!

Make sure you check all these things *before* installing or using a new CD-ROM or DVD drive.

Fixing CD-ROM and DVD Problems

Okay, you have your new CD-ROM or DVD drive installed and ready to spin. But what do you do if it doesn't spin right? As usual, it's time to sift through the potential problems and offer a few timely solutions.

Problem 1:

Your CD-ROM/DVD drive isn't recognized by Windows—it doesn't appear in either My Computer or Windows Explorer

This is typically a driver-related problem of some sort. The first thing to check is if your CD-ROM/DVD drive shows up in the System Properties dialog box. Start by selecting the **System** icon in **Control Panel**; when the System Properties dialog box appears, select the **Device Manager** tab and look for the CD-ROM or DVD entry. Look for an entry for CD-ROM or DVD; if no such entry exists, your system doesn't know that it has a CD-ROM or DVD drive attached. Use the **Add New Hardware Wizard** to properly install the drivers for your drive; you might also want to see if there's an installation program (on diskette) that came with your drive, and if there is, use it *first*, before you run the Add New Hardware Wizard.

What if there *was* a CD-ROM or DVD entry in the System Properties dialog box? In this instance, double-click the **CD-ROM** or **DVD** entry; if the entry is blank (no driver displayed) you'll need to reinstall your drive via the **Add New Hardware Wizard**. If a driver *is* displayed, delete it (via the **Remove** button) and then reinstall it with the **Add New Hardware Wizard**.

In other words, if your system isn't recognizing your CD-ROM or DVD drive, you need to either install or delete and then reinstall your drive.

Problem 2:

Your CD-ROM/DVD drive doesn't work—nothing happens

First, have you inserted a CD-ROM or DVD disc into your drive? Do you have the disc inserted *properly* (label side up)? If you're using an external drive, is it plugged in and powered on? Have you accessed the disc properly?

If you think you're doing everything right, you probably have some sort of power problem with your CD-ROM/DVD drive. If you're using an internal drive, you should check all the connections inside your system unit; not only should the drive be plugged into a drive controller, but it should also be plugged into your computer's power supply. If you're using an external drive, make sure all the connections are solid and that the drive actually has power (make sure the power light is on).

If you do have power and still can't get the drive to work, see Problem 3.

Problem 3:

Your CD-ROM/DVD drive doesn't work—the drive spins, but you can't access the disc

Let's assume that you have power to your drive and have a CD-ROM or DVD inserted properly (right side up). Have you accidentally inserted a DVD disc into a CD-ROM drive? Most DVD drives will read CD-ROM discs, but not vice-versa.

If you still can't access the disc, you probably don't have the correct driver loaded into system memory. Open the Windows **Control Panel** and select the **System** icon. When the System Properties dialog box appears, select the **Device Manager** tab, click the + next to the CD-ROM or DVD entry, and see if the device listed is the device actually installed on your system. If it's not the right driver, delete it and install the proper driver via the Add New Hardware Wizard. If you have the right driver but think you might need an updated version, highlight the driver in the System Properties dialog box, click the **Properties** button, and when the Device Properties dialog box appears, select the **Driver** tab and click the **Update Driver** button.

Finally, check for DMA and port conflicts with your CD-ROM/DVD drive. This is easy to do within Windows 98. Just click the **Start** button, select **Help**, and when the Windows Help window appears, select the **Contents** tab and select **Troubleshooting, Windows 98 Troubleshooters, Hardware Conflict**. All you have to do now is follow the Troubleshooter's onscreen instructions to find and resolve any conflicts you're having. In the end, if you have a conflict, you'll need to change the DMA or port assignment for one of the conflicted devices.

Problem 4:

Your CD-ROM or DVD drive doesn't work—you receive an error message

Error messages generally result from DMA or port conflicts. Make sure that your assignments are not used by other devices, and then change them if they are.

Problem 5:

Your CD-ROM or DVD drive freezes your system

Again, the culprit is most likely a DMA or port conflict. Check your assignments and change any conflicting ones.

Problem 6:

Your CD-ROM or DVD drive causes another peripheral to malfunction— or vice versa

No doubt about it—you have a conflict! One or more of your port or DMA channel assignments is used by another device on your system. Begin by changing the port assignment; then reboot your computer and see what happens. If that doesn't do it, change the DMA assignment (or try another port assignment), and so on and so on. I know, this can get tedious, but it's just about the only way to figure out what is conflicting with what, short of calling in a professional computer guru-type—which isn't a bad idea, actually!

Problem 7:

Your CD-ROM or DVD drive is slow

Yeah, that's true. CD-ROM and DVD drives *are* slow—much slower than most hard disk drives—and not much faster than a good diskette drive. There are a few things you can do to speed up your CD-ROM/DVD performance, however, including the following:

➤ Get a faster drive. This is the blatantly obvious solution. If you have an older drive, you can upgrade to a newer 40× drive and vastly improve your playback performance.

➤ Add more memory to your system. All data transfer utilizes system memory at some point, and the more you have, the faster things go.

➤ Remove any old CD-ROM drivers from your system files. If you've upgraded an older system to Windows 95 or Windows 98, it's possible that older 16-bit drivers for your CD-ROM drive are still being loaded by either your AUTOEXEC.BAT or CONFIG.SYS files. Check these files and either delete or "remark" out any references to the older drivers.

➤ Get a faster computer. Yeah, it's drastic, but a faster computer will make all your peripherals *seem* faster, at least.

Problem 8:

Your CD-ROM or DVD doesn't always read data accurately

Inaccurate data can result from several problems—most likely a scratched or dirty disc. You can buy commercial CD/DVD cleaners that will remove surface dirt and debris; scratches are less easily fixed—if at all.

It's also possible that the laser beam inside your CD-ROM/DVD drive is dirty or out of alignment. You can try to "blow" the dirt out of the drive with compressed air, or—in some cases—wipe the laser lens with a cotton swab. However, your best bet is to see a repair person ASAP to get this puppy fixed.

Problem 9:

You can't read a rewritable CD in a read-only CD-ROM drive

First, are you trying to read a CD-RW disc in a CD-ROM drive? If so, you can't do it; CD-RW discs use a special data format that can only be read by CD-RW drives.

If you're having trouble reading a CD-R disc in a CD-ROM drive, you could have a simple incompatibility problem. Generally, this is more of a problem with playing CD-R discs on older, slower CD-ROM drives, or with discs recorded on older CD-R drives. If you encounter this kind of incompatibility, there's not much you can do about it, save for trying the disc in another machine.

Finally—and I hate to even suggest this—make sure that the CD-R or CD-RW disc actually has data on it. If could be that you're trying to read a disc that hasn't had data "burned" into it yet!

Problem 10:

You can't play music CDs on your CD-ROM or DVD drive

To get audio from your CD-ROM or DVD drive, an audio cable must be connected between your drive and your sound card. If you haven't connected this cable, you won't hear audio from *any* CD or DVD discs you play!

10 Do's and Don'ts for Using Your CD-ROM or DVD Drive

1. *Do* use your CD-ROM/DVD drive to play standard audio CDs, and your DVD drive to play DVD movies—you might as well enjoy yourself while you're stuck in front of your computer!

2. *Don't* assign your CD-ROM/DVD drive to ports or channels used by other devices in your system.

3. *Do* make sure your CD-ROM/DVD drive is compatible with your sound card.

4. *Don't* try to play computer CD-ROMs in your normal audio CD player; not only will the resulting squeals and noise be really annoying, but they could damage your speakers!

5. *Do* think about upgrading to a CD-R or CD-RW drive; a 650MB backup device is quite useful!

6. *Don't* forget to configure Windows to load the proper device drivers for your CD-ROM/DVD drive.

7. *Do* invest in the fastest CD-ROM or DVD drive you can afford; when you're accessing data, a 24× drive is twice as fast as a 12× drive.

8. *Don't* use your CD-ROM or DVD drive tray as a cup holder!

9. *Do* treat your CD-ROM and DVD discs with care; damage and debris can affect playback.

10. *Don't* get concerned if your CD-ROM/DVD drive appears slow—optical access *is* slower than normal hard disk drive access.

The Least You Need to Know

➤ CD-ROMs are read-only devices; to write or record your own data on a CD, you need a CD-R or CD-RW drive.

➤ DVDs work just like CD-ROMs, except they store much more data—enough data to hold a complete movie!

➤ Most CD-ROM/DVD problems are caused by port or DMA channel conflicts.

Chapter 19

What to Do When... Your Sound System Doesn't Sound Right

In This Chapter

➤ Learn about the many different types of audio generated by Windows

➤ Find out how to hook up and configure your system for the best possible sound

➤ Discover how to find and fix most audio-related problems

Seems like every time you click something in Windows, it makes a sound. Your computer talks to you when something good happens ("You've got mail!") and buzzes at you when something bad happens (that awful noise associated with error messages). You listen to music on your system via audio CDs, and depend on background sounds to entertain and direct you on a variety of Web pages.

So what do you do when you can't hear the sounds anymore—or if the songs you hear are the wrong ones? If your system develops audio problems of any sort, it's time to quit listening and start reading!

Looking at (or Listening to) PC Sound

All computers come with a built-in speaker. This is a lousy little speaker, and delivers not much more than tiny beeps and buzzes. If you want *good* sound from your system, you need to supplement the built-in speaker with a better audio system—which typically consists of a sound card and two or more external speakers.

Pick a Card, Any Card

You install a sound card the same way you would any other add-in card—open up your system's case and slide the card into an open slot. It's pretty simple, really. (In some cases you may also need to configure some jumpers or switches on the card itself; make sure you follow the manufacturer's instructions when installing the card.)

Once the sound card itself is installed, you also need to load the appropriate device driver for the card into your system's memory. If Plug and Play doesn't recognize your sound card when you reboot your computer, use the Add New Software Wizard to add the drivers manually.

Don't Forget the Speakers!

Now, a sound card in and of itself won't do you much good—you need to hook up a set of external speakers to get the most out of your system's new sound capabilities. Here's where it pays to check out several models before you buy; don't just assume that bigger speakers mean better sound! Some smaller speakers deliver *terrific* sound, especially when accompanied by a *subwoofer* for the lower bass frequencies.

An external speaker setup—especially one with a subwoofer—can sometimes get a little complicated. You'll need to make sure you plug in the *right* speaker into the *right* jack (and the *left* one into the *left* jack), and that any cable running *between* the speakers is connected properly, and that the subwoofer and the other speakers all have power. Just follow the wiring diagram supplied with the speakers as closely as possible—then make sure you have the speakers positioned for the best possible sound.

Configuring Windows' Audio Properties

After you install a new sound card, you may want to tweak its basic configuration. You do this in the Multimedia Properties dialog box, as shown in the next figure. (You open the Multimedia Properties dialog box by selecting the **Multimedia** icon in the Windows **Control Panel**.)

Maximizing MIDI

If you *really* want to get into high-quality audio, look into something called MIDI. MIDI, which stands for *musical instrument digital interface*, is a standard used by professional musicians to record and play back music digitally. Most sound cards come with basic MIDI capabilities; pro musicians might opt for a more fully featured dedicated MIDI card, most of which are compatible with the Roland MPU-401 standard. With a MIDI setup, you can connect your computer to digital keyboards and other synthesized instruments—and use your computer to "sequence" and play back music through the attached musical instruments.

Of course, you don't need a complete MIDI setup to get basic musical instrument playback capabilities. Several companies make add-on piano keyboards that are compatible with the basic MIDI capabilities found on most standard sound cards. One of these keyboards functions just like a normal piano, and can also be used (with accompanying software) to teach you basic piano techniques.

Go to the **MIDI** tab to add and configure MIDI instruments.

Go to the **CD Music** tab to configure audio CD playback.

Configure your system's audio in the Multimedia Properties dialog box.

Click to display the Master Volume Control.

Click to display the Recording Control.

Check to display a volume control in the Taskbar Tray.

Click to select your speaker setup or configure playback properties.

Click to configure recording properties.

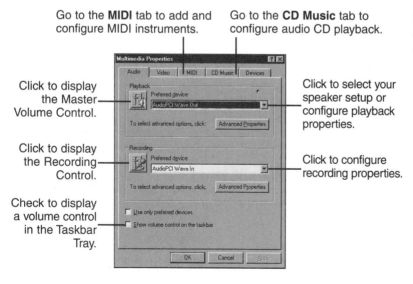

Here is some of what you can configure in the Multimedia Properties dialog box:

➤ To change the playback volume, select the **Audio** tab and click the **Playback** button to display the Master Volume Control. Click and drag the volume sliders to the desired levels for each type of playback. (Depending on your make and model of sound card, this dialog box may include sliders for different audio devices on your system; use the main volume slider to control the overall volume.)

➤ To display a volume control icon in the Taskbar Tray, select the **Audio** tab and select **Show Volume Control On The Taskbar**.

➤ To change the preferred playback device, select the **Audio** tab and select a new device from the **Preferred Device** list in the Playback section. To change the preferred recording device, select a new device from the **Preferred Device** list in the Recording section.

➤ To change the quality of sounds recorded on your system, select the **Audio** tab and click **Advanced Properties** in the Recording section. When the Advanced Audio Properties dialog box appears, adjust the Sample Rate Conversion Quality slider from **Good** to **Best**; moving the slider to the right (Best) improves recording quality, but also uses more disk space and slows down your overall system performance.

➤ To add a new MIDI instrument to your system, select the **MIDI** tab, click the **Add New Instrument** button, and follow the instructions in the MIDI Instrument Installation Wizard.

➤ To fine-tune your system's playback of audio CDs, select the **CD Music** tab and make changes to the appropriate settings.

➤ To check the settings for any audio-related device on your system, select the **Devices** tab, select the device in question, and then click the **Properties** button.

Configuring Regular Windows Sounds

In addition to Windows' fancy-shmancy audio playback capabilities, you also have to deal with the run-of-the-mill sounds generated when you execute selected system actions. These sounds are stored in .WAV files, and specific .WAV files are associated with specific tasks in the Sounds Properties dialog box, shown in the following figure. (To access this dialog box, go to the Windows **Control Panel** and select the **Sounds** icon.)

There are really three ways to associate sounds with events. First, you can go to the Sounds Properties dialog box and select a unified sound *scheme* from the **Schemes** pull-down list. With a sound scheme, all the sounds for all the events are preselected and related.

Second, you can select an entire desktop *theme*, which includes related colors, fonts, wallpaper, and sounds. (Themes are included as part of Windows 98, but had to be added to Windows 95 as part of the Windows 95 Plus! pack.) To change a theme (and associated sounds) in Windows 98, open the **Control Panel** and select the **Desktop Themes** icon. (In Windows 95 you'll have to go the **Plus!** menu—if you purchased and installed the Plus! pack—and select the **Desktop Themes** option.) When the Desktop Themes dialog box appears, select a new theme from the pull-down list, and make sure the **Sound Events** box is checked.

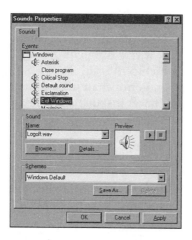

Associate sounds with events in the Sounds Properties dialog box.

Finally, you can associate individual sounds with individual events. Just go to the Sounds Properties dialog box, select an action from the **Events** list, then either select a sound from the **Name** pull-down list or click the **Browse** button to browse for a specific sound file. When you have a sound selected, you can listen to it by clicking the **Arrow** button in the **Preview** section.

What Can Go Wrong with Your System's Sound

The most common problems with your system's sound are often similar to the problems you find with CD-ROM or DVD drives.

➤ Things might not be hooked up right. Remember to seat all the cards and connect all the cables—including the power cables for your powered speakers!

➤ Things might not be configured properly. Don't forget to configure Windows for your specific sound card—and make sure you have the latest sound driver loaded!

➤ Things might be in conflict—in particular, ports (also called input/output addresses), interrupts, and DMA channels! It's very important to make sure that your sound card is set up so that it doesn't use ports, channels, or interrupts assigned to other devices on your system. If you have conflicts, you might find that *several* devices don't work right!

➤ Things might not be properly associated. If you find events that used to make noise have suddenly become silent, chances are the .WAV file has been deleted or moved. Check the Sounds Properties dialog box to make sure that real sounds are associated with all key events and actions.

Direct Memory for Your Sound

Your sound card, like most peripherals, uses a direct memory access (DMA) channel to pipe information directly to your system's memory, bypassing the microprocessor. Most systems have eight DMA channels available.

When you're adding a "standard" sound card to your system, you run into a basic problem—there really is no such thing as a "standard" when it comes to multimedia computing. Every sound card seems to work with a different set of parameters than other cards, and there's no way to know which card really does what. This means that installing a sound card requires more trial-and-error than most other add-on devices— although higher-priced cards typically have fewer installation/configuration issues. I wish it were different, but it's not. Sorry.

Fixing Audio Problems

Okay, you have your new sound card and speakers all fired up and ready to go. But what do you do if they *don't go?* Well, let's take a look at the most common sound problems you may encounter.

Problem 1:

Your sound card doesn't work—you don't get any sound

Let's look at the simple stuff first. Is the card installed properly in your system unit? Have you connected the audio cable from your CD-ROM/DVD drive to your sound card? Are speakers (or headphones) hooked up to the card? Are the speakers plugged in and turned on? (And are they plugged into the correct jack? You don't want to plug your speakers into your microphone jack!) Are you performing a task on your PC that actually produces sound? Is the volume turned up loud enough (both on your speakers and in Windows)?

Okay, now that the easy stuff is out of the way, let's turn to something more difficult. The most likely cause of no sound is some sort of conflict. One by one, change your card's DMA, IRQ, and port settings. (This may entail resetting some jumpers on the card itself, as well as making some software-based changes.)

Problem 2:

Your sound card freezes or crashes your system

If you've just installed your sound card, you may not have the card properly installed. Check your installation (is the card properly seated and connected?) and then reboot your system.

If this doesn't fix it, you have something wrong in your setup. Check your software setup to make sure you have the same DMA, IRQ, and port assignments as selected on your sound card itself (usually via DIP switches or jumpers). If the settings are correct, you probably have a conflict of some kind. You should methodically change the DMA, IRQ, and port assignments in Windows so that they don't conflict with the assignments for other devices on your system.

Problem 3:

When you launch Windows, you get an error message about your sound card

There are a number of error messages you can receive about your sound card when you launch Windows. Perhaps the most common is one that looks something like this:

```
SOUNDCARD ERROR: DRIVER.XXX not installed
```

This error message occurs when the driver file for your sound card either isn't found or is incorrect. The obvious fix is to make sure the driver is being loaded properly, using the System Properties dialog box.

This message can also be generated when you have an interrupt conflict between your sound card and another device. If this is your problem, change the IRQ setting for one of the two devices.

Problem 4:

Sound from your sound card skips or plays continually

This problem generally results from an IRQ conflict. Change the interrupt setting for your sound card to one not used by another system device and then reboot your system. You may want to change the sound card's interrupt to one between 3 and 8; some systems using a higher interrupt (between 9 and 15) may cause playback problems.

Problem 5:

You only get sound from one channel of a stereo setup

The most likely cause of this problem is using the wrong kind of plug for your powered speakers. It's possible that you're using a mono plug; you need a stereo plug to connect to your sound card's stereo jack.

Let's not overlook the obvious, either—make sure you actually have both speakers connected! (Most speaker hookups are terribly confusing; even *I* have occasionally plugged the wrong plug into the wrong jack—or left one of the speakers accidentally unplugged!) And don't forget to check the balance slider in the Master Volume Control (accessible from the Multimedia Properties dialog box) and make sure that the balance isn't set all the way to the left or the right.

This problem also can occur if you don't have the proper driver for your sound card loaded into memory. Check your Windows configuration to make sure you have the proper driver installed and selected.

Problem 6:

The volume level from your sound card is too low or too high

This is normally a simple problem with a simple solution. First, try adjusting the volume on your powered speakers. If this isn't the problem, you need to adjust the volume within Windows; use the Master Volume Control, accessible from the Multimedia Properties dialog box.

Next, check your setup to make sure you have the right sound driver loaded. Next, try moving your speakers farther away from your video monitor; electrical "noise" from your monitor might be affecting the speakers' sound. Finally, try moving your sound card to another slot inside your system unit. Sometimes proximity to another card can cause your sound card to generate poor-quality sound.

Of course, poor-quality sound could simply be the result of using poor-quality speakers with your system. You may want to invest in some better speakers if you're really picky about this sort of thing.

Problem 7:

Program- or event-specific sounds don't play

If you can't play .WAV files from a specific program (for example, if you don't hear "You've Got Mail" when you log onto America Online), check the association in the Sounds Properties dialog box. It's possible that the sound file has been moved (this might happen when you upgrade to a newer version of a program, and the upgrade is made to a different directory or folder) or even deleted.

If the sound file exists and is associated properly, make sure you can actually play the sound; click the **Preview** arrow in the Sounds Properties dialog box to check out the sound. If you can hear the sound in the dialog box but *not* in the associated program, then you have a program-specific problem; check with the technical support department of your software's manufacturer for help.

If you can't hear a specific sound with the Multimedia Properties Preview but other .WAV files play properly, you have a corrupted .WAV file. The only way to fix a corrupted file is to reinstall it, either from your Windows installation CD or from a specific program's installation media.

It's possible that two applications on your system are trying to generate sounds at the same time—and they're essentially canceling each other out. Stop or close all open applications (particularly games and the Windows Media Player) and then see if you can hear your normal system sounds.

If you can't hear *any* .WAV sounds—or if all .WAV sounds play back incorrectly—you have a bigger problem. Your sound card may not be capable of playing .WAV files, or may not be configured properly for .WAV playback. There could also be some sort of resource conflict between your sound card and another device installed in your computer that only affects .WAV playback. (Don't laugh—I've seen it happen.) Check all your sound configuration settings and make any necessary changes.

10 Do's and Don'ts for Quality Sound

1. *Do* install a good sound card and hook up a quality pair of powered speakers to your PC system; it's a lot better than using the cheap speaker built into your system unit!

2. *Don't* assign your sound card to ports, channels, or interrupts used by other devices in your system.

3. *Do* add a subwoofer to your PC speaker system; you'll be amazed at the powerful bass delivered by a quality subwoofer!

4. *Don't* hesitate to listen to a variety of speaker systems before you make your choice; the sound quality varies *wildly* from system to system, and you can't go by size or price alone.

5. *Do* use the Master Volume Control in the Multimedia Properties dialog box to set the volume for all types of playback separately.

6. *Don't* forget to properly configure Windows for your specific sound card.

7. *Do* add a volume control to the Windows Taskbar by checking that option in the Multimedia Properties dialog box.

8. *Don't* get unrealistic expectations about your PC system's sound capabilities; despite all the hype, the sound won't be near as good as that with a high-quality home audio system.

9. *Do* check out all of your sound card's capabilities, including hookups for MIDI keyboards.

10. *Don't* waste *too much* time playing with Windows sound files—you can get carried away assigning sounds to obscure Windows events!

The Least You Need to Know

➤ PC sound is generated from a sound card and typically fed to an external speaker system; these speaker hookups are often confusing and the cause of many problems.

➤ Sound cards can be one of the most temperamental devices in your system; I/O address, DMA, and IRQ conflicts are common.

➤ Most Windows audio settings are configured from the Multimedia Properties and Sounds Properties dialog boxes.

Chapter 20

What to Do When...Your Files Are Funky

In This Chapter

➤ Learn how to copy, move, delete, rename, preview, and associate files

➤ Find out how to *undelete* files you've accidentally deleted

➤ Discover how to find and fix file-related problems

All your data is stored in files. All the good things you do with your computer involve files, and some of the bad things do, too. This means you must be careful when working with your files, because any mistake you make can cause your files—and your valuable data—to disappear.

The Least You Need to Know About Files

The next few sections are like a refresher course in file management. Feel free to skip these pages if you're comfortable with your file-management skills.

A file is nothing more than a collection of data of some sort. Everything on your computer's hard drive is a separate file, with its own name, location, and properties. The data (information) in a file can be a document from an application (such as an Excel worksheet or a Word document), or it can be the executable code for the application itself.

Every file has its own unique name. A defined structure exists for naming files, and its conventions must be followed for Windows to understand exactly what file you want when you try to access one. Each filename must consist of three parts, as described in Table 20.1.

Table 20.1 Parts of a Filename

Filename Part	Description
Name	The first part of the filename, which can include either letters or numbers.
Period	The period following the file's name acts as a divider between the name and the extension.
Extension	This is the last part of the name, used to denote various types of files.

Putting it all together, you get filenames that appear onscreen something like this: **FILENAME.EXT**.

Before Windows 95, filenames had to conform to what was called the "eight dot three" (8.3) convention—eight characters for the name, then the period, then a three-character extension. In Windows 95 and Windows 98, the filename can now contain up to 256 characters, in any combination—including multiple periods—and spaces!

Folders Used to Be Directories

Prior to Windows 95, what are now called folders were then called *directories*. So if I sometimes slip and tell you to look in a certain directory, what I mean is to look in a certain folder, okay?

Windows stores files in *folders*. A folder is like a master file; each folder can contain both files and additional folders. The exact location of a file is called its *path* and contains all the folders leading to the file. For example, a file named FILENAME.DOC that exists in the SYSTEM folder that is itself contained in the WINDOWS folder on your C drive has a path that looks like this: **C:\WINDOWS\SYSTEM\FILENAME.DOC**.

Mastering files and folders is a key aspect of using your computer. You may need to copy files from one folder to another, or from your hard disk to a floppy disk. To do this, you use one of Windows' two file-management tools—My Computer or Windows Explorer.

Using My Computer and Windows Explorer to Manage Your Files

My Computer is a file-management tool that lets you manage your hard drive(s), mapped network drives, peripheral drives, folders, and files. My Computer is extremely versatile; in Windows 98 you can use My Computer to view the contents of the Control Panel and Printers folders, as well as to browse pages on the World Wide Web. To open My Computer, just select the **My Computer** icon on your desktop.

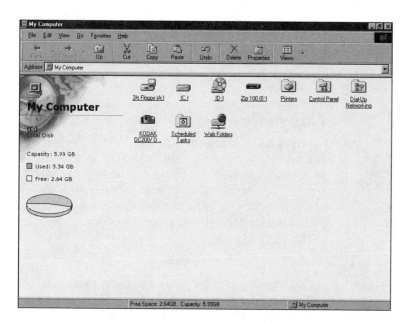

To manage your files, use My Computer...

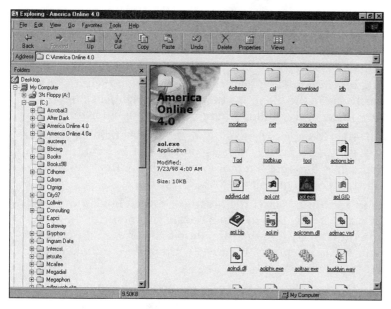

...or use Windows Explorer; they both perform the same file-management tasks.

Windows Explorer is another Windows file-management tool, similar to My Computer. It differs from My Computer in that it displays two different *panes* of information; the left pane contains a directory tree of all the folders on your system, and the contents for selected items are displayed in the right pane. Windows Explorer is a little more difficult to open; click the **Start** button, select **Programs**, and then select **Windows Explorer**.

Too Many Explorers

Don't confuse Windows Explorer—which you use to view and manipulate folders and files—with Internet Explorer, Microsoft's Web browser.

Know that both My Computer and Windows Explorer do the same things and work pretty much the same way. Use whichever one you're most comfortable with.

Copy Files

Copying a file or folder is how you place a copy of it at another location (either in another folder or on another disk) while still retaining the original where it was. Copying is different from moving in that when you copy an item, the original remains; when you move an item, the original is no longer present in the original location.

There are nine different ways you can copy a file in Windows:

➤ **The toolbar method**   From My Computer or Windows Explorer, highlight the file to copy and click the **Copy** button on the toolbar; paste the copy into a new folder by navigating to the folder and then clicking the **Paste** button on the toolbar.

➤ **The pull-down menu method**   Select the file to copy then pull down the **Edit** menu and select **Copy**; paste the copy into a new folder by pulling down the **Edit** menu and selecting **Paste**.

➤ **The pop-up menu method**   Right-click the file to copy and select **Copy** from the pop-up menu; paste the file into a new folder by right-clicking anywhere in the new folder and selecting **Paste** from the pop-up menu.

➤ **The Send To method**   To copy a file to another disk drive, right-click the file to copy, select **Send To**, then select the drive (typically A or B) from the pop-up menu. (This method copies files into the root folder of the destination drive; you can't select a different destination folder.)

➤ **The drag-and-drop method**   Select the file to copy, then hold down the **Ctrl** key while you drag it to the new location; release the mouse button and the **Ctrl** key to drop the copy. (If you drag and drop a file onto a *different drive*—from C to A, say—the file is automatically copied without need to hold down the **Ctrl** key during the operation.)

➤ **The right-drag method**   Select the file to copy, then *right-drag* the file to the new location. (Right-dragging is dragging while holding down the *right* mouse button.) When you release the mouse button, you'll be presented with a pop-up menu; select **Copy Here**.

➤ **The shortcut key method 1**   Select the file to copy, then press **Ctrl+Insert**; press **Shift+Insert** to paste the copied file.

➤ **The shortcut key method 2**   Select the file to copy, then press **Ctrl+C**; press **Ctrl+V** to paste the copied file.

➤ **The DOS method**   Open a DOS window and type the following at the DOS Prompt: **copy *filename.ext c:\newlocation***, where *filename.ext* is the name of the file to copy, and *newlocation* is the folder you want to copy to.

Refreshing!

If you have moved, copied, or deleted some files and folders but don't see the changes, update your display by pulling down the **View** menu and selecting **Refresh**—or just press the **F5** key.

Moving Files

Moving a file or folder is different from copying a file or folder. Moving deletes the item from its previous location and places it in a new location; copying leaves the original item where it was *and* creates a copy of the item elsewhere. In Windows there are seven different ways to move a file:

➤ **The toolbar method**   From My Computer or Windows Explorer, highlight the file to move and click the **Cut** button on the toolbar; paste the file into a new folder by clicking the **Paste** button on the toolbar.

➤ **The pull-down menu method**   Select the file to move, pull down the **Edit** menu, then select **Cut**; paste the copy into a new folder by pulling down the **Edit** menu and selecting **Paste**.

➤ **The pop-up menu method**   Right-click the file to move and select **Cut** from the pop-up menu; paste the file into a new folder by right-clicking anywhere in the new folder and selecting **Paste** from the pop-up menu.

➤ **The drag-and-drop method**   Select the file to move, then drag it to the new location; release the mouse button to drop the file into a new folder. (Note that this procedure, if used to drag files to a different drive, actually *copies* the file, rather than moving it; this method only works when moving a file to a different directory on the same drive.)

➤ **The right-drag method**   Select the file to move, then *right-drag* the file to the new location. When you release the mouse button, you'll be presented with a pop-up menu; select **Move Here**.

➤ **The shortcut key method**   Select the file to move, then press **Ctrl+X**; press **Ctrl+V** to paste the file into a new folder.

➤ **The DOS method**   Open a DOS window and type the following at the DOS Prompt: **move *filename.ext x:\newlocation***, where *x* is the destination drive and *newlocation* is the destination folder.

Deleting Files

Because disk space is a resource you don't want to waste, you should delete files and folders you no longer need. Note that deleting a file is different from cutting a file. When you cut a file (in preparation for a move), you keep it in memory for pasting; when you delete a file, you send it to the Recycle Bin.

235

There are eight different ways to delete a file in Windows:

➤ **The delete key method**   Highlight the file and press the **Del** key on your keyboard.

➤ **The *permanent* delete key method**   Highlight the file and press **Shift+Del**; this will bypass the Recycle Bin and permanently delete the file, with no restoration possible.

➤ **The toolbar method**   From My Computer or Windows Explorer, highlight the file to move and click the **Delete** button on the toolbar.

➤ **The pull-down menu method**   Select the file to move, pull down the **File** menu, then select **Delete**.

➤ **The pop-up menu method**   Right-click the file to move and select **Delete** from the pop-up menu.

➤ **The drag-and-trash method**   Select the file to move, then drag it to the Recycle Bin.

➤ **The drag-and-*permanently*-trash method**   Select the file to move, then hold down the **Shift** key and drag it to the Recycle Bin; this will bypass the Recycle Bin and permanently delete the file, with no restoration possible. (Note, however, that since you can also use the **Shift** key to select multiple files, you may want to start the drag maneuver before you press the **Shift** key for permanent deletion.)

➤ **The DOS method**   Open a DOS window and type the following at the DOS Prompt: **del *filename.ext*** where *filename.ext* is the file you want to delete.

Recycling Is for Hard Disks Only

The Recycle Bin only holds files deleted from your hard disk. Files deleted from other drives—diskette drives and Zip drives, for example—do *not* get placed in the Recycle Bin. When you delete files from non-hard disk drives, they're really deleted—*permanently!*

Undeleting Files

If you delete a file and later decide you made a mistake, you're in luck. Windows stores deleted files in the Recycle Bin for a period of time—if you have deleted the file recently, it should still be in the Recycle Bin.

As long as a deleted file is still in the Recycle Bin, you can easily restore it to its previous location. Start by opening the Recycle Bin by selecting its icon on the desktop. When the Recycle Bin opens, locate the file or folder you want to restore. Right-click the item's icon and choose **Restore** from the pop-up menu.

If you open the Recycle Bin and you can't find the file you're looking for, you're out of luck—you waited too long, and the file has been permanently deleted from your hard disk.

Files do not stay in the Recycle Bin indefinitely. By default, the deleted files in the Recycle Bin can occupy 10 percent of your hard disk space. (You can change this setting by right-clicking the **Recycle Bin** icon, selecting **Properties** from the pop-up menu, and adjusting the slider in the Recycle Bin Properties dialog box.) When you have enough deleted files to exceed 10 percent of your disk space, the oldest files in the Recycle Bin are completely deleted from your hard disk.

Deleting Files—Permanently

If you want to free up some extra disk space, you can manually empty the Recycle Bin. Doing so permanently removes deleted files from your hard disk. Just right-click the **Recycle Bin** icon and, when the pop-up menu appears, select **Empty Recycle Bin**. When the Confirm File Delete dialog box appears, click **Yes** to completely erase the files, or click **No** to continue storing the files in the Recycle Bin.

In addition, if you use **Shift+Del** to delete a file (or hold down the **Shift** key while dragging a file to the Recycle Bin), the file will be permanently deleted without first being stored in the Recycle Bin.

Go Wild

You can use "wildcard" characters when performing searches with the Find utility. For example, if you use * in place of multiple characters, searching for FILE* will find FILE-NAME, FILETYPE, and FILES. If you use ? in place of a single character, searching for FILE? will find only FILES.

Finding Files

Locating a specific file can sometimes be difficult, especially if you have a large drive or several drives to search. Fortunately, Windows includes a Find utility to search through a drive for you.

Click the **Start** button, select **Find**, then select **Files or Folders**. When the Find dialog box appears, select the drive you want to search or the drive and folder you want to search. Enter the name of the file or folder you want and click the **Find Now** button. When the search is complete, the dialog box expands to display any matching files or folders. You can open, move, copy, or delete any files listed.

Naming Conventions

Windows 95 and Windows 98 allow folder and filenames to include up to 256 characters—including many special characters. Some special characters, however, are "illegal," meaning that you *can't* use them in folder or filenames. Illegal characters include the following:

\ / : * ? " < > |.

If you need to share a long filename file with someone who does *not* have Windows 95 or Windows 98, you have two options. (1) Rename the file to the older 8.3 convention. (2) Let Windows rename the file for you; it will keep the first six characters, then add a "~x," where x is a number that keeps track of multiple files with the same first six characters. (If you want to see what a long filename looks like to non-Windows 95/98 users, open the MS-DOS box and issue the DIR command; this will list files in their 8.3 versions.)

You Can't View *Everything*...

Windows does not include viewers for all file types. If the Quick View option—or, for some graphics file types, a *Preview* option—does not appear on the pop-up menu, no viewer is available for that particular file type.

Renaming Files and Folders

File and folder names should ideally describe the contents of the file or folder. Sometimes, however, the contents may change or the file or folder may contain a revision number that needs updating. If you have a file or folder with a name that just isn't right, you can rename it.

Just locate the file or folder you want to rename. Right-click the file or folder icon, and choose **Rename** from the pop-up menu; the filename is now highlighted. Type a new name for your folder (which overwrites the current name) and press **Enter**.

When you rename a file, however, avoid changing its extension—you could mess up the file's association and perhaps make it unreadable by some applications.

Unprotecting Read-Only Files

If you have a file that you want to edit or delete but you can't, chances are the file is designated as *read-only*. Read-only files can't be changed or deleted; you can read them, but you can't touch them. If you need to edit or delete a read-only file, you need to change that file's *attributes*.

Select the file or folder you want to change and right-click its icon. Choose **Properties** from the pop-up menu and, when the Properties dialog box appears, select the **General** tab—and then select or deselect the desired attributes. For example, to make a read-only file editable, deselect the **Read-only** check box. After you've made the desired changes, click the **OK** button.

Previewing Files with Quick View

If you would like to view the contents of a file—but you don't want to wait for the associated application to launch—you can take advantage of Quick View. Quick View is a special viewing utility that lets you see the contents of a file from within My Computer or Windows Explorer.

To "quick view" a file, select the file (in either My Computer or Windows Explorer), right-click the file's icon, then choose **Quick View** from the pop-up menu. This will start the viewer, in which you can look at the contents of the file. If it is a file you want to edit, click the associated application icon on the left side of the toolbar.

Working with File Types

As you use My Computer and Windows Explorer to browse files and folders, you'll notice that some files have specific icons. These icons let you know what *type* the file is.

The file type determines more than just the icon, however; it also determines the description you see if you look at the file's details and the application that will be used to open the file. (This is called the *file association*.) Windows also uses the characters in the extension of a filename (the characters to the right of the period in the filename) to determine a file's file type.

Note that, depending on how you have Windows configured, file extensions may not be visible when you look at files with My Computer or Windows Explorer. To display all file extensions, click the **Start** button, select **Settings**, then select **Folder Options**. When the Folder Options dialog box appears, select the **View** tab and *uncheck* **Hide File Extensions for Known File Types**. Click **OK** to register this new setting.

Table 20.2 shows you some of the icons you'll encounter when you open My Computer or Windows Explorer and their corresponding file types and typical extensions.

Table 20.2   Icons and File Types

Icon	File Type and Typical Extension
	System file (.SYS)
	Configuration settings file (.INI)
	Text file (.TXT)
	Microsoft Word document file (.DOC)
	Microsoft Excel worksheet file (.XLS)
	Microsoft PowerPoint presentation file (.PPT)
	Web page file (.HTM or .HTML)
	Sound file (.WAV)
	MIDI music file (.MID)

continues

Table 20.2 CONTINUED

Icon	File Type and Typical Extension
	Bitmap image file (.BMP)
	TrueType font file (.TTF)
	System font file (.FON)
	Help file (.HLP)
	MS-DOS application (.EXE)
	Unknown file type (or has no extension)

Displaying or Hiding File Types

Windows has the capability to *not* display files of a certain type—such as sensitive system files. Because you don't want to accidentally delete or change a system file, hiding them can be a good idea. You may, however, need to edit a system file, so you should know how to unhide the files.

Click the **Start** menu, select **Settings**, and then select **Folder Options**. When the Folders dialog box appears, select the **View** tab and double-click the **Hidden Files** icon to expand this section. (If the section is already expanded—if the three options below the folder are visible—you don't need to double-click the icon.) If you want to see hidden files, select **Show All Files**. If you don't want system files displayed, select **Do Not Show Hidden or System Files**. Click **OK** to register your changes.

The Default Is Bold

The default action for a file type appears as bold in the **Actions** list when you edit the file type. You can change the default action by selecting the new default action in the **Action** list and clicking the **Set Default** button.

Associating a File Type with an Application

When you install a new application, it usually registers its file types automatically—that is, Windows associates that file type with a specific application. If you create files with custom or special extensions, however, you need to register these special extensions as a file type.

When you associate a file type with a particular program, you also designate the *actions* that are performed on the file—whether the file can be opened or edited, and so forth. You can have more than one action for any particular file type. These actions will all be displayed when you right-click a file of the registered type; the action that will be performed when you click the file is the *default* action.

To associate a file type with an application, begin by clicking the **Start** menu, selecting **Settings**, and then selecting **Folder Options**. When the Folders dialog box appears, select the **File Types** tab, and click the **New Type** button. Enter any comments about the file type in the **Description of Type** text box, the file type's extension in the **Associated Extension** text box, and the content type, if applicable, in the **Content Type** box. (It's okay to leave all but the **Associated Extension** box blank.) Now click the **New** button under the **Actions** list. Enter an action (open, edit, close, and so on) into the **Action** box, and then enter the path and program file used to perform this action into the **Application Used to Perform Action** box. (You can also click the **Browse** button to select the application.) Click the **OK** button when you've finished.

Removing File Types

If you have file types registered that don't even exist on your system (due to uninstalling a particular program), or if you want to delete the current registration and start again, you can remove the file type from Windows.

Note, however, that deleting a file type does not delete any files with that extension from your system. When you delete a file type, all you do is remove the association between that file extension and the corresponding application.

Begin by clicking the **Start** menu, selecting **Settings**, and then selecting **Folder Options**. When the Folders dialog box appears, select the **File Types** tab. Choose the file type you want to remove from the **Registered File Types** list and click the **Remove** button.

When Files Get Vile

Many things can go wrong with files, but, fortunately, you can prevent most of the problems yourself. (This is mainly because you cause most of the problems in the first place!)

What file problems might you encounter? Let's see... You can accidentally delete a file you really didn't want deleted, or you can inadvertently copy one file over another existing file, which erases the latter. (There's not much you can do about this one, I'm afraid.) In fact, if you try hard enough, you can even sabotage your entire hard disk by using Windows file commands incorrectly. (Scary thought, isn't it?)

But before you become too frightened to use My Computer or Windows Explorer at all, take heart in the knowledge that Windows normally gives you ample warning (in the form of an onscreen message) before it carries out most of these commands. If you heed the onscreen warning, you can halt any such operation before it destroys your files.

Know also that hard disk problems can inflict severe damage on your files. Bad sectors on a hard disk, for example, can scramble the data in affected files, making them unreadable. And, of course, computer viruses can cause the same type of damage to your files—and in many cases, even worse. Because all your efforts at your computer depend on the integrity of your files, it's imperative that you understand how fragile their existence can be.

But don't worry—many ways exist for you to protect your files from potential catastrophes. That's why you bought this book, isn't it?

What to Do When You Have File Problems

Most file problems are caused by you. Either you mistype something, or click the wrong item, or use the wrong command, or just plain mess up an operation. The most important information you need to know about file problems, then, is how to recover from your own mistakes!

Problem 1:

You accidentally deleted an important file

Deleting an important file can be one of the most disconcerting errors you will make in the course of using your computer. How could you do that?

In Windows 95 and Windows 98, all deleted files are temporarily stored in the Recycle Bin. To undelete a file in the Recycle Bin, select the **Recycle Bin** icon on your desktop, then when the Recycle Bin window opens, right-click the item you want to undelete and select **Restore** from the pop-up menu.

If a file has been "permanently" deleted from the Recycle Bin, there still might be a way to bring the missing file back from the dead. You see, just because a file isn't accessible doesn't mean that it's been physically deleted from your hard disk. In fact, all deleted files continue to reside on your hard disk, although all reference to the data in the file allocation table (FAT) has been removed—at least until the reference data has been overwritten by newer data. There are several third-party programs—including Norton Utilities, my favorite—that include special "undelete" utilities. These utilities will recover any existing data from the FAT and thus "restore" the deleted file back to your hard disk.

Prior to Windows 95, Windows itself contained an undelete utility. If you're still running Windows 3.1 (or have upgraded from Windows 3.1 on your current PC), you can access this utility by opening the Microsoft Tools program group and double-clicking on the **Microsoft Undelete for Windows** icon. When Microsoft Undelete launches, select the drive and directory where the undeleted file resides (by clicking on the **Drive/Dir** button), and click on the file to be undeleted. When you click on the **Undelete** button, you'll be asked to enter the first character of the file (shown as a "?"). Do so, and click **OK**. Your deleted file will now be automatically undeleted!

Prior to Windows, the Microsoft DOS operating system (versions 5 and 6) also contained an undelete utility. If your system is *really* old, you may still have this utility somewhere on your hard disk. You use this utility by opening a DOS window, changing to the directory where you deleted the file, then typing **UNDELETE** and pressing **Enter**. When you issue this command, DOS attempts to undelete all previously deleted files in the current directory. (You can specify a particular file to undelete by typing the path and filename after the main command, like this: **UNDELETE C:\DIR01\FILENAME.EXT**.)

Problem 2:

You can't find a file

Is it possible to actually lose a file on your hard disk? Of course it is. When you have thousands of different files in dozens of different directories and subdirectories, you can easily forget where you stashed a certain file.

Windows makes it easy to find specific files, however. Just click the **Start** button, select **Find**, then select **Files or Folders**. When the Find dialog box appears, enter all or part of the filename in the **Named** box, select the drive(s) you want to search from the **Look In** pull-down list, make sure **Include Subfolders** is checked, then click the **Find Now** button. Windows will now return a list of files that match your search parameters.

If this doesn't find the file you're looking for, the file may actually be on another disk (maybe on a diskette instead of your hard disk), or you may have accidentally deleted the file. To look for a possibly deleted file, just open the Recycle Bin; any files you find here can be undeleted, following the steps outlined in Problem 1.

Problem 3:

You can't tell which is the most recent copy of a file

You find two files with the same name on your hard disk (in different folders, of course). Which is the newer file? The answer is simple—look at the date and time the file was last edited.

If you're using Windows 98 and have **View As Web Page** enabled, selecting the file in My Computer or Windows Explorer will display the date and time the file was last modified. You can also display this (and more) information by right-clicking the file's icon and selecting **Properties** from the pop-up menu.

Problem 4:

You can't delete a file

You tried to delete a file, but it won't delete. This problem can occur for one of three reasons:

➤ The file is currently in use by another program. Try closing that program and then deleting the file.

➤ You're trying to delete a file from a diskette that is write-protected. If you're trying to delete a file on a 3 1/2-inch diskette, slide the tab in the lower-left corner so that the hole is closed, then try the procedure again.

243

➤ The attributes of the file have been set so that you can't delete it. Every file has multiple attributes; one such attribute makes a file read-only, meaning that you can't delete it or write to it. To change a file's attributes, right-click the file in My Computer or Windows Explorer and select **Properties** from the pop-up menu. When the Properties dialog box appears, uncheck the **Read-Only** attribute, then click **OK**.

Problem 5:

You try to access a file and find that its data is scrambled or incomplete

Scrambled data can be caused by a number of factors. The most likely reason is that you accidentally rebooted or turned off your system while that file was being accessed, causing the file to become corrupted. Another cause for scrambled data is a bug in a software program or a computer virus. Whatever the cause, you can't do much about it—once data is scrambled, it's scrambled.

Restoring Those Scrambled Programs

Of course, if a program file gets scrambled, you can always reinstall the program from your program's original installation CD or diskettes.

It's possible that your data isn't *really* scrambled, however. If you try using an old version of a software program to open a document saved with a *newer* version of that program, it may appear (from within the old version of the program) that the file is scrambled. In reality, the file is fine, it's just saved in a format that your version of the program can't read. Make sure you're using the newest version of a program—or that someone saves the file in question "down" to an older version, for compatibility.

If you have a backup copy of the data on another disk (or on a backup disk) you can always use that copy to replace your scrambled copy. See Chapter 8, "Recovering When "The Big One" Hits," for more information on restoring backup data.

Problem 6:

You attempt a file operation and get a Windows error message

Windows error messages often appear to let you know that you incorrectly typed something, so if you get such a message, the first action is always to try the operation again, typing more carefully this time. However, even when you type it correctly, you can still get error messages. Chapter 28, "Windows Error Messages...What They Mean and How to Deal with Them," gives a more complete listing of error messages; Table 20.3 presents those you're most likely to encounter when working with files.

Table 20.3   Windows File-Related Error Messages

Error Message	Probable Cause and Solution
`Cannot find file`	The most common cause for this message is that the file in question is either missing or corrupted. Use the **Find** command to search for the file; reinstall the file in question if necessary.
`Cannot read from drive x`	Windows is looking for a file on drive *x:* (probably drive A) and there isn't a diskette in the drive. Insert any diskette to end the Windows look loop. If a diskette *is* in drive *x:* and you get this error message, you either have a bad (or unformatted) diskette, or something wrong with your diskette drive.
`Folder xxx does not exist`	You have specified a folder that does not exist. Check the spelling of the folder and pathname. You might also try pulling down the **View** menu and selecting **Refresh** to refresh the file/folder display.
`File already exists. Overwrite?`	You're trying to create or save a file with a name that already exists. Windows is asking if you want to overwrite the existing file. If so, answer yes. If no, answer no, and assign a new name to your file.
`File is missing`	When Windows loads, it tries to load any programs that are included in the StartUp folder. This message is generated when one of these files no longer exists or has been entered incorrectly. Use My Computer or Windows Explorer to open the **StartUp** folder and check all programs and associations, removing or editing those that are not correct.
`Not a valid filename`	You typed an invalid filename. Try again.
`The specified path is invalid`	You typed an incorrect path for a file operation. Check the path and retype the command.
`Write protected disk`	You're trying to perform a file operation on a diskette that is write protected. Change diskettes, or slide the write-protect tab into the down position (on 3 1/2" diskettes).

10 Do's and Don'ts for File Management

1. *Do* create a toolbar for My Computer on your desktop (in Windows 98 only) by dragging the My Computer icon to one side of your screen and then releasing your mouse button. This places all the contents of My Computer on your desktop, all the time.

2. *Don't* accept the default font in Windows Explorer. To change Explorer's font, right-click on the desktop to open the Display Properties dialog box; select the **Appearance** tab, select **Icon** from the **Item** list, and then select a new font or font size.

3. *Do* hold down the **Shift** key in My Computer or Windows Explorer to select multiple contiguous files—more than one file, all in a row. Hold down the **Ctrl** key in My Computer or Windows Explorer to select multiple non-contiguous files (more than one file *not* in a row).

4. *Don't* forget whether you're copying or moving or whatever when dragging and dropping; hold down your right mouse button when dragging and dropping and you'll see a pop-up menu of choices when you release your mouse button.

5. *Do* create a desktop shortcut for Windows Explorer so it's always on your desktop, too.

6. *Don't* let others see files you've deleted (especially if they're private files you want to *keep* private)—remember that the Recycle Bin holds copies of all deleted files for several days. If a file is truly private, empty the Recycle Bin before anyone else can take a peek—or use **Shift+Del** to bypass the Recycle Bin and permanently delete the file.

7. *Do* use the **Send To** option on most pop-up menus to automatically copy files to selected devices or locations.

8. *Don't* turn off your computer while you're in the middle of a file operation; the data will probably get scrambled.

9. *Do* use wildcards (such as * and ?) when you're searching for a file and you don't know the exact filename.

10. *Don't* use any of the following illegal characters when naming a file:

    + = / [ ] ' : ; , ? * \ < > |.

The Least You Need to Know

➤ There are multiple ways to perform most file-related operations in Windows 95 and Windows 98—when in doubt, just highlight the file, right-click your mouse, and choose an option from the pop-up menu.

➤ File types must be associated with applications in order to launch an application by selecting a specific file.

➤ Files you delete from your hard drive are temporarily stored in Windows' Recycle Bin; you can *undelete* files as long as they're still in the Bin.

Chapter 21

What to Do When... Your Software Is Hard to Use

In This Chapter

➤ Find out five ways to launch programs and six ways to close them

➤ Learn how to associate file types with specific applications

➤ Discover how to find and fix software-related problems

Hardware is important. No doubt about it.

Hardware by itself is nothing more than a collection of useless chips and transistors inside a fairly ugly off-white case, topped off by a blank, unstaring picture tube. Even though hardware is important, it's not much at all without software. Software, after all, makes your computer go.

So let's get going and figure out what kinds of problems you can encounter with your software...and how you can fix 'em!

What You Need to Know About Software

Software is a part of your system that you can't touch directly. Software comes in a package and is encoded on CDs or diskettes. In most cases you transfer the program files from the CD/diskette to your hard disk, where your computer can access them and load them into its system memory. You interact with the programs with your keyboard and mouse, and you follow your progress on the computer screen. When you're done, you can print out the results on your printer. Put simply, software is how you get stuff done. Without software applications, you wouldn't have any need for your keyboard, your mouse, your monitor—or anything else that makes up your computer system.

Five Ways to Launch a Windows Application

When you install a Windows-compatible program, a shortcut to that program is automatically created on the **Start** menu—most often in the **Programs** menu. Some programs automatically create a desktop shortcut during installation, as well.

Assuming that you have both **Start** menu shortcuts and desktop shortcuts to your program, there are five ways you can launch a Windows-compatible program from within Windows:

➤ **The Run menu method**   Click the **Start** button and select **Run**. When the Run dialog box appears, type the path and name of the file you want to launch (or click the **Browse** button to search for the file), and then click **OK**.

➤ **The My Computer/Windows Explorer method**   Launch either My Computer or Windows Explorer and find the file you want to launch. Click the file to launch the program.

➤ **The desktop shortcut method**   If the program created a desktop shortcut during installation, all you have to do to launch the program is click on the shortcut icon. (To create a desktop shortcut for this program, use My Computer or Windows Explorer to find the file you want to launch, and then right-click on the file and—when the pop-up menu appears—select **Send To**, and then select **Desktop as Shortcut**.)

➤ **The Start menu shortcut method**   Assuming the program created a shortcut on the Start or Programs menu during installation, all you have to do to launch the program is click on the menu item. (To add a menu item for this program, open **My Computer** or **Windows Explorer** to find the file you want to launch, and then drag the file and drop it on the **Start** button; a menu item for this program will now appear at the top of the Start menu.)

➤ **The "launching a document" method**   If you open **My Computer** or **Windows Explorer** and click on a document associated with a program (for example, .DOC files are associated with Microsoft Word; .XLS files are associated with Microsoft Excel), the associated program will be launched with the selected document open.

Six Ways to Properly Exit a Windows Application

After you've finished using a Windows-compatible application, there are six ways you can close the application:

➤ **The close window method**   Click the **X** button in the window's upper-right corner.

➤ **The Control Menu method 1**   Double-click the icon in the window's upper-left corner (the **Control Menu** button).

➤ **The Control Menu method 2**   Click the icon in the window's upper-left corner (the **Control Menu** button), and then select **Close** from the drop-down menu.

➤ **The File menu method**   Pull down the application's **File** menu, and then select **Exit**.

➤ **The taskbar button method**   Right-click the window's **Taskbar** button and choose **Close**.

➤ **The shortcut key method**   From within the application, press **Alt+F4**.

There is also a seventh method, not typically recommended: the "emergency shutdown" method. You only use this method if the program fails to close using one of the normal methods—press **Ctrl+Alt+Del**, and when the Close Program dialog box appears, select the program in question and click **End Task**. Closing programs in this fashion can make your system unstable, so you should reboot your computer if you have to close a program this way.

Five Ways to Switch Between Windows Applications

When multiple applications are open, you can determine which is the currently active window by the color of its title bar—the title bar for the active application is usually brighter than that of an inactive application. If applications are overlapped on your desktop, the active one is on top. Also, the active window's Taskbar button appears lighter and looks like it is pressed in.

If you have multiple applications open, there are five ways to switch between applications:

➤ **The taskbar button method 1**
Click the application's Taskbar button.

➤ **The taskbar button method 2**
Press **Windows+Tab** to switch from one Taskbar button to another; press **Enter** to actually switch to the selected application. (The Windows key is the special key on newer Windows-compatible keyboards that has the Windows logo on it.)

Save Before You Close!

If you attempt to close an application window without saving a document, the application will warn you and give you an opportunity to save the document. You must choose to save or not save the document before the application window will close.

➤ **The title bar method**   Click the application's title bar. (This method only works if the application's title bar is visible on your desktop!)

➤ **The "open real estate" method**   Click almost any other part of the window that is visible. (Again, it has to be visible; this method doesn't work if the window is hidden.)

➤ **The shortcut key method**   This is the method I use, by the way. Hold down the **Alt** key and then press the **Tab** key repeatedly until the application window you want is selected. (This cycles through all open windows.) When you're at the window you want, as shown in the little dialog box in the middle of the desktop, release the **Alt** key.

Note, however, that if you run too many applications at the same time you may run into some performance problems; your computer may not possess enough memory to run all the programs you want at one time. It's also possible that two or more programs running simultaneously may attempt to use the same memory space, resulting in memory conflicts. If you frequently run up against these types of problems, try running fewer programs at the same time.

Things That Can Go Wrong with Your Windows Software

In addition to memory conflicts, you can experience several other problems with your software, such as:

➤ The program may not be compatible with your version of Windows.

➤ The program may not be configured correctly for your system and existing peripherals.

➤ The program may have system-performance requirements that your system doesn't provide or require components your system doesn't incorporate.

➤ The program itself may contain bugs that keep it from operating correctly—or may not have all its components installed on your system.

➤ And finally, you just may not know how to operate your software. (Really!)

Any of these problems can be darned annoying. Read on for hints on how to drastically reduce your annoyance level.

What to Do When You Have Software Problems

It's impossible in the course of a few pages to discuss everything that can go wrong with every software package currently available—so I'm not even going to try. Instead, I'll simply examine a few common problems shared by all software programs.

Problem 1:

Your software doesn't work

Several factors can cause a Windows application to refuse to run:

➤ The program may not be compatible with your version of Windows. Some Windows 3.0 and 3.1 programs are incompatible with Windows 95 and Windows 98. If a Windows 3.x application won't run and gives you a General Protection Fault error message, you probably have an incompatible program. You'll need to upgrade this software to a Windows 95 or Windows 98 version.

➤ Your system may not have enough memory available to run the program. Try closing other Windows applications before you start this one, or try adding more memory to your system.

➤ Your computer may not have enough disk space to run the program. Windows employs extra disk space as virtual memory. If there isn't enough free disk space available, you may not be able to run some programs. Try deleting unused files from your hard disk before you restart the program.

If you can't get a certain program to run, first make sure that the program is referenced properly from the menu item or icon you selected. Right-click on the item or icon and select **Properties** from the pop-up menu; when the Properties dialog box appears (see the figure) select the **Shortcut** tab and note the file and path entered in the **Target** box. Now use My Computer or Windows Explorer to go to that location, and confirm that the target file actually is where it's supposed to be. If the target file *isn't* there, use the **Find** command to find the file, and then enter the correct location in the shortcut's **Target** box.

Use the Properties dialog box to make sure the right target file is referenced by any given shortcut.

If the file is where it's supposed to be but doesn't launch when selected, exit Windows, restart your computer, and try launching the program again. This "fixes" your problem quite often, surprisingly.

If your program still doesn't launch, check to ensure that the program is installed correctly. If you have your doubts, uninstall the program (by selecting the **Add/Remove Programs** icon from the Windows **Control Panel**) and then reinstall it. (You'd be surprised how many problems get solved by reinstalling the software!)

You should also be certain that this particular program is compatible with your computer's particular hardware configuration. Your machine may need more memory, a faster microprocessor, or a higher-resolution video card before your finicky new program consents to run on it.

If all else fails, consult the instruction manual or Web site for this particular piece of software, or call the software publisher's technical support line.

Problem 2:

Your software crashes or freezes

Everything works fine, but then—all of a sudden—your software bombs! Fortunately, Windows 95 and Windows 98 are relatively safe environments; when an individual application crashes or freezes, it seldom messes up your entire system. You can use a special command to close the problem application without affecting other Windows programs.

When a Windows application blows up, follow these steps:

1. Press **Ctrl+Alt+Del**.

2. When the Close Program dialog box appears, select the application that is frozen from the list, and then click **End Task**. (It probably has the words [not responding] next to it.)

3. After a few seconds, a Wait/Shutdown window appears; confirm that you want to shut down the selected application.

4. Click the **End Task** button.

Is It Safe?

Even though you can continue working in Windows after an application freezes, it is safer to close all remaining applications, exit Windows, and then restart your computer. This will protect you just in case Windows has become unstable due to the application problem.

This will close the offending application and let you continue your work in Windows.

Unfortunately, programs sometimes crash with annoying frequency in Windows. The causes are myriad and often difficult to pin down. They include the following:

➤ Your system may have run out of memory. Try running the program while no other Windows programs are running, or add more memory to your system.

➤ The program may be getting caught in a memory conflict with another Windows program. Try running the program by itself.

➤ The program may be an older version that's incompatible with your version of Windows. Upgrade the program to its latest version.

➤ Windows was just feeling cantankerous. Start the program again and hope for the best.

➤ You have a bug in your software—or even a corrupted program file. If nothing else pans out, try reinstalling your program from scratch. If this doesn't fix the problem, call the knowledgeable folks at the software publisher's technical support line for assistance. After all, that's what they're there for.

If you have multiple applications that crash on a regular basis, the situation probably can be attributed to insufficient memory. See your computer dealer about adding more RAM to your system.

Problem 3:

You can't launch a document file

The number one cause for this problem is that the file is no longer where it was—or where Windows thinks it is. For example, if you've deleted or moved a file, the filename can still appear in the Documents menu (off the Start menu); clicking the filename for this deleted file will simply result in an error message.

It's also possible that the document file type is not associated with a program type. When you select a document file, it should launch the associated program, with the selected document pre-loaded. It's possible that, however, Windows may display the Open With dialog box, or a dialog box with this message:

Taking Advice

When you call a software manufacturer's technical support line, be prepared for their questions. Have all pertinent information about your program handy, including which version you're using. Also be prepared to answer questions about your system setup—what kind of PC you have, what peripherals you have hooked up, and so on. And finally, be prepared to jot down any instructions they give you for future use. The folks on these lines can be really helpful—if you give them a little help, too!

```
Cannot Run Program
No application is associated with
this file.
Choose Associate from the File menu
to create an association.
```

If you see the Open With dialog box, select an application to associate with the file, check **Always Use This Program to Open This File**, and click **OK**.

If you receive the error message, that means you need to manually create an association for the particular document type at hand. Start by clicking the **Start** menu, selecting **Settings**, and then selecting **Folder Options**. When the Folders dialog box appears, select the **File Types** tab, and click the **New Type** button. Enter any comments about the file type in the **Description of Type** text box, the file type's extension in the **Associated Extension** text box, and the content type, if applicable, in the Content Type box. Now click the **New Button** under the **Actions** list. Enter an action (open, edit, close, and so on) into the **Action** box, and then enter the path and program file used to perform this action into the **Application Used to Perform Action** box. Click the **OK** button when you've finished.

If you still can't launch the file, something is probably screwy with the program file itself.

Problem 4:

You can't open certain types of files in a specific application

Most applications let you import a variety of different file types, in addition to their native file types. (For example, Microsoft Word's native file type is .DOC, but you can also import HTML files and plain text files and even WordPerfect files.) Obviously,

253

not every program can import every type of file, but chances are an *import filter* exists for the file type you're trying to import. If you can't find the file type you're trying to import listed in your application's Open dialog box, try reinstalling the program and choosing a *custom* installation. You should find a list of filters or *converters* available; make sure you select to install import filters for all file types you may be importing.

Problem 5:

You have trouble running certain DOS applications under Windows

First, a question: Why are you still running that old DOS program, anyway? Are you a member of some historical preservation society or something?

Now that I have that off my chest (sorry...), it's worth pointing out that Windows 95 and Windows 98 really weren't designed with DOS programs in mind. Oh, they'll run those old programs (sometimes!), but not without a bit of work—and a lot of problems.

There are a number of reasons why you might not be able to load a particular DOS program, including:

➤ The program may not be compatible with your version of Windows. There are some types of DOS programs that just won't run under Windows because they need full control of your system to do their job. These programs—which include "disk doctor" and anti-virus programs—simply shouldn't be used under Windows.

➤ Your computer may not have enough memory available to run the program. Try closing any other open programs, and then restart the DOS program. Examine the program's configuration settings, with particular attention to memory-related settings.

➤ You may be running the program in a window when it needs to run full screen. Change the program's configuration settings so that it always runs in full-screen mode.

If you can start a DOS program but it then freezes or crashes on you, you probably need to check the configuration of the DOS program. Many DOS programs simply don't run well in Windows and require a special configuration—of memory, or display properties—to work at all.

To configure the way a DOS program runs within Windows, open **My Computer** or **Windows Explorer**, find the DOS program file (typically with an .EXE extension), right-click the file icon, and select **Properties** from the pop-up menu. When the Properties dialog box appears, make the appropriate changes on the **Font**, **Memory**, **Screen**, and **Misc** tabs.

10 Do's and Don'ts for Software

1. *Do* use the most up-to-date version of a software program; if you need to upgrade, then *upgrade!*

2. *Don't* expect your software to read your mind; make sure *you* read all the instructions and documentation so you can tell the program to do what you want it to do.

3. *Do* keep your original software CD or diskettes and documentation in a safe place for future reference.

4. *Don't* attempt to run multiple copies of the same software at one time; you're just asking for trouble.

5. *Do* visit the software manufacturer's Web site to see if there are any recent updates or bug fixes you should download and install.

6. *Don't* pirate software; if you're using a program, pay for it. It's the right thing to do.

7. *Do* install and configure your software correctly for your specific system's setup.

8. *Don't* forget to read the README files included with most packages before installation.

9. *Do* buy a Que book for each software package you own—two, or three, if you can afford them!

10. *Don't* run old DOS programs in Windows unless you really have to; if a Windows version exists, get it!

The Least You Need to Know

➤ There are numerous ways to open and close software programs; make sure you close your applications properly, to avoid losing unsaved data.

➤ If a program freezes, press **Ctrl+Alt+Del** to manually shut down the frozen program.

➤ File types must be associated with a particular application if you want to launch the application by clicking a document file.

Chapter 22

What to Do When... Your New Software Causes New Problems

In This Chapter

➤ Learn the right ways to install—and *uninstall*—software programs in Windows

➤ Find out how to install Windows components that weren't installed automatically when you first installed Windows

➤ Discover how to find and fix problems caused when you upgrade your software

---

The only thing worse than trying to get your existing software to work right is getting *new* software to work right! When you install new software on your system—even if it's just a new version of a current program—you introduce the opportunity for lots of *new problems*!

Things to Do *Before* You Upgrade Your Software

Before you install any program, there are a few precautions you should take.

First, make sure you back up important data on your hard disk—*particularly* the data files associated with any programs you may be upgrading. (You'll remember how to back up your hard disk from Chapter 7, "Preparing a PC Survival Kit," of course.)

Next, make copies of your key system files, either to a diskette or to a "safe" directory on your hard disk. New programs will often rewrite these files, so it's nice to have copies you can return to in case the installation goes south. I recommend you make copies of these files, found in either your root folder or the **\windows** folder:

➤ AUTOEXEC.BAT
➤ CONFIG.SYS

➤ SYSTEM.DAT

➤ SYSTEM.INI

➤ USER.DAT

➤ WIN.INI

Recovering from a Bad Installation

If your new software installation, for whatever reason, doesn't work out right, the first thing to do is to copy these "saved" files back to their original locations.

Not All Programs Are Compatible

Not all older programs will run successfully with newer versions of Windows. If you're running Windows 98, a list of programs with known incompatibility problems with Windows 98 is found in the PROGRAMS.TXT file in the \windows folder.

Finally, be sure to read all the instructions for the new software, including some special documentation that you will normally find tucked away on the software's installation CD or diskette. This last-minute documentation often is contained in a file named README, README.TXT, or READ.ME. These files (normally in plain-text format, so you can read them with Notepad or WordPad) contain information about the program that cropped up *after* the printed documentation was completed. You often discover a few last-minute installation instructions in these files, as well as information on any known bugs in the software.

It also doesn't hurt to visit the software publisher's Web site. Even more up-to-date information can sometimes be found there, along with recent patches or updates you can download to your system.

Installing New Software Programs

Installing a new Windows application is as easy as running the automated Setup or installation program included with most programs. When you insert the installation CD for a new program in your CD-ROM drive, the Setup program should start automatically; just follow the instructions onscreen to complete the installation. If it doesn't start automatically, you'll have to launch the Setup program manually; just click the **Start** button, select **Run**, type *x:***setup** (or *x:***install**, if that doesn't work) in the Run dialog box (where *x* is the letter of your CD-ROM drive), and then click **OK**.

If you're installing from 3.5-inch diskettes, you launch the Setup program by inserting the first diskette into your diskette drive, clicking the **Start** button, selecting **Run**, typing **a:****setup** in the Run dialog box, and then clicking **OK**.

If the program you're installing doesn't have an automated Setup program, or if you prefer to install a new program manually, you can run Windows 98's Install Programs Wizard. You launch this wizard by selecting the **Add/Remove Programs** icon from the Windows **Control Panel**, and then selecting the **Install/Uninstall** tab, clicking **Install**, and following the wizard's onscreen instructions.

Uninstalling Software—the Right Way

Removing a Windows application can be easy—or it can be complicated. Most newer Windows programs include their own utilities to uninstall the program automatically. You should use this publisher-supplied utility, if it exists, to uninstall the program. You can generally find the program's uninstall utility in the folder where the program's other files reside.

If you want to remove a Windows application that doesn't include its own uninstall utility, the process has been simplified with the addition of the Add/Remove Programs Properties utility (shown here), accessible from the Windows **Control Panel**. This built-in utility identifies every component of the application you want to remove and deletes them from your hard disk automatically. All you have to do is highlight the program you want to remove, and then click the **Add/Remove** button; the rest of the uninstallation is done automatically.

Don't Uninstall the Data Files!

An uninstall program should *not* remove your personal files, even if they are stored in the application's folders. The files deleted during the automatic uninstall are not moved to the Recycle Bin. Just to be safe, however, you should move files you want to keep to a new folder before removing the application.

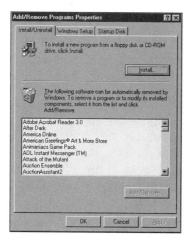

The right way to delete programs—the Add/Remove Programs Properties utility.

Note, however, that only applications that provide uninstall programs appear in the list for removal. If the Windows program you want to remove does *not* have an automatic uninstall utility, you have to delete the files for the program manually, using My Computer or Windows Explorer. The problem with this method is that miscellaneous files associated with the program are often scattered throughout various folders on your hard disk; you may want to purchase a third-party uninstall program to find and remove all program remnants from your system.

Upgrading Your Windows Installation

When you first install Windows (or if you bought a new PC with Windows pre-installed), the most-used components are automatically installed by default. There are other Windows components, however, that are available for installation on your system. As long as you have your original Windows installation CD, you can add these extra components to your system at any time in the future.

What's Installed—and What's Not

In the Windows **Setup Components** list box, a check mark next to an item indicates that the component is already installed on your system. If the check box is gray with a check mark in it, one or more subcomponents are installed. If there is no check mark, the item is not installed. You can install all or part of the unchecked items and their components.

Use the Add/Remove Programs utility (found in the Windows Control Panel) to add any uninstalled Windows components—and to remove any previously installed components. From the Add/Remove Programs Properties dialog box, select the **Windows Setup** tab, and then select the component you want to add or remove from the **Components** list. (Click the name, not the check box.) The **Description** box near the bottom of the dialog box displays a description and the number of components that are selected. If the component you selected has subcomponents, click the **Details** button to view the subcomponents. Choose **OK** to confirm changes on subcomponent selections. When you have finished selecting components and subcomponents, choose **OK** in the Add/Remove Programs Properties dialog box. If prompted, insert your original Windows installation CD; you also may be prompted to restart your computer to complete the installation.

In addition to the uninstalled Windows components discussed previously, there are also some uninstalled components in Windows 98 that Microsoft doesn't tell you about. These are called *unlisted* components because they're not listed in the **Components** list in the **Windows Setup** page of the Add/Remove Programs Properties dialog box. The best way to discover unlisted components is to browse your Windows 98 installation CD for .INF files.

To install an unlisted component, open the **Add/Remove Programs Properties** dialog box, select the **Windows Setup** tab, and then click the **Have Disk** button. In the **Copy Manufacturer's Files From** box, type the path to the setup information file (.INF file) for the Windows component that you want to install. (Choose **Browse** if you need to look for the file, of course.) In the Have Disk dialog box, select the items you want to install from the **Components** list, and then choose **Install** and click **OK** to install the component.

New Things That Can Go Wrong

You might think that the easiest program installation would be an upgrade for an existing program. Of course, you would be wrong.

The list of things that can go wrong with a software upgrade is only slightly longer than the list of what can go wrong with a new installation:

➤ The new program may have a different name or extension, or may reside in a different directory, so that existing shortcuts might not launch the new version.

➤ The new program may be configured differently than the old version for your system.

➤ The new program may have system-performance requirements different from the old version, and your system may not be compatible or sufficient anymore. (You can bet that new versions of old programs will require more disk space and more memory—without fail!)

➤ The new program's installation procedure may alter your system files in such a way that the operation of other programs is adversely affected.

➤ The upgrade may not accept data files created with the older version.

➤ As usual, the program itself may contain bugs that keep it from operating correctly.

➤ And, finally, you just may not know how to operate the new software— especially if it's radically different from the old version.

And you thought upgrading an existing program would be simple!

What to Do When You Have Upgrade Problems

In addition to the normal software problems discussed in Chapter 21, "What to Do When...Your Software Is Hard to Use," take a look at these potential problems that can happen when you add *new* software to your system.

Problem 1:

You installed new software, and now your other programs don't work

New programs can affect the way older programs work—and never for the better. If you've recently installed a new program and can't get existing programs to run correctly (or run at all), you should check all relevant points of configuration, including your printer, your keyboard, your mouse, and your display. It's not uncommon for a new program to seize control of your system components and configure them the way *it* wants them configured, your previous configuration be damned! If this happens, you'll have to go back and manually put things back the way they were.

It's possible, too, that the new program has introduced a memory conflict with an existing program. If only one of your older programs is affected, it's relatively easy to isolate the problem. If several programs are affected, however, the problem may be more widespread. Unfortunately, such multiple-program conflicts are the most difficult problems to diagnose and solve; you may have to call in professional help on this one.

Problem 2:

After installing the new version, you can't use (or find) the pre-upgrade version of your software

This is normal. In most cases, the upgrade is installed *over* the old version of the software—meaning it just doesn't exist anymore. If you want to revert back to your old software version, you'll have to delete the new version from your hard disk and reinstall the previous version from scratch!

Of course, if you want to keep your old version around after you install the upgrade version, you'll want to install the upgrade to a *new* folder—one different from your existing program directory. In most cases, you can instruct the software installation program to install to a different directory than the default—but only if you choose the **Custom** option during the installation process.

Problem 3:

Your new software doesn't work with files from a previous version

Sometimes when you upgrade a program to its latest version, it turns out that the newer version uses a file format different from that of the older version. If so, your old files won't run in the new version. If this happens to you, check the upgrade's documentation or check with the software publisher for instructions on how to convert your older files to the new format.

Another possibility is that the new version of the program simply doesn't know where to look for your old files. Remember, just because you had configured the old version to your liking doesn't mean that the new version is using the same configuration information. Check the program's setup to make sure it knows where to look for all your files.

The Last Word on New Software

In dealing with new software problems, the main thing to keep in mind is to trace your steps. If you've installed a new program and now something else in your system refuses to work, trace your steps back to see if you can deduce how the new program may have affected your wayward software or hardware. Even if you must call in a pro to untangle things for you, this little piece of detective work can help you help your rescuer identify—and fix—the problem that much faster.

10 Do's and Don'ts for Software Upgrades

1. *Do* keep a copy of your old software, *just in case!*

2. *Don't* install the new program without making copies of your key system files—and your existing data files and documents!

3. *Do* keep both the installation CD and documentation for your new software in a safe place for future reference.

4. *Don't* attempt to run the old version and the new version of your software at the same time; your system probably won't know how to handle this.

5. *Do* allocate enough time to do the installation; a few hours might be necessary to install and tweak and troubleshoot and possibly reinstall *just in case* it doesn't work right the first time around.

6. *Don't* expect the new software to work just the same as the old version; most new versions upgrade their operations as well as their features.

7. *Do* change any appropriate system configurations necessary for the new software.

8. *Don't* forget to read the README files included with most packages before installation—and to visit the software publisher's Web site for even more current information.

9. *Do* buy a Que book for your new software version—don't expect the old Que book to work with the new software!

10. *Don't* let this new program intimidate you; most programs use a similar logic in the way they operate.

The Least You Need to Know

➤ Most Windows programs have automatic installation routines; those that don't can be installed from the Add/Remove Programs Properties dialog box.

➤ Expect new versions of old programs to require more hard disk space and system memory.

➤ When upgrading a program, back up all your old data files and documents—just in case the upgrade overwrites all your old files.

Chapter 23

What to Do When... Your Hardware Upgrade Downgrades Your System

In This Chapter

➤ Find out what you should do *before* you upgrade your computer system

➤ Learn the proper way to add new devices to your system

➤ Discover how to find and fix upgrade-related problems

For some reason, you've decided to upgrade your computer system. You want to add more memory, or a DVD drive, or a new sound card, or a bigger monitor, or...well, one or more of a dozen possible things. If you're like me, you're a little daunted by the thought of taking your system unit apart, and a trifle anxious about what sort of problems you may encounter.

As well you should be—because any time you poke around inside your computer, you're just asking for trouble!

Why Should You Upgrade Your Computer?

If your PC is more than a year old, chances are you can significantly improve its performance by upgrading one or more components. Whether you're adding more memory, moving to a larger hard disk, adding a faster modem, or changing audio or video cards, you can keep your system up-to-date without buying a completely new system.

Fortunately, Windows 95 and Windows 98 include Plug and Play technology that makes it relatively easy to add new components to your system. That isn't to say you might not run into problems; that's why Plug and Play is sometimes referred to as "plug and *pray*." However, if you're willing to take the case off your system unit and get your hands dirty, you can improve your system's performance without buying a whole new PC!

What sort of things can you upgrade on your computer system? Take a look at this list:

➤ Microprocessor chip
➤ Memory chips
➤ Video card
➤ Sound card
➤ Game controller card
➤ Hard disk drive
➤ Diskette drives
➤ Other portable storage drives (such as Zip or Jaz drives)
➤ CD-ROM and DVD drives
➤ Tape drive
➤ Modem
➤ External speakers
➤ Monitor
➤ Keyboard
➤ Mouse or other input device
➤ Joystick or other game controller
➤ Scanner
➤ Printer

In short, just about anything on your system you can unplug or unscrew, you can upgrade!

Before You Upgrade—Taking Precautions

Now, I won't even pretend to show you how to upgrade every single component in your system in this single chapter. However, I will point out some things you'll want to do *before* you upgrade, to reduce your chances of experiencing major problems!

Prepare a PC Survival Kit

I won't bore you with the details of this again. (However, if you don't mind getting a little bored, just turn back to Chapter 7, "Preparing a PC Survival Kit," for more information.) Suffice to say, you need to create a Window Emergency Startup Disk, in case you knock out your key system files while upgrading.

Back Up Your Important Data Files

Again, before you do anything major to your system, you need to back up any important files from your hard disk. (In fact, if you have a large enough storage medium, I recommend a complete hard disk backup.) See Chapter 7 for instructions on how to back up your key files.

Record Your CMOS Information

Some critical information about your system is stored on a special chip inside your computer. This battery-powered chip is called a *CMOS* chip, and it holds all the configuration information about your system in permanent memory. You need to record the information from this chip, *just in case* something goes south during your upgrade and fries this chip (or its battery).

Most newer PCs have a *setup program* available in ROM. One of the very first messages you see when you turn on your computer will indicate how you access this program. (This message will typically occur before or during the memory check—when those numbers flip by real quickly on your screen—but before accessing any of your disk drives.) You need to access this setup program.

Which Key for Me?

Different computers use different keystrokes to access the CMOS setup program. Some manufacturers require you to press the **Delete** key when your system is booting (during the memory check); other vendors require you to press **Ctrl+Alt+S** or **Ctrl+Alt+Esc**, and still others use a simple function key, such as **F1**. If these don't work, you should refer to your system documentation or call the vendor where you purchased the system.

When you access your setup program, you'll see your CMOS information displayed onscreen. Now you should write down the information in a safe place so you can get it when you need it.

If, while upgrading, your CMOS chip loses its memory, you'll need to access the setup program again. Referring to the information you gathered here, reset all your CMOS parameters.

Obtain the Proper Tools

To do the upgrade right, you'll need the right tools. (It just won't do to use an old butter knife in place of a proper screwdriver!) Take a look at the contents of Miller's Recommended Minimum Upgrading Toolkit:

➤ **Phillips-head screwdriver** A #2 (or "medium sized") is the preferred size.

➤ **Flat-blade screwdriver** Try to find one with a blade about an eighth of an inch wide. (*Don't* use a magnetized screwdriver!)

➤ **Pliers** The "needle-nose" type, small enough for prying things loose inside your PC.

➤ **Tweezers** The kind for plucking eyebrows will work just fine.

More Power!

If you think you will be working on your PC system quite a bit, invest in a small power screwdriver. It will make your life a lot easier—and, besides, we all need *more power!*

Reduce the Risk of Static Electricity

Another danger in poking around inside your PC is damaging the very sensitive chips by giving them a jolt of static electricity. (You can build up enough static electricity walking across a carpet to do hundreds of dollars worth of damage to your system unit!) Before you shock something that shouldn't be shocked, head down to your local computer shop and pick up an anti-static "strap," or anti-static spray, or an anti-static mat, or anything else to ground yourself and drain the static electricity from your body *before* you touch those expensive chips!

➤ **Chip pulling tool**   But only if you're really serious about this sort of thing. (Otherwise, the pliers or tweezers will do an adequate job.)

➤ **Small flashlight**   Good for finding your way around the dark insides of your system unit.

➤ **Large, soft cloth**   A good place to put all your delicate parts.

Turn Off the Power!

It goes without saying—*Don't mess with your computer until you turn off the power!*

Enough said.

Doing the Deed

Once you have everything prepared, it's time to do the actual upgrade. I discussed the upgrade procedure in detail back in Chapter 2, "Hardware Basics for the Technically Timid," so I'll refer you back to that chapter rather than repeating everything here. In general, however, here are the steps you should take when performing any type of hardware upgrade:

1. Back up key files and record key system settings.
2. Turn off your computer.
3. Remove the old component (if you're replacing a component).
4. Install the new component per the manufacturer's directions.
5. Restart your system. (But *don't* seal up your system unit—wait until everything checks out before you put the box back together.)
6. If necessary (see the instructions provided by the device's manufacturer), enter your PC's Setup program and reconfigure the CMOS settings.
7. After Windows starts, it should recognize the new device and automatically install the appropriate driver. If Windows does not recognize the device or installs the incorrect driver, run the **Add New Hardware Wizard**.
8. After everything is up and running properly, power down your PC and button up your system unit.

Most new peripherals sold today are Plug and Play, meaning that Windows should recognize them automatically the next time it starts. For these older devices, you'll most probably need to use the Add New Hardware Wizard, described in Chapter 2. It's also possible that you'll need to run a setup program specific to your new peripheral, if so supplied.

After You Upgrade—Common Problems

Okay. You've plugged in your new card, or new memory chips, or new peripheral. You put your computer back together, plug it in, turn it on, and...

Something goes wrong.

Such as:

➤ You forgot to plug your computer back in—or plug everything back into your system unit.

➤ You didn't connect something properly.

➤ Some part of your system isn't compatible with your new component.

➤ You broke something while you were inside your system unit.

➤ You left something loose inside your system unit, like a wire or a screw.

➤ You need to change your system configuration to recognize your new upgrade.

➤ The device driver for your new component conflicts with an existing device driver in Windows.

Sometimes the best way to troubleshoot an upgrade problem is to uninstall the device that you just upgraded, and then reinstall it. Sometimes it takes Windows two (or more!) tries to get the configuration right. Sometimes you may need to consult with a technical professional to hunt down a pesky device conflict—or throw in the towel and not add the particular device that is giving your problems.

Before you do any of these things, however, finish reading this chapter and see if you can fix it yourself. (You should also check out Chapter 29, "Getting It Right...System Settings and Technical Maintenance," which includes all sorts of information on tracking down device driver conflicts.)

It's a Test!

Before you reassemble your system, you should fully test everything related to what you upgraded. If, for some reason, something doesn't work, you should retrace your steps to try and figure out what you may have done wrong. It's good procedure to remove the last device you installed and then restart your system. Going backwards step-by-step will help you identify which component is causing your current problems.

Fixing Upgrade Problems

Just as I couldn't cover all the details about upgrading in one chapter, I also can't cover all the problems you might encounter in this limited space. Some upgrading problems are actually covered in other, more specific sections of this book. I'll just try to cover the most common problems here.

Problem 1:

Your upgrade doesn't work

This could be one of a number of things. If you installed a new card, it may not be properly seated in the slot. You may not have all your cables connected properly. You may have broken something while you were diddling about inside your PC. You may have a bad part. You may not have *completed* the installation or setup. Windows might not have recognized your new hardware—or may have installed the wrong driver by mistake. The driver installed may be corrupted, or may need to be updated.

Whew! That's a lot that can go wrong!

It's also possible that your system doesn't recognize your new component. Depending on what you installed, you may have to do one of several things:

➤ Change CMOS settings (most common for memory and disk drives)

➤ Load new drivers via the Add New Hardware Wizard

➤ Adjust specific jumpers or switches on your motherboard or other specific component

Remember, after you make any of these changes you'll need to reboot your system in order for the changes to take effect.

The important thing to remember is to retrace your steps *backwards* through your installation, and try to determine if everything was done correctly. If all else fails, call the technical support line for your new component, or consult with a technical professional.

Problem 2:

After you upgrade, an existing part of your system no longer works properly

This is probably caused by some sort of resource conflict between your new and old components. The most common resource conflicts involve IRQ or port settings.

If you're adding an external component, you may be able to fix this by simply changing ports. If this doesn't fix it (or if you installed an internal device), you'll need to change IRQ settings for one or both of the devices in conflict.

Also note that conflicts can occur when devices hooked up to two *nonconsecutive* ports are used at the same time. In other words, if you have two devices trying to use COM1 and COM3 (or COM2 and COM4) simultaneously, both could freeze up. (I've had this happen with a mouse hooked up to COM1 and a modem hooked up to COM3.) If this is your problem, change the port for one of the devices.

Problem 3:

After you upgrade, your existing software doesn't work right

This is normally a simple setup problem. Make sure that Windows is configured properly for your new device; and that you select and configure the new device from within your software program, if possible.

It's also possible that your old software simply won't work with your new hardware. If you suspect this is the case, put in a call to the software manufacturer and see if they have a quick solution; if not, you may have to upgrade to a newer version of your software.

Problem 4:

You installed new memory, and now your entire system doesn't work (you may receive an error message on system startup)

When you added memory, you didn't tell your computer about it. The solution is simple—tell your computer!

You do this by accessing your CMOS information (discussed earlier in this chapter) via your system's startup program. When you've access the CMOS info, you need to change the settings to reflect your new memory settings.

(Fortunately, many new systems will automatically recognize the new memory setup during the power-on procedure.)

Problem 5:

You added a new video card, and now your monitor doesn't seem to work right

The problem here could be one of three things. Thing one: You didn't set up your card correctly to work with your monitor. Check the setup program (or the documentation) for the card for more information.

Thing two: Your monitor isn't compatible with your video card. It's more likely than not that you have a higher-resolution card (SVGA, per-

Getting the Jump

On some older PCs you may need to adjust jumpers or switches on the motherboard to get your system to recognize your new memory.

haps) and a monitor that can only display a lower-resolution picture. If this is the case, run the card at a lower resolution, can the new card, or buy a new monitor.

Thing three: Windows isn't configured properly. Open the **Display Properties** dialog box and make sure the right video card is selected, and that the display settings are properly configured.

271

10 Do's and Don'ts for Hardware Upgrading

1. *Do* use the proper tools when disassembling your system unit.

2. *Don't* forget to plug everything back in properly when you're finished upgrading.

3. *Do* take proper precautions before upgrading your system—such as making a PC Survival Kit and backing up key data and system files.

4. *Don't* be afraid to call in expert help if you're having big problems.

5. *Do* remember to reconfigure your system to recognize your new components.

6. *Don't* forget to ground yourself so you don't release a static charge and fry your computer chips.

7. *Do* record your CMOS information, just in case.

8. *Don't* be a total klutz and break anything inside your system unit!

9. *Do* upgrade to Windows 98 *before* you attempt a major hardware upgrade; not only is Plug and Play more reliable than with previous versions of Windows, it also includes some new utilities to help you track down and fix any problems that might develop.

10. *Don't* even attempt a difficult upgrade if you're not totally confident of your abilities; it's better to be safe than sorry and let a professional do the dirty work.

The Least You Need to Know

➤ Before you upgrade a system component, note your current system settings, assemble the proper tools, and back up all critical data files.

➤ Make sure you turn off your system's power before you open up the case and add a new component—and test your installation before you put the case back on your system unit.

➤ If Plug and Play doesn't recognize the new peripheral, use the **Add New Hardware Wizard** to add the new device manually.

Chapter 24

What to Do When... Your Internet Connection Goes Offline

In This Chapter

➤ Find out how your computer connects to the Internet

➤ Learn how to configure your modem and create an Internet connection

➤ Discover how to find and fix modem-related problems

Everybody's going online. The Internet is essential for tens of millions of users; if you can't connect, you can't communicate. But if online computing is deceptively simple, it's also fraught with potential problems—any of which can put you offline and out of touch. So if you want to stay wired, turn the page—and learn how to avoid Internet-related problems!

All About the Internet

When talking about the Internet, there's one thing you should keep in mind—the Internet isn't a thing. You can't touch it or see it or smell it; you can't put it in a box and buy it. The Internet is like the huge power grid that provides electricity to homes across the country—it exists in-between the points that matter.

If the Internet isn't a physical thing, what is it? It's really more simple than you might think; the Internet is nothing more than a really big computer network. In fact, it's a computer network that connects other computer networks—what some would call a "network of networks." Computers and other devices connect to the Internet, and thus have access to other computers and devices that are also connected to the Internet. Once you're connected, you can access anything or anybody else also connected to the

Internet, seamlessly and practically invisibly. With a single click, you connect through the Internet to a computer down the street or half-way around the world; on the Internet, distance doesn't matter.

Just being connected to the Internet, however, really doesn't do much. It's much the same as having electricity run to your home—that wall outlet doesn't do anything until you plug something into it. The same thing with the Internet; the Internet itself just kind of sits there until you plug something into it that takes advantage of it.

There are many applications that are plugged into—or sit on top of—the Internet. *Email* (discussed in Chapter 25, "What to Do When...Your Email Works More Like Snail Mail") takes advantage of the Internet's interconnections to deliver electronic messages from one user to another. Usenet utilizes computer servers connected to the Internet to host electronic message boards (called *newsgroups*) for communities of users. Chat servers connect to the Internet and allow users to "talk" to each other (via their keyboards, over the Internet) in real-time. And the World Wide Web (discussed in Chapter 26, What to Do When...Your Web Surfing Wipes Out") uses the Internet to connect literally millions of computers and devices in a "web" of linked sites and pages.

America Online—It's Not the Internet, Although It's Connected to It

You probably know someone who is connected to America Online and uses AOL to connect to the Internet. You may even be an AOL subscriber yourself.

Well, here's the skinny on AOL. America Online is a *commercial online service*, in that it exists independent to the Internet, with its own distinct connections and its own proprietary software, content, and interface. However, AOL also functions as a *gateway* to the Internet, so that AOL users can connect to the Internet through the AOL service. So you can use AOL to connect to the Internet, just as you would any ISP.

The Internet itself doesn't do any of these things—but it does *enable* these things to happen. And when *you* connect to the Internet, you have access to all these activities, and more.

How an Internet Connection Works

How does your personal computer connect to the Internet? First, your PC connects to an *Internet service provider* (ISP) via standard telephone lines. (If you use your computer at work to connect to the Internet, you actually go through your company's local area network to a dedicated line to the Internet, bypassing conventional phone lines.) Your PC uses a piece of hardware called a *modem* to translate the signals from your keyboard to signals that can be sent over standard phone lines; your ISP has a modem on the other end of the line that converts the signals back into digital format for transmission over the Internet.

An Internet service provider is a company that does nothing more than connect individual users to the Internet. Some ISPs (such as America Online) are also commercial online services, and provide their users with an easy-to-use onscreen interface and proprietary content and navigation. But these commercial online services also function as traditional ISPs, consolidating thousands of incoming telephone lines into a single gateway to the Internet for their individual users.

So you use your modem to connect to an ISP via your phone line, and your ISP then plugs you into the Internet. Once you're on the Internet, you're on your own, free to use (or not to use) individual Internet services, to visit (or not to visit) individual sites and servers connected to the Internet, and to communicate (or not) with individual users who are also plugged into the Internet. Once you disconnect from your ISP (that is, hang up your phone line), you're no longer connected to the Internet, and you can't access any Internet services or contact any other users—and they can't contact you, either—until you connect again.

How Modems Work

A modem (which stands for *mo*dulator-*dem*odulator) is, in essence, a little electronic telephone that enables your PC to transmit computer data over standard telephone lines. It can be installed either on a card inside your system unit or outside the unit, hooked up to a communications, or COM, port. Because computer information is stored digitally and phone lines can only transmit analog data, your modem must convert (modulate) the digital data into analog format—or, when receiving data, demodulate the analog data back into digital format.

Your modem is connected to a specific communications port on your system unit. (Remember that your mouse also is hooked up to a COM port; these two devices can conflict with one another, so be careful not to set them for the same port!) When you configure your modem, make certain that it really is configured for the port that it's plugged into. See both your computer and modem instruction manuals for detailed setup instructions.

Different modems transmit data at varying rates; the faster the transmission rate, the more expensive the modem. Transmission speed is measured in bits per second (bps); the current standard is 56Kbps, although many older PCs have slower modems installed.

There are other ways to connect to the Internet besides standard phone lines, however. Most local phone companies offer *ISDN* (Integrated Services Digital Network) access, a digital alternative to standard phone service access, which connects you to the Internet at 128Kbps. Also available—from *some* phone companies—is a new technology called DSL, which promises faster-than-ISDN speeds over normal phone lines.

Outside of phone-based connections, you can also connect to the Internet via a cable modem (if your cable company offers such service), through your company's local area network (which can be really fast if your company is connected to the Net via a T1 or T3 line), or you can get ultra-fast downloads via a DirectPC digital satellite dish. All these non-standard services are rather expensive, however, so you'll have to balance the cost versus speed question to best serve your particular interests.

Configuring Your System for Internet Use

To connect to the Internet, then, you need a modem installed in your system—and your modem has to be configured properly to connect to you Internet service provider.

When you install a new modem in your system, Windows installs device drivers that use a series of default settings that work best for most computer systems. However, you still need to tell Windows about your dialing defaults—area code, calling card number, and so on—and, in some instances, you may need to edit your modem configuration to be compatible with specific online services.

Installing New Modem Drivers

If Windows doesn't recognize your modem during installation, you can install new modem drivers manually from the diskette supplied by your modem manufacturer.

Isn't That IDSN?

Windows 98 is automatically configured for use with ISDN. If you have a previous version of Windows, however, you'll probably need to install ISDN services on your PC before you connect to an ISDN line. For more information about using ISDN, go to Microsoft's ISDN Web page at www.microsoft.com/windows/getisdn/.

Go to the **Control Panel** and select the **Modems** icon. When the Modem Properties dialog box appears, click the **Add** button. When the Install New Modem Wizard appears, select **Don't Detect My Modem; I Will Select It From a List** and click the **Next** button. If your new modem is not in the **Manufacturers** and **Models** list boxes and you have the drivers from the manufacturer, click the **Have Disk** button. Insert the diskette that has the appropriate installation (.INF) file in drive A and click **OK**. (If you have downloaded new drivers from an online service to your computer, instead of inserting a diskette, click the **Browse** button to select the folder that the drivers were downloaded into.) Click the **OK** buttons to return to the Install New Modem Wizard and then click **Next**. Select the communications port the modem is set for or connected to (if it is external), click **Next**, and then click the **Finish** button in the last screen of the Wizard to return to the desktop.

Configuring Your Modem

When you need to make changes to your modem settings, possibly because a specific ISP requires different settings, use the Modem Properties dialog box (accessed by selecting the **Modems** icon in the Windows **Control Panel**). Select the **General** tab, highlight the modem to be configured, and click the **Properties** button. When the Properties dialog box displays, as shown in the next figure, click the **General** tab and then click the **Port** drop-down list box to select from the available communications ports. To change the speed that your modem uses to communicate with your computer, click the **Maximum Speed** drop-down list box and select from the speed options.

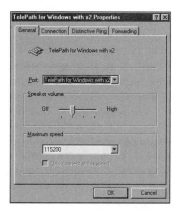

Change your modem's port assignment and connection speed in the Modem Properties dialog box.

The **General** tab lets you configure those settings that most often need configuring; more technical settings can be found on the **Connection** tab. Here you can set the **Data Bits**, **Parity**, and **Stop Bits** values, or click the **Port Settings** button to open the Advanced Port Settings dialog box and modify the **Receive Buffer** and **Transmit Buffer** settings. You can also click the **Advanced** button to open the Advanced Connection Settings dialog box; check **Use Flow Control** and select either **Hardware(RTS/CTS)** or **Software(XON/XOFF)** to enable flow control and indicate the type of control.

Plug and Play = Fewer Things to Configure

If your modem is Plug and Play, you may not have the option to change port or speaker volume settings.

Fortunately, you really don't have to know what data bits and parities and buffers are because the default settings used when Windows first installed your modem work just fine in most instances. However, if you're having serious connection problems, check your modem's instruction manual or your ISP's installation instructions for details on which of these more technical settings to enable in specific circumstances.

Configuring Windows' Dialing Options

Before you can connect to anything—to the Internet, to a private bulletin board system, or to another computer—you need to tell Windows how and from where you're connecting. Start by selecting the **Modems** icon in the Windows Control Panel; when the Modems Properties dialog box appears, select the **General** tab and click the **Dialing Properties** button.

When the Dialing Properties dialog box appears (see the following figure), enter your area code in the **Area Code** field and select the country or region you are setting up in the **I Am In This Country/Region** field to define the default location. If you want to disable call waiting while you're using your modem (a good idea), select the **To Disable Call Waiting, Dial** box and select the necessary dialing code. If you want to use a calling card for your modem calls, select the **For Long Distance Calls, Use This Calling Card** box, and then click the **Calling Card** button and enter the appropriate information. If you have to dial a number to access an outside line, enter the appropriate numbers in the **For Long Distance Calls** and **For Local Calls** fields. Click **OK** when done.

Use the Dialing Properties dialog box to configure your system for all modem-based calls.

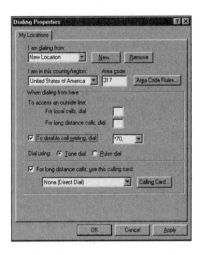

Windows Pauses for a Comma

You may want to insert a comma after the digit(s) you use to access an outside line; this instructs Windows to pause slightly before it dials the actual number, thus allowing a smooth transfer to the outside line.

The information you enter in the Dialing Properties dialog box is used by all Windows telecommunications programs, such as Phone Dialer, HyperTerminal, and Dial-Up Networking.

Creating a New Internet Connection—Automatically

To connect to the Internet, you need to establish an account with an Internet service provider (ISP); when you dial up your ISP via modem, your computer will automatically be connected to the Internet. Before you create your new Internet connection, however, you need to gather various pieces of information from your Internet service provider. Here's what you need to know:

➤ Area code and telephone number of your Internet service provider (*not* their voice number; their dial-up number)

➤ Your username and password as assigned by your ISP

➤ Your email address (in the form of *xxx@xxx.xx*) as assigned by your ISP

➤ The names of your ISP's incoming and outgoing email servers (may be the same)

➤ Your email POP account name (normally the part of your address before the @ symbol) and password as assigned by your ISP (typically the same as your general ISP username and password)

➤ The name of your ISP's news server

➤ If your ISP offers LDAP "white pages" service (not all do), the name of your ISP's LDAP server

The *Internet Connection Wizard* is a special utility found in Windows 98 (and with later versions of Internet Explorer) that automates the creation of a new Internet connection. The Wizard makes it easy to establish a new connection; all you need to do is input some connection information provided by your Internet service provider, and the Wizard does the rest of the setup—including setting up your email and Usenet newsgroup accounts.

To use the Wizard, click the **Start** button, select **Programs**, select **Accessories**, select **Communications**, and then select **Internet Connection Wizard**. If you haven't chosen an ISP yet, select the first option, **I Want To Sign Up for a New Internet Account**, and click the **Next** button; the Wizard will then dial a toll-free number and display a list of ISPs from which you can choose to establish an account. If you already have established an account with an ISP, choose the third option, **I Want To Set Up My Internet Connection Manually**, and then click the **Next** button; follow the remaining steps in the Wizard to complete your new Internet connection.

Creating a New Internet Connection—Manually

Although most users will prefer to use the Internet Connection Wizard to automate their Internet setup, Windows does let you create a connection manually—and, of course, that's the only way to create a connection in Windows 95. You use Windows' Dial-Up Networking to manually create a new connection; begin by opening **My Computer** and selecting the **Dial-Up Networking**. When the Dial-Up Networking window opens, click the **Make New Connection** icon.

When the first screen of the Make New Connection Wizard appears, give the new connection a name, select which modem you want to use, and click **Next**. Enter the area code and the telephone number of the service to which you want to connect, and then click **Next**. When the last Wizard screen is displayed, click **Finish** to complete the dial-up networking connection setup.

Multiple Connections for Multiple ISPs

Windows lets you create multiple connections to multiple ISPs. You then have the choice of selecting which ISP you want to dial into for a specific Internet session.

Connecting to Your Internet Service Provider

After you've created your Internet connection, all it takes to get online is a click of your mouse. Just click the **Start** button, select **Programs**, select **Accessories**, select **Communications**, and then select **Dial-Up Networking**. (Alternatively, open **My Computer** and select the **Dial-Up Networking** icon.) When the Dial-Up Networking window appears, click the icon for your Internet service provider. When the Connect To dialog box appears, enter your username and password and click the **Connect** button.

Connect Automatically

If you launch some Internet applications (such as Internet Explorer, Outlook Express, or Netscape Navigator) before you establish your dial-up connection, they will automatically launch Dial-Up Networking and establish a connection to your ISP.

Windows now will dial your ISP and automatically establish a connection. When the connection is established, an icon, indicating the nature of your connection, will appear in the Taskbar Tray. Now you can launch the appropriate Internet software, such as Internet Explorer or Outlook Express.

To close the connection, right-click the connection icon in the Taskbar Tray and choose **Disconnect** from the pop-up menu.

What Can Go Wrong with Your Internet Connection

Okay, you're convinced. You can't wait to join the Internet revolution and use your computer to cruise the information superhighway. After all, what can go wrong?

Lots, actually. First, you can hook up your modem incorrectly. Maybe you fail to seat an internal modem securely into its slot on the motherboard, or perhaps you plug an external modem into the wrong port on your system unit. It *has* been done before. Oh, and if you attempt such tasks too early in the morning, before you finish your first cup of coffee or otherwise completely wake up, I suppose you can even forget to connect the modem to a working telephone jack. (If you're reading this book, you're undoubtedly too sharp to overlook something so simple, but I mention it, just in case...).

Next, you can sabotage your setup, partially or entirely, by configuring the modem's switches or Windows modem settings—or both—incorrectly. Given all the different settings possible, such mistakes in setup aren't difficult to make. It's possible, too, to create a COM port conflict by designating your modem and your mouse for either the same COM port or a conflicting COM port.

You can also be cursed with a noisy telephone line. You'd be surprised at the amount of trouble this seemingly minor annoyance can cause—everything from slowing down your connection speed to thwarting your connection altogether. Even if you get everything else right, Ma Bell can send you back to square one with just a little line noise.

Finally, your ISP may not be operating up to par. Now that the Internet is experiencing astronomic growth, it's not uncommon to run into "traffic jams" at popular sites, and access in general often slows down during the heaviest-trafficked times of the day.

Diagnosing Modem Problems

If you think you have a modem-related problem, it's probably because of a resource conflict between your modem and another hardware device, or because your modem has not been configured properly. If you're using Windows 98, you have access to an extremely useful modem diagnostic tool that can help you find and fix these types of problems.

From the Modems Properties dialog box, select the **Diagnostics** tab. Now highlight the communications port that the modem is attached to in the Port list, and click the **More Info** button to open the More Info information box. Review the information in the Port Information group at the top and in the Modem Response Code group at the bottom of the dialog box. Click **OK** to return to the Modem Properties dialog box.

Click the **Driver** button to view the communications driver currently used by Windows. Compare this data with that provided by your modem manufacturer. Click **OK** to return to the Modems Properties dialog box. Click the **OK** or **Cancel** button to close the Modems Properties dialog box.

Most modem problems are caused by either incorrect configuration or conflict with other hardware devices. If you can't locate the cause of your problem here, you should use the Modem Troubleshooter. Click **Start** and select **Help**; when the Help window appears, select the **Contents** tab, select **Troubleshooting**, select **Windows 98 Troubleshooters**, then select **Modem**. When the Modem Troubleshooter appears, follow the onscreen instructions to track down the cause of your particular problem.

If you're using Windows 95, of course, you don't have either of these wonderful troubleshooting utilities—which means you have to track down your problems the old-fashioned way, from the Modems Properties and System Information dialog boxes.

What to Do When Your Internet Connection Goes Offline

Online communications can sometimes give you fits. Everything from incorrect setups to faulty connections to noisy phone lines can make your telecommunicating go awry. Take some time, therefore, to examine the following sections. They describe some of the most common Internet-related problems you may experience—and what can cause them.

Problem 1:

Your modem doesn't work—nothing happens

If you attempt to use your modem but it does nothing at all, start by checking all your connections—especially the connection to the phone line. A malfunctioning modem usually results from a bad connection. If you use an external modem, make sure that it's hooked to the correct port in the back of your system unit. Make certain, too, that the modem is plugged into a power source (if necessary) and connected to a phone line. If you use an internal modem, check to ensure that the card is firmly seated in its slot. You should also try hooking a normal phone to the line hooked to your computer, just to make sure that you have a dial tone. After you've taken care of a poor or overlooked connection, you may need to reboot your system to recover from the problem.

Next, you should check to see if your modem is communicating with your computer. In Windows 98 you can do this by going to the Modems Properties dialog box, selecting the **Diagnostics** tab, highlighting the port used by your modem, then clicking the **More Info** button. If you receive a series of OK responses, your modem is communicating properly and you should proceed to the solutions presented in Problem 2. If you don't receive positive responses, then you have a hardware problem—your modem is either not connected properly, not powered up, or not working properly.

To perform this same test in Windows 95 you use HyperTerminal, a manual dialing program. Begin by clicking **Start**, selecting **Programs**, selecting **Accessories**, selecting **Communications**, and then selecting **HyperTerminal**. When the HyperTerminal window opens, select **Hypertrm.exe** to launch HyperTerminal. When the Connection Description dialog box appears, click **Cancel**; you should now be at the main HyperTerminal window, in manual mode. Type **AT** and press **Enter**. If you get no response, you have a hardware problem. If you receive an OK message, however, your modem is working fine, and you have other problems—so continue on to Problem 2.

If you've determined that you have a modem hardware problem, here are a few things to try. First, confirm that your modem is seated properly (if it's an internal modem) or that it has power (if it's an external modem). Make sure all cables are connected properly, and that no cables or connectors are bent or broken. Next, go to the **Device Manager** tab in the System Information dialog box and see if your modem is in conflict with another device. (If so, a yellow exclamation point will be listed next to both your modem and the conflicting device.) Next, try uninstalling your modem from Windows, and then manually reinstalling it. Make sure the modem is installed on a functioning, non-conflicting COM port. If all this fails, you may have a defective modem.

Problem 2:

Your modem is working, but it doesn't dial

After you've confirmed that your modem is working and communicating with your computer—but you still can't dial a number—you should confirm that you're not trying to make one Internet connection while a previous connection is still open.

(You can dial two places at the same time!). Then make sure that the phone line your modem is connected to is working by disconnecting your modem and hooking a working telephone to the same phone line; if the phone doesn't pick up a dial tone, neither will your modem. Try another phone line, or call the phone company for repairs.

If you have voice mail on your phone line, some voice mail systems change the dial tone to indicate when you have messages waiting. This modified dial tone may not be recognized as a real dial tone by some modems; answer your voice mail to change the tone back to normal, and then try dialing again.

It's also possible that you have your phone line plugged into the wrong jack at your modem. Most modems have two jacks—one labeled "line" and the other labeled "phone." Make sure that the phone line is plugged into the one labeled "line."

If your problem persists and it clearly isn't caused by a bad connection, an inoperable phone line, or a defective modem, the most likely source of your woes is an incorrect configuration within Windows. Make certain that you've selected the correct COM port and check the modem initialization string; your modem's documentation lists the correct commands to use for your device. Also check the Maximum Speed setting in the Modem Properties dialog box; you might try *reducing* this setting if your modem is having difficulty communicating with your computer. And check for any COM port conflicts between your modem and another device, such as a mouse.

If Windows appears to be configured correctly (or it wasn't and you've fixed it) but your modem still doesn't dial, check your hardware. Many modems have physical switches that must be set in certain positions for the device to operate. Refer to your modem's documentation for the correct switch settings for your system.

Problem 3:

Your modem dials, but it doesn't connect

Many common causes for this problem are the same as for Problem 2—either your hardware or software is set up incorrectly. If you think this is the case, see Problem 2 for troubleshooting instructions.

It's also possible that your modem is dialing an incorrect phone number, or that something is screwy at your ISP. Make sure that your modem's speaker is enabled, and then listen to the connection in process. If you hear your modem dialing, dialing, dialing—and it receives no answer from your ISP—then check the phone number you entered for your ISP. If the phone number is correct, it's possible that your ISP is having problems

> **It's ImPORTant!**
>
> If you're running Windows, you should always check the port settings from within Windows to make sure that they're configured correctly. Simply open **Control Panel** and select the **System** icon. From the System Information dialog box, select the **Device Manager** tab and examine the Properties for ports COM1 through COM4.

and temporarily can't accept incoming calls. (Dial your ISP's voice support line to confirm or report this problem.) If you hear a busy signal after dialing, that means that too many people are trying to dial in at one time, and your ISP can't accept any more incoming calls right now; wait a few minutes and try dialing in again.

Problem 4:

Your modem dials and connects, but nothing else happens

Yes! Your modem dials the number and makes contact with your ISP—but then it just sits there, doing nothing. What gives?

First, it's possible that you've entered an incorrect username or password, and your ISP doesn't recognize you. Check these settings before you dial again.

As with all modem-related problems, an incorrect setup can be behind this one, too. Double-check all configuration parameters against your ISP's preferred settings; if in doubt, call your ISP's voice support line and have them walk you through the setup for their system.

If none of the above fixes your problem, check again for COM port conflicts in your system. Remember that two devices cannot be configured to use the same COM port. Remember, too, that a mouse hooked up to COM1 occasionally interferes with a modem connected to COM3; if you experience this type of trouble frequently, reconfigure your modem's COM settings for another port and see what happens.

Problem 5:

You connect to your ISP, but at a slower speed than desired

There are many factors that determine which speed you actually connect at. The most common cause of slower-than-expected connections is line noise. I run into this problem a lot when traveling; many older hotels have very noisy phone systems, which cause my modem to connect at speeds as slow as 14.4Kbps.

In addition, the busier your ISP is, the more likely that you'll connect at a slower speed. If you try to connect during "prime time" (from just after dinner to bed time in your specific time zone) chances are you'll get a slower connection than if you try to connect after midnight.

If you want to speed up your Internet connections, the obvious solution is to get a faster modem! Remember—the faster the modem, the shorter the access and download times while you're online.

What do you do if you install a fast modem and still think the Internet is too slow? Here are some things you can try to speed up your Internet sessions:

➤ Add more memory to your system.

➤ Create a bigger cache for your Web browser—and flush your cache from time to time.

➤ Get a bigger hard disk drive (for bigger Web page caches).

➤ Turn off your Web browser's graphics loading.

➤ Avoid Internet multitasking; don't send email, read newsgroup articles, and surf the Web all at the same time—that's cramming a lot of data into a small pipe!

➤ Find a faster ISP.

➤ Consider upgrading to an ISDN, DSL, or cable modem connection.

At the end of the day, sometimes the Internet *is* slow, no matter what you do or how you connect. That's why the WWW is sometimes referred to as the World Wide *Wait*.

Problem 6:

Your session gets unexpectedly disconnected

You can get disconnected in the middle of a session if you have more than one phone in your house hooked to the same phone line. If someone picks up an extension while your modem is online, the resulting interruption can scramble the connection. Sometimes the problem can be rectified simply by hanging up the extension; other times, you must cancel the current modem session and start over again.

Call Waiting can also be the cause of disconnect problems. When the Call Waiting signal comes down the line it stands a good chance of either scrambling your modem session or disconnecting your modem completely. While you can simply abstain from ordering the Call Waiting service, you can also turn it off temporarily by dialing ***70** right before your online session—or configuring the Dialing Properties dialog box to insert this code for you whenever you initiate a connection.

Some ISPs and commercial online services (AOL is notorious for this) will disconnect you if you've been idle for too long. (They don't like users staying connected without actually doing anything.) If you want to stay connected, do *something* every few minutes, even if it's just checking your email inbox or clicking to a different Web site.

In addition, Windows itself will disconnect you if you're idle too long, if that's how you configured things. Go to the **Connection** tab in the Properties dialog box for your modem and *uncheck* the **Disconnect a Call if Idle** box (or enter a larger time increment).

Sometimes a Windows-related problem can cause your modem session to shut down. If Windows is low on memory, it may not have enough resources to let your modem do its thing. If you think this is the problem, try closing a few Windows applications and then restarting your modem. If you have continual modem problems under Windows, you may need to add more memory to your system.

Another increasingly common cause of this problem is a noisy phone line. If you have frequent trouble connecting or staying connected, it might not hurt to have your local phone company check your line for excess noise.

Problem 7:

Your communications become garbled during an online session

Garbled communications—all of a sudden receiving gibberish in a chat room, or experiencing a mangled file download—can have several possible causes. Using different settings on your system than those required by your ISP is one cause. Always make sure beforehand that your setup matches in stop bits, parity, and other such technical settings as those of the system you're attempting to access.

Interrupted and Corrupted

If your modem is interrupted while downloading data of any kind, the communication breakdown usually corrupts the data, making it unusable. You'll need to download the file again to ensure that you get a clean copy.

Dealing with a Noisy Host

Sometimes line noise doesn't originate at your end, but in the line feeding the system you're trying to access. If you experience isolated line noise when dealing with a particular ISP, call (using your regular phone, not your modem!) your ISP and inform them of the problem.

A second potential cause of this problem is that something isn't hooked up properly. If you haven't done so already, check all your cables—including your telephone cords—to ensure that they're securely fastened. If any older cables are hooked into the line, replace them. Old cables can eventually go bad, resulting in difficulties with your data communications.

A final cause of this type of communications breakdown—and a common one, at that—is excess noise on your telephone line. If you often endure noisy connections when you talk on the telephone, your computer is likely to experience the same noisy connections when it uses the same phone line. Although usually a mere annoyance in person-to-person calls, a similarly poor connection between your computer and another system can totally foul up its online transmissions; any lost data that results can destroy a downloaded file or cause an online session to end in a disconnect.

Fortunately, you can take several steps to minimize line noise. For example, check your telephone cable from the wall to your computer. Is the cable new and firmly connected? You may try replacing the cable if it's not new. If feasible, remove any nearby electrical devices or appliances from the vicinity of your phone cord. Blenders, TVs, radios, electric shavers—all can create interference that increases line noise. If you've tried these steps but you still have a problem with line noise, call your local telephone company.

Problem 8:

You can't disconnect your modem

Sometimes this really happens—your modem just doesn't seem to want you to hang up. Your first concern is, of course, to break the connection; then you can try to figure out what went wrong. If you can't disconnect when you click the **Disconnect** button, try shutting down the program manually (by pressing **Ctrl+Alt+Del** and using the Close Programs dialog box). If your modem *still* stays connected, you'll have to shut down your computer to disconnect the current call.

Now to discover why you couldn't hang up. Guess what, folks—the most common cause of this failure is improper software or modem settings. So get out your manuals and look up those settings—your disconnect code is probably incorrect.

Problem 9:

Using your modem causes your mouse to act funny—or vice versa

This is actually a common problem and results from weird hardware bugs that force two different COM ports to use some of the same system resources. As the following paragraphs explain, however, resolving the conflict is simple.

First, check the port settings for your mouse and your modem. If they're both configured for the same COM port, change one of the devices' settings so that it can use a different port.

Now, check that they're not both set for COM ports with even numbers (COM2 and COM4). If so, reconfigure one of the devices to use an odd numbered port.

At the same time, check that the two devices aren't both configured for COM ports with odd numbers (COM1 and COM3). If so, reset one of the devices to use an even number.

It's As Easy As 1-2-3...

If you're using Windows and running your modem on COM2—and there is no COM1 on your system—you may not be able to get your modem to work at all. This is because Windows looks for COM ports in order, and if COM1 doesn't exist...well, you've got problems. Reassign your modem—or some other accessory—to COM1, and you'll fix your problem.

Problem 10:

Your computer acts oddly soon after you've downloaded a file

What now? You've just pulled several files—including a great new game—from this new Internet site you found, and now your computer acts as though it needs to be decked out in an electronic straitjacket. It doesn't seem to have any problems with loose connections, incorrect settings, or excess line noise; your online session went without a hitch—flawlessly, in fact. So what's wrong?

Well, along with your nice new files, you have probably downloaded a not-so-nice computer virus! Any time you download a file, access the file, and find your computer starting to do strange things (running more slowly, mysteriously losing files, displaying unusual messages onscreen), you may have accidentally infected it with a virus. If the symptoms seem to match, refer to Chapter 10, "Germ Warfare— Protecting Your Computer from Viruses," for what to do next.

10 Do's and Don'ts for Connecting to the Internet

1. *Do* make sure that Windows is configured properly for your specific modem and for your Internet service provider.

2. *Don't* limit yourself to connecting to the Internet only via America Online; stand-alone Internet service providers often provide faster and more reliable connections— and let you use whatever Web browser and email program you want.

3. *Do* invest in the highest-speed modem you can afford; if you have ISDN, DSL, or cable modem service in your area, investigate changing to one of these ultra-fast services.

4. *Don't* forget to disable call waiting when you're connecting to the Internet; an incoming call waiting call can disconnect you in the middle of an online session!

5. *Do* obtain local access numbers for your ISP if you're going to be traveling; the last thing you want to do is connect to your ISP via a long-distance call, or by using a (normally extra-charge) 800 number.

6. *Don't* download program files from unfamiliar or suspicious Internet sites; such files may hide covert computer viruses.

7. *Do* install a separate telephone line for your modem if you can afford it. (It frees up your regular line so that you can talk and type at the same time.)

8. *Don't* configure your modem to use the same COM port as any other device in your computer system, such as a mouse.

9. *Do* make sure that your modem is connected correctly to both your computer *and* your telephone line—and that you actually have a dial tone on the line.

10. *Don't* let yourself get *too* addicted to the Internet; conversing with friends around the world is nice, but talking with the folks next door (or your family members in the same room!) can be even better.

The Least You Need to Know

➤ Your modem must be configured properly (via the Modem Properties dialog box) to establish an online connection, as must Windows' dialing properties (from the Dialing Properties dialog box).

➤ Before you can connect to the Internet, you must have an account with an Internet service provider, and an associated Windows dial-up networking connection. (Use the Internet Connection Wizard to create a new connection.)

➤ If you're having trouble connecting to the Internet, look for configuration mistakes, incorrect settings, and noisy phone lines—and try to connect when your ISP isn't so busy!

Chapter 25

What to Do When... Your Email Works More Like Snail Mail

In This Chapter

➤ Learn how email messages are sent across the Internet

➤ Discover how to track down most email-related problems

➤ Find out if there is anything you can do about "spam" email messages

---

Email is the most-used Internet application. More users send and receive email messages every day than access Web pages, or chat, or exchange messages in Usenet newsgroups.

Because it's the most widely used application, it's also the Internet application that causes the most problems. If you've ever had problems sending or receiving email, you know what I'm talking about!

How Email Works

Electronic mail (*email*) is a means of communicating with other Internet users via letter-like messages, written and delivered electronically over the Internet. While email messages look a lot like traditional letters, email itself is a lot different from the so-called "snail mail" delivered by the United States Postal Service.

When you send an electronic "letter" to another Internet user, that letter travels from your PC to your recipient's PC (via the Internet) almost *instantly*. Your messages travel at the speed of electrons over a number of phone lines and Internet connections, automatically routed to the right place just about as fast as you can click the "send" button. That's a *lot* different from using the U.S. Postal Service, which can take days to deliver a similar message.

To make sure your message goes to the right recipient, you have to use your recipient's email *address*. Every Internet user has a unique email address, composed of three parts:

➤ The user's **login name**
➤ The @ sign
➤ The user's **domain name** (usually the name of the Internet service provider)

What Do All Those Initials Mean?

SMTP (Simple Mail Transfer Protocol) is the general protocol for transmitting all email across the Internet. You send email from your PC using SMTP; email sent from one server to another also uses SMTP.

When it comes to retrieving the email stored on your ISP's server, there are two different protocols that can be used. With *POP3* (Post Office Protocol 3), your email messages are stored on the ISP's server only until your email program retrieves them, at which time they are deleted from the server. With *IMAP* (Interactive Mail Access Protocol), you don't actually download messages to your computer; instead, you view your email messages as they're stored on the ISP's server. Both POP3 and IMAP protocols are supported by most major email programs.

To keep things straight, just remember that you use SMTP to *send* messages, but you use POP3 or IMAP to *retrieve* messages waiting for you on your ISP's mail server.

As an example, if you used America Online as your Internet provider and your login name was goofyjoe, your email address would be goofyjoe@aol.com.

You use an email application (or *client*)—such as Microsoft Outlook, Outlook Express, Netscape Messenger, or Eudora—to create, send, receive, and read email messages. You don't actually transmit a message directly from your PC to its recipient; your email program connects to a mail server located at your ISP, which stores, sends, and receives messages on your behalf.

Because your ISP is the "middleman" in the email equation, you have to configure your email program so that it knows the name of your ISP's mail server (normally in the form of mail.domain.com). Some ISPs maintain two servers, an *incoming* mail server (also called a POP3 or IMAP server) and an *outgoing* mail server (also called an SMTP server). If your ISP only has a single server, use that address for both the incoming and outgoing settings.

In addition to standard ISP server-based email, you can also send and receive email from special Web-based email services. These services—such as the ever-popular Hotmail (www.hotmail.com)—let you access your email from *any* computer, using any Web browser; if you use a PC at work or on the road, this is a convenient way to check your email at any time of day, no matter where you are. Second, you can use this auxiliary email account as a second Internet identity, distinct from your normal email address; some users use their Web-based email to access the Internet under an assumed name, for privacy purposes. Third, these Web-based email accounts are free—which is reason enough for some people.

What Can Go Wrong with Your Email

The most common problem with email is an incorrect address. It's easy to mistype an address, or to get the wrong address from someone. If you're having trouble getting a message to another user, try to verify the email address with the recipient personally.

In addition, sometimes the Internet just sort of bogs down and things don't get to where they're supposed to go. This can be caused by problems at your ISP's mail server, or at your recipient's mail server, or anywhere inbetween. So if you get an email message bounced back to you and you know it was addressed correctly, try resending it.

Speaking of mail server problems, you won't be able to send or receive email at all if you don't configure your email program with the correct mail server information. Make sure you have the right server name from your ISP—for both incoming and outgoing email.

Finally, email messages are increasingly becoming a conduit for computer viruses. Plain-text email messages themselves can't carry viruses, but files attached to messages can. Be extra safe, and don't open any file attachments to messages from people you don't know—and you might even be cautious with attachments from friends, as well.

What to Do When Your Email Works More Like Snail Mail

Email is your lifeline to other Internet users; what do you do when sending and receiving messages is problematic? Here are the most common email-related problems, along with their probable causes.

Problem 1:

You can't connect to your email server

This problem is most often caused by an incorrect configuration in your email program. Make sure you have the right incoming and outgoing mail server names for your ISP, as well as the correct username (typically your email address) and password, if required. (And remember that some ISP's use case-sensitive usernames and passwords.)

If you have everything configured properly, it's possible that there is some sort of problem with your ISP's mail server. Wait a few minutes and try connecting again. If you continue to have problems connecting, call your ISP's voice support line and report the problem.

Problem 2:

Your email program connects to your ISP, but you have trouble sending or receiving an email message

Just because you connect to your ISP doesn't mean you can actually send or retrieve messages. Again, check your email program's configuration; be especially sure that you have the right protocols (POP3, IMAP, and so on) selected.

If you receive a "timeout" message after connecting, there may be problems with the ISP's mail server. Things can really slow down during busy times of the day; if it takes too long to complete an action (such as downloading a list of messages), your program "times out" and reports an error. Try clicking the **Send/Receive** button again to initiate a new upload/download of messages. (If you receive a lot of timeout messages, reconfigure your email program to allow more time before timing out.)

Sometimes a really large message (or a message with a large attachment) can take so long to retrieve that it times out your email program. (Any message more than 1MB in size could cause this sort of problem on a normal 56Kbps connection.) The really bad thing is, if you can't download this message, it clogs up your message retrieval so you can't grab any other message after this one, either. If you run into this sort of problem, call your ISP's voice support line and ask them to remove the extra-large message from the queue so you can retrieve the rest of your message. (And email the person who sent the large message and ask them to either compress it—using a Zip utility—or break it up into several smaller messages.)

Problem 3:

An email message you sent is returned as "undeliverable"

This may be the most common Internet-related problem, period—and the one with the simplest solution.

If you get an email message bounced back to you, there is a very good possibility that the recipient's email address was incorrect. (This is just like when you get a letter returned from the postal service as "addressee unknown.") Double-check the email address (perhaps by calling the recipient and inquiring by voice), correct it, and resend the message.

It's also possible that the address was correct but there was a problem with the recipient's mail server. If you're positive you have the right address, go ahead and resend the message and hope the server problem has been corrected.

You can sometimes track down the cause of the error by carefully deciphering the error message that accompanies many returned messages. You'll often find specific reasons that the message was returned, which can help you formulate your reaction.

Finally, know that Internet users often move from one email account to another as they play a game of musical chairs with multiple ISPs. It's possible that you sent your message to what was formerly a viable address, but one that has since been abandoned by the user. Again, checking with recipients personally (*not* via email!) may be the only way to get their current email address.

Problem 4:

You have trouble sending an attachment to an email message

Most email programs let you "attach" files to your email messages. You can use this feature to send pictures, word processing documents, and even complete executable programs along with your email messages.

Note, however, that some email programs might set a limit on the size of your email attachments, and that some ISPs might not let their users receive attachments. (For example, AOL lets users select whether they want to receive attachments or not; some parents turn off the attachment-receiving option for their children's email accounts.) Also note that overly large (more than 1MB) attachments may cause retrieval problems for your intended recipient(s). It might not be a bad idea to contact your recipients ahead of time to warn them that a really large email is on its way; they can then prepare themselves for what will be an annoyingly long download.

It's also possible that you have your email program configured incorrectly for sending attachments. Your attachments should be sent in ASCII mode, using the MIME protocol. If your program is configured to use binary mode for attachments, many other email programs will be unable to decode the attachment.

Problem 5:

You can't open an attachment sent with an email message

If you try to open a file attachment and either can't open it or open it and discover a bunch of garbage, it's likely that it was sent in binary format, rather than the standard MIME format. When your email program tries to deal with it, it reads the binary numbers as ASCII characters, thus the onscreen garbage. The easiest thing to do is to ask the sender to resend the attachment in MIME format. Otherwise, you need to obtain a binary conversion utility to try to convert the file back yourself—which, trust me, is not the easiest thing in the world to do.

It's also possible that the file was sent correctly but somehow got trashed in its trip across the Internet, typically at either the sending or receiving server. Again, asking for the file to be resent is the simplest course of action.

If you have trouble opening an attachment from within your email program, try saving it to your hard disk instead, and then opening it normally from there. It's possible that your email program simply can't handle the type of file that was sent as an attachment.

Finally, Windows itself may not be able to recognize the file that was sent as an attachment. If you try to open a file type that doesn't have a corresponding association in Windows, you'll receive a message that Windows doesn't recognize the file type. See Chapter 20, "What to Do When...Your Files Are Funky," for more help on this particular Windows-related file problem.

Problem 6:

You opened an email attachment and then started experiencing problems with your computer

You know what happened, don't you? You just opened an attachment that contained a *virus*. Computer viruses are often inserted into executable program files (files with an .EXE extension); when you open the attachment, you launch the program—which activates the virus.

Once a virus has invaded your system, there's not much you can do about it, especially if it's a malicious virus that deletes key system files from your hard disk. The best protection against computer viruses of all sorts is an anti-virus program, such as those discussed in Chapter 10, "Germ Warfare—Protecting Your Computer from Viruses." Better still—don't open any email attachments (especially .EXE files) from senders who aren't familiar to you!

Problem 7:

You didn't receive a message someone said they sent you

Just as you sometimes get email bounced back to you as undeliverable, people sending *you* email sometimes receive an "undeliverable" message in return. The causes are the same, of course—the sender could have an incorrect email address for you, or there may have been temporary problems with your ISP's mail server that bounced the message back to the sender.

It's also possible that the message is still in transit. We kind of expect email delivery to be instantaneous, but sometimes ISPs get a bit of a backlog going, which can hold up email delivery anywhere from a few minutes to a few days. The solution, of course, is to be patient—and to ask the sender to resend the message anyway, just in case.

In addition, don't forget that extra-large messages (over 1MB, in many cases) can screw up your mail delivery. One large message can clog your entire retrieval, blocking dozens of other messages from being downloaded to your inbox. If you think you have a message that you haven't actually received, it doesn't hurt to call your ISP's voice support and have them check on it.

Problem 8:

You can't find the email address for a specific person

One of the biggest complaints about email is that it's difficult to look up someone's email address. Unfortunately, there is no central repository for email addresses on the Internet; every ISP, every commercial online service, and almost every Internet domain server issues and controls its own email addresses, and doesn't send them to any central directory.

There are, however, sites where you can search for email addresses. Some of the sites that offer email directory services are quite good, even though they can only list those email addresses they actually know about—which might be just a fraction of the total number of email addresses actually available.

Here are some of the more popular email directories on the Internet:

➤ 411Locate (www.411locate.com)

➤ Bigfoot (www.bigfoot.com)

➤ Email Address Book (www.emailbook.com)

➤ InfoSpace (www.infospace.com)

➤ Internet Address Finder (www.iaf.net)

➤ Switchboard (www.switchboard.com)

➤ The Ultimates (www.theultimates.com)

➤ WhoWhere (www.whowhere.lycos.com)

➤ World Email Directory (www.worldemail.com)

➤ Worldpages (www.worldpages.com)

➤ Yahoo! People Search (people.yahoo.com)

In addition, there is one surefire way to find out someone's email address: *Ask them for it!*

Problem 9:

You're getting tired of junk emails filling your inbox

If you've been using the Internet for any time at all, you've probably started to receive unwanted emails—and lots of them. These junk emails—referred to as *spam*—eat up telephone time while they download, clog up your inbox, and generally just annoy the heck out of you.

The easiest way to deal with a spam message is to simply delete it. But if you get several—or dozens—of spam messages daily, even the task of deleting the messages can be time-consuming.

So how do you stop the spam?

First, you have to recognize where the spammers get your email address. Any time you put your email address on the Internet, you have potentially supplied your address to a spammer. When you register for a service on a Web page, or create your own personal Web page, or post an article in a newsgroup, or participate in a mailing list discussion, you leave your email address—which can be fodder for future spammers. So the first step in fighting spam is to limit the number of places where you post your email address.

Another spam-fighting technique is to use a phony email address. Whenever possible, *don't* leave your real email address; enter something else instead—as long as you *don't* want to receive replies!—to throw off the spammers.

You can also *alter* your email address when you post to newsgroups or mailing lists, using something called a *spamblock*. Because most spammers use software programs (called *spambots*) to automate the name-retrieval process, manually adding "NOSPAM" (the spamblock) to your address will throw off the spambots, yet still be manageable for any human beings who want to respond to your message. Just write your address like this: **myname@domain.NOSPAM.com**; real users will see to take out the spamblock in their reply, while the so-called *spambots* will be totally thrown off.

In addition, don't encourage the spammers. Don't answer their emails. Don't visit their Web pages. Don't buy their products and services. If no one patronizes them, they won't make any money, and they'll eventually go away.

Don't Reply!

Here's something *not* to do: Don't reply to any spammer's invitation to remove your name from their mailing lists. If—and it's a big if, because spammers' email addresses are typically phony—your message actually gets through, chances are your name will only be *added* to other mailing lists, not removed!

If you want to complain about a particular piece of spam, forward the message to the postmaster from where the mail was sent. Use the domain name of the address in the From: field, and address the message to either **postmaster@*domain.name*** or **abuse@*domain.name***—or both. In the text of your message, complain that you didn't solicit this mail, and you don't want to receive any more in the future. This may or may not have any effect; most spammers jump around from ISP to ISP with annoying regularity.

The bottom line is that it's very difficult, if not impossible, to stop all junk emails, just as it's difficult to stop postal junk mail. The best thing to do is limit the exposure of your email address, and learn to ignore the spam.

10 Do's and Don'ts for Effective Email

1. *Do* check your email frequently, and respond to your messages promptly; other users expect timely responses to their messages.
2. *Don't* send HTML-formatted email to people using plain-text email applications (such as cc:Mail and older versions of Eudora).

3. *Do* be careful about opening attachments to email messages, especially from people you don't know—that attachment could contain a devastating computer virus!

4. *Don't* give out your email address indiscriminately, or in Usenet news postings; this is where the spammers gather addresses for all their junk emailings.

5. *Do* consider signing up for a Web-based email service, such as Hotmail; it's good to have a backup email address, and it's convenient if you need to check email when you're away from home.

6. *Don't* worry too much about POP3, IMAP, SMTP, and all those other email initials; just make sure you get the right configuration information from your ISP, and then plug that info into your email program.

7. *Do* remember to "quote" relevant parts of the original message when you're replying to an email message; this helps the author of the original message remember what it is you're replying to.

8. *Don't* get discouraged if you can't find a specific address when searching an email directory; most email addresses simply aren't listed in these directories.

9. *Do* learn how to participate in topic-specific email mailing lists, and obtain a list of mailing lists from Liszt (`www.liszt.com`).

10. *Don't* believe all those myths and "urban legends" floating around in random email messages, and don't perpetuate them by forwarding the messages to anyone else. Continuing a chain letter via email won't make you rich, Bill Gates won't send you money if you pass along that message, the U.S. Congress isn't going to start charging for use of the Internet any time soon, and the sick little boy who wanted to get in the *Guinness Book of Records* by receiving as many cards or emails as possible got well a long time ago.

The Least You Need to Know

➤ Email messages are sent from your computer through your ISP to the recipient's ISP, and then downloaded to the recipient's personal computer; you download your waiting email messages from your ISP's mail server.

➤ "Undeliverable" email typically results from problems at your recipient's ISP mail server, or an incorrect email address.

➤ Files attached to email messages can be used to send documents to other users, but can also be used to transmit harmful computer viruses.

➤ Junk email, or "spam," is annoying, widespread, and almost impossible to stop.

Chapter 26

What to Do When... Your Web Surfing Wipes Out

In This Chapter

➤ Find out what can keep you from accessing a Web site

➤ Learn what all those Web-related error messages mean

➤ Discover the secrets of successful Web searchers

The World Wide Web is the cool part of the Internet. Web pages—and there are hundreds of millions of them—are colorful and graphical and sometimes multimedia-enabled. They're linked to each other, one after another, and offer just about any type of information you can imagine. You can find corporate Web pages and personal Web pages, archived pages and real-time pages, fun pages and serious pages, pages with audio clips and pages with movie clips, pages that make you think and pages that make you laugh.

The Web is so-called because all of these pages and sites and servers are interlinked, all criss-crossing each other like some sort of global spider's Web. Any one page can link to any other page anywhere on the Web; geography matters not.

It's this interlinking that makes the Web so cool, and that causes so many problems. Read on to learn more.

How the World Wide Web Works

I find that cruising the Web is like browsing through an encyclopedia. Invariably when I'm reading one article in an encyclopedia, I find a reference to a related article that interests me. When I turn to the new article, I find a reference to another article, which references another article—and, before I know it, I have all 24 volumes open in front of me. When you're on the Web, it's the same sort of experience. In the course of a single session, it's not unusual to discover that you've visited more than a dozen different sites—and still have lots of interesting places to go!

Pages, Sites, and Hyperlinks

At the heart of the Web is the Web *page*. A Web page is nothing more than a document, like a word processing document or any other computer file that resides on a Web *server*. (A server is just a computer that is constantly connected to the Internet, and accessible to all other Internet users.) Each Web page has a unique address (called a *URL*, or *Uniform Resource Locator*), and the server *hosts* the page and makes it available to other Web users.

When you have multiple related pages together, you have a Web *site*. Typically, the main page—called the *home* page—of the site owns the "top level" address; all other pages on the site are "underneath" the home page, in terms of hierarchy. Most home pages have navigational buttons or links to the other key pages on the site.

A Web page is created using a special code, kind of a low-level programming language. This code, called *HTML* (for *HyperText Markup Language*), describes what each element on the Web page looks like, and how it behaves. Users never see the HTML code; it operates in the background. Instead, you see the result of the code—the Web page itself.

Thanks to HTML codes, Web pages can include more than just plain text. Different codes let Web page developers add color and pictures and sounds and even movie clips to Web pages. Codes can also be inserted for *hyperlinks*, which link one Web page to another. When users click on a hyperlink, they are automatically transported to the linked page. Hyperlinks can connect Web pages on the same site or on different sites—even in different countries!

You view a Web page with a Web *browser*. The two most popular browsers today are Microsoft's Internet Explorer and Netscape Navigator (part of the Netscape Communicator suite). Both of these browsers work pretty much the same way, and have pretty much the same features.

How to Read a URL

A Web address—otherwise known as a URL—precisely points to a single Web page, through the use of addressing standards. The first part of the URL is the `http://`, which tells Web browsers that what follows is a Web page. (There are other prefixes for other types of Internet sites—`ftp://` for FTP sites, for example.)

Following the prefix, in most instances, is the site address, in the form of `www.site.com`. This is *not* a standard, however; site addresses can start with something other than `www.` and end with something other than `.com`. (For example, sites for non-profit organizations often end in `.org`, educational sites end in `.edu`, government sites end in `.gov`, and sites from other countries end in specific country codes—such as `.uk` for the United Kingdom.)

When you enter a site address, you'll automatically be taken to the home page of that site. In most cases, the home page has an address that looks like this: www.*site*.com/ index.html. You don't have to enter the index.html because your Web browser automatically looks for and loads the index.html page when you just enter a site address.

The index.html is an example of a filename used as part of a Web address. In this case, the address for that page references the index.html *file* on the www.*site*.com *site*. If there were a page with the filename bob.html on that site, its address would be www.*site*.com/bob.html.

If a site has a lot of pages, the pages might be organized into *directories* or "child sites," with each directory representing a specific topic. Each directory will be preceded by the "backslash" symbol, and the directory's contents (including any subdirectories within the directory) will follow a backslash.

So, if you had the directory frank on our hypothetical site, its address would be www.*site*.com/frank/. If the frank directory had another subdirectory named bob that contained the bob.html file, the address for that file would be www.site.com/ frank/bob/bob.html.

When you enter a URL into your Web browser's **Address** box, you have to enter the address exactly as given. If you misspell a word or leave out a backslash, it will have the same effect as leaving a number out of your street address—it will cause your browser to look for the wrong address.

What Can Go Wrong on the Web

The biggest problem with the Web is connecting to the right Web page. URLs can be long and convoluted, and easily mistyped (either by you, in your browser's **Address** box, or by the person coding a hyperlink on another Web page). Chances are if you have trouble accessing a page, you have the wrong URL.

In addition, Web sites are constantly revising their content, design, and navigation. So it's not uncommon to click on a link and get a different page than what you were expecting—or no page at all! Server and traffic issues can also temporarily block access to overloaded Web sites. (Only so many users can connect to a server at one time, no matter how large the site—and servers sometimes are taken "offline" for maintenance.) If you can't connect to a site now, check your URL and try again a little later.

Sometimes your problem isn't whether you can connect, but rather how long it takes you to connect. There can be several causes of slow loading—a slow Internet connection (via your phone line), lots of traffic on the Internet (too many users online at the same time), lots of traffic to a particular site or page (too many users wanting to look at the same thing), or very large graphics files on the destination Web page. If you think a page is taking *too* long to load, click your browser's **Stop** button to cancel the loading, then click the **Refresh** or **Reload** button to try accessing the page again. Sometimes just trying again will get you to the page faster!

It's also possible that your connection problems aren't site related. Try connecting to more than one site; if you can't connect to *any* site, you could have a problem with your connection to your ISP. See Chapter 24, "What to Do When…Your Internet Connection Goes Offline," for more instructions.

What to Do When Your Web Surfing Wipes Out

Web surfing can be both fun and productive—if you're not wasting all your time tracking down bad URLs and dead links! Read on to discover the most common Web-related problems, and how to solve them.

Problem 1:

Your Web browser won't connect to any Web site

If you try connecting to one site, then another, then another—all unsuccessfully— you know you don't have a problem with a single URL or Web server. When you can't connect to *anything*, there's either a problem between you and your ISP, or between your ISP and the Internet.

Try doing something non–Web-related on the Internet; check your email, or try to access a chat room. If you can do other Internet-related tasks, your ISP has a problem with its gateway to the Web. You may have to wait a few minutes (or hours!) for the gateway to unclog; if the problem persists, call your ISP's voice support line and report the problem.

If you also can't perform other Internet-related tasks (if you get errors when trying to check your email, for example), your problem lies in your connection to your ISP. End your current connection, then reconnect. Often times establishing a new connection solves this type of problem. If you continue to lack Internet access on subsequent connections, check your configuration information, as detailed in Chapter 24, "What to Do When…Your Internet Connection Goes Offline." If the situation persists, call your ISP's voice support line and report the problem.

Problem 2:

Your Web browser won't connect to a specific Web site

The first thing to check if you can't connect to a specific site is the URL. If you entered the URL manually, it's possible you mistyped it; try reentering the address, more carefully this time. It's also possible that the address doesn't actually exist; either the URL is wrong, or the page *used to* exist but has been taken offline for some reason or another. (Dead pages are an increasing problem on the Web.) Next, the link to the page may be incorrect (someone had to manually enter the code for the link when the page was being created; human beings sometimes make mistakes!). And, finally, the page may be *temporarily* unavailable (sometimes Web servers "go down"—break—and leave all the pages they host unavailable until repairs are made); trying again later is the best suggestion in this situation.

One trick to try if you can't access a specific page on a Web site is to try to access other pages on the site. You can do this by *truncating* the URL. For example, if you couldn't access www.*mysite*.com/*mydirectory*/*mypage*.html, then truncate the last part of the URL and try accessing www.*mysite*.com/*mydirectory*/. If that doesn't work, keep truncating until you get to the main site URL (in this case, www.*mysite*.com). On many sites, the home page contains a search function you can use to find specific pages on the site; it's possible you can search for the page that you couldn't access, in case the site administrator changed URLs on you.

If you receive an error message when you try to access a page, it's easier to track down the cause of the problem. Proceed to Problem 3 for more details.

Problem 3:

Your Web browser gives you an error message when you try to connect to a specific Web site

More often than not, your browser will display an error message when it can't access a specific Web page. Learning how to decipher these messages will help you determine *why* the page in question is inaccessible.

Table 26.1 details the most common Web error messages, what they mean, and what to do about them.

Table 26.1   Web Error Messages

Error Message	Cause	Recommended Action
400 - Bad request	Page can't be found; URL is incorrect	Reenter URL; check uppercase and lowercase
401 - Unauthorized	Page is protected and you're not on the "guest" list—or you entered an incorrect password	If you're not on the "guest" list, you can't get in; if you are on the "guest" list, recheck and reenter your password
403 - Forbidden	Page is protected and you're not on the "guest" list—or you entered an incorrect password	If you're not on the "guest" list, you can't get in; if you are on the "guest" list, recheck and reenter your password
404 - Access denied	Page is protected and you're not on the "guest" list—or you entered an incorrect password	If you're not on the "guest" list, you can't get in; if you are on the "guest" list, recheck and reenter your password

continues

Table 26.1 CONTINUED

Error Message	Cause	Recommended Action
`404 - Not found`	Page can't be found; URL is incorrect	Reenter URL; try going one level up in site directory
`503 - Service unavailable`	Something in between you and the page is down, probably either the site's server or your ISP's Internet gateway	Wait a few minutes and try connecting to the page again
`Bad file request`	Your browser isn't compatible with a form on the page	Upgrade your browser to the latest version
`Cannot open... You do not have permission to open this item`	Page is protected and you're not on the "guest" list—or you entered an incorrect password	If you're not on the "guest" list, you can't get in; if you are on the "guest" list, recheck and reenter your password
`Connection refused by host`	Page is protected and you're not on the "guest" list; you typed an incorrect password; or this page is blocked to your ISP	If you're not on the "guest" list, you can't get in; if you are on the "guest" list, recheck and reenter your password; if this site is blocked to your ISP, complain to your ISP
`Connection reset by peer`	The Web site reset your connection for some reason	Reload or refresh the Web page
`Connection timed out`	Either the site or your Internet connection stopped responding	Wait a few minutes and try reloading the page; if you get this message at multiple sites, close your current connection, wait a few minutes, and then reconnect to your ISP
`Failed DNS lookup`	Page can't be found; URL is bad or there are temporary connection problems	Recheck the URL and try again; if the URL is correct, try again a few minutes later
`File contains no data`	You have the right site, but there's nothing there	It's possible the site may be updating its pages, so try again in an hour or so; it's also possible the site has been closed down, even though the domain name is still active

Error Message	Cause	Recommended Action
Helper application not found	Your browser isn't capable of reading a particular file	Update your browser to the latest version, or add the "plug-in" to read this particular file type
Host unavailable	The site you're trying to access is "down"	Try accessing the site in a few minutes or hours; if you continue to get this message, the site may have been closed
Host unknown	The site you're trying to access is "down," or you have an incorrect URL	Recheck and reenter your URL, then try accessing the site in a few minutes or hours; if you continue to get this message, the site may have been closed
Network connection was refused by the server	The site's server is too busy to handle any more users	Wait a few minutes, then try again
Permission denied	You're trying to upload a file to an FTP site and you can't get in, either because of a bad password or the site is too busy	Recheck and reenter your password, and try accessing a few minutes later
Socket is not connected	Somewhere in between your PC and the target site is a bad connection	Try connecting to another site; if you get the same error message, disconnect from your ISP, wait a few minutes, and then reconnect
Too many connections - try again later	The site's server is too busy to handle any more users	Wait a few minutes, then try again
Too many users	The site's server is too busy to handle any more users	Wait a few minutes, then try again
Unable to locate host	The site you're trying to access is "down"	Try accessing the site in a few minutes or hours; if you continue to get this message, the site may have been closed
Unable to locate the server	Page can't be found; URL is bad or there are temporary connection problems	Recheck the URL and try again; if the URL is correct, try again a few minutes later

continues

Table 26.1 CONTINUED

Error Message	Cause	Recommended Action
Unable to open http://www.*site*.com/*page*... The site reports that the item you requested could not be found.	The overall site exists, but the individual page you want doesn't	Make sure you have the correct page URL; try truncating the URL to access a higher-level directory
Viewer not found	Your browser isn't capable of reading a particular file	Update your browser to the latest version, or add the "plug-in" to read this particular file type

Problem 4:

You connect to a Web page, but it only partially loads

There can be a number of causes if a page "hangs" while loading. First, the page may actually still be loading, but it's a really big page. Click the **Stop** button on your browser and then try reloading the page. If the page still takes too long to load, try turning off graphics in your browser, so that you only load text. (Also note that pages that load background sounds and music can *appear* to be hung, but are actually just waiting for the music file to download.)

Second, the connection to this site may have gone bad in mid-load. Try reloading the page; if you still have trouble loading this and other pages, disconnect from your ISP, wait a few minutes, and then reconnect.

Third, the problem may be with your Web browser. Try "flushing" your browser's cache and history files to clear disk space and memory.

Problem 5:

You connect to a Web page, but parts of the page don't display properly

Some pages incorporate advanced technologies—such as Java and Macromedia Shockwave—that may not be compatible with all Web browsers. If you get a blank space on your page, try reloading—but then check to make sure your browser is capable of displaying these elements. (That might mean adding a "plug-in" to your browser, or upgrading to a more recent version.)

It's also possible that parts of the page referenced in its HTML code actually aren't there. This is somewhat common when dealing with graphics files; site designers will reference .JPG and .GIF files elsewhere on the site (or on another site) that subsequently disappear. Try right-clicking on the empty space and selecting **Load Picture** from the pop-up menu; if the picture still doesn't load, it's a problem with the page, not with your browser.

Problem 6:

You can't find the information or site you're looking for

Users spend more time on the Web searching than they do in any other activity. It takes most users so long to search because they don't know the *best* ways to search— or even the best *places* to search.

When you're searching the Web, you have the choice of using a *search engine* or a *directory*. A search engine uses a special type of software program (called a *spider* or *crawler*) to roam the Web automatically, creating giant indexes of sites that you can then search; the most popular search engines on the Web are AltaVista (www.altavista.com), Excite (www.excite.com), HotBot (www.hotbot.com), and Northern Light (www.northern-light.com). A directory is a hand-picked and categorized collection of Web sites; Yahoo! (www.yahoo.com) is the most-popular directory on the Web. Search engines typically index anywhere from 50 million to 100 million individual Web pages; directories typically catalog less than a million pages, but organize them in tightly defined categories.

Whether you use a large search engine or a well-organized directory, here are some tips to help you improve your Web searches:

➤ **Think like the creators.** Web sites are created by human beings. That isn't necessarily a good thing, since human beings are less than logical—and less than perfect. Did the person writing about Internet Explorer call it "Internet Explorer," or "Microsoft Internet Explorer," or just "Explorer," or "IE," or "IE5" (including the version number), or was it simply called a "browser" or a "Web browser" or even (somewhat incorrectly) a "navigator"? The best search engines in the world can't anticipate human beings who use alternate words, or (heaven forbid!) use the wrong words by mistake. So when you construct your queries, think through all the different ways people refer to the topic you're looking for. *Visualize* the results you'd like to find, and what they might look like on a Web page. Then, and only then, should you construct your query, using the keywords and operators and modifiers you need to return the results you visualized.

For Better Searches, Buy the Book!

If you really want to power-up your Web searches, read my recent best-seller from Que, *The Complete Idiot's Guide to Online Search Secrets.* In this book you'll find tips and techniques that will help you perform more efficient and more effective searches—on practically *any* search site!

➤ **Use the right words.** When you construct your query, you do so by using one or more *keywords*. You should choose keywords that best describe the information you're looking for—using as many keywords as you need. Think of it as describing something to a friend—the more descriptive you are (that is, the more words you use), the better picture your friend has of what you're talking about. Also, think about alternative ways to say what it is that you're looking for. If you're looking for a *car*, you could also be looking for a *vehicle* or an *automobile* or an *auto* or for *transportation*. It doesn't take a search guru to realize that searching for **car vehicle automobile auto transportation** will generate better results than simply searching for **car**.

➤ **When you don't know the right words, use wildcards.**   What if you're not quite sure of which word form to use? Many search sites let you use *wildcards* to "stand in" for parts of a word that you're not quite sure about. In most instances, the "asterisk" character (*) is used as a wildcard to match any character or group of characters, from its particular position in the word to the end of that word. So, in our previous example, entering **auto*** would return all three words—auto, automobile, *and* automotive.

➤ **Modify your words with +, -, and " ".**   A *modifier* is a symbol that causes a search engine to do something special with the word directly following the symbol. There are three modifiers used almost universally in the search engine community: + (for when a keyword *must* be included for a match), - (for when a keyword must *never* be part of a match), and " " (for when an exact phrase must be found).

➤ **Use AND, NOT, and OR in a Boolean search.**   Modifiers are nice, but they're not always the most *flexible* way to modify your query. The preferred parameters for serious online searching are called *Boolean operators*. While not all search sites allow Boolean searches, those that do will probably allow these operators: **AND** (a match must contain *both* words), **OR** (a match must contain *either* of the words), and **NOT** (a match must *exclude* the next word). Boolean searching also lets you use parentheses, much like you would in a mathematical equation, to group portions of queries together to create more complicated searches.

10 Do's and Don'ts for Better Web Surfing

1. *Do* make sure you're using the latest version of Internet Explorer or Netscape Navigator; some Web sites incorporate features that only work with the latest Web browsers.

2. *Don't* limit yourself to AOL's built-in browser if you're an America Online subscriber; once you launch AOL, you can run *any* Web browser (or any other Internet application) while you run AOL in the background.

3. *Do* learn the proper methods for effective searching; you can find all sorts of useful tips and techniques in my bestselling book, *The Complete Idiot's Guide to Online Search Secrets*.

4. *Don't* be concerned about giving out your credit card number to Web retailers using secure servers; secure Web sites are actually safer than handing your credit card to a nameless waiter in a fancy restaurant.

5. *Do* "bookmark" your favorite sites in your Web browser, so you can revisit them with a single click.

6. *Don't* bother typing **http://** every time you enter a URL; most Web browsers assume this first part of the address, so you don't have to enter it.

7. *Do* double-check the URL if you have trouble accessing a Web site; if the URL is correct, wait a few seconds and try again, just in case there was a temporary traffic clog on the Web.

8. *Don't* settle for the default start page configured in your Web browser; you can set *any* page on the Web as your browser's start page.

9. *Do* create your own personal Web page; sites such as GeoCities (`www.geocities.com`) and Tripod (`www.tripod.com`) make it easy to create a Web page without HTML, and for free.

10. *Don't* become a Web addict; if you find yourself surfing for hours at a time for no particular reason, it's time to seek professional help!

The Least You Need to Know

➤ If you can't access a particular Web site, double-check the URL and try reaccessing it at a later time.

➤ If a particular Web page appears to be missing, try looking for other pages on the same site—or emailing the site administrator about the missing page.

➤ If you can't access *any* Web page, your ISP is having trouble with its gateway to the Internet.

HOLY MACARONI...

Chapter 27

What to Do When... Your Kids Uncover Naughty Bits Online

In This Chapter

➤ Find out which major search engines offer content-filtered searches

➤ Discover software programs that block access to offensive Web sites

➤ Learn the best ways to protect your children online

The Internet contains an almost limitless supply of information; some of it is good, and some of it is potentially bad. There are sites with sexual content, and violent content, and hateful content, and content that you couldn't even imagine until it popped up on your computer screen. Some of this stuff isn't just adult, it's disgusting!

So how do you protect your family from the bad stuff on the Internet—while still allowing access to all the good stuff? This chapter will provide a few suggestions...

How to Make the Internet Safe for Children

I'll be the first to voice the opinion that the Internet shouldn't be censored; in my view, the good on the Net far outweighs the bad, and I don't want anyone anywhere telling me what I can and can't access. But I also know that there's a lot of content out there that children probably shouldn't be accessing. Balancing "freedom of the Net" with the responsibility of protecting impressionable children is the challenge.

It's probably not possible to shield every child from every inappropriate page on the Web. Dedicated content pushers will always find a way around whatever content blocks are enacted—and determined kids will find the stuff you don't want them to find. (I know I would have, when I was a kid!) The best we can do, I believe, is to create an environment that encourages *appropriate* use of the Internet, and discourages deliberate searching for inappropriate content.

Although there are technological tools you can employ to keep inappropriate content away from your kids, nothing replaces good old parental supervision. At the end of the day, you have to take responsibility for your children's online activities. Provide the guidance they need to make the Internet a fun and educational place to visit—and you'll all be better for it.

The Family-Friendly Web Site Solution

There are numerous Web sites that apply filters to weed out inappropriate content and search results. These sites are often good to use as your browser's start page because they're a launching pad to safe content for your children.

The best of these family-friendly Web sites are:

➤ **AltaVista—AV Family Filter** (www.altavista.com)   This is a filtered version of the AltaVista search engine; adult and other inappropriate sites are deleted from normal search results. (To activate the filter, go to the main AltaVista page and click the **Family Filter** link.)

➤ **Ask Jeeves for Kids** (www.ajkids.com)   A unique service where you enter your queries via a plain-English question, and Ask Jeeves provides the answer via a short list of highly qualified and filtered Web sites—recommended!

➤ **EdView SmartZone** (school.edview.com/search/)   A collection of over seven million teacher-reviewed kid-safe Web pages, categorized by subject and grade level.

➤ **Family Web Files** (www.familywebfiles.com)   Links to family-friendly Web sites, in both English and Spanish.

➤ **infoplease Kids' Almanac** (kids.infoplease.com)   One of the largest and coolest information-oriented kids sites on the Web.

➤ **Infoseek—GOguardian** (infoseek.go.com)   This is a filtered version of the standard Infoseek search engine; adult and other inappropriate sites are deleted from normal search results. (To activate the filter, go to the main Infoseek page and click the **GOguardian** link.)

➤ **Lycos—Search Guard** (www.lycos.com)   This is a filtered version of the Lycos site; adult and other inappropriate sites are deleted from normal search results. (To activate the filter, go to the main Lycos page and click the **Parental Controls** link.)

➤ **OneKey** (www.onekey.com)   A directory of kid-safe sites, organized in over 500 different categories; each site has been personally reviewed.

➤ **Searchopolis** (www.searchopolis.com)   One of the newer filtered search engines.

> ➤ **Super Snooper (supersnooper.com)** A new search engine that filters out inappropriate results; you'll find some good filtering here.

> ➤ **Yahooligans! (www.yahooligans.com)** Yahoo! for kids, designed for ages 7 to 12, with sites hand-picked for appropriateness—recommended!

These sites all work pretty much the same way. Someone, somewhere, compiles a list of offensive words and topics. Then software at the site (or, in some cases, a *person* at the site) searches through the site's index for pages that contain those words or topics, and exclude them from the newly filtered site index. That way, when you do a search at that site using that filter, you never see any offensive Web pages that might otherwise have been included in your results.

My two favorite sites here are Ask Jeeves for Kids and Yahooligans! Yahooligans! is a good high-quality directory that is very easy to browse, and Ask Jeeves lets kids search the way they're inclined to search—using plain-English questions. As with the main Ask Jeeves site, it's an efficient and effective way to find the Web sites that contain the answers to your questions—and, with the kids' version, the content is filtered for appropriateness.

The Safe-Surfing Software Solution

Another way to protect your family from inappropriate Internet content is to install software on your computer that performs filtering functions for all your online sessions. These safe-search programs guard against either a preselected list of sites or a preselected list of topics, and block access to sites that meet the selected criteria.

The following are five of the most popular filtering programs:

> ➤ **Cyber Patrol (www.cyberpatrol.com; $29.95)** Blocks access to a preselected list of Web sites; also detects sites with objectionable words or images.

> ➤ **Cyber Snoop (www.pearlsw.com; $29.95)** Tracks where your child has visited and saves the list as an activity log for parents to review; it can also block access to specified Web sites and Usenet newsgroups.

> ➤ **Cybersitter (www.solidoak.com/cysitter.htm; $39.95)** Blocks access to a preselected list of Web sites, FTP sites, and Usenet newsgroups; also detects offensive words and phrases. One of the most popular filter programs, with more than 1.7 million users—recommended!

> ➤ **Net Nanny (www.netnanny.com; $39.95)** Blocks access to a preselected list of Web sites, Usenet newsgroups, and chat rooms.

> ➤ **SurfWatch (www.surfwatch.com; $49.95)** Blocks access to a preselected list of Web sites, Usenet newsgroups, and chat rooms; large initial list of banned sites (25,000 URLs)—recommended!

Of these, I tend to like Cybersitter and SurfWatch the best—Cybersitter for its ease of use and SurfWatch for its massive list of suspect URLs. Note, however, that these filtering programs can also block access to sites you *don't* want filtered; one of the editors on this book mentioned that Cyber Patrol has actually blocked his access to www.nbc.com!

What to Do When Your Kids Uncover Naughty Bits Online

Given that you can't protect your children from 100 percent of the bad stuff on the Internet, how can you minimize their exposure to inappropriate content in their everyday surfing?

Problem 1:

Your search engine returns X-rated sites when you do a G-rated search

One of the problems with searching the Web is that adult-oriented sites (sex sites, in other words) keep popping up in your search results. The people that run these sites are experts at "promoting" and describing their sites in such a way that they seem to match just about any search query.

If you want to weed out offensive content from your normal search results, three of the major search sites offer special filters for kid-friendly searching:

➤ AltaVista—AV Family Filter (www.altavista.com)

➤ Infoseek—GOguardian (infoseek.go.com)

➤ Lycos—Search Guard (www.lycos.com)

When you access these sites, you'll have to click the link that turns on their filtering or parental control options.

Although search filters are the best way to avoid objectionable content, they can also filter out sites that you actually want to visit. Instead, you might try using your own search filters by adding parameters to your queries that exclude certain words and phrases from your search results. This approach has the added benefit of filtering the queries you make at any search site, whether the site offers built-in filtering or not.

Which words should you exclude from your queries? Some of the more common words used in the titles and META tags of adult Web sites are "sex" and "hardcore." If you tell a search engine to exclude these words from your search (by using either the - command or the **NOT** Boolean operator), any pages containing these two words won't be returned.

Let's see how this works. Pick a search engine and enter a search for **breasts**. Chances are that you'll get a few adult sites mixed in with a results list that also includes sites about breast cancer and breast feeding. Now enter this search: **breasts -sex -hardcore** (or, in a Boolean search, **breasts NOT sex NOT hardcore**) and see what you get. It should be a slightly cleaner search.

Note that this isn't a perfect tactic, because not all adult sites include the words "sex" and "hardcore" in their META tags; in addition, some adult sites use splash pages that tend to foil filtering schemes of all types. Still, it helps a little, so you might want to give it a try.

Problem 2:

You're receiving adult-oriented emails in your inbox

Spam is bad enough; pornographic spam (what I call sexspam) is even worse. Unfortunately, spam of any type is near impossible to stop; it's the online equivalent of trying to stop junk mail from cluttering your real-world mail box. You can complain to your ISP about it, but as soon as they go after one sexspammer, another one pops up—or the first one simply changes ISPs. See Chapter 25, "What to Do When...Your Email Works More Like Snail Mail," for more advice on how to handle spam, but don't get your hopes up.

Problem 3:

A family member is being "stalked" online

This can be a scary situation; your child logs on to the Internet, and immediately receives threatening or suggestive email messages, instant messages, or private messages in chat rooms. Obviously, whoever is "cyberstalking" knows your child's private email address, IM username, and chat nickname. You can only hope that this person doesn't know your home phone number or street address.

The only surefire way to stop a cyberstalker is to stop using the Internet. Drop your Internet account and disconnect the phone line from your PC. You can't be stalked online if you're not online.

Set Your Own Rules for Online Use

I have a friend (Hi, Jeff!) who was a late convert to letting his children online. He finally came up with a formal agreement that he presented to his kids, where they agreed (in writing) to certain standards of behavior online; in return, he let them have Internet access. I like this approach; he didn't dictate to his kids, they agreed together to what they would and wouldn't do while connected to the Internet. (The agreement was also fairly detailed; remember that children can get very literal in their interpretation of rules and restrictions!)

There's too much valuable information (and too many potentially good relationships) on the Internet to completely deny children access. The best way to emphasize the good and protect against the bad is to make Internet use a true family activity, with everything out in the open, no secrets. When you surf with your kids, you'll know they're getting the best of the Net—and you get to share some quality time, besides.

A less drastic solution is to simply change your child's email account and username. Completely
abandon your child's old identity, and give him or her a new online identity.

317

You can also try to track down the cyberstalker, by carefully examining the headers of the offensive email messages. You can try reporting the cyberstalker to your ISP, and to the stalker's ISP (if that can be determined). Unfortunately, a *smart* cyberstalker will know how to disguise his identity by using anonymous remailing services, so it may be difficult if not impossible to track him down.

If the threats get too worrisome, don't hesitate to contact your local authorities. There have been instances of online stalking leading to real-world situations; where your children are concerned, it's better to be safe than sorry.

Of course, the best solution is to prevent this sort of situation from ever developing. Train your children to never reveal their real identities online, and to hide behind multiple usernames and nick names and email addresses. (I like signing up the kids for Web-based email, such as Hotmail, which is practically impossible to trace to a specific ISP account.) If your kids are careful, the Internet can be a very safe place to play.

10 Do's and Don'ts to Protect Your Kids on the Internet

1. *Do* make sure your children know never to give out any identifying information (home address, school name, telephone number, and so on) or to send their photos to other users online.

2. *Don't* allow your children to arrange face-to-face meetings with other computer users without parental permission and supervision. If a meeting is arranged, make the first one in a public place and be sure to accompany your child.

3. *Do* consider making Internet surfing an activity you do together with your children—or make it a family activity by putting your PC in a public room, rather than in a private bedroom.

4. *Don't* hesitate to set reasonable rules and guidelines for computer use by your children; consider limiting the number of minutes/hours they can spend online each day.

5. *Do* consider giving each of your children an online pseudonym so they don't have to use their real names online.

6. *Don't* be afraid to monitor your children's Internet activities. Ask them to keep a log of all Web sites they visit; oversee any chat sessions they participate in; check out any files they download; even consider sharing an email account (especially with younger children) so that you can oversee their messages.

7. *Do* teach your children that people online may not always be who they seem; just because someone says she's a 10-year-old girl doesn't necessarily mean that she really is 10 years old, or a girl.

8. *Don't* let your children respond to messages that are suggestive, obscene, belligerent, threatening, or that make them feel uncomfortable—and encourage your children to tell you if they receive any such messages.

9. *Do* install content-filtering software on your PC, and set up one of the family-friendly Web sites as your browser's default start page.

10. *Don't* assume that Internet access is a right; it should be a privilege earned by your children, and kept only when their use of it matches your expectations.

The Least You Need to Know

➤ Several major search sites (AltaVista, Infoseek, and Lycos) provide filtered search options that try to remove offensive Web pages from their search results.

➤ There are numerous "kid-friendly" Web sites—such as Ask Jeeves for Kids and Yahooligans!—that provide either filtered searches or hand-picked directories of non-offensive sites.

➤ Filtering software—such as Cybersitter and SurfWatch—blocks access to sites that contain offensive topics and words.

➤ All these tools aside, the best way to protect your children online is to make Internet surfing a family activity.

Part 3

A Quick Course in Problem Solving: Technical Details for the Technically Timid

This is the most technical part of a generally non-technical book. If you don't mind dealing with device drivers, messing about with error messages, and rummaging about in the Windows Registry, then read these chapters for a more technical approach to finding and fixing your system's problems.

Chapter 28

Windows Error Messages...What They Mean and How to Deal with Them

---

In This Chapter

➤ Discover the causes behind the most common Windows error messages

---

Windows uses error messages to try and tell you why something bad has happened. Sometimes the messages are easy to decipher. Sometimes they're not.

Because Windows can display literally thousands of error messages—some of them fairly obscure—I've tried to narrow it down to the most common messages you're likely to encounter with Windows and sort them in alphabetical order. (I've avoided including program-specific error messages, or else this book would expand by a few hundred pages or so.)

If your message isn't in this list, don't despair—it just means you have something *really weird* happening with your system. Write down the message and call a competent computer technician. They'll be glad to help you out.

Understanding Common Error Messages

When Windows messes up, it often displays an error message designed to help you figure out this particular problem. The bigger problem is that Windows' error messages are often indecipherable.

So, to help you figure out what Windows is trying to tell you, this section lists the most common messages you're likely to encounter with Windows, in alphabetical order—along with the most probable cause(s) of the message.

For Windows Help, Go to the Source

The best place to look up Windows-related error messages is in the Microsoft Knowledge Base. You can access the Knowledge Base at support.microsoft.com/support/ search/c.asp.

A fatal exception <XY> has occurred at xxxx:xxxxxxxx

Windows does not cause these fatal exception errors; these messages are just Windows' way of reporting a problem encountered by your system's microprocessor, often caused by faulty RAM. In almost all cases, a fatal exception error will freeze or crash your entire system, and you'll have to reboot to continue. If you encounter frequent fatal exception errors, you may need to replace your system's memory chips.

A TSR is installed

Windows does not work with many DOS-based terminate-and-stay-resident (TSR) programs. If you receive this message, remove any TSRs from your system's memory and edit your AUTOEXEC.BAT file so TSRs are not automatically loaded when your system is booted. (And why are you still using that old DOS program, anyway?)

Abnormal termination

This message occurs when a Windows application crashes unexpectedly, most often due to memory problems. Sometimes this kind of program crash will also crash Windows itself.

Another application is using communication port

You are running two programs that are both trying to access a single communication port, such as two communications programs. Close one of the two programs to avoid the current conflict.

Application execution error: Cannot find file Check to ensure path and filename are correct

This message results when Windows tries to load a program that either doesn't exist or isn't located where Windows thinks it is. If this message appears when you start Windows, it means you have an incorrect file inserted in your Startup menu. Check all the programs in this group to make sure the filename and path are correct.

Application execution error: No association exists for this file

If no program file is associated with a data file you're trying to launch, you receive this message. To associate a program file with a file type, click the **Start** button, select **Settings**, then select **Folder Options**. When the Folder Options dialog box appears, select the **File Types** tab. Add a new file type by clicking the **New Type** button and filling in the blanks in the Add New File Type dialog box.

Application is still active

You're trying to exit Windows while an application is still running. Close the program and then exit Windows.

Attempt to load duplicate device

Windows is trying to load a device that is already loaded. Check your SYSTEM.INI file for duplicate lines and eliminate them.

BIOS failed to initialize

This message may appear after you have installed a new program or otherwise changed your system's configuration. Try starting your machine in Safe mode, then edit both the CONFIG.SYS and AUTOEXEC.BAT files, deleting any references to the SMARTDRV.EXE file.

Call to undefined dynalink

This message results when a Windows program tries to use an incompatible DLL file. You'll probably need to wipe the program from your hard disk and reinstall it from scratch. It's also possible that an old printer driver can cause this problem. The solution is similar; erase the old driver and install an updated version.

Cannot communicate with modem

For some reason, Windows cannot access your modem. Check all connections and setup configurations to make sure that your modem is working and properly setup.

Cannot copy file

For some reason (generally something wrong with either the original or the destination disk) the current file cannot be copied. If you encounter this message when installing Windows, try to continue without copying the file.

Cannot find a device file that may be needed

This message is typically followed by a filename (often with the .VXD extension), and indicates that a virtual device driver (VXD) file is missing or corrupted. If you recently installed a new device or program, uninstall it and then reinstall it; if the problem persists, you may need to obtain a new or updated version of the driver file.

Cannot find the file "XXX" or one of its components.

The most common cause for this message is that the file in question is either missing or corrupted. Click the **Start** button and select **Find** to search for the file. Reinstall the program in question if necessary.

Cannot format disk

Windows generates this message when you try to format a diskette that is write-protected. Change diskettes or slide the write-protect tab into the down position (on 3 1/2-inch diskettes).

This message can also appear when you're trying to use a damaged diskette, or if the diskette contains a virus. If either of these are the case, you probably want to throw away this particular diskette and start again with a new one.

Cannot print. SoftRIP error.

Some printers print an entire page as a graphics image, forming that image in memory before printing. If your system doesn't have enough memory, this message is generated. Close any other open applications to free up additional memory.

Cannot read from drive x

Windows is looking for a file on drive *x*. If no diskette is in drive *x*, insert any diskette to end the Windows look loop. If a diskette is already in drive *x*, you either have a bad (or unformatted) diskette, or a bad diskette drive. If the message refers to drive C (your hard disk), your hard disk is going bad.

Cannot replace xxxx: Access Denied.

A common cause of this message is if you tried to copy a file to a write-protected diskette or to a drive that doesn't have a diskette inserted. Make sure the diskette is inserted correctly before you resume the operation or change the diskette's write-protect status.

In addition, this message can be generated if you try to access a file that is in use by another application—or, on a network, by another user.

Cannot run program – No application is associated with this file

If no program file is associated with a document you're trying to launch, you receive this message. To associate a program file with a file type, click the **Start** button, select **Settings**, then select **Folder Options**. When the Folder Options dialog box appears, select the **File Types** tab. Add a new file type by clicking the **New Type** button and filling in the blanks in the Add New File Type dialog box.

Cannot run program – Out of system resources

Resources include system memory as well as space taken by everything you see on your screen—icons, fonts, dialog boxes, and so on. When too much is going on at one time, Windows runs out of resources. Try closing any open programs or simplifying your screen in any way—minimizing windows, closing dialog boxes, and so on.

Cannot start application

Windows cannot start the desired application. Check to make sure the correct directory path and filename was specified. It's also possible that sufficient memory was not available to run this application.

Cannot start more than one copy of xxx

Some programs cannot be loaded twice in Windows. If a program is already running, avoid starting a second instance of the program.

Could not print page x

Windows could not print a particular page in your printout. This is often due to low memory or insufficient disk space to print a page with lots of graphics. Try printing this page at a lower resolution.

Deleting this file will make it impossible to run this program

This message appears when you try to delete a program file. Make sure you *really* want to delete this program before you proceed.

Destination disk drive is full

You receive this message when you're trying to copy data to a diskette that has run out of free space. Either delete files from the diskette, or use another diskette that has more free space.

Disk error

If Windows generates a disk error message, it's normally because you're trying to use a bad or unformatted disk. If you receive a disk error message while reading or writing from a diskette, try another diskette. If you receive this error message regarding your hard disk, it's possible that it is starting to fail. Run **ScanDisk** to find any hard disk errors, and consider replacing your hard disk, after you've backed up your critical data, of course!

Divide by zero

This message generally results from software bugs. When it occurs, close Windows, reboot your computer, and then restart Windows and the problem application. If this message occurs with frequency, consult the publisher of the software.

Drive x: is inaccessible

This message is displayed when a specified drive can't be accessed. Make sure you actually have a diskette correctly inserted in the drive and that the diskette is formatted. If the drive does exist, there may be a problem with your Windows setup.

Explorer caused a fatal exception xxxxxxx in module KERNEL32.DLL at xxxx:xxxxxxxx

This message is displayed when either Windows Explorer or Internet Explorer (they both use the same base code) has misbehaved. If you receive this error frequently, try upgrading to a newer version of Internet Explorer (which upgrades all the underlying code). This error can also be caused by a faulty KERNEL32.DLL file in Windows 95 (*not* Windows 98!); you can download a "fix" for this file from www.microsoft.com/windows95/downloads/ contents/wuadmintools/s_wunetworkingtools/w95kernel32/default.asp?site=95.

Explorer caused an invalid page fault in module comctl32.dll

This is a well-known bug that sometimes appears if you're running Microsoft Office 97 and have Microsoft's IntelliPoint software version 2.0 installed on your system, and you move the mouse pointer out of the Office program window and onto the open desktop. You can minimize the chances for this bug to appear by opening the **Mouse Properties** dialog box and unchecking the **Focus** and **SmartSpeed** options.

Error 20

You're trying to print a document with a considerable amount of graphics or a large number of fonts to a Hewlett-Packard or HP-compatible printer. Your printer doesn't have enough memory to print the entire page, and your output will be incomplete. Simplify your document or print at a lower resolution.

Error 21

See *Error 20*.

Extremely low on memory, close applications and try again

This message results when your system doesn't have enough memory to run the application or perform the operation you specified. Just like the message suggests, close some applications and try the operation again. You may also need to exit Windows (to free up some unreleased memory), restart Windows, and then run the application or perform the operation.

This message can also be caused when you have too little free space left on your hard disk. (Windows uses your hard disk for virtual memory; too little hard disk space equals too little virtual memory.) Try deleting unnecessary files to free up hard disk space.

File already exists. Overwrite?

You're trying to create or save a file with a name that already exists. Windows is asking if you want to overwrite the existing file. If so, answer yes. If no, answer no and assign a new name to your file.

Insufficient disk space

Your system is short on hard disk space. Try deleting some unneeded files and then restarting the operation at hand.

Insufficient memory to run this application

You're trying to launch a program but don't have enough free system memory to do so. Try closing down any open applications before relaunching the new application; if this message occurs again, reboot your system to clear up memory clogs.

Invalid destination specified

Windows displays this message when you try to copy a file to a folder or drive that doesn't exist. Check your commands and try this operation again.

Invalid VxD Dynamic Link Call

This message is generated when a device driver is either missing, corrupted, or incompatible with your version of Windows. If you recently installed a new device or program, try uninstalling and reinstalling it to fix the driver file. If the problem continues, contact the manufacturer of the problem device for an updated driver file.

The problem that causes this message can sometimes stop Windows from loading. If so, you'll need to restart in Safe mode to remove the device.

Invalid system disk, replace the disk, and then press any key

This message appears when you've tried to start your system with a non-bootable diskette in your A drive. Remove the diskette and press any key to continue.

Keyboard error. Press F1 to continue

This error is generated when your computer can't find a keyboard attached to your system during startup—or if one of your keys is stuck. Make sure your keyboard is connected (and the keys unstuck) and then reboot with the power button/switch on your system unit. (Because your keyboard is recognized, you actually can't press **F1** to continue!)

No association exists for this file

If no program file is associated with a data file you're trying to launch, you'll receive this message. To associate a program file with a file type, click the **Start** button, select **Settings**, then select **Folder Options**. When the Folder Options dialog box appears, select the **File Types** tab. Add a new file type by clicking the **New Type** button and filling in the blanks in the Add New File Type dialog box.

No COM ports available

You're trying to add a new device to your Windows and all of your COM ports are filled. You'll need to uninstall one of your current devices before you can add the new device.

Not a valid filename

You typed an invalid filename for a file operation. Remove any illegal characters from the filename.

Not enough disk space

There isn't enough free space on the current disk to continue with the operation. Delete some files and try again.

Not enough memory

This error occurs when you try to launch an application but your system is low on available memory. Here are some solutions to try:

➤ Close any open applications—including "background" utilities—and then restart the latest program. The more applications you have open, the less system memory you have available for additional applications.

➤ Close all applications, exit Windows, and restart your computer. Sometimes Windows applications don't free up all their memory when they close. This memory "leakage" can build up over time and drain your system resources. Exiting and relaunching Windows frees up this stolen memory.

➤ Free up extra disk space on your system. You can do this by emptying the Recycle Bin or deleting unused files or applications. Because Windows uses extra disk space as virtual memory, having too little disk space free can result in insufficient memory problems.

It's also possible that you are trying to launch a DOS program that needs more memory than is currently allocated.

Open With

Windows displays this message when you try to open a document and there is no file type associated. Choose a program to open the file with from the list in the dialog box, or click the **Other** button to choose from other programs on your system.

Out of memory

Windows has trouble running under low memory conditions. When this message is generated, try closing some open applications to free up memory space. If Windows continues to generate this message, exit Windows and reboot your system to free up any unreleased memory.

Parity error

This message most often results when something is wrong with your system memory. It's also possible that a power supply problem can cause this message. Whatever the cause, rebooting your system and restarting Windows generally clears things up.

Port already open

See *Port in use.*

Port in use

This message is generated when you try to use a communications program (such as Dial-Up Networking) after you improperly quit a previous online session; chances are that a program named RNAAPP.EXE is stuck in your system's memory. Press **Ctrl+Alt+Del** to display the Close Program dialog box, then click **RNAAPP** and click the **End Task** button. After you close RNAAPP.EXE you should be able to start a new communications session.

Print queue is still active

You're trying to exit Windows while a print job is still in progress. Either finish or cancel the print job before you try exiting again.

Rundll32.exe has performed an illegal operation

The error message is caused by a problem with your modem driver. You may need to uninstall and then reinstall your modem to continue.

Sector not found reading drive X

Windows encountered a problem reading one of your drives, most likely due to a bad sector on the disk. If the drive is your hard drive, you may be developing a serious hard drive failure. Call a computer technician for advice.

Setup detects that an earlier version of SetupX.dll or NetDi.dll is in use

While installing a new version of Windows, you have one or more applications open. Close the open applications and then continue with your installation.

Setup cannot create files on your startup drive and cannot set up Windows. There may be too many files in the root directory of your startup drive, or your startup drive letter may have been remapped (SU0018)

This is an odd problem you may encounter while installing Windows. The root folder of a drive holds a maximum of 512 files or folders, and your root folder apparently contains more files/folders than this. Move or delete some files to continue the installation.

Setup could not back up your system files

You're trying to install a new version of Windows, but your hard drive does not have enough free space to back up the previous system files. Because you need up to 75MB free to continue, try deleting as many files as you can.

System Error

When some piece of hardware in your system stops working, this message is generated. You'll see it often when something is wrong with your disk drives—like you're using an unformatted diskette or you forgot to close the diskette drive door. Cancel out and fix your problem before retrying the operation.

The file or folder that this shortcut refers to cannot be found

When you see this message, it means that the file associated with this shortcut has been moved or deleted. If the file's location has changed, right-click the **Shortcut** icon, select **Properties** from the pop-up menu, select the **Shortcut** tab when the Properties dialog box appears, and enter a new location in the **Target** box. If the file has been deleted, delete the shortcut by dragging the shortcut icon into the Recycle Bin.

The network could not validate your user name

This message is generated when you are starting up Windows on a network, or when you are logging on to the network after another user has logged off, and tells you that either the username or password you entered was incorrect. Check both and try logging in again. If you're sure you entered the correct information, contact your network's administrator for assistance.

The printer on LPT1 is offline or not selected

This message appears when your printer is not ready to print. It may be offline or out of paper. Check your printer and click the **Retry** button to resume the print job.

The string specified by the workgroup (or computer name) keyword in the registry is too short

This message is sometimes generated if you didn't properly specify your network workgroup or computer name when you set up Windows. To fix this, select the **Network** icon from the Windows Control Panel; when the Network dialog box appears, select the **Identification** tab, and enter proper names in the **Computer Name** and **Workgroup** boxes.

There is no viewer capable of viewing this file

You see this message when you use the Quick View option to view files in My Computer or Windows Explorer, but Quick View isn't capable of viewing this particular file type. Use the file's application to view the file instead.

There was an error writing to LPT1:

This message appears when something is wrong with your printer or your printer setup. Here are some possible solutions to the problem:

➤ Make sure your printer is actually turned on and is online.

➤ Make sure you have paper in your printer. If not, refill your paper tray.

➤ Check your printer for paper jams.

➤ Double-check all cable connections; make sure both ends of the printer cable are securely fastened.

If these simple solutions don't fix your problem, check your printer configuration.

This filename is not valid

This message appears when you type an illegal name for a filename. An illegal name would include characters that you can't use for filenames. Remove any illegal characters from the filename and save the file again.

This program has performed an illegal operation and will be shut down

This message appears when a program has ceased proper operation, for whatever reason (typically untraceable). Click the **Close** button to close the offending program.

That Character Is Illegal!

The following characters (called "illegal" characters) cannot be used to name a file in Windows: **/ \ * | < > ? " :.**

Unrecoverable Setup Error. Setup cannot continue on this system configuration. Click OK to quit Setup:

If this error occurs when you're installing a new version of Windows, you'll have to continue with the installation from DOS.

Windows Explorer is Dangerously Low on Resources

This problem is caused by a major memory leak in your system; chances are you won't be able to shut down Windows normally, and will have to force a manual reboot. In reality, a faulty KERNEL32.DLL file in early versions of Windows 95 contributed to this problem; you can download a free "patch" for this file from `www.microsoft.com/windows95/downloads/contents/wuadmintools/s_wunetworkingtools/w95kernel32/default.asp?site=95`.

Pre-Windows 95 Messages: GPFs and UAEs

With Windows 95, Microsoft started issuing error messages that provided more specific information about the problem at hand. Prior to Windows 95, the system's error messages were more generic.

In Windows 3.1 the most common error message was a General Protection Fault (GPF). This message was displayed when an individual application crashed or froze. GPFs seldom shut down Windows itself, serving instead to alert users to a problem that had frozen a Windows application.

The Windows 3.0 equivalent of a GPF was an Unrecoverable Application Error (UAE). Unlike a GPF, a UAE more often than not caused all of Windows to crash.

Windows Setup was unable to update your system files

You may see this message if you're trying to install (or reinstall) Windows and you're running anti-virus software. This can also be caused if you have "Boot Sector Protect" enabled in your system's CMOS settings; check your BIOS on system startup to disable this setting.

Windows was not properly shut down

Windows displays this message the next time you restart your computer after you've improperly exited Windows (and then runs ScanDisk). Remember to shut down Windows properly next time by clicking the **Start** button, selecting **Shut Down**, and—when the Shut Down Windows dialog box appears—selecting the **Shut Down the Computer?** option.

Write protected disk

You're trying to perform a file operation on a diskette that is write protected. Change diskettes, or slide the write-protect tab into the down position (on 3 1/2-inch diskettes).

X:/ is not accessible. The device is not ready

This message appears when a disk drive is not yet ready; the *X* represents the drive with the problem. If the problem is with a diskette, CD-ROM, or DVD drive, insert the proper diskette or disc in the drive. If the problem is with a hard disk drive, you may have some major problems with your system; consult a technician for more information.

You cannot format the current drive

You're trying to format a diskette that is write protected. Change diskettes or slide the write-protect tab into the down position (on 3 1/2-inch diskettes).

The Least You Need to Know

➤ Windows generates error messages when it encounters most common (and uncommon!) problems.

➤ When you receive an error message, read it carefully and *write it down*—then proceed as instructed.

Chapter 29

Getting It Right... System Settings and Technical Maintenance

In This Chapter

➤ Find out how to display the properties for all the devices in your computer system

➤ Discover Windows' "hidden" system utilities

➤ Learn advanced technical troubleshooting techniques

➤ Reference the most common Windows settings

Throughout this book we've talked about a lot of different system settings. I thought it might be a good idea to take all the common system settings and put them in one place.

In addition, I might as well show you how to get to these system settings, and how to perform some slightly more technical types of maintenance—and troubleshooting—than you've done up till now.

In other words, this is a chapter for those who are *not* technically timid! If you're at all intimidated by the technical aspects of your computer system, feel free to let somebody else read this chapter. If you're fearless and pure of heart, however, turn the page and read on!

Keep an Eye on Your System's Performance (from a Technical Standpoint)

If you really want to keep on top of things, Windows provides several technical utilities that let you monitor—and, in some cases, change—the configuration and performance of your computer's system components. These utilities will keep you informed as to how your components are performing, and when you may need to look closer to improve performance or fix a major problem.

Spy on Your System with the System Monitor

You can use the System Monitor utility to check your computer's current performance. If you are having problems with your system locking up or slowing down, you can use the monitor to tell you which device is using resources when the problems occur.

Start by clicking the **Start** button, selecting **Programs**, selecting **Accessories**, selecting **System Tools**, and then selecting **System Monitor**.

On launch, System Monitor automatically shows your processor usage. If you want to monitor other system items, pull down the **Edit** menu and select **Add Item**. Select the category you want to monitor from the **Category** list, and then select the specific item to monitor from the **Item** list. Click the **OK** button. (If you want to remove an item from the Monitor list, pull down the **Edit** menu, select **Remove Item**, select the item you want removed, and click **OK**.)

System Monitor is an easy tool to use, but it's not the only tool available to monitor the performance of your system. Read on...

Look at Everything with System Properties

The performance of your system can also be reviewed and modified through the System Properties utility, found in the Control Panel.

Just open the **Control Panel** and select the **System** icon. When the System Properties dialog box appears, select the **Performance** tab.

The Performance Status group displays the current Memory, System Resources, File System, Virtual Memory, Disk Compression, and PC Cards (PCMCIA) status. See Table 29.1 for explanations of these settings.

Table 29.1   System Properties Settings

Setting	Explanation
Memory	The amount of random access memory (RAM) on your system.
System Resources	The percentage of resources (such as windows, images, icons, and virtual memory) currently available for use. (The higher the number, the better.)
File System	Specifies whether you are using a 32-bit or MS-DOS compatibility mode (real-mode) file system.

Setting	Explanation
Virtual Memory	Specifies whether you are using 32-bit or 16-bit disk-based virtual memory.
Disk Compression	Specifies whether you have enabled disk compression.
PC Cards (PCMCIA)	Specifies whether you have any PCMCIA PC Card sockets installed on your system.

To see additional information, or to change the File System, Graphics, or Virtual Memory settings, click the appropriate button in the **Advanced Settings** group at the bottom of the dialog box.

Look at Even More System Settings with Microsoft System Information

In addition to System Monitor and the System Properties dialog box, Windows 98 contains a new utility, Microsoft System Information, that organizes a lot of different system information and maintenance tools into one handy utility.

Click the **Start** button, select **Programs**, select **Accessories**, select **System Tools**, and then select **System Information**. When Microsoft System Information appears, click on the item in the left-hand pane you want to examine. The contents of that view will appear in the right-hand pane (as seen in this figure).

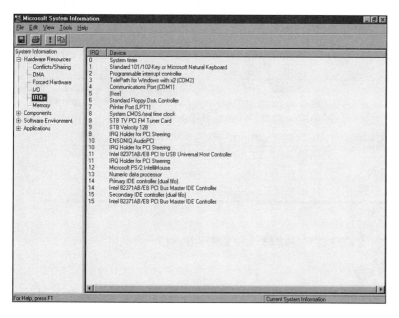

Use Microsoft System Information to examine your system's configuration in painful detail— and to access many of Windows 98's "hidden" system tools.

Monitor Things You Didn't Know You Could Monitor with Windows 98's "Hidden" System Tools

While Microsoft System Information gives you a snapshot of your entire system configuration, Windows 98 includes even *more* utilities to monitor various aspects of your system's performance. (The System Configuration Utility, discussed later in this chapter, is one such utility.) All of these "hidden" tools are accessible from the **Tools** menu in the Microsoft System Information utility, and are described in Table 20.2.

Table 29.2   Microsoft's Secret System Tools

Tool	Description
Windows Report Tool	Used to create a report that can be sent to Microsoft Technical Support, detailing the specifics of a given problem.
Update Wizard Uninstall	Uninstalls the latest changes downloaded via the System Update utility.
System File Checker	Verifies system file integrity, restores corrupted system files, and extracts compressed files from the Windows 98 installation CD.
Signature Verification Tool	Locates certified ("signed") and uncertified ("unsigned") files on your system.
Registry Checker	Used to find and fix errors in the Windows Registry.
Automatic Skip Driver Agent	Identifies drivers that have caused Windows 98 to stop responding on previous startups, then marks them so that they are bypassed on subsequent startups.
Dr. Watson	A familiar tool to experienced Windows users; takes a snapshot of your system whenever a system fault occurs, aiding diagnoses of tricky problems.
System Configuration Utility	Automates major system troubleshooting.
ScanDisk	Finds and fixes errors on your hard disk drive.
Version Conflict Manager	Used to restore old drivers that have been replaced by newer versions.

Troubleshooting Hardware Problems— the Technical Way

To be truly effective, you need to move beyond passive monitoring and into active troubleshooting. Now, I've already offered you hundreds of pages of advice on how to troubleshoot problems with your computer system, but my advice has been more practical than technical. If you don't mind getting a little more technical, however, you can take advantage of some of the troubleshooting utilities Microsoft has included as part of the Windows operating system. Some of these utilities (such as the Windows 98 Troubleshooters) are relatively easy to use; others require a bit of technical expertise.

Find and Fix Easy Problems with Windows Troubleshooters

Windows 98 (*not* Windows 95!) includes several *Troubleshooters* (wizards, actually) to help you walk through device conflicts on your system. Using one of these Troubleshooters is an easy way to find and fix hardware problems. You're led step-by-step through a series of questions designed to track down the solution to your specific problem. All you have to do is answer the interactive questions in the Troubleshooter, and you'll be led to the probable solution to your problem.

In most cases, Windows 98's Troubleshooters can help you diagnose and fix common system problems. Always try the Troubleshooters before you pick up the phone and dial Microsoft's Technical Support line—or start trying to track down device conflicts manually.

The following Troubleshooters are included with Windows 98:

➤ Dial-Up Networking
➤ Direct Cable Connection
➤ DirectX
➤ Display
➤ DriveSpace 3
➤ Hardware Conflict
➤ Memory
➤ Modem
➤ MS-DOS Programs
➤ Networking
➤ PC Card
➤ Print
➤ Sound
➤ Startup and Shutdown
➤ The Microsoft Network

To run a Troubleshooter, click the **Start** button and select **Help**. When the Help window appears, click the **Contents** tab, click **Troubleshooting**, then click **Windows 98 Troubleshooters**. Select the Troubleshooter for your specific problem in the left pane; the Troubleshooter itself will be displayed in the right pane. All you have to do now is follow the interactive directions to troubleshoot your particular hardware problems.

Working through a modem-related problem with the Windows 98 Modem Troubleshooter.

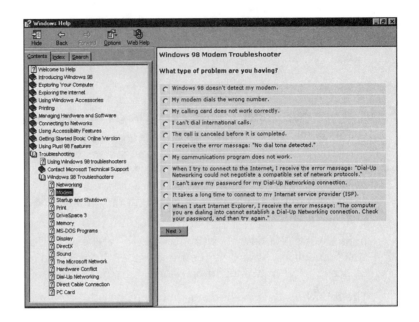

Find and Fix Shared IRQs with Microsoft System Information

Sometimes a new piece of hardware will inadvertently try to share an IRQ with another previously installed component, with predictably bad results. In Windows 98 you can use the Microsoft System Information utility to examine any and all shared IRQs on your system.

To open this utility, click the **Start** button, select **Programs**, select **Accessories**, select **System Tools**, then select **System Information**. When the Microsoft System Information window appears, Click the **+** next to Hardware Resources in the System Information pane, then select **Conflicts/Sharing** to see a list of all shared IRQs. Identify the device causing your problem, and either reconfigure or reinstall the device to use a different IRQ.

Find and Fix Driver Problems with the Device Manager

For any piece of hardware to work with Windows, Windows has to install and configure a special file, called a device driver. Windows includes driver files for most popular devices; if you have a newer or less widely used peripheral, however, the manufacturer may have to provide its own drivers for Windows to use.

In most cases, Windows automatically recognizes your new device and installs the proper drivers; even when Plug and Play doesn't work, the Add New Hardware Wizard can be used to install the proper drivers for new devices. However, in a worst-case situation where nothing happens as it should, it is possible to add new drivers manually—and to update your existing drivers with new, higher-performance versions.

Whether you're using Windows 95 or Windows 98, the Device Manager (found in the System Properties dialog box) is where you can review your various hardware settings and determine which devices may have conflicts or other problems.

You open the System Properties dialog box by selecting the **System** icon in the Windows Control Panel. When you select the **Device Manager** tab, any resource conflict will be highlighted within the problematic Class group. Click the **+** next to the hardware device type to view all corresponding devices. If there is a problem with a specific device, it will be identified with one of the following symbols:

➤ A black exclamation point (!) on a yellow field indicates that the device is in what Windows calls a "problem state." Note that a device in a problem state can still be functioning, even though it has some sort of problem, explained by the accompanying problem code.

➤ A red "X" indicates that the device is currently disabled. This means that the device is physically present in your system, but doesn't have a driver loaded.

➤ A blue "i" on a white field indicates that the device is not using the automatic settings, but has a manual configuration instead. (This icon isn't necessarily bad because it doesn't indicate a problem, only a different type of configuration.)

If you have a device conflict, highlight that device and click the **Properties** button; this displays the Properties dialog box. If you now click the **General** tab you'll see a message indicating the basic problem and the steps Windows recommends to solve the problem. The message may also display a problem code and number that can be useful when consulting with a technical support specialist.

New Windows 98 Drivers

Windows 98 uses a new type of device driver, called the Win32 Driver Model (WDM). Both Windows 98 and Windows NT (soon to be called Windows 2000) use WDM, so hardware manufacturers can now write one driver that will work on both operating systems. Note that Windows 98 will still work with non-WDM drivers; it's expected, however, that most new hardware will be WDM-compliant.

Not All Cards Are Played Face Up

For various reasons, some sound and video cards don't always report all the resources they're using—which can cause Device Manager to show only one device in conflict, or to report no conflicts when in fact there is a conflict. The only way to get a complete handle on this situation is to disable the sound or video card and see if a suspected conflict is resolved.

To reconfigure a device, highlight the device and click the **Properties** button to display the Properties dialog box. When the Properties dialog box appears, select the **Resources** tab. (If your device does not have a **Resources** tab, either you cannot change its resources or it isn't using any resource settings.) Select the resource you want to change, deselect **Use Automatic Settings** (if selected), and then click the **Change Setting** button. When the Edit Resource dialog box appears, edit the system resources appropriately. Click **OK** when done.

Update *All* Your Drivers with Windows Update

Windows is constantly changing. Microsoft often releases updated versions of critical system files to improve performance or fix bugs; peripheral manufacturers often issue updated versions of their driver files.

How do you make sure your system has the latest versions of these critical files? Windows 98's new Windows Update utility compares the files on your computer system with a database of files on Microsoft's Web site—and automatically downloads and installs any new or updated files your system needs for best operation.

You launch Windows Update by clicking the **Start** button and selecting **Windows Update**; Windows 98 now starts Internet Explorer and navigates to the Windows Update Web page. Click the **Product Updates** link to scan the files on your hard disk and update those drivers that have newer versions available.

To update a device driver, highlight the installed driver and click the **Properties** button to open the Properties dialog box. When the Properties dialog box appears, select the **Driver** tab, and then click the **Update Driver** button. When the Update Device Driver Wizard appears, click the **Next** button; when asked what you want to do next, select **Search for a Better Driver**, and then click **Next**. You'll now be prompted as to *where* you want to search for an upgraded driver. If you have new driver software from your hardware's manufacturer, select either **Floppy Disk Drives** or **CD-ROM Drive**, as appropriate. Insert the diskette or CD-ROM and click **Next**, and then follow the onscreen instructions to install your specific driver.

If you are using Windows 98 and prefer to search Microsoft's Web site for an upgraded driver, select **Microsoft Windows Update**, and then click **Next**. Windows will now connect to the Internet and retrieve any updated drivers that exist. The Wizard tells you whether it found an updated driver. If no better driver was found, click **Next** to keep your current driver. If an updated driver is available, click **Next** to install the new driver, following the appropriate onscreen instructions.

Find and Fix Memory Problems with Virtual Memory

Windows augments your system's random access memory (RAM) with *virtual memory*. Virtual memory is hard disk space that is viewed by Windows as random access memory, so when Windows runs low on RAM it simply begins to store transient data on your hard drive.

Most of the time you don't have to worry about virtual memory because Windows does the configuration automatically. If you are running low on hard drive space, however, you can decrease the amount of hard drive used for virtual memory and give yourself more storage room for your permanent data.

To access Windows' virtual memory settings, go to the **Control Panel** and select the **System** icon. When the System Properties dialog box appears, select the **Performance** tab and click the **Virtual Memory** button.

When the Virtual Memory dialog box appears, you'll see that **Let Windows Manage my Virtual Memory Settings** is already selected. If you want to override the automatic settings, select **Let Me Specify My Own Virtual Memory Settings**. You can now choose the hard disk you want to use for virtual memory, and then specify the **Minimum** and **Maximum** number of megabytes you want Windows to use for virtual memory. Click the **OK** button when done.

Windows Knows Best

In general, you should let Windows determine how to best manage virtual memory because Windows is built to use it as efficiently as possible. Because specifying the wrong settings can impair your system's performance, inexperienced users should not change Windows' default virtual memory settings.

The hard disk you specify for virtual memory must have at least as much free space as the maximum amount of virtual memory you set. If you are low on hard disk space, a large virtual memory space can cause problems, such as not having enough space to save or copy a file.

You can also choose to disable virtual memory, but this could prevent your computer from running certain applications or opening large files—or, in some instances, running Windows itself.

Find and Fix Big Problems with the System Configuration Utility

If your problem is so major that you can't fix it with the Troubleshooters or the Device Manager, you need to turn to a more powerful tool. Included with Windows 98 is just such a tool: the *System Configuration Utility*.

The System Configuration Utility duplicates the procedures used by Microsoft Technical Support staff when they're trying to diagnose system configuration problems. You work through a series of steps that, one-by-one, disable various system components until you track down the one that's causing your specific problem. Use the System Configuration Utility when you have major problems with your system, particularly problems that appear after you've installed a new piece of hardware.

Launch the System Configuration Utility by clicking the **Start** button, selecting **Programs**, selecting **Accessories**, selecting **System Tools**, then selecting **System Information**. When the Microsoft System Information window appears, pull down the **Tools** menu and select **System Configuration Utility**.

I won't go into all the troubleshooting options available in this feature-rich utility—especially because most of them are for technical professionals. Suffice to say that you can literally work through your system operations one step at a time, and thus isolate *where* problems are being introduced into your system. If you're a tech pro (or *very* comfortable with the inner workings of Windows and your computer system), explore the System Configuration Utility when you have hard-to-find problems.

System Settings: Technical Settings for Technical Stuff

Generally, system settings—such as IRQ and DMA assignments—are a little too technical for the average user. However, when you're installing a new peripheral for your system, you may be asked to select one or more of these settings. So, if you know a little bit about this stuff, you may be able to fake your way through it.

The following tables (29.3 through 29.6) list some of the most common system settings you may run into. When in doubt, default to these settings when reconfiguring the various parts of your system. (Note, however, that the settings for your particular system or configuration may be different.)

Table 29.3   Standard IRQ Assignments

IRQ	Purpose	Common Devices
0	CMOS clock (system timer)	
1	Keyboard controller	
2	Cascade to second IRQ controller	Mouse, scanner, network adapter
3	COM2 or COM4	Mouse, modem, network adapter, video, scanner
4	COM1 or COM3	Mouse, modem, CD-ROM, scanner
5	LPT2	Sound card, mouse, modem, scanner
6	Diskette controller	Tape drive
7	LPT1	Network adapter, mouse, sound card
8	Real-time clock	
9	*Unused*	SCSI adapter, scanner
10	*Unused*	Network adapter, mouse, sound card, SCSI adapter
11	*Unused*	Mouse, sound card, scanner

IRQ	Purpose	Common Devices
12	Motherboard mouse port	Mouse, video, SCSI adapter, scanner
13	Math coprocessor	Mouse
14	Hard disk controller	SCSI adapter
15	*Unused*	Mouse, SCSI adapter

Table 29.4 Standard DMA Channel Assignments

Channel	Purpose
0	*Unused*
1	*Unused*
2	Diskette controller
3	*Unused*
4	First DMA controller
5	*Unused*
6	*Unused*
7	*Unused*

Table 29.5 Standard Serial Port Addresses and Assignments

Port	I/O Address	IRQ
COM1	3F8h	IRQ4
COM2	2F8h	IRQ3
COM3	3E8h	IRQ4
COM4	2E8h	IRQ3

Table 29.6 Standard Parallel Port Addresses and Assignments

Port	I/O Address	IRQ
LPT1	3BCh	IRQ7
LPT2	378h	IRQ5
LPT3	278h	None

347

The Least You Need to Know

➤ The Device Manager in the System Properties dialog box can be used to monitor and edit most key system settings.

➤ The Microsoft System Information utility includes many technical troubleshooting tools, as well as access to "hidden" system utilities.

➤ Windows 98's Troubleshooters can be used to interactively find and fix many common problems.

Chapter 30

The Course of Last Resort...Editing the Windows Registry

In This Chapter

➤ Learn all about the Windows Registry, where all Windows settings are stored

➤ Find out how to fix a corrupted Registry file

➤ Discover how to edit your Registry settings with the Registry Editor

Most of the configuration information for your system is stored in a special database called the Windows Registry. This file includes the properties set in the Control Panel, settings installed by all of your Windows applications, and hardware detected by the Add New Hardware Wizard. When you configure these properties via normal means (dialog boxes and the like), the changes are automatically stored in the Registry.

You can also make changes directly in the Registry by using a utility called Registry Editor. Editing the Registry directly is recommended only if you are a very experienced Windows user and know how to recover from any mistakes—but may be necessary to correct some hard-to-fix problems.

More Than You Ever Wanted to Know About the Windows Registry

First, some history.

In the pre-Windows days of personal computing, DOS (also known as MS-DOS) was the operating system used by practically all PCs. Under DOS, system configuration was stored in two system files that ran automatically whenever you turned on your

PC. These two files (CONFIG.SYS and AUTOEXEC.BAT) were filled with command line after command line that instructed DOS how to manage various devices and software programs.

With the advent of Windows 3.0, two new files were created to store configuration settings for the Windows operating system. These files (WIN.INI and SYSTEM.INI) served much the same function as CONFIG.SYS and AUTOEXEC.BAT did under DOS, and ran automatically whenever Windows was launched.

Windows 95 (and, subsequently, Windows 98) replaced all these configuration files with the Windows Registry. Settings for new devices and new software programs—Windows 9X-compatible items, at least—were written directly to the Registry files.

However, Windows 95/98 had to maintain compatibility with older hardware devices and software programs. If you're running an older DOS program on your PC, it will still write its settings to the CONFIG.SYS and AUTOEXEC.BAT files; if you're running an older Windows 3.X program, it will write its settings to the WIN.INI and SYSTEM.INI files. So Windows 95 and Windows 98 still have to maintain all those older configuration files, even though they're only used for older programs and devices that may (or may not) be installed on your system.

To make a long story short, all new hardware and software use the Registry; older hardware and software use the older configuration files. (And Windows reads *all* these files on startup—which is why you still have to check those older files if Windows generates an error message on startup!)

Back Up the Registry Before You Do *Anything* Major

Many experienced users back up the Registry before installing any new Windows application. Because programs write new information to the Registry during setup, the Registry could be in jeopardy every time you install an application, even if the application displays the "Designed for Windows" logo.

Managing the Windows Registry—Without Editing It

Most users will never have to touch their Registry. And, if you've ever looked at the darned thing, you'll know that you really don't *want* to mess with it, unless you really have to. Still, some hardcore problems can only be fixed by editing the Registry, so it pays to know a little bit about it—*just in case.*

Backing Up Your Registry

Because making changes to the Registry is risky—even for very experienced Windows users—you should back up the contents of the Registry before you begin editing. That way you can restore the preedited Registry in case something goes wrong.

The Registry itself is composed of two files: SYSTEM.DAT and USER.DAT. These files are hidden files located in the **windows** folder.

Before you can back up the Registry files, you first have to "unhide" them. You do this by clicking the **Start** button, selecting **Settings**, and selecting **Folder Options**; when the Folder Options dialog box appears, select the **View** tab then check **Show All Files**.

Once you can see the Registry files, use **My Computer** or **Windows Explorer** to create a new subfolder in the `\windows` folder and name it **registry**. Now copy the SYSTEM.DAT and USER.DAT files from the `\windows` folder to the `\windows\registry` folder. To be extra safe, you can use a Zip utility (such as WinZip) to copy the Registry files to a diskette; this will allow you to keep a copy of your Registry away from your computer system.

Restoring Your Registry

If you encounter Registry problems, all you have to do is restore the backup copy of your Registry to return your system to the state it was in prior to encountering problems. However, you can't do this from regular Windows mode; you have to do it from either Safe mode or MS-DOS mode.

Begin by rebooting your system and pressing **F8** during the boot process; select **Safe Mode** from the Windows Startup menu to start up in Safe mode. While in Safe mode, use **My Computer** or **Windows Explorer** to copy the SYSTEM.DAT and USER.DAT files from the `\windows\registry` folder back into the `\windows` folder. Now you can reboot your computer in normal mode, and your system will be restored to its previous condition.

Reverting to a Previous Copy of the Registry

Even though you should still make manual backups of your Registry files before attempting major Registry changes, Windows 98 (but not Windows 95) automatically makes backup copies of the Registry files every time you start your computer. When Windows 98 starts, a hidden program called Registry Checker automatically scans your Registry for errors; if it notices a problem, it replaces the current version of the Registry with the "clean" backup copy.

If your Registry appears to be beyond fixing, you can use Registry Checker to manually restore the backup copy made the last time you started your computer. Note, however, that you need to use Windows' MS-DOS mode to restore this Registry backup.

While Windows is running, click the **Start** button and select **Shut Down**; when the Shut Down Windows dialog box appears, select **Restart in MS-DOS Mode** and click **OK**. Your computer will now restart in a special non-Windows MS-DOS mode.

When you see the `c:\>` prompt, type **cd c:\windows\command** and press **Enter**. You should now see a prompt that reads: `c:\windows>`. Type **scanreg/restore** and press **Enter**. Registry Checker will now restore the backup copy of the Registry. When it finishes doing so, press **Ctrl+Alt+Del** to restart your computer.

Using Registry Checker to restore a backup has its plusses and its minuses. On the plus side, it's easier than restoring a backup manually. On the minus side, it may not be able to restore the most recent backup of the Registry; any backup you make after Windows starts will be more up-to-date than the backup made at startup. In addition, if a prior version of the Registry was corrupt, Registry Checker will blindly restore the corrupt version.

Fixing a Corrupted Registry

Registry Checker (in Windows 98 only, remember) is a versatile utility; you can also use it to manually fix a corrupted Registry. Run the Registry Checker before trying to restore your backup copy of the Registry; if the problems are minor, it can fix them without the hassle of restoring a backup.

Just click the **Start** button and select **Run**; when the Run dialog box appears, type **scanreg** in the **Open** box, and click **OK**. Registry Checker will now scan your Registry for errors, fixing them automatically. When it is done scanning your Registry, it will ask if you want to make another backup of the Registry. Click **Yes** to do so.

Cleaning Up the Registry

Microsoft has developed a special utility that can remove errors from the Registry—corrupted keys, unused settings, and so on. RegClean works by finding Registry keys that contain erroneous values, and then removing them. Note that RegClean does not fix *all* Registry problems; in particular, it cannot fix a "corrupt" Registry. It is, however, a good tool to run periodically to find and fix simple Registry errors.

Where to Get RegClean

RegClean is not included on the Windows installation CD. You have to download it from Microsoft's Web site at support.microsoft.com/support/downloads/dp3049.asp.

When you launch RegClean, it will display a progress dialog box; during this process RegClean is scanning your Registry for errors. Depending on the size of your Registry, this can take anywhere from 30 seconds to 30 minutes.

If RegClean found no errors, select **Exit**. If RegClean found errors, click the **Fix Errors** button. When RegClean is finished, click **Exit**.

To undo any changes made by RegClean, just open **My Computer** or **Windows Explorer** and select the **UNDO.REG** file created by RegClean; this reverses all the changes and returns the original values to the Registry.

Editing the Registry

Most of the time you can affect changes to Windows's settings via normal means—through the Control Panel, or through specific system or software configuration routines. When worse comes to worst, however, there are some parameters that can only be accessed via the Registry. When that time comes, you need to know how to edit the Registry—using Registry Patches or Windows's Registry Editor.

Using Registry Editor

The Registry Editor gives you power to configure Windows features that are available only by editing the Registry. The settings in the Registry are called *keys*, and all keys have numerous *subkeys*. Each subkey has a specific set of values; the values store the configuration information for that item.

To start the Registry Editor, click the **Start** button and select **Run**. When the Run dialog box appears, type **regedit** in the **Open** box and click **OK**. The Registry Editor window opens, as shown in this figure.

Be Careful!

You will not find the Registry Editor on any menu because inexperienced tampering with it could render your computer unusable; you always have to start it with the **Run** command. When you launch the Registry Editor, make any changes carefully. There is no **Undo** command, nor any opportunity to close without saving. Every change you make is the real thing!

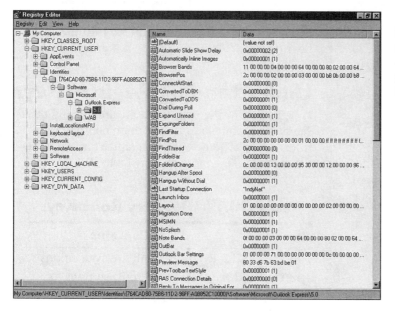

Using the Registry Editor; the left pane shows the hierarchy of keys and subkeys, and the right pane shows the values for the selected subkey.

353

Open the levels of keys and subkeys the same way you open folders and subfolders in Windows Explorer, clicking on the + next to a specific item. Highlight the subkeys in the left pane and edit the values in the right pane. Settings are changed *as you make the changes*; there is no "save" command in Registry Editor.

Close the Registry Editor by clicking its **Close** button. You may have to restart Windows to see the effect of some edits.

Changing Registry Entries with Patches

A Registry Patch is a way to make changes to the Registry using an "add-on" file, rather than editing the Registry directly. Registry Patches are files with .REG extensions, which are "absorbed" into the Registry when selected. Registry Patches are typically used to transfer precise settings from one system to another system.

Other Registry Tools

The tools described in this chapter are not the only tools available for editing or managing your Registry. Here are five of the most popular Registry-related freeware/shareware programs, all available from CNET's Download.com Web site (www. download.com):

➤ **Extension Manager** lets you edit file associations in the Registry.

➤ **Extension Viewer** lets you check and analyze settings in the Registry.

➤ **JumpToRegKey** lets you jump directly to your most-used Registry keys.

➤ **RegBackup** lets you quickly and easily back up the Windows Registry.

➤ **Tweak Reg** lets you edit the functionality of the Registry.

To create a Registry Patch, open the **Registry Editor**, select the key or keys you want to use, then pull down the **Registry** menu and select **Export Registry File**. Choose a name for the Patch, and click **Save**.

To apply a Registry Patch on another PC, copy the .REG file to the other PC, and then use My Computer or Windows Explorer to select the Patch's icon. You will receive a message indicating that the Patch has been successfully entered into the Registry.

Understanding Registry Keys

When you edit the Registry, there are literally thousands of separate keys that contain configuration information. These keys are organized into a handful of "root" keys, as shown in Table 30.1.

Table 30.1   Registry Root Keys

Key	Contains
HKEY_CLASSES_ROOT	All file associations
HKEY_CURRENT_USER	Profile settings for each user on this PC
HKEY_LOCAL_MACHINE	Settings for this specific PC
HKEY_USERS	Settings used by all users

Key	Contains
HKEY_CURRENT_CONFIG	Universal system preferences
HKEY_DYN_DATA	Hardware status and driver settings

While you can always search for specific keys or settings (by pulling down the Registry Editor's **Edit** menu and selecting **Find**), it's helpful to know where specific types of data are stored.

The Least You Need to Know

➤ The Windows Registry is where all Windows configurations are stored.

➤ You can fix a corrupted Registry with the Registry Checker utility, or clean up a messy registry with RegClean.

➤ You use the Registry Editor to edit settings in the Registry.

The OOPS! Glossary: Technical Terms for the Technically Timid

address   The pointer to a particular Web page (also known as a *URL*). Also the specific identifier for a person's email inbox.

applet   A small program in Windows that performs a common task.

application   Another word for a computer software program.

audio   Sound.

backup   The process of creating a compressed copy of the data on your hard disk, to be used in case of an emergency.

baud rate   One measure of modem transmission speed; one baud is equal to 1K bits per second (bps).

BIOS   The basic input/output system that interacts with computer hardware.

board   A device that plugs into your system unit and provides auxiliary functions. (Also called a *card*.)

Boolean logic   A system of operators (AND, OR, NOT, NEAR, and so on) that work with words in much the same way that arithmetic operators (addition, subtraction, and so on) work with numbers. (Also known as Boolean algebra or Boolean query or Boolean search.)

boot   The process of turning on your computer system. To *reboot* is to turn your system off and then back on, which can be done by pressing **Ctrl+Alt+Del** or pressing your PC's **on/off** button.

bootable disk   A disk or diskette that can be used to start your system because the disk contains certain system files. See *system disk*.

browser   A software program that lets a computer or other device access HTML pages on the World Wide Web. Netscape Navigator and Microsoft's Internet Explorer are the two most popular computer-based browsers today.

buffer   Memory-based storage for pending computing tasks; multiple print jobs are sent to a buffer where they wait in a queue for the printer to execute them.

bus   A hardware "gateway" that lets you connect hardware devices to your PC.

button   A raised object in a dialog box that can be "pressed" (by clicking it with a mouse) to perform certain operations.

byte   A measurement of space (on disk or in memory); one byte is pretty much equal to one character. One thousand bytes is called a *kilobyte* (KB), one million bytes is called a *megabyte* (MB), and one thousand megabytes is called a *gigabyte* (GB).

C prompt   The prompt issued by the DOS command interpreter when it is waiting for you to input a command.

card   A device that plugs into your system unit and provides auxiliary functions. You can add video cards, modem cards, and sound cards to your system. (Also called a *board*.)

CD-R   Compact disc—recordable. A type of CD drive that lets you record *once* onto CD discs, which can then be read by any CD-ROM drive.

CD-ROM   Compact disc—read-only memory. CD-ROM discs contain large volumes of information and are read by lasers.

CD-RW   Compact disc—rewritable. A type of CD disc that can be written to multiple times. CD-RW discs can only be read on CD-RW drives; they cannot be read on standard CD-ROM drives.

central processing unit   Also known as the CPU. See *microprocessor*.

chat   Text-based real-time Internet communication, typically consisting of short one-line messages back and forth between two or more users. Users gather to chat in chat rooms or channels.

click   The process of selecting an item onscreen; what you do with a mouse button.

client   A software program that runs on a personal computer and makes requests from another "server" computer.

component   A part of Windows incidental to the main program. A component can be an applet like HyperTerminal or Notepad, or a utility like the DVD driver.

computer   That big beige thing on your desk that's causing you all the problems.

copy   To place data in a different location, without deleting the original data.

cursor   The highlighted area or pointer that tracks with the movement of your mouse or arrow keys onscreen.

cut   To erase data from a location while still keeping it in Windows memory (called the Clipboard) for pasting into a different location.

cyberspace   Where all online communications take place.

dead link   A hyperlink on a Web page that doesn't lead to an active page or site—probably because that page no longer exists.

defragment   To restructure a disk so that files are stored in contiguous blocks of space, rather than dispersed into multiple fragments at different locations on the disk.

delete   Erase. Kill. Zap. Get rid of.

desktop   The entire screen area on which you display all of your computer work. The Windows desktop can contain icons, a taskbar, menus, and individual application windows.

device   A Windows file that represents some object—physical or nonphysical—installed on your system.

dialog box   An onscreen window that either displays a message or asks for user input.

Dial-Up Networking   The Windows component that allows you to connect one computer to another computer (or network of computers) using a modem and traditional phone lines.

directory   (1) An index to files you store on your disk. Also known as a *folder*. (2) A search site that collects and indexes Web pages manually, either by user submission or editorial selection. Yahoo! is the Web's most popular directory.

disk   A device that stores data in magnetic format.

disk compression   To take the information that is stored, or will be stored, on a disk and compact it so that it takes less space to store. Disk compression in Windows is handled by the DriveSpace utility.

diskette   A portable or removable disk.

document   A piece of information in a computer file. A Web page is one kind of document.

domain   The name of a site on the Internet. Domains are hierarchical, and lower-level domains often refer to particular Web sites within a top-level domain. Examples of domains are .com, .edu, .gov, and .org.

DOS   The pre-Windows operating system for IBM-compatible computers.

double-click   Clicking a mouse button twice in rapid succession.

download   The process of receiving information or data from a server on the Internet.

driver   The program support file that tells a program how to interact with a specific hardware device, such as a hard disk controller or video display card.

DriveSpace   A Windows utility that compresses the data on a hard disk—while still leaving it accessible for day-to-day use.

DSL   Digital Subscriber Line, a new ultra-fast Internet connection using standard phone lines. Download speeds can approach 32Mbps. Often proceeded by another letter, denoting the type of DSL connection; for example, ADSL stands for Asymmetric Digital Subscriber Line, and SDSL stands for Symmetric Digital Subscriber Line.

DVD   A new optical storage medium, similar to CD-ROM but with much higher storage capacity. (The acronym DVD actually doesn't stand for anything anymore; at one time it stood for Digital Versatile Disk, and at another Digital Video Disk.)

e-commerce   *Electronic commerce*, or business conducted over the Internet.

email   Electronic mail, a means of corresponding to other computer users over the Internet through digital messages.

error message   An onscreen message that Windows or a specific application issues to tell you that you did something wrong or that a command was not able to be executed correctly.

e-tailer   A retailer engaging in e-commerce; an online merchant.

FAQs   See *Frequently Asked Questions*.

FAT   File Allocation Table. A special section of your disk that stores tracking data to help Windows locate files.

FAT32   The 32-bit File Allocation Table used in Windows 98.

FDISK   The DOS-based utility that creates one or more partitions on a hard disk drive.

file   A collection of data, with its own unique name and location; files can be documents or executable programs.

File Allocation Table   See *FAT*.

file type   A specific type of file, associated with a specific application.

filename   The formal name assigned to a file; in Windows 95 and Windows 98 a filename can be up to 256 characters long.

floppy disk   Another term for *diskette*.

folder   A way to group files on a disk; each folder can contain multiple files or other folders (called subfolders).

format   The process that prepares a disk for use.

frames   An HTML technique for combining two or more separate HTML documents within a single Web page.

Frequently Asked Questions   Also known as a FAQ, this is a document that answers the most commonly asked questions about a particular topic. FAQs are often found in newsgroups and on some Web sites as a preparatory answer to the common questions asked by new users.

FTP   File Transfer Protocol, an older, non–Web-based convention that enables files to be downloaded from other computers on the Internet.

full-motion video   The display of movie clips on your PC in as realistic a form as possible.

function key   One of the special keys labeled **F1** to **F12**, located at the top of your computer keyboard.

graphical user interface   The look and feel of an operating system that uses graphical elements instead of character-based elements. Also known as the GUI (pronounced "gooey").

graphics   Picture files. Pictures, photographs, and clip art are all commonly referred to as graphics.

hard disk   A piece of hardware that stores large amounts of data for future access.

hardware   A piece of electronic equipment that you can actually touch. Your personal computer and all its peripherals are hardware; the operations of your PC are controlled by *software* (which you *can't* touch).

heading   The initial portion of an HTML document, specified by a special code.

home page   The initial page screen of a Web site.

host   An Internet server that houses a Web site.

hover   In Windows 98, the act of selecting an item by placing your cursor over an icon *without clicking*.

HTML   HyperText Markup Language, the scripting language used to create Web pages.

HTTP   HyperText Transfer Protocol, the protocol that enables communication between Web servers and Web browsers.

hyperlink   Special text or graphics on a Web page that, when clicked, automatically transfers the user to the another Web page.

IBM-compatible   All personal computers that are compatible (that is, can share software and operating systems) with the original IBM PC.

icon   A graphical representation of an object onscreen. Typically, you *click* on an icon to initiate a function.

IEEE 1394   Also known as FireWire, this new type of bus lets you connect multiple high-bandwidth devices to your PC.

Inbox   The virtual container where unread email is stored.

install   How you get software from its box to your hard disk.

instant messaging   Text-based real-time one-on-one communication over the Internet. Not to be confused with *chat*, which can accommodate multiple users, instant messaging (IM) typically is limited to just two users.

Internet   The global "network of networks" that connects millions of computers and other devices around the world. The World Wide Web and Usenet are both parts of the Internet.

Internet Explorer   Microsoft's PC-based Web browser software.

Internet service provider   Also known as ISP, is a company that connects individual users (calling in via traditional phone lines) to the Internet. Some Internet service providers—such as America Online—also provide unique content to their subscribers.

IRQ   Interrupt ReQuest, a signal used by a device to gain the attention of your system's microprocessor when it needs processing resources. Most PCs have 16 different IRQs, labeled 0 through 15.

ISDN   Integrated Services Digital Network, an ultra-fast digital alternative to traditional telephone service.

ISP   Internet service provider, a company that provides Internet access via modem or direct lines for a fee.

Java   A programming language used to develop sophisticated interactive Web pages.

Jaz drive   A portable storage medium from Iomega that can hold up to 1 gigabyte of data.

key   A folder that contains specific settings in the Windows Registry.

keyboard   The thing that looks like a typewriter that you use to type instructions to your computer.

keyword   A word which forms all or part of a search engine query.

kilobyte   One thousand bytes, more or less. (Actually, it's 1,024 bytes). Also known as KB, as in 640KB.

launch   To start a program.

LDAP   Lightweight Directory Access Protocol, a type of service that acts like a virtual "white pages" to directories of email addresses.

legacy   Older hardware that is not compliant with the Plug and Play standard.

link   See *hyperlink*.

log in   The requirement that one "registers" with one's computer or network before being granted access.

mailing list   A discussion group conducted via email.

megabyte   Approximately one million bytes. Also known as MB.

megahertz   One million hertz. (A hertz is a measurement of frequency; in the case of computers, the speed of a microprocessor is measured in megahertz, abbreviated MHz.)

memory   Temporary storage for data and instructions, via electronic impulses on a chip.

menu   A selection of items or services.

Meta search   A search of searches; a process where queries are submitted to multiple search engines or directories simultaneously.

microprocessor   The chip inside your system unit that processes all the operations your computer can do.

Microsoft   The company that developed and publishes the Windows operating system and hundreds of other bestselling programs, including Office, Excel, and Word.

Microsoft Fax   The fax client included with Windows 95 but *not* included with Windows 98.

MIDI   Musical Instrument Digital Interface, a protocol for high-quality digital sound, used in various computer applications and by musicians.

mirror sites   One or more copies of a Web site, located on different servers. Many sites "mirror" their information on multiple servers to prevent overloading of their main site.

modem   *Mo*dulator-*dem*odulator. A hardware device that enables transmission of digital data from one computer to another over common telephone lines via modulating and demodulating.

modifier   A symbol that causes a search engine to do something special with the word directly following the symbol. There are three modifiers used almost universally in the search engine community: +, -, and " ".

monitor   The thing that looks like a TV screen that displays all your computer text and graphics.

motherboard   The big board that makes up the bulk of the insides of your system unit. The motherboard holds your main microprocessor and memory chips and also contains slots to plug in additional boards (cards).

mouse   The hand-held device with a rollerball and buttons you use to navigate through Windows and other graphical applications.

move   To place data in a different location, and delete it from its original location.

MS-DOS   The Microsoft-specific version of DOS.

multimedia   The combination, usually on a computer, of interactive text, graphics, audio, and video.

multitasking   The capability to run more than one application at a time.

My Computer   The chief file management utility in Windows, with its own shortcut on the desktop.

Netscape Communicator   The PC software suite that contains the Netscape Navigator Web browser.

Netscape Navigator   Netscape's PC-based Web browser software.

network   Two or more computers connected together. The Internet is the largest network in the world.

newsgroup   A special-interest discussion group, hosted on Usenet.

OLE   Object Linking and Embedding. The Microsoft standard for creating automatically updated links between documents; also the standard for embedding a document created by one application into a document created by another.

online communications   Any and all communications between one computer and another over phone lines, via modem.

Oops!   The sound you make when something goes wrong with your computer.

operating system   The core system software that lets you (and your software programs) communicate with your hardware.

parallel   A type of external port used to connect printers and other similar devices.

password   A special encrypted "word" (comprised of any combination of letters and numbers) that one enters to obtain access to a computer, network, or Web site.

paste   To place data cut or copied from another location into a new location.

path   The collection of folders and subfolders (listed in order of hierarchy) that hold a particular file.

PC   See *personal computer.*

peripheral   Add-on hardware device for a computer system, such as a printer or a modem.

personal computer   A multi-function hardware unit that includes a hard disk, memory chips, microprocessor chip, and monitor. Personal computers perform tasks when enabled by *software* entered into memory.

pixel   The unit of measurement used in measuring the quality of screen displays.

Plug and Play   Hardware that includes its manufacturer and model information in its ROM, enabling Windows to recognize it immediately upon startup and install the necessary drivers if not already set up.

pop-up menu   The context-sensitive menu that appears when you right-click an object.

port   A fancy name for those connectors that stick out of the back of your system unit. Also refers to the system assignment of specific devices.

portal   A Web site that provides a gateway to the Internet, as well as a collection of other content and services. Most of today's portals (Yahoo!, Excite, and so on) started life as search engines or directories.

Print Manager   The Windows component that manages all print jobs.

printer   The piece of computer hardware that lets you create hard copy printouts of your documents.

protocol   An agreed-upon format for transmitting data between two computers.

pull-down list   A button with a down arrow that, when clicked, displays a list of further options or items.

query   A word, phrase, or group of words, possibly combined with other syntax or operators, used to initiate a search with a search engine or directory.

queue   The list of print jobs that are ready for printing, paused, or currently printing. (Not to be confused with Que, the company that published this book!)

RAM   Random access memory. A type of temporary memory used in your computer.

read   How data is absorbed from a disk to your system's memory.

Recycle Bin   The "trash can" on the Windows desktop that temporarily holds deleted files.

RegClean   A utility used to delete erroneous values in the Windows Registry.

Registry   The Windows registration file that stores all configuration information.

Registry Checker   An autorunning utility that checks, backs up, and restores Registry files whenever your PC is turned on.

Registry Editor   A utility used to edit the Windows Registry.

resolution   The size of the images on a screen; how the quality of screen displays is measured.

restore   The process of returning a backed-up file to its previous location, often from a disk or tape to a hard drive.

right-click   The act of hovering over an item and then clicking your right mouse button; this often displays a pop-up menu of commands related to the object selected.

robot   See *spider*.

root directory   The main directory or folder on a disk.

screen saver   A utility that prolongs the life of your monitor by blanking the screen—or providing a continuously moving image—while your monitor is not in use.

search   To look for information in an orderly fashion.

search box   The text box on a search site where you enter your search query.

search engine   A Web server that indexes Web pages, then makes the index available for user searching. Search engines differ from directories in that the indexes are generated using *spiders,* where directories are assembled manually. Search engine indexes typically include many more Web pages than are found in directories.

search site   Generic term for a Web site that offers either a search engine or directory (or both).

search term   See *query.*

secure server   A Web *server* with the capability for protected credit card transactions.

serial   A type of external port used to connect communication devices, such as modems, PalmPilots, and so on.

server   A central computer that responds to requests for information from one or more client computers. On the Internet, all Web pages are stored on servers.

setup   How you configure your system (or individual software or hardware).

Shortcut   (1) A combination of two keys on your keyboard that, when pressed simultaneously, execute a specific function. (2) An icon on the desktop used to represent an application; click a shortcut to launch an application, or right-click to view and modify its properties.

site   A unified collection of Web pages on the Internet.

snail mail   Traditional U.S. Postal Service (USPS) mail.

software   A digital program that instructs a piece of hardware to perform a specific task.

spam   Email or newsgroup messages that are unsolicited, unwanted, and generally irrelevant.

spamming   The act of sending large numbers of unsolicited email message.

spider   A software program that follows hypertext links across multiple Web pages, but is not directly under human control. Spiders scan the Web, looking for URLs, automatically following all the hyperlinks on pages accessed. The results from a spider's search are used to create the indexes used by search engines.

spool   To line up multiple print jobs in queue. These print jobs are said to be "spooled" to the printer.

standby mode   A special mode on newer computer systems that powers down disk drives and monitors without actually shutting off the computer itself; often called *sleep* mode.

Start menu   The menu used to start most Windows programs and utilities; visible when the **Start** button is clicked.

Startup diskette   A special diskette used to start Windows if something is wrong with the information on your hard disk.

SuperDisk   A portable storage medium from Sony that can hold up to 120MB of data; SuperDisk drives can read and write information to and from older 3 1/2" diskettes.

surge suppressor   A device that protects your system from unwanted power line surges.

system disk   A disk containing the operating system and all files necessary to start your computer.

system files   The files whose presence are necessary for Windows to start; normally hidden from user view or editing.

system unit   That part of your computer system that looks like a big beige box. The system unit contains your microprocessor, system memory, hard disk drive, floppy disk drives, and various cards.

tab   The top of a "page" in a dialog box; many dialog boxes display multiple sets of data on a series of tabs.

table   A collection of data organized into rows and columns.

Taskbar   The bar at the bottom of the screen (normally) in Windows; the **Start** button and temporary buttons for active applications appear on the Taskbar.

TCP/IP   Transmission Control Protocol/Internet Protocol. The protocol used for communications on the Internet.

telecommunications   How your computer talks to other computers, using a modem.

toolbar   A menu bar, containing icons representing programs or commands, that can be "docked" to the Windows Taskbar.

Tray   The area of the Windows Taskbar that holds icons for "background" utilities, such as the Windows clock.

undelete   Unerase. Bring back from the dead. Save your skin.

uninstall   To delete a software application—and all its associated files, drivers, and associations—from a computer system.

unlisted   A Windows component that is not only not automatically installed, but is also not listed in the Add/Remove Programs list.

upgrade   To add a new or improved peripheral or part to your system hardware. Also to install a newer version of an existing piece of software.

upload   The act of copying a file from a personal computer to a Web site or Internet server.

URL   Uniform Resource Locator; the address of a Web page.

USB   Universal Serial Bus, a new type of bus that lets you connect new external devices to your system and have them recognized without first rebooting your computer.

Usenet   A subset of the Internet that contains topic-specific *newsgroups*.

value   The program setting that defines a specific key in the Windows Registry.

VGA   Today's basic color display standard; 640×480 pixels.

virtual memory   Hard disk space used by Windows as transient memory.

virus   A bad, nasty, evil computer program that can cause untold damage to your data.

WDM   Win32 Driver Model (WDM). A new type of device driver that works with both Windows 98 and Windows NT/2000.

Web   See *World Wide Web.*

Web browser   See *browser.*

Web view   A display mode for My Computer or Windows Explorer that displays all icons and files as Web links.

wildcard   A character that substitutes for one or more characters within a query. For example, the * wildcard typically substitutes for any combination of characters.

Windows   The generic name for all versions of Microsoft's graphical operating system.

Windows 95   The version of Microsoft's Windows operating that was released in 1995.

Windows 98   The latest version of Microsoft's Windows operating system, released in 1998.

Windows 2000   The new name for Microsoft's *Windows NT* operating system; where Windows 95/98 is designed for individual consumer PCs, Windows 2000 is designed for networked PCs in a corporate environment.

Windows Explorer   The dual-paned file management utility in Windows; Windows Explorer is not to be confused with the *Internet Explorer* Web browser.

Windows Messaging   The email and messaging subsystem included in Windows 95 but not included in Windows 98; Windows Messaging used Microsoft Fax as its fax client.

Windows NT   An operating system from Microsoft designed for networked computers in a corporate environment; the new version of Windows NT is called *Windows 2000.*

World Wide Web   A subset of the Internet that contains HTML pages.

write   How data is placed on a disk.

Zip drive   A portable storage medium from Iomega that can hold up to 100MB of data.

Online Troubleshooting and Help Resources

Site	URL	Comments
Annoyances.org	www.annoyances.org	Effective solutions to Windows 95/98 annoyances
CMPnet	www.cmpnet.com	Resources for technical professionals from the CMP magazine group (*BYTE, InformationWeek, Windows Magazine*, and so on)
CNET	www.cnet.com	One of the top full-service tech portals, with links to tech news, file downloads, and how-to information—recommended
EarthWeb	www.earthweb.com	A network of sites targeting developers and IT professionals; sites include Developer.com, HTMLGoodies, Gamelan (for Java programmers), Y2Kinfo, and ITKnowledge
FixWindows.com	www.fixwindows.com	A great site for finding and fixing all Windows-related problems; check out the very helpful Troubleshooting Flowcharts
IDG.net	www.idg.net	News and resources from the IDG family of magazines (*PC World, MacWorld, InfoWorld*, and so on)

continues

Site	URL	Comments
informIT	`www.informit.com`	New site from Pearson Education and Macmillan Computer Publishing (the owners of Que, who published this book) that lets you read complete libraries of computer books online—both on a free and on a subscription basis
Internet.com	`www.internet.com`	Internet and Web developer news and resources, from the company that runs the InternetWorld trade shows
ITKnowledge	`www.itknowledge.com`	A complete online library for the IT professional, from EarthWeb
Kim Komando's Komputer Klinic	`www.komando.com`	Online help from the popular tech radio show host
Macmillan Computer Reference	`www.mcp.com`	Major computer book publishers (Que, Sams, Hayden, and more) offer free chapters of online books, plus information on their complete catalog
Microsoft Knowledge Base	`support.microsoft.com/ servicedesks/ directaccess/`	Click the `Support Online` link to enter the Knowledge Base, where you can search for official solutions to problems you may have with any Microsoft products—including all versions of Windows and Office
Microsoft Personal Support Center	`support.microsoft.com`	The home page for all of Microsoft's support services
Microsoft Windows 98 Automated Personal Support Assistant	`support.microsoft.com/ support/windows/faq/98/ default.asp?FR=0`	A new interactive tool (from Microsoft) to help you find answers to your Windows 98-related questions/problems
MyDesktop	`www.mydesktop.com`	News, information, support, and more in an online community for technical users
PcTips.com	`www.pctips.com`	Articles and forums offering online help for all major software and operating systems platforms

Site	URL	Comments
Techni-Help	www.freepchelp.com	Free online help from a group of self-professed computer nerds; includes links to other tech support-oriented sites
TechSupportSites	www.techsupportsites.com	A huge directory of links to all the major tech support resources on the Internet; essentially a vendor directory with more than 1,000 links—recommended
TechWeb	www.techweb.com	Tech news and resources, associated with CMPnet
Tom's Hardware Guide	www.tomshardware.com	A great PC hardware site, lots of info on souping up your system
VirtualDr	www.virtualdr.com	Technical support and information for all versions of Windows, DOS, and all types of hardware
Windows 98 Troubleshooter	members.aol.com/Knows98/index.htm	Windows 98 information and help, plus easy-to-use links to articles and troubleshooters in the Microsoft Knowledge Base
WinDrivers.com	www.windrivers.com	Windows-related hardware support and a huge library of downloadable Windows device drivers
ZDNet	www.zdnet.com	A portal that combines all the technology news and information from Ziff-Davis Publishing magazines (*PC Week, PC Magazine,* and so on); also features ZD University Web-based training
ZDNet Help	www.zdnet.com/zdhelp/	Tips, tricks, secrets, downloads, and FAQs to help you solve computer-related problems, from Ziff-Davis Publishing

Go to the Manufacturer!

If you're having problems with a particular piece of hardware or software, one of the best places to go for help is the manufacturer's site! Most manufacturer sites have tech-support links, which often include downloadable fixes, patches, and drivers, answers to common problems, and links and forms that let you contact the manufacturer directly with your own specific problem. For a good list of manufacturer tech-support sites, check out the TechSupportSites site (www.techsupportsites.com).

Index

D

387